D0173681

Environmental problems in Third World cities

Environmental problems in Third World cities

Jorge E. Hardoy
Diana Mitlin
David Satterthwaite

EARTHSCAN
Earthscan Publications Ltd, London

First published 1992 by
Earthscan Publications Limited
120 Pentonville Road, London N1 9JN

British Library Cataloguing-in-Publication Data

A catalogue record for this book is available from the British Library

ISBN 1 85383 146 8

Typeset by Saxon Graphics Ltd, Derby.
Printed by Biddles Ltd., Guildford and Kings Lynn.

Earthscan Publications Ltd is an editorially independent subsidiary of Kogan Page Limited and publishes in association with the International Institute for Environment and Development and the World Wide Fund for Nature.

Contents

List of illustrations

BOXES

FIGURES

TABLES

About the authors

Jorge E Hardoy is President of the *Instituto Internacional de Medio Ambiente y Desarrollo* (IIED–América Latina), an international non-profit NGO based in Buenos Aires. He is also President of the National Commission for Historic Monuments in Argentina and editor of the journal *Medio Ambiente y Urbanizacion.* Qualifying as an architect in 1950 with a Masters and PhD from Harvard University in City and Regional Planning, he has written widely on both historical and contemporary urban issues. Among his former publications with Earthscan are *Squatter Citizen: Life in the Urban Third World* (with David Satterthwaite), published in 1989 and *The Poor Die Young; Housing and Health in Third World Cities* (edited with Sandy Cairncross and David Satterthwaite), published in 1990. He is a former President of the Inter–American Planning Society, twice a Guggenheim fellow and has recently served on the Board of the International Development Research Centre (IDRC) in Canada. He was an advisor of the World Commission on Environment and Development (the Brundtland Commission) and also advises the World Health Organization on links between health and environment in cities.

Diana Mitlin is an economist with the Human Settlements Programme (a joint programme of the International Institute for Environment and Development in London and IIED–América Latina) and managing editor of its journal, *Environment and Urbanization.* With a first degree in economics and sociology from Manchester University and a Masters in economics from Birkbeck College (University of London), she has a special interest in the role of NGOs and voluntary organizations in housing and environmental action in Third World cities. She worked with David Satterthwaite in advising the United Nations Centre for Human Settlements (Habitat) on the links between sustainable development and human settlements.

David Satterthwaite coordinates the Human Settlements Programme of the International Institute for Environment and Development and IIED–América Latina and is Editor of its journal *Environment and Urbanization*. Trained as a development planner at University College London with a first degree in history, he was an advisor to the World Commission on Environment and Development (the Brundtland Commission) and more recently has worked with the World Health Organization, UNICEF and the UN Centre for Human Settlements (Habitat) on the links between environment, health and development in cities.

Preface

This is the third book about urban issues in the Third World which we have published since 1989. The first, *Squatter Citizen*, sought to describe the vast and complex process of urban change in the Third World and considered its impact on the lives of its poorer citizens. This contained a description of the growing gap between the 'legal city' and the 'illegal city' including its origins in colonial policies and its reinforcement by post-colonial governments. It also reviewed the inappropriate and ineffective ways in which governments have sought to solve urban problems and described the growing scale of forced evictions. It also analyzed recent urban trends in Africa, Asia and Latin America and the role of small and intermediate urban centres within regional and rural development. The second book, *The Poor Die Young: Housing and Health in Third World Cities* (edited with Sandy Cairncross) described the scale of ill health, disablement and premature death in Third World cities and the links with housing and living conditions. This also highlighted the extent to which such problems can be prevented, even within constrained investment budgets. Different chapters by specialist authors discussed different options for safe and sufficient water, sewers (or other means to remove human wastes), drainage, garbage collection and disposal, the control of disease vectors and the provision of emergency life saving services.

This book is an expanded and extended version of a report that we prepared for the Earth Summit (the United Nations Conference on Environment and Development) in Rio de Janeiro in June 1992, at the request of the UK Overseas Development Administration. Its structure is similar to the two chapters in *Squatter Citizen* on environmental problems – although the information has been much expanded and updated and new sections have been added: the scale of urban change; natural disasters and their consequences (at neighbourhood and city level); drainage; who bears the costs of environmental degradation; using each city's natural resource base; the institutional constraints; cities and the global commons; and sustainable development and cities. We hope that this expanded work on environmental problems does justice to the enormous increase in the literature about this subject which has become available since 1989. This literature and the greater interest shown by governments and international agencies in environmental problems in Third World cities (and their links to sustainable development) both before and after the Earth Summit encouraged us to prepare this volume.

We are also working on a fourth volume, *The Future City*. Its main theme is the need for new forms and channels of funding and technical support from governments and international agencies towards community level initiatives – as the most appropriate response to current conditions and trends in most Third World cities. These are issues also raised in this book, but which need further development. This volume will also consider how such an approach would fit within the broader city context and the changes needed in administrative structures and in intersectoral and inter-municipal coordination.

We are grateful to many friends and colleagues for their help in its preparation. Special thanks are due to the UK Overseas Development Administration (especially Gerry Duffy and Ian Haines) and to the Swedish International Development Authority (especially Goran Tannerfelt) for the support given to our research programme on environmental problems in Third World cities. The UK ODA also helped fund the report on which this book is based for the Earth Summit. However, the views expressed in this book do not necessarily represent the views of these agencies.

Within IIED, Jules Pretty, Koy Thompson, Charles Secrett, Virginia Diaz Jimenez, Mick Kelly and Christine Barton also made invaluable suggestions for this book's improvement. This report also draws on the work of research teams in Africa, Asia and Latin America with whom we have worked over the years; special mention should be made of the groups with whom we are currently working on the scale and range of environmental problems and their health and ecological impacts: Lagos Group for the Study of Human Settlements, Mazingira Institute (Kenya), the Centre for Science and Environment (Delhi) and the Muslim University of Aligarh. This book also draws on our collaboration with Sandy Cairncross at the London School of Hygiene and Tropical Medicine and on advice from Carolyn Stephens (also from the London School) on the links between environmental problems and health.

We have also learnt much about this link between health and environment from our collaboration with the World Health Organization (and the WHO Commission on Health and the Environment), UNICEF and UNCHS (Habitat) in the preparation of material for the Earth Summit. Special thanks are due to Francesco Sella, Greg Goldstein, Wilfrid Kreisel, Pietro Garau, Dr Padmini and Yin Yin Nwe. This book draws to a considerable degree on *Our Planet, Our Health*, the Report of the WHO Commission on Health and Environment (WHO, Geneva,

1992) and background papers prepared by WHO staff for this Commission; we worked with WHO and this Commission in the preparation of this book.

Special acknowledgement should be made of recent publications by Gordon Conway and Jules Pretty, Ian Douglas, Mike Douglass, Christine Furedy, Gordon McGranahan, Arif Hasan, William Rees and Richard Stren (which are listed in the References) which proved particularly important in helping us update and expand our earlier work.

Jorge E. Hardoy, Instituto International de Medio Ambiente y Desarrollo (IIED–América Latina), Buenos Aires.

Diana Mitlin and David Satterthwaite, Human Settlements Programme, International Institute for Environment and Development, London.

1

A new environmental agenda for cities?

INTRODUCTION

Cities can provide healthy and stimulating environments for their inhabitants without imposing unsustainable demands on natural resources and ecosystems. A successful city, in this sense, is one which meets multiple goals. Such goals include healthy living and working environments for the inhabitants: water supply, provision for sanitation and garbage disposal, drains, paved roads and other forms of infrastructure and services essential for health and for a prosperous economic base; and a sustainable relationship between the demands of consumers and businesses and the resources and ecosystems on which they draw. Their achievement implies an understanding of the links between the city's built environment, the physical environment in which it is located (including soils, water resources and climate) and the biological environment (including local flora and fauna) and how these are changing. Such an understanding is essential if environmental hazards are to be minimized, and environmental capital not depleted.[1]

There are many other important environmental goals whose achievement would make city environments more pleasant, safe and valued by their inhabitants. These often include a sense among the inhabitants that their culture and history are valued and reflected in the city's form and layout. They certainly include city environments which are more conducive to family life, child development and social interaction. It is difficult to be precise about the forms they should take since these goals vary greatly depending on culture and climate and within a city, with housing quality; public spaces and facilities become more important in densely populated areas with overcrowded housing. The precise nature of the interaction between environmental factors and human wellbeing is also poorly understood. But all city environments need a range of public facilities such as open spaces within walking distance of residential areas where young children can play and socialize, easily supervised by adults, and community-centres which serve the particular needs of their inhabitants (for instance as meeting places, mother and child centres, places for child activities and places where social events can be organized). These also need community or public provision for their maintenance. Sites are also required in all residential areas where older children, adolescents and adults can gather, socialize, explore, and play sports; these sites also need to be accessible, safe and well-maintained. Cities need parks, beaches (where these exist) and sites of natural beauty which preserve the character of a city's natural landscape and to which all citizens have access. In hot climates, open spaces with trees can give welcome relief from the heat, especially when combined with lakes, streams or rivers which can provide more comfortable micro-climates.[2]

Achieving a balance between these different goals implies the need for a representative political and administrative system through which the views and priorities of citizens can influence policies and actions both within the district or neighbourhood, where they live and at city level. Good governance is critical for successful cities. It provides the means through which citizens reach agreement on how to meet multiple goals. City government also has to represent the needs and priorities of its citizens in the broader context – for instance in negotiations with provincial and national governments, international agencies and businesses considering investments there.

The quality of governance also determines the extent to which a city takes advantage of being a centre of concentrated production and population, and avoids the potential disadvantages. This concentration greatly reduces the unit costs of providing each building with piped water, sanitation, garbage collection, paved roads, electricity and drains. It also greatly reduces unit costs for health services and the provision of schools, pre-school centres and child development centres.[3] Even in most squatter settlements, population densities are not so high as to pose problems for the cost-effective provision of such infrastructure and services.

Industrial concentration in cities reduces the cost of enforcing regulations on environmental and occupational health and pollution control. It also lessens the cost of many specialized services and waste-handling facilities – including those which reduce waste levels or which recover materials from waste streams for reuse or recycling. The concentration of households and enterprises in cities makes it easier for public authorities to collect taxes and charges for public services, while in prosperous cities there is a larger revenue base, a larger demand and a larger capacity to pay. This same concentration of people can make it easier for them to be fully involved in electing governments at local and city level and to take an active part in decisions and actions within their own district or neighbourhood. Only in the absence of effective governance, including the institutional means to ensure that infrastructure, services and pollution controls are provided, are environmental problems greatly exacerbated.

It is also within cities that a high proportion of the Third World's[4] emissions of greenhouse gases (including stratospheric ozone depleting chemicals) are released. Their current and historic contributions to global greenhouse gas emissions remains much smaller than those from Europe, North America, Japan and Australasia.[5] But if major limitations on such emissions prove necessary to limit climatic change and its deleterious consequences, some of the most cost-effective means of limiting each nation's emissions will be found in its cities. Measures taken now to promote healthy, resource efficient, minimum-waste cities in the South can ensure a high quality of life, without the enormous (and probably unsustainable) levels of resource use and waste generation currently associated with urban centres in the North.

While the contribution of Third World cities to global environmental problems remains small relative to their share in the world's urban population, urban environmental problems in terms of their impact on human health and damage to local resources and ecosystems are far more serious that in cities in Europe, Japan or North America.

Rapid urban change in itself need not produce serious environmental problems. Certain cities in the North (for instance Milton Keynes in the UK) have been among the world's most rapidly growing cities in recent decades and they do not have serious environmental problems. A city such as Curitiba in Brazil is another rapidly growing city which has much less serious environmental problems than many cities which have grown far more slowly.[6] Environmental problems become particularly serious where there is a rapid expansion in urban population with little or no consideration for the environmental implications, and for the institutional framework to ensure these implications are addressed. In most Third World countries, urban populations have expanded without an associated expansion in the services and facilities essential for an adequate and healthy urban environment. This has usually occurred with little or no effective pollution control – and with forms of urban governance which cannot begin to meet their responsibilities. Neither has much regard been given to the environmental implications of such rapid urban expansion – including the modifications to the earth's surface (and to local ecology), the changes wrought in the natural flows of water, and the demands made on the surrounding region for building materials for roads, car-parks, industries and other components of the urban fabric (see Box 1.1). Urban expansion has often taken place over lands ill-suited for this purpose while large metropolitan centres and industrial centres have developed in areas where dispersal of air pollutants is difficult.

Box 1.1 The environmental impact of urban development

Urban development directly transforms large areas of the earth's surface. Hillsides may be cut or bulldozed into new shapes, valleys and swamps may be filled with rocks and waste materials, water and minerals may be extracted from beneath the city, and soil and groundwater regimes modified in many ways. The construction of buildings, roads and other components of the urban fabric modifies the energy, water and chemical budgets of the affected portions of the earth's surface. As cities expand, they not only alter the earth's surface but create new landforms (as in the case of reclaimed land).

Urban developments greatly affect the operation of the hydrological cycle, including changes in total runoff, alteration in peak-flow characteristics and a decline in water quality. As such, they also greatly affect the processes of erosion and sedimentation. To these changes must be added the network of pipes and channels for water collection, treatment, transmission, regulation and distribution – and the culverts, gutters, drains, pipes, sewers and channels of urban waste water disposal and stormwater drainage systems. Urbanization affects stream channels and flood plains, often causing water to flow through cities at a high velocity.

Temperatures in urban areas are affected by many factors including the way in which the walls and roofs of buildings, and the concrete or roadstone of paved areas, behave in terms of high conductivity, heat capacity and ability to reflect heat as well as their heat storage capacity which is higher than natural soils. Also important are: the input of artificial heat generated by machinery, vehicles, heating and cooling systems; the way in which a large extent of impervious surface sheds rainwater rapidly, altering the urban moisture and heat budget; and the ejection of pollutants and dust into the urban atmosphere. The urban heat balance affects rain producing mechanisms and the rate of snow melt over and within cities.

The creation of a city involves massive transfers of materials. These include major earth-moving activities which involve modifications to the hydrological cycle and to the weight of materials on the ground surface. This redistribution of stresses in an urban area alters the natural movement of groundwater and dissolved matter. The process of building a city changes the nature of land cover both temporarily and permanently and induces changed relationships between the energy of falling rainwater and the amount of sediments carried into streams. This leads in turn to an increase or decrease in the sediment in the water supply to stream channels. This will affect the stability of those stream channels and the consequent pattern of downstream channel erosion.

This rearrangement of water, materials and stresses on the earth's surface requires careful assessment, as the impacts are often felt off-site, down-valley, downstream or downwind. Terrain for urban development requires careful evaluation as past changes in geomorphic conditions may cause problems if the land is disturbed by ill-planned earthworks. Each type of geomorphic process has special limitations for urban construction, but previous phases of urban land use may leave unstable fills, poorly drained valley floors and weakly consolidated reclaimed land. Urban sediment requires special control measures.

Source: Drawn from Douglas, Ian (1986) 'Urban Geomorphology' in P G Fookes and P R Vaughan (eds), *A Handbook of Engineering Geomorphology*, Surrey University Press (Blackie and Son), Glasgow, pp. 270–283 and Douglas, Ian (1983) *The Urban Environment*, Edward Arnold, London.

Rapid urban expansion without effective urban governance means that in virtually every urban centre – from large cities and metropolitan areas to regional centres and small market towns – a substantial proportion of the population is at risk from natural and human-induced environmental hazards. For instance, in most major cities a high proportion of the population lives in shelters and neighbourhoods with little or no provision for supplying their needs for water or for ensuring the safe disposal of their solid and liquid wastes. Provision for drainage – including that to cope with storm and surface runoff – is often deficient. A large proportion of the urban population live in poor quality housing, for instance whole households might live in one or two rooms in cramped, overcrowded tenements, cheap boarding houses or shelters built on illegally occupied or subdivided land. Many people live on land subject to periodic floods, landslides or some other natural hazard, while human induced changes have often increased the risks.

An increasing proportion of the urban population in Africa, Asia and Latin America may now be living in regions or zones where the ecological underpinnings of urban development are fragile. For instance, in Latin America a considerable proportion of the rapid growth in urban population has taken place in areas which, only a few decades ago, were sparsely settled. Many of the world's most rapidly growing urban centres over the last 40 years have been those which developed as administrative and service centres in areas of agricultural colonization or mining or logging in what were previously uninhabited or sparsely populated areas. Again in Latin America, urban development has spread only in the last few decades to the hot and humid regions in the interior of Brazil, Bolivia, Paraguay and Venezuela, Central America and Mexico, to the Chilean and Argentine Patagonia region, and to the Dominican Republic interior. Among the reasons why most of these regions had remained sparsely populated was the greater environmental hazards or soils less suited to sustained commercial exploitation.[7]

One result is that environment-related diseases and injuries frequently cause or contribute to disablement and premature deaths among infants, children, adolescents and adults in urban areas. In many cities and most poor urban districts, they are the leading cause of death and illness. In many poor city districts, infants are 40–50 times more likely to die before the age of one than in Europe or North America, and virtually all such deaths are environment-related. Over 600 million urban citizens in Africa, Asia and Latin America live in 'life and health threatening' conditions because of unsafe and insufficient water, overcrowded and unsafe shelters, inadequate or no sanitation, no drains and garbage collection, unstable house sites, risks of flooding and other environment-related factors.[8] Most of the diseases and injuries which result are preventable at a low cost.

Addressing such environmental problems can even mean enormous cost savings in terms of time and effort, in addition to improvements to health. Regular supplies of water piped into the home mean that the people no longer have to fetch and carry large volumes of water from public standpipes. A readily available water supply and the means to heat it makes laundry, personal hygiene and many household tasks easier, more convenient and less time-consuming. Better public transport means people no longer have to walk long distances to and from work or shops or spend long hours travelling. More accessible health care centres improve health but also eliminate the need for long journeys to and from distant hospitals. For tens of millions of city dwellers living in areas subject to floods each year, basic site drainage and flood protection can remove not only the health risks of flooding but also the disruption to their daily lives and work which floods always cause.

Environmental problems around the city also exist. In most Third World cities and many smaller urban centres, serious environmental degradation affects soils, crops, forests, freshwater aquifers and surface water, fisheries and other natural resources. This arises from demands for natural resources, changes brought to water flows, and air and water pollution and solid wastes generated by urban enterprises and consumers. Most such environmental degradation can also be prevented or much reduced at relatively low cost.

The scale and severity of environmental problems in Third World cities reflect the failure of governments. In most Third World nations, both national and urban governments have failed in three essential environmental actions: to enforce appropriate legislation (including that related to environmental health, occupational health and pollution control); to ensure adequate provision for water supply and solid and liquid waste collection and treatment systems; and to ensure adequate health care provision to treat not only environment-related illnesses but also to implement preventive measures to limit their incidence and severity. The policies and actions that governments take in regard to the urban environment have profound implications for the health and wellbeing of urban citizens and, in the longer term, for the ecological sustainability of cities and the urban and regional systems of which they are part. The extent to which good environmental quality is achieved in cities may be one of the most revealing indicators of the competence and capacity of city and municipal government, and of the extent to which their policies respond to their populations' needs and priorities.

But there are the factors far beyond the competence and capacity of city and municipal governments which influence the quality of city environments. The very poor environmental conditions evident in most Third World cities are also an expression of the difficult circumstances in which most Third World countries find themselves. Stagnant economies and heavy debt burdens do not provide an appropriate economic base from which to develop good governance. Governments from the North and international agencies may promote environmental policies but there is little progress in changing the international economic system which would permit more economic stability and prosperity among the poorer Third World nations. Many Third World economies have no alternative but to increase the exploitation of their natural resources to earn foreign exchange to meet debt repayments, especially in the face of the protective barriers around the world's largest consumer markets which limit their exports of industrial goods.

A NEW ENVIRONMENTAL AGENDA

A new environmental agenda is needed in Third World cities, one which centres on enhancing the capacity of city authorities, professional groups, NGOs and community organizations to identify and address their environmental problems. This would not only reveal some of the underlying causes of ill-health and premature death, it would also limit the damage arising from city-based demands and city-generated wastes on the local, regional and global environment. A new agenda would also permit agreements to be reached about how the city can be a safer, more convivial place to live and work. The last few years have brought some signs that a new environmental agenda may be emerging. There's evidence of this in a growing volume of literature on the subject and in new policies or projects by certain governments and development assistance agencies. But this emerging urban environmental agenda appears weak and is not underpinned by any significant initiative to relieve the economic stagnation and debt burdens which hardly promote stable, competent and democratic governance.

The growing interest in urban environmental problems is based too much on Northern perceptions and precedents. It appears biased towards addressing the environmental problems which Third World cities have in common with cities in Europe and North America. This often means a greater attention to chemical agents in the air, rather than biological agents in water, food, air and soil – including those responsible for diarrhoeal diseases, dysentery and intestinal parasites. This bias often means that critical environmental problems such as the control of disease vectors which spread malaria, dengue fever, filariasis and yellow fever are forgotten. It can mean more attention to the loss of agricultural land due to urban spread than to the fact that half, or more, of the urban population lack access to safe and sufficient water supplies. As a recent report by the WHO Commission on Health and the Environment points out, it is biological pathogens in the human environment plus the high proportion of people who lack access to fresh water and other essential natural resources which represent far more serious environmental problems than chemical contamination, both in urban and in rural areas (see Box 1.2).

Box 1.2 The main links between health and the environment

The most immediate environmental problems in the world are the ill health and premature death caused by biological agents in the human environment: in water, food, air and soil. They contribute to the premature death of millions of people (mostly infants and children) and to the ill health or disability of hundreds of millions more. The problems are most acute in Third World countries where:

- four million infants or children die every year from diarrhoeal diseases, largely as a result of contaminated food or water
- two million people die from malaria each year and 267 million are infected
- hundreds of millions of people suffer from debilitating intestinal parasitic infestations.

In addition, all countries have serious environmental health problems, affecting:

- hundreds of millions of people who suffer from respiratory and other diseases caused or exacerbated, both indoors and outdoors, by biological and chemical agents in the air
- hundreds of millions who are exposed to unnecessary chemical and physical hazards in their home, workplace or wider environment.

Health also depends on whether people can obtain food, water and shelter and over 1000 million people lack the income or land to meet such basic needs.

Source: World Health Organization, (1992) *Report of the WHO Commission on Health and the Environment: Summary*, WHO/EHE/92.1, Geneva.

Insufficient attention is given by governments and aid agencies to two critical environmental problems: biological pathogens in the urban environment; and people's lack of access to natural resources (especially fresh water and safe land for housing). These two problems underlie millions of preventable deaths every year, and contribute to serious ill-health or disablement for hundreds of millions. Similarly, urban land markets in most cities mean that between one third and two thirds of the population are unable to afford safe, healthy and legal housing. These are the environmental problems which deserve a high priority.

Most environmental problems are political problems. They arise not from some particular shortage of an environmental resource such as land or fresh water but from economic or political factors which deny poorer groups both access to it and the ability to demand changes. In most cities, poorer groups' lack of piped water supplies is not the result of a shortage of fresh water resources but the result of governments' refusal to give a higher priority to water supply (and the competent organizational structure its supply, maintenance and expansion requires). There are some cities or metropolitan areas with critical shortages of fresh water resources (for instance Mexico City) but rarely are supplies so constrained that they prevent piping sufficient supplies for health to poor households. The same is true for land; most cities or metropolitan areas in the Third World have sufficient unused or under-utilized land sites within the current built-up area to accommodate most low-income households currently living in very overcrowded conditions. The many poor households who live in settlements on dangerous sites such as floodplains or steep slopes choose such sites not in ignorance of the dangers but because the authorities failed to plan for and allocate more suitable sites. Again, there are cities with critical land shortages because of special site characteristics but even here, governments could do much more to reduce risks for those in hazard-prone areas.

A failure of governance underlies most environmental problems – failure to control industrial pollution and occupational exposure, to promote environmental health, to ensure that city-dwellers have the basic infrastructure and services essential for health and a decent living environment, to plan in advance to ensure sufficient land is available for housing developments for low-income groups and to implement preventive measures to reduce environmental problems or their impacts. This is often, in turn, linked to the national economy's weakness; effective governance in ensuring a healthy environment for citizens is almost impossible without a stable and reasonably prosperous economy. Strong support for efficient resource use, minimum waste, cities and urban systems which limit the need for private automobiles and maximum recovery of materials from waste streams can ensure that increasing prosperity does not also mean increasing environmental degradation.

Other priorities are to strengthen the process within each city and city district through which environmental problems and their causes can be identified, their relative importance assessed and choices made about how limited resources are best used to address them and who should make those decisions. For instance, too much attention is given to describing individual environmental problems and to particular technical solutions with little support for enhancing city governments' capacity to act effectively and democratically. Very little support is channelled directly to low-income groups and their organizations for community initiatives to improve environmental conditions. Yet in most cities, the homes and neighbourhoods developed by lower-income groups (most of them illegally) remain a major influence on the planning, building and development of most new homes and neighbourhoods. Their capacity to build, to work collectively in addressing common problems and to negotiate effectively with local, city and (often) national government will continue to have the greatest influence on the quality of their living environment. Since they make up a high proportion of the population of most cities and an even higher proportion of additions to the city, the quality of low-income housing and living environments will be a major influence on the quality of the whole city's environment. Yet institutions which respond to this fact and which make available appropriate kinds of technical and financial support are very rare.

The long term solution to any city's environmental problems depends on the development within that city of a competent, representative local government. Democratic structures remain among the best checks on the misallocation of resources by city and municipal governments. Outside agencies – whether national ministries or international agencies – often misunderstand the nature of the problem and the range of options from which to choose the most appropriate solutions. External agencies can bring knowledge, expertise, capital and advice – but they cannot solve most environmental problems without effective local institutions.

The pressure for environmental action in Third World cities coming from international research, activist groups and donor agencies in Europe and North America neglects the environmental health agenda. Measures to prevent or limit the transmission of diarrhoeal diseases, typhoid, cholera and other waterborne, water-washed or water-based diseases and acute respiratory infections, tuberculosis and vector borne diseases such as malaria, dengue fever and yellow fever have critical environmental components. These must remain high up the urban environmental agenda.

In addition, the particular problems that are documented may not be the most serious in terms of their impact on health or local ecosystems but simply those which are more easily documented or those which a particular research project or institution chose to document. One example is the fact that there is far more data on ambient air pollution levels for cities for (for instance) sulphur dioxide than on the extent to which city populations are served by sewers (or other effective sanitation systems) and storm drains. Yet the current health impact of inadequate sanitation and drainage is much greater than the health impact of current levels of sulphur dioxide. There is also a tendency for authors writing about environmental problems in Third World cities to extrapolate from their knowledge of cities in the North. Much of the general literature on environmental problems in Third World cities is written by authors from the North; although there is an increasing wealth of literature on environmental problems in Third World cities written by Third World specialists, they rarely write about more than the problems within their own cities or nations. Detailed documentation of the scale and nature of environmental problems exists for only a tiny proportion of the Third World's urban centres – and almost certainly, a highly unrepresentative sample. Despite this fact, generalizations about the most serious environmental problems 'in the Third World' are routinely made. Most general works about environmental problems in the South tend to extrapolate from the environmental problems of cities in the North, even to the point where one recent paper suggested that tropospheric ozone reduction should receive a high priority in Third World cities because of the evidence of its health impact in Los Angeles.[9] Very few Third World cities are likely to have a concentration of ozone at ground level which would constitute one of their most serious environmental problems – not least because only a handful have a comparable concentration of population and industrial production, none have a comparable concentration of automobiles and most have enormous deficiencies in such basic things as water supply, sanitation and drainage, and health care.

The growing pressure for action on environmental problems in Third World cities must include all urban centres. The recently growing enthusiasm among governments and aid agencies for urban issues (including the role of urban economies and urban environmental problems) gives too much attention to the largest cities. Most of the Third World's urban population live in urban centres with fewer than half a million inhabitants; in many countries, half or more of the urban population live in urban centres with fewer than 100,000 inhabitants. Yet most of the discussion on environmental problems in Third World cities is on environmental problems in a handful of the largest metropolitan centres. Improved water supplies, sanitation, solid and liquid waste management, control of disease vectors, capacity to plan and manage new urban developments and preventive health care services are needed in virtually all urban areas, including the tens of thousands of small and intermediate sized urban centres in which a high proportion of the Third World's urban population lives.

A theme to which this book will constantly return is that each city and urban centre has its own unique range of environmental problems and effective action demands local capabilities to identify problems and their causes and decide the best use of limited resources. In many societies, far more support needs to be channelled directly to citizen and community action groups. This not only delivers immediate benefits to poorer groups more cheaply and effectively than most state actions. It also strengthens society, by reinforcing democracy and participation, and by developing partnerships between community based organizations, NGOs and municipal governments.

Many Third World NGOs have pioneered new, more participatory approaches to working with low-income groups and their community organizations in improving environmental health and installing infrastructure and services. Some have achieved remarkable cost reductions when compared with conventional projects; one example is the Orangi Pilot Project in Karachi and its support for sewage systems. Tremendous potential exists for new partnerships between local governments, local NGOs and local community organizations, but national governments and international agencies have yet to fully recognize this.

There is a need for new attitudes among architects, planners, engineers and other professionals whose training should help equip them to work cooperatively with low-income households and the community organizations they form. If more support is to be channelled to citizen-directed, community-level initiatives, professionals will need to learn how to work cooperatively at community level. New tools and methods are needed for community-based actions which guide professionals in how to work with low-income groups and their community organizations in identifying problems and their underlying causes, and developing appropriate solutions.

A joint programme involving the North and the South to address environmental problems must have the long-term goal of building the capacity within each society to identify, analyze and act on their own environmental problems. Building such a capacity, in turn, demands action by the North on such issues as unrealistic debt-repayment levels and the removal of protectionist barriers around the North's own markets; more prosperous, stable economies in the Third World with citizens no longer suffering constantly from environment-related diseases, injuries and premature deaths should be preconditions for agreement on tackling global issues such as atmospheric warming.

Working together on the most immediate and serious environmental problems including those in cities would lay an appropriate foundation for joint action to protect the global commons. Only through joint actions to tackle the environmental problems which pose the greatest threats to poorer citizens (in both rural and urban areas) can they share First World citizens' longer term environmental concerns. Only through a redistribution of decision-making powers and resources in their favour both within and between nations will they be able to do something about both.

THE STRUCTURE OF THE BOOK

This book reviews the scale and scope of environmental problems in Third World cities and their surrounds, and draws some conclusions as to the priorities for action. The second half of this chapter outlines the urban context and stresses the number and diversity of urban centres where action is needed. Chapter 2 describes environmental problems and their consequences on two different geographic scales: the house and workplace and their immediate surrounds; and the wider neighbourhood or district. Chapter 3 describes the environmental problems of cities in general such as air and water pollution.[10] Both Chapters 2 and 3 include a discussion of natural disasters and the extent to which their incidence and the severity of their impacts are linked to human-induced changes, with Chapter 2 considering such disasters at district level and Chapter 3 at city level.

Chapter 4 considers the environmental impacts of cities on their wider regions and on the global commons. This includes a consideration of resource and waste flows between a city and its region, and the contribution of city-based production and consumption to environmental degradation worldwide, and to climatic change, especially global warming.

Chapter 5 discusses how these problems might be resolved, with a particular emphasis on the institutional structure and processes which can achieve this, rather than on particular technical solutions. What is needed is the means by which groups of people in each neighbourhood, municipality and city can reach a consensus on environmental problems and address them. This chapter includes a discussion of the role of public and private suppliers of infrastructure and services, and of ways to mobilize action by Third World citizens and their governments on international concerns such as global warming. It also points to the serious political and institutional constraints which inhibit action. At city level, they centre on the fact that most city and municipal governments are weak, ineffective and unrepresentative. At national level, these include unrepresentative governments; an economic climate which discourages long term measures; and a shortage of foreign exchange with which to import pollution-control equipment or new 'clean' technologies. Governments' responsibilities for environmental health, pollution-control and land use management far exceed their powers and the resources available to them. At international level, a major constraint is the low priority given by most aid agencies and development banks to addressing the most serious environmental problems and to strengthening the capacity of Third World societies to identify and tackle these problems themselves. However, there are many innovative projects which show how much could be done if funds were channelled in different ways.

Chapter 6 considers the implications for cities of achieving the sustainable development goals outlined by the World Commission on Environment and Development. It highlights contradictions which need to be resolved, including the contradiction between local and global sustainability and between development and sustainability goals. It also discusses the national and international frameworks which will be needed to resolve such contradictions and to encourage the pursuit of global and local sustainability goals, as well as development goals, within each city and municipal government.

Chapter 7 draws some conclusions and develops points raised in this chapter about a new environmental agenda. It stresses that any new environmental agenda must become driven by the specific needs and priorities of citizens, with sufficient power and resources allocated to those who suffer most from environmental problems to ensure their resolution. This means an environmental agenda within each urban centre and region which responds to the specifics of that particular area.

Some comment is needed about rural areas. The fact that this book concentrates on environmental problems in urban areas should not be taken to imply that there are not very serious environmental problems in rural areas. Indeed, as Chapter 4 will elaborate, it is difficult to separate urban and rural environmental issues since many of the environmental problems in one, impact so much on the other. Nor indeed should this book be interpreted as a request to necessarily divert limited resources from rural to urban areas. Much of this book is about building or strengthening capacity for governance at local and city level so more appropriate actions can be taken, using existing resources. Implementing existing environmental legislation to reduce pollution, more effective controls on occupational health problems, meeting the demands of poorer groups for improved water, drainage and sanitation with cost-effective solutions and increasing the capacity of city and municipal governments to raise their own revenues are among many measures recommended which do not need a large increase in funding. The belief that it is a lack of funds which inhibits local and city actions has drawn attention away from more important issues of governance, accountability, participation and the right of all citizens to protection by law from enterprises which pollute their home, work and city environment.

THE SCALE OF URBAN CHANGE

Between 1950 and 1990, the population of Africa, Asia and Latin America grew from 1.7 billion to close to four billion, while its urban population grew from 286 million to more than 1.5 billion; this urban population is now larger than the total population of Europe, North America, Japan, the former Soviet Union and Australasia combined. UN projections suggest that the Third World's urban population will grow by more than 700 million persons between 1990 and 2000; by contrast, the urban population in the rest of the world is projected to grow by little more than 70 million (see Table 1.1). These UN projections also suggest that urban populations are growing so much faster than rural populations that 80 per cent of the growth in the world's population between 1990 and 2000 will be in urban areas.

Table 1.1 Trends and projections in urban populations, by region, 1950–2000

REGION	1950	1970	1990	2000
Urban population (millions of inhabitants)				
Africa	32.2	82.7	217.4	352.4
Latin America & Caribbean	68.8	163.6	320.5	411.3
Asia (not incl Japan)	184.4	406.8	975.3	1,485.7
Other	0.2	0.7	1.4	2.1
Third World total	285.6	653.8	1,514.7	2,251.4
Rest of the world	448.2	698.6	875.5	946.2
Percentage of population living in urban centres				
Africa	14.5	22.9	33.9	40.7
Latin America & Caribbean	41.5	57.3	71.5	76.4
Asia (not incl Japan)	14.2	20.4	32.6	41.5
Other	7.5	17.5	23.1	27.3
Third World total	17.0	24.7	37.1	45.1
Rest of the world	53.8	66.6	72.6	74.9

Source: United Nations (1991) *World Urbanization Prospects 1990; Estimates and Projections of Urban and Rural Populations and of Urban Agglomerations*, United Nations, ST/ESA/SER.A/121, New York.

One component of this rapid growth in the Third World's urban population has been an increase in the number of large cities. In 1950, there were just ten cities with more than one million people; by 1990, there were around 171.[11] Many of these million-cities have populations which have grown more than tenfold in these same 40 years – including Abidjan, Amman, Curitiba, Dar es Salaam, Dhaka, Khartoum, Kinshasa, Lagos, Manaus, Nairobi and Seoul. Brasilia, the federal capital of Brazil, did not exist in 1950 and now has more than two million inhabitants. By 1990, there were over 30 urban agglomerations with more than five million inhabitants and most were in the South; in 1940, no Third World city had attained this size and in the North, only two cities (London and New York) had more than five million inhabitants. Never in history have so many new urban dwellers been added each year to the population of existing cities.

However, certain aspects of this urban change have elements of continuity with the past. Most of the largest urban centres in Latin America, Asia and North Africa today have been important urban centres for centuries. In addition, a high proportion of the largest cities are in a few of the Third World's most populous countries. In 1990, there were nine Third World agglomerations with populations estimated at more than ten million inhabitants: Mexico City, São Paulo, Buenos Aires, Rio de Janeiro, Shanghai, Calcutta, Bombay, Seoul and Beijing. Six were in just three nations: China, India and Brazil, the first, second and fourth most populous countries in the Third World in 1990. Fourteen cities had between five and ten million – all but three (Cairo, Lagos and Lima) in Asia. Of the 23 largest urban agglomerations in the Third World (with five million or more inhabitants in 1990), three were in China, four were in India, two were in Brazil and one was in Indonesia. Among these 23 largest cities in the Third World, nine were also among the world's largest cities in 1800 and most of the rest were already important urban centres.[12]

Drawing on UN estimates for 1990,[13] 171 urban centres in the South have more than one million inhabitants: 24 in Africa, 109 in Asia[14] and 38 in Latin America and the Caribbean. In 1990, they concentrated some 510 million inhabitants. A high proportion of these are also in a small group of the most populous nations. Of the 171 'million-cities', China had 38, a quarter of the Third World's total; India had 24; while Brazil had 14. These three countries and Indonesia, which are the most populous Third World nations had close to half of the Third World's largest 171 cities. More than two thirds of these cities had been founded by 1600; more than a third have histories stretching back more than 1000 years.[15]

While many Third World governments discuss urban strategies (which are rarely the most appropriate for those in greatest need, or for promoting a stronger economic base), metropolitan areas like Karachi, Bombay, São Paulo and Mexico City are currently growing by 250,000 or more inhabitants each year. Although our analyses of recent census data and long-term urban trends suggest that the Third World will be less urbanized and far less dominated by 'mega-cities' by the year 2000 and beyond than has been suggested by many sources, these analyses still imply a large and, in most countries, rapidly growing urban population in the next few decades.[16]

However, three inaccurate assumptions about urbanization in the Third World pervade most discussions about their environmental problems:

- most of the problems (and much of the urban population) are in huge mega-cities;
- the high concentration of population and production is a major cause of environmental problems; and
- existing documentation of environmental problems is an accurate representation of such problems. Each of these is considered briefly below.

Mega-Cities

Highlighting trends in these large cities obscures the fact that in 1990, only a third of the Third World's urban population (and 12.5 per cent of its total population) lives in cities with one or more million inhabitants. Many cities with less than a million inhabitants have also grown very rapidly in recent decades. There are hundreds of cities in the South with between 250,000 and one million inhabitants; many were only small urban centres 40 years ago. There are thousands of urban centres with under 250,000 inhabitants; many did not exist or were villages or small towns with only a few thousand inhabitants 40 years ago.

Most of the Third World's urban population live in urban centres with fewer than half a million inhabitants; in most of the less populous and the less urbanized nations, it is common for half the urban population to live in urban centres with fewer than 100,000 inhabitants. Close to 50 independent Third World countries have no urban centre which had reached 500,000 inhabitants in 1990. Table 1.2, below, presents the distribution of the Third World's urban population divided between different size settlements.

According to UN estimates, less than 3 per cent of the Third World's population live in 'mega-cities' of ten or more million inhabitants (see Table 1.2); this is also borne out by the census data for 1990 and 1991 which has recently become available for many of the Third World countries with very large cities. This is not surprising, in that mega-cities can only develop in countries with large non-agricultural economies and

Table 1.2 Third World population, by region, for 1990 and its distribution between rural areas and different size urban centres

	Third World	*Latin America & Caribbean*	*Asia*	*Africa*
Total population (million inhabitants)	4,086	448	2,989	642
Urban population	1,515	320	975	217
Rural population	2,571	128	2,014	425
Proportion of total population living in:				
Rural areas	62.9	28.5	67.4	66.1
Urban areas with less than 1 million inhabitants	24.6	41.8	22.0	24.7
Urban areas with 1–2 million inhabitants	3.2	5.6	2.8	3.4
Urban areas with 2–5 million inhabitants	3.8	9.4	3.1	3.1
Urban areas with 5–10 million inhabitants	2.6	1.4	2.7	2.6
Urban areas with 10 million plus inhabitants	2.4	8.8	1.9	0.0

Source: The urban statistics above are derived from statistics in United Nations (1991) *World Urbanization Prospects 1990*, New York. This statistical compendium presents population estimates for all urban agglomerations with one or more million inhabitants in 1990. By aggregating their populations, by region, and taking the total population figures, by region, from this compendium, it is possible to calculate the above. The statistics for Asia do not include Japan. Figures for Third World also include Third World Oceania.

large national populations; most nations in the South have too small a population and too weak an urban-based economy to support mega-cities. A city of ten million can only exist if there is an economy which can provide incomes (however inadequate) for a population concentration of that size. The vast majority of Third World nations are never likely to have the population and the economic base to permit the development of a mega-city with ten million or more inhabitants; indeed, close to half do not even have national populations which exceed ten million inhabitants.

Recent censuses show that the population growth rate in many of the largest cities fell dramatically during the 1980s. Several of the mega-cities are likely to have substantially smaller populations by the year 2000 than the often-quoted population projections for this year made by the United Nations in the mid 1980s, including some like Mexico City and Calcutta with several million inhabitants less.[17]

The role of population density

At the beginning of this chapter, we noted the advantages for environment and health that the concentration of population and production in cities can bring: the greatly reduced unit costs for most forms of infrastructure and service which contribute to a healthy environment (piped water, sanitation, garbage collection, roads, and drains) and which provide people with protection from environmental hazards. Other potential advantages of concentration were also noted, including the cheaper unit costs for waste reduction and management and lower costs for regulation enforcement and revenue raising.

Most Third World cities (including most of the largest) are not very densely populated (in terms of persons per unit area). Indeed, as Chapter 4 will discuss in more detail, in many areas within most cities or metropolitan areas, densities are so low or settlement patterns so varied (with open spaces and low density areas interspersed with small areas of high density development) that the costs per household of providing infrastructure and services are much increased.

In all cities, there are particular problems in certain densely populated districts or settlements and where there are serious deficiencies in infrastructure and service provision. In some – for instance very dense squatter settlements – no public provision may be evident. In others, some provision may exist but it is insufficient. For instance, many Third World cities have inner-city tenement districts or districts where cheap boarding and rooming houses have developed. Even where the buildings have provision for piped water, sewers and drains, these are often in a poor state of repair and used so intensively (with many households sharing each bathroom and WC) that major improvements are necessary. But such problems are rarely the result of an overall shortage of space within the city; they are much more the result of the concentration of a high proportion of the city's population (those with low incomes) in a very small area. For instance, a recent estimate for Metro Manila in the Philippines suggested that the poorest 45 per cent of the population lived in over 600 squatter settlements which take up just 5.3 per cent of the land area.[18] A study of environmental problems in Nairobi (Kenya) highlights the very high population densities in particular illegal/informal settlements which house a substantial proportion of the city's population – which contrast with the relatively low population density of the city itself; recent estimates for Mathare Valley suggest a population density of around 500 persons per hectare, while in Kibera/Woodley, estimates suggest 157 persons per hectare; for Nairobi as a whole, the average population density is around 20 per hectare.[19] Shanghai and Colombo are among the many Asian cities with low population densities when their total population is divided by their total area, but very high population densities in certain central districts and in other specific areas.[20]

Perhaps surprisingly, even in most squatter settlements, population densities are not too high to have posed problems for the cost-effective provision of infrastructure and services, especially if provision for these had been made in advance of the settlement's development.[21] What is often expensive and time consuming, is installing infrastructure and services in densely populated illegal or informal settlements. Where these developed without sufficient space left for access roads, public space and community facilities and without a site plan which keeps down the costs of piped water, drains and other infrastructure, the costs of improving infrastructure and services to the standards needed for a healthy environment are often high. But this high cost is not because of high population densities but because the provision of adequate infrastructure and services was not made beforehand.

It is only in the absence of the institutional means to ensure that infrastructure, services and pollution controls are provided, that a high concentration of population and industrial production greatly exacerbates environmental health problems. In the absence of effective governance, a high concentration of industries and motor vehicles (and, on occasion, coal or biomass-fuelled household fires or furnaces) can also mean high levels of air, soil and water pollution. Good governance is critical for cities, both to ensure that the potential environmental health advantages of concentration are fully exploited and that potential disadvantages are avoided.

Inadequacies in the information base

Most existing documentation on urban environmental problems comes from Europe, North America and Japan. Most of the documentation on Third World cities that does exist comes from a handful of the largest Asian and Latin American cities. Generalizations about environmental problems in Third World cities are usually derived from these. They are almost certainly inaccurate because they fail to reflect the great diversity of urban centres within each nation: from capital cities (usually the largest cities) to dozens or even hundreds of small urban centres. There are tens of thousands of urban centres in the Third World: India, China and Brazil alone each have several thousand urban centres within their national boundaries which range from the world's largest, to thousands of small market and administrative centres. Brazil alone has a dozen cities or metropolitan areas with a million or more inhabitants and over 50 others with more than 100,000. It also has over 600 urban centres with between 10,000 and 100,000 inhabitants and thousands more with under 10,000 inhabitants.[22] Even relatively small and predominantly rural countries can have dozens of urban centres: Ghana with 14 million inhabitants in 1984 had 189 urban centres, each with 5,000 or more inhabitants.[23]

Each urban centre will have its own particular mix of environmental problems whose scale and scope are influenced by such factors as population size and density; scale and nature of production base; climate, soil and site characteristics; water resources and surface water flows; and the type and distribution of flora and fauna in and around the urban centre. Generalizations are often invalid, even within urban centres in the same country; what appears as a particularly pressing problem in one urban centre may represent very minor problems in other centres in that same country.

2

Environmental problems in the home, workplace and neighbourhood

INTRODUCTION

This chapter concentrates on three kinds of environmental problem in relation to the home, workplace and neighbourhood:[1]

- Pathogens or pollutants in the human environment (in air, soil, food or water) which can damage human health;
- Shortages of natural resources essential to human health (for instance sufficient fresh water); and
- Physical hazards within the city (for instance the risk of flooding for housing built on floodplains or of mudslides or landslides for housing built on steep slopes).

These are all environmental problems amenable to human intervention. Chapter 3 describes these environmental problems at the city level, and also considers other environmental problems such as noise pollution, lack of provision for public space and facilities and characteristics of urban environments which contribute to stress and psycho-social problems.

Chapter 4 widens the discussion of environmental problems to include the impact of city-based production, consumption or waste generation on the health of rural dwellers and on natural resources and ecosystems. Broader issues about the aggregate impact of cities and urban systems on global climate and natural resources are discussed in Chapter 6.

Although many of the examples given in this and subsequent chapters reveal very serious environmental problems in terms of disease, disablement, premature death and damage or destruction of natural resources, these may not be the 'worst cases' since many of the worst cases have probably never been documented. Very few nations have a range of citizen groups working on environmental issues comparable to those in Europe, North America and Japan. In the First World, it is largely through the efforts of individual activists, citizen groups and NGOs that attention has been drawn to environmental problems. Although First World governments have been slow to react, the fact that most have taken some action despite the opposition of powerful vested interests is a demonstration of democratic processes at work. Such democratic processes are controlled or even repressed in many Third World nations.

THE INDOOR ENVIRONMENT AT HOME

The fact that a high proportion of the Third World's urban population live and work in very poor conditions is too well known to need much elaboration. In most cities, between one third and two thirds of the population live in inadequate housing units. These people live in unsafe structures without adequate protection from the elements, sufficient space (relative to the number of people living there), piped water supplies, provision to remove excreta, household liquids and solid wastes, drainage, and all-weather roads. Despite the many different forms of housing used by poorer groups – from rooms rented in tenements or illegal settlements, beds rented in boarding houses and houses or shacks built on illegally occupied or subdivided land or rudimentary temporary shelters on some piece of open space – almost all are characterised by three factors which contribute to poor environmental health. The first is the presence in the human environment of pathogens because of a lack of basic infrastructure and services such as sewers, drains or services to collect solid and liquid wastes and safely dispose of them. The second is a lack of safe and sufficient water supply. The third is overcrowded, cramped living conditions which increase the risk of transmission of airborne infections and increase the risk of accidents.

Water and sanitation

A lack of readily available drinking water, of sewage connections (or other systems to dispose of human wastes hygienically), of garbage collection and basic measures to prevent disease and provide primary health care can result in many debilitating and easily prevented diseases becoming endemic among poorer households. These include diarrhoea, dysenteries, typhoid, intestinal parasites and food poisoning. When combined with under-nutrition (as is often the case), these can so weaken the body's defences that measles, pneumonia and other common childhood diseases become major causes of death.[2] Cholera remains a threat for poorer groups in many urban centres. Table 2.1, drawn from a recent WHO report, lists the water-related diseases and estimates their impact on mortality and morbidity and, where they exist, the size of the population

Table 2.1 Examples of the main water-related infections with estimates of morbidity, mortality and population at risk

DISEASE (Common name)	(name)	MORBIDITY	MORTALITY (No of deaths/year)	POPULATION AT RISK
1. WATERBORNE (and water-washed; * also foodborne)				
Cholera	Cholera*	More than 300,000	More than 3000	
Diarrhoeal diseases	This group includes salmonellosis,* shigellosis,* campylobacter,* E coli, rota-virus, amoebiasis* and giardiasis*	700 million or more infected each year	More than five million	More than 2000 million
Enteric fevers	Paratyphoid			
	Typhoid	500,000 cases; 1 million infections (1977–8)	25,000	
Infective jaundice	Hepatitis A*			
Pinworm	Enterobiasis			
Polio	Poliomyelitis	204,000 (1990)	25,000	
Roundworm	Ascariasis	800–1,000 million cases; 1 million cases of disease	20,000	
Leptospirosis				
Whipworm	Trichuriasis			
2. WATER-WASHED				
Skin and eye infections				
Scabies	Scabies			
School sores	Impetigo			
Trachoma	Trachoma	6–9 million people blind		500 million
Leishmaniasis	Leishmaniasis	12 million infected; 400,000 new infections/year		350 million
Other				
Relapsing fever	Relapsing fever			
Typhus	Rickettsial diseases			
3. WATER-BASED				
Penetrating skin				
Bilharzia	Schistosomiasis	200 million	Over 200,000	500–600 million
Ingested				
Guinea worm	Dracunculiasis	Over 10 million		Over 100 million
4. WATER-RELATED INSECT VECTOR				
Biting near water				
Sleeping sickness	African Trypanosomiasis	20,000 new cases annually (thought to be an underestimate)		50 million
Breeding in water				
Filaria	Filariasis (lymphatic)	90 million		900 million
Malaria	Malaria	267 million (107 million clinical cases)	1–2 million (three quarters children under 5)	2100 million
River blindness	Onchocerciasis	18 million (over 300,000 – blind)		85–90 million
Yellow fever	Yellow fever	10–25,000		
Breakbone fever	Dengue fever	30–60 million infected every year		

Source: Adapted from WHO (1992) *Our Planet, Our Health*, Report of the World Commission on Health and Environment, Geneva. Derived from Cairncross, Sandy and Richard G Feachem (1983) *Environmental Health Engineering in the Tropics – An Introductory Text*, John Wiley and Sons, Chichester; and White, GF, Bradley DJ and White, AU (1972) *Drawers of Water: Domestic Water Use in East Africa*, University of Chicago Press, Chicago. Figures for morbidity, mortality and population at risk from WHO (1990) *Global Estimates for Health Situation Assessment and Projections 1990*, Geneva.

at risk. As this report noted, the health effects of these diseases are heavily concentrated in the Third World and, within the Third World, among the poorer urban and rural households of poorer countries.[3]

Many health problems are linked to water – its quality, the quantity available, the ease with which it can be obtained and the provisions made for its removal, once used. Hundreds of millions of urban dwellers have no alternative but to use contaminated water, or at least water whose quality is not guaranteed (see Box 2.1). A small minority have water piped into their homes while rather more have to collect water from a standpipe nearby. As one specialist commented, 'those not served are obliged to use water from streams or other surface sources which in urban areas are often little more than open sewers, or to purchase water from insanitary vendors. It is little wonder that their children suffer frequently, often fatally, from diarrhoeal diseases'.[4]

Box 2.1 Inadequacies in Third World cities' water supply and sanitation

Accra (Ghana): Most of the population has access to piped water but the piped water systems are often not operational. There is a central sewage system but much of the population is not connected to it, because of high connection charges; an estimate in 1985 suggested that only 30 per cent of the population were connected. New residential areas often use septic tanks for sanitation while in other unconnected areas, pan or bucket latrines are used with the contents emptied into night-soil containers provided by the city council which are then emptied at a shoreline tipping station. In many poor settlements, there are very few public or private sanitation facilities, even in settlements with many thousands of households. The city's open drainage system collects surface runoff, domestic discharges (other than sewage) and some industrial discharges (often illegally) and in some areas, may also (unofficially) receive wastes from latrines.

Bangkok (Thailand): About one third of the population has no access to public water and must obtain water from vendors. Only 2 per cent of the population is connected to a sewer system; human wastes are generally disposed of through septic tanks and cesspools with their effluents, as well as wastewater from sinks, laundries, baths and kitchens discharged into stormwater drains or canals.

Calcutta (India): Some three million people live in 'bustees' and refugee settlements which lack potable water, endure serious annual flooding and have no systematic means of disposing of refuse or human wastes. Some 2.5 million others live in similarly blighted and unserviced areas. Piped water is only available in the central city and parts of some other municipalities. The sewage system is limited to only a third of the area in the urban core. Poor maintenance of drains and periodic clogging of the system have made flooding an annual feature.

Dakar and other Senegalese towns: Senegalese towns have no provision for the removal of household and public waste. Of the five urban centres with sewage systems, generally only the inner urban population has access to facilities. In Dakar, the capital, a survey in 1980/81 found that 28 per cent of households have private water connections while 68 per cent rely on public standpipes and 4.2 per cent buy water from carriers. A survey in Pikine, the outer part of Dakar, found an average of 696 persons per standpipe with 1513 in one neighbourhood. In Dakar, nearly one sixth of human solid wastes is dumped away from proper toilet facilities.

Dar Es Salaam (Tanzania): From a survey of 660 households drawn from all income levels in 1986/87, 47 per cent had no piped water supply either inside or immediately outside their houses while 32 per cent had a shared piped water supply. Of the households without piped water, 67 per cent buy water from neighbours while 26 per cent draw water from public water kiosks or standpipes. Only 7.1 per cent buy water from water sellers. Average water consumption per person is only 23.6 litres a day. For sanitation, only 13 per cent of the dirty water and sewage is regularly disposed of. Of the 660 households, 89 per cent had simple pit-latrines. Most households have to share sanitary facilities. Overflowing latrines are a serious problem, especially in the rainy season, and provisions to empty septic tanks or latrines are very inadequate.

Jakarta (Indonesia): Less than a third of the population have direct connections to a piped water system; around 30 per cent depend solely on water vendors whose prices per litre of water are up to 50 times that paid by households served by the municipal water company. Over a third of the population rely on shallow wells (most of which are contaminated), deep wells or nearby river water. Over half of all dwellings have no indoor plumbing and much of the population has to use drainage canals for bathing, laundry and defecation. The city has no central waterborne sewage system. Septic tanks serve about 68 per cent of the population with 17 per cent relying on pit latrines or toilets which discharge directly into ditches or drains, 6 per cent using public toilets (generally with septic tanks) and about 9 per cent with no formal toilet facilities.

Kampala (Uganda): Most inhabitants do not have piped water close to their homes; a household survey in 1981 found only 18 per cent of households with potable water within 100 metres. Many people have to rely on springs, streams or wells, many of which are polluted by human wastes or waste waters from drainage channels. Very few have adequate sanitation systems; the survey in 1981 showed that 81 per cent of the population used pit latrines and in some poor neighbourhoods, up to 40 persons use each latrine.

Karachi (Pakistan): Only 38 per cent of the population have water piped to their homes; 46 per cent rely on standpipes and a further 16 per cent purchase it from vendors who supply if from water tankers. In most areas served with a piped supply, water is only available for a few hours a day.

Khartoum (the Sudan): The water supply system is working beyond its design capacity while demand continues to rise. The coverage is poor, with low-income groups in squatter settlements paying the most for water, often bought from vendors. Breakdowns and cuts in the supply system are common. The municipal sewage system serves only about 5 per cent of the Khartoum urban area. Even that system is susceptible to breakdowns when waste is discharged either directly into the river or onto open land.

Kinshasa (Zaire): There is no sewage system in Kinshasa. Around half the urban population (some 1.5 million people) are not served by a piped-water network. High-income areas are often 100 per cent connected while many other areas have 20–30 per cent of houses connected – essentially those along the main roads. The sale of water flourishes in areas far from the network – in these areas water is usually obtained from wells or the river.

Madras (India): Only two million of the 3.7 million residential consumers within the service area of the local water supply and sewerage board are connected to the system. On average, they receive some 36 litres per day per capita. The rest within the service area must use public taps which serve about 240 persons per tap. Another million consumers outside the service area must rely on wells, but supplies are inadequate too because of falling groundwater levels. The sewage system serves 31 per cent of the metropolitan population.

Metro Manila (Philippines): Only 15 per cent of the population is served with sewers or individual septic tanks. Some 1.8 million people lack adequate water supplies, and educational, health and sanitary services.

Sources: Accra: Sangsore 1992 and IIED 1992; Bangkok: Sivaramakrishnan and Green 1986; Phantumvanit and Liengcharernsit 1989 and United Nations 1987. Calcutta and Madras: Sivaramakrishnan and Green 1986. Dakar and other Senegalese towns: Ngom 1989. Dar es Salaam: Kulaba 1989. Jakarta: Sivaramakrishnan and Green 1986 and Clarke, Hadiwinoto and Leitmann 1991. Karachi: Sahil 1988; United Nations 1988. Kampala: UNEP 1988. Khartoum: El Sammani, El Hadi Abu Sin, Talha, El Hassan and Haywood 1989. Kinshasa: Mbuyi 1989. Manila: Jimenez and Velasquez 1989. Full references given in the bibliography.

The quantity of water available to a household and the price which has to be paid can be as important to a family's health as its quality.[5] The cost of water and the time needed to collect it influence the quantity used. Where public agencies provide no water supply – as is common in illegal settlements – the poor often obtain water from private vendors and can pay 4–100 times the cost per litre paid by richer groups with piped supplies (see Table 2.2).[6] Water vendors probably serve between 20 and 30 per cent of the Third World's urban population.[7]

Table 2.2 Differentials in the cost of water (ratio of price charged by water vendors to prices charged by the public utility)

City	*Water price ratio private vendors: public utility*
Abidjan	5:1
Dhaka	12:1 to 25:1
Istanbul	10:1
Kampala	4:1 to 9:1
Karachi	28:1 to 83:1
Lagos	4:1 to 10:1
Lima	17:1
Lome	7:1 to 10:1
Nairobi	7:1 to 11:1
Port-au-Prince	17:1 to 100:1
Surabaya	20:1 to 60:1
Tegucigalpa	16:1 to 34:1

Source: World Bank (1988), *World Development Report 1988*, p. 146.

Where there is a public supply – a well or public standpipe – the quantity used per person will depend on the time and energy needed to collect and carry water back to the home. There are often 500 or more persons for each tap; in one part of Dakar, a survey in the late 1980s found that there were 1513 persons per tap.[8] Very often, water will only be available in the piped system for a few hours a day.

Since water is very heavy, consumption levels are influenced by the distance that it has to be carried. Low-income people often work very long hours, so queuing at a tap or carrying water takes away from time which is already in short supply. Limited quantities of water mean inadequate supplies for washing and personal hygiene, and for washing food, cooking utensils and clothes. Eye and ear infections, skin diseases, scabies, lice and fleas are very difficult to control without sufficient supplies of water. So too is a good standard of personal hygiene.

Removing and safely disposing of excreta and wastewater is also a critical environmental health need. No drains or sewers to take away wastewater and rainwater can lead to waterlogged soil and stagnant pools which can transmit diseases like hookworm. Pools of standing water can convey enteric diseases and provide breeding grounds for mosquitoes which spread filariasis, malaria and other diseases. Inadequate or no drainage often means damp walls and living environments.

Around two thirds of the Third World's urban population have no hygienic means of disposing of excreta and an even greater number lack adequate means to dispose of wastewaters.[9] Most cities in Africa and many in Asia have no sewers at all. This is not only in the smaller cities;

many major cities with a million or more inhabitants have no sewers. Rivers, streams, canals, gullies and ditches are where most human excrement and wastewater ends up, untreated. For those cities with sewers, rarely do they serve more than a small proportion of the population – typically the richer residential, government and commercial areas. Box 2.1 provides many illustrations of this; the majority of people in major cities such as Jakarta, Calcutta, Dar es Salaam, Accra, Khartoum, Kampala and Manila live in housing lacking adequate sanitation. In India, defecating in the open is common practice since one third of the urban population (over 50 million people) have no latrine of any kind while another third rely on bucket latrines. A third may use latrines connected to sewers but only 10 per cent have sewage connections to their homes.[10] Removing and disposing of excreta in ways which prevent human contact is central to reducing the burden of disease.

Official government or United Nations statistics often suggest that people in urban areas are better served than those in rural areas but public provision to remove and safely dispose of human excreta is usually no better in poor urban neighbourhoods than in rural ones. The health problems that arise in urban areas are usually more serious because higher densities and larger populations make it more difficult to dispose of excreta in ways which ensure no possibility of human contact. For instance in Dar es Salaam, virtually all the population rely on pit latrines but these regularly overflow and the public authorities only have the equipment to empty a tiny proportion of them.[11] In Jakarta, there is no waterborne sewage system, so much of the population uses the canals for bathing, washing clothes and defecation.[12]

Even in larger and richer cities where a higher proportion of homes are connected, millions suffer; for instance, although 70 per cent of metropolitan Mexico City's population live in housing served by sewers, there are still three million people not served.[13] In Buenos Aires metropolitan area, recent estimates suggest that four million of the 11.3 million inhabitants lack piped water and close to six million are not connected to the sewer system.[14]

It is common for official statistics to overstate the proportion of people adequately served; for instance, people in neighbourhoods with public latrines are often considered 'adequately served' when there are 100 or more persons per latrine and maintenance and cleaning are so poor that the latrine itself is a major health hazard and many people avoid using it. In addition, no one who knows Bolivia or Kenya can take seriously official government figures which suggest that 100 per cent of their urban populations were adequately served with piped water in 1980.[15] Criteria for 'adequate service' often seem more appropriate for exaggerating the impact of government or aid programmes than for meeting poor households' needs. A family of six needs at least 300–400 litres of water a day to meet all its needs, the equivalent of 30–40 buckets a day. One of the most widely used criterion for judging whether a water supply is adequate is the existence of a communal tap within 100 metres. It is not appropriate to claim that a household has an adequate supply for its health and convenience when household members have to fetch and carry two bucketfuls of water for 100 metres, 15–20 times a day (and no doubt queue to get to the water tap). The existence of a water tap within 100 metres does not mean that the tap works or that water is available from it 24 hours a day.[16]

Overcrowding

Another characteristic common to most homes of poorer groups is crowded, cramped conditions. Many health problems affecting poorer groups are associated with overcrowding, including household accidents, acute respiratory infections (of which pneumonia is perhaps the most serious), tuberculosis and other airborne infections.[17] In the predominantly low-income residential areas in Third World cities, there is often an average of four or more persons per room and in many instances less than one square metre of floorspace per person.[18] Diseases such as tuberculosis, influenza and meningitis are easily transmitted from one person to another. Their spread is often aided by low resistance among inhabitants due to malnutrition and by frequent contact between infective and susceptible people.

Acute bacterial and viral respiratory infections account, with tuberculosis, for some five million deaths annually; tuberculosis is responsible for more than half of these deaths.[19] In Kanpur, one of India's major industrial centres, the development authority estimates that 60 per cent of children in 'slums' have tuberculosis.[20] Box 2.2 describes the impact of tuberculosis on health and its association with housing. A child who contracts bronchitis or pneumonia in the Third World is 50 times more likely to die than a child in Europe or North America.[21] A recent WHO report summarised the problem:

> Acute respiratory infections tend to be endemic rather than epidemic, affect younger groups, and more prevalent in urban than in rural areas. The frequency of contact, the density of the population and the concentration and proximity of infective and susceptible people in an urban population promote the transmission of the infective organisms. Poorer groups ... are much more at risk because of the greater proportion of younger age groups, limited health and financial resources, and overcrowded households in congested settlements with limited access to vaccines and antibacterial drugs.[22]

Box 2.2 The impact of tuberculosis on health and its association with housing

About 20 million people worldwide have active cases of pulmonary tuberculosis, a contagious chronic disease of the lungs caused by a bacterium transmitted through the air when infected people cough or sneeze. If untreated, the fatality is close to 50 per cent, mostly among young adults. Nearly three million people die each year from tuberculosis, more than from any other infectious disease. Virtually all these deaths are in Third World countries: over 60 per cent of them in Asia and over 20 per cent in Africa. 1.4 per cent of these deaths take place in the First World and most of these deaths are among the elderly, ethnic minorities and migrants.

Each year, there are eight million new cases of tuberculosis; four million of these are infectious. Countries with the largest number of TB cases are Bangladesh, Brazil, China, India, Indonesia, Nigeria, Pakistan, the Philippines and Vietnam. Sub-Saharan African countries tend to have proportionately the highest incidence of cases.

In most Third World countries, the incidence of TB has been declining, although it increases in absolute numbers as the population increases. In some East and Central African countries, there has been a rapid increase in the number of TB cases reported, almost doubling in the last 4–5 years. One of the main reasons is the spread of infection with the human immunodeficiency virus; when people infected with TB are also infected with HIV, TB is more likely to become active. An estimated three million people with HIV infection are also TB infected. In people with TB, the time it takes for HIV to develop into AIDS is shortened dramatically.

Household members living with an infectious case are at greatest risk. The highest incidence of TB tends to be among populations living in the poorest areas where families are usually large, housing inadequate and overcrowded, nutrition levels low and health care limited or unavailable. Household, social or work contacts are at greatest risk from infection as the number of infective cases increases; density of population also accelerates transmission rates. Overcrowded housing conditions and poor ventilation often means that TB infection is transmitted to more than half of family members.

The cost of immunization against TB is less than US$6 per person. The cost of drugs to treat TB is only some US$30–50 per patient and high cure rates are possible; in Tanzania, a TB programme using short course chemotherapy has achieved an 85 per cent cure rate for diagnosed cases.

Sources: Drawn from WHO (1992) *Our Planet, Our Health*, Report of the Commission on Health and Environment, Geneva. This drew from Cauthen, GM, Pio, A and ten Dam, H G (1988) *Annual Risk of Tuberculosis Infection*, World Health Organization, Geneva; and WHO (1990) *Global Estimates for Health Situation Assessment and Projections 1990*, Geneva.

The vaccine-preventable 'childhood' diseases such as mumps, measles, diphtheria and whooping cough also spread more rapidly in overcrowded urban areas: while measles holds few worries for children in richer households, among poorer households it is often one of the most common causes or contributory factors to infant or child death. Meningococcal meningitis is another airborne infection, the transmission of which is partly due to overcrowding.[23]

Crowded, cramped conditions, inadequate water supplies and facilities for preparing and storing food greatly exacerbate the risk of food contamination.[24] In a review of environmental problems at the household level in Third World cities, Gordon McGranahan notes that

> microbially contaminated food contributes to a high incidence of acute diarrhoea in Third World countries and foodborne diseases including cholera, botulism, typhoid fever and parasitism ... microbial activity generally contributes to food spoilage while unsafe chemicals may deliberately be added to retard or disguise spoilage ... food contamination is intimately linked to the sanitary conditions of food preparation, processing and even production.[25]

He also notes that the risk of contamination and spoilage is all the greater in warm climates, where bacterial multiplication is extremely rapid.[26]

A recent WHO report noted that 'within the home, there are likely to be numerous interconnections and interactions among water, sanitation, flies, animals, personal hygiene and food that are responsible for diarrhoea transmission'.[27]

A high proportion of the population in most low-income settlements or districts have intestinal worms. For hookworm alone, estimates suggest some 700–900 million people infested with 1.5 million cases of disease and 50,000 deaths a year.[28] Studies in poor urban communities in Lagos,[29] Manila,[30] Kuala Lumpur,[31] and Allahabad[32] have shown the high prevalence of intestinal worms, especially in children.

Accidents

Accidents within the home are also common in overcrowded conditions, perhaps not surprisingly when there are often five or more persons living in one room and there is little chance of giving the occupants (especially children) protection from fires, stoves and kerosene heaters. Accidents were found to be one of the five leading causes of death in an analysis of the causes of mortality in ten Third World nations;[33] while accidents in the home may not cause as many deaths as road accidents, they are more numerous, and for every death, there are several hundred accidental injuries.[34] Overcrowded conditions can also increase the risk of accidental poisonings; it is hardly possible to prevent children from coming into contact with harmful chemicals used in the household (for instance bleach or kerosene) or to keep medicines in a secure place, when whole families live in one or two rooms.

Indoor air pollution

Where open fires or relatively inefficient stoves are used indoors for cooking and/or heating, smoke or fumes from coal, wood or other biomass fuels can cause or contribute to serious respiratory problems. Chronic effects include inflammation of the respiratory tract which in turn reduces resistance to acute respiratory infections, while these infections in turn enhance susceptibility to the inflammatory effects of smoke and fumes.[35] Exposure to carcinogens in emissions from biomass fuel combustion has been confirmed in studies in which exposed subjects wore personal monitoring equipment. Women who may spend 2–4 hours a day at the stove must be at risk. Infants and children may be heavily exposed because they remain with their mothers; the added exposure to pollutants combined with malnutrition may retard growth, leading to smaller lungs and greater prevalence of chronic bronchitis.[36]

Health impacts

Increasing numbers of health studies in Third World cities show the degree to which lower-income groups' lives are dominated by ill-health, disablement or premature death and the extent to which environmental factors are major causes or contributors. According to the World Health Organization, in many illegal settlements, a child is 40–50 times more likely to die before the age of five than a child born in a Western nation.[37]

In many cities, the incidence of tuberculosis, diarrhoeal diseases and other health problems related to poor quality living environments has been shown to be much higher in squatter settlements or inner-city tenements than in the city as a whole. Studies of the health problems faced by poorer groups point not only to the high proportion of infant and child deaths but also high rates of death, disablement and serious injury from household accidents, and high proportions of people in each age group suffering from ill health for substantial proportions of their lives. The studies also suggest that it is in the house and its immediate surrounds that most injuries and diseases are contracted. The scale of the health differentials within cities will be discussed in the final section of chapter 3, after all environmental problems within cities have been discussed.

THE WORKPLACE

Environmental hazards arising in the workplace are also a major problem in Third World cities, and are evident in workplaces from large factories and commercial institutions down to small 'backstreet' workshops and people working from home. They include dangerous concentrations of toxic chemicals and dust, inadequate lighting, ventilation and space, and lack of protection for workers from machinery and noise. One global estimate suggests that there are 32.7 million occupational injuries each year with about 146,000 deaths.[38] Environmental hazards in the workplace are made all the more serious by the lack of social security; there is little or no provision by most employers of sick pay or compensation if workers are injured or laid off.

Many industries have long been associated with high levels of risk for their workforce from toxic chemicals – for instance in factories extracting, processing and milling asbestos, chemical industries, cement, glass and ceramics industries, iron and steel industries, factories making rubber and plastics products, metal and non-ferrous metal industries and textile and leather industries.[39] Some of the most common environment-related occupational diseases are silicosis, byssinosis, lead and mercury poisoning, pesticide poisoning, noise-induced hearing loss and occupational skin diseases.[40]

Many case studies can be cited which show a high proportion of the workers in particular industries or industrial plants whose health is affected by workplace exposures. For instance, a recent study of Egyptian pesticide factorys found that 'about 40 per cent of the workers had problems related to pesticide poisoning, ranging from asthma to enlarged livers.'[41] In most countries, the scale of occupational injuries and diseases is almost certainly greatly under-reported. For instance, the Mexican Social Security Institute reported an average of 2000–3000 cases of work-related illnesses across the country in 1988 but a study in just one large steel mill found 4000–5000 cases alone, with more than 80 per cent of the workers exposed to extreme heat, noise and toxic dust.[42] A paper on Bangkok's environmental problems noted that a remarkable number of Thai workers are exposed to poor working environments but that the number of workers suffering from occupational diseases is small. 'This may be a reflection of the difficulties of linking disease to working conditions rather than revealing a satisfactory condition'.[43]

This point has wider relevance since people's long term exposure to dust, excessive noise, inadequate lighting and pollutants in the workplace often contributes much to ill health, disablement and premature death but it is difficult to prove the link, if compensation is being sought. There are many examples of industrial workers killed or permanently injured by chemicals they handle or inhale at work[44] but the health impacts which take longer to become apparent are more worrying in that these affect such a large number of industrial workers. A report in 1983 stated that one third of those working in asbestos factories in Bombay suffer from asbestosis while many of those working in cotton mills suffer from byssinosis (brown lung).[45] A study of workers in the Bombay Gas Company found that 24 per cent were suffering from chronic bronchitis, tuberculosis and emphysema.[46] There is also an increasing number of studies documenting serious health problems from environmental hazards in small workshops. One example is the informal enterprises in Jamaica that recycle and repair lead-acid batteries, resulting in exposure of both workers and the wider public to lead.[47] Many people working in informal enterprises use chemicals that should only be used under carefully controlled conditions with special safety equipment. One example is the rise in leukaemia among leather workers in Turkey after the introduction of a cheaper benzene-containing glue in making leather goods; over 50 deaths have been documented and many thousands of leather workers were put at risk.[48]

A review of occupational health issues in Latin America, after listing many examples of serious health problems affecting high proportions of the workforce of particular industries, commented that:

> Few health standards are applied to limit work-place exposures; in most of the region's countries, the standard-setting process is either just beginning or has not yet begun. In those nations where standards regulating work practices or toxic exposure do exist, the standards are often not enforced, either for political or economic reasons or because of a lack of trained inspectors.[49]

It is also appropriate to consider environmental problems associated with work in 'the home' in that many poor city-dwellers use their homes as a workshop to produce goods for sale or as a store for goods sold on the street, or as a shop, bar or café. Environmental problems here are too diverse to be covered in a short summary. But briefly, there are often problems with levels of light and ventilation, as well as major problems for many home-workers arising from the use of toxic or flammable chemicals in the home as part of the work done there. One common way in which this happens is through out-working; here, well-organized (and often large) enterprises commission people (usually women) working in their homes to fabricate some product – for instance, sandals or articles of clothing. These enterprises will often supply the out-workers with raw materials and chemicals and collect the finished articles. Many of these chemicals are a serious fire hazard and should be used in carefully controlled conditions in factories with special provisions to limit inhalation or skin contact and to guard against fire hazards. The advantages of such homeworkers to the enterprise are obvious: low wages, no costs involved in building and running factories, no costs for social security and few problems with labour unrest since the workforce is too scattered to allow them to organize.

Certain groups are particularly at risk from occupational hazards. For instance pregnant women and their unborn children are particularly vulnerable to certain toxic substances. Human vulnerability to environmental factors precedes conception since both the mother's ova and the father's sperm may be damaged by radiation or certain chemical pollutants. Environmental factors also exert a strong influence on the child in the womb, for instance through the mother's exposure to toxic chemicals; methyl mercury, certain pesticides, PCBs and carbon monoxide are among the chemicals known to harm the foetus when transferred through the placenta.[50] Many light industries prefer to employ young women in assembling products, and hazardous chemicals are often used without adequate safeguards; these often pose particular threats to foetuses.[51]

The fact that child labour is widespread means that tens of millions of children are also exposed to environmental hazards at work. Children are more susceptible than adults to accident, injury and industrial disease.

> Small, weak and inexperienced workers are more at risk from dangerous machinery and materials, heavy weights and the heat of industrial processes; and more prone to chemical poisoning and respiratory complaints caused by the many airborne hazards.[52]

One example is the widespread employment of minors in the shoe industries in Novo Hamburgo, Brazil; with 30 major factories and 170 smaller ones, the industry employs over 35,000 people and at least 12,000 are minors. Benzene-based solvents are widely used in the shoe factories. There is normally inadequate ventilation so the vapour hangs around the work floor. It is also common for packed lunches to be brought, stored and eaten on the shop floor.[53] Box 2.3 gives additional examples of the occupational health hazards for children at work.

THE NEIGHBOURHOOD ENVIRONMENT

Added to health risks associated with the presence of toxic substances or pathogens inside the home are those which arise from the sites on which many poorer households live. The two are not easily separated since deficiencies in environmental protection in one will impact on the other – for example a lack of sewers to remove excreta and wastewater from each house results in open drains which then present hazards for the whole

Box 2.3 Examples of environmental hazards for children at work in India.

Brass moulding industry A report on the workers who make brass instruments in Roorkee (Uttar Pradesh) mentions that 400 children are engaged in this industry, mainly in packing and moulding. In the moulding, gas escapes and is inhaled by the young workers; they are also burnt by sparks and accidental spillage from molten metal.

Carpet weaving In Kashmir's carpet weaving industry, some 6500 children between the ages of eight and ten work in congested sheds in long rows behind giant looms; the air is thick with particles of fluff and wool and 60 per cent suffer from asthma and TB.

Agate processing The agate processing industry in Khambat, Gujarat, employs some 30,000 workers including many children. A study of 342 workers included 35 children and half the children surveyed had lung diseases while five had pneumonoconiosis.

Match industries Match factories in or around Sivakasi employ as many as 45,000 children of between four and 15 years of age. Twelve hour days are common, working within cramped environments with hazardous chemicals and inadequate ventilation. A supervisor commented that 'we prefer child labour. Children work faster, work longer hours and are more dependable; they also do not form unions or take time off for tea and cigarettes.'

Glass industries In and around Firozabad, there are some 200,000 people working in glass industries; roughly a quarter are children. Among the environmental hazards are exposure to silica and soda ash dust, excessive heat, accidental burns, accidents caused by defective machines or unprotected machinery, cuts and lacerations caused by broken glass.

Sources: UNICEF (1992) *Environment, Development and the Child*, Environment Section, Programme Division, UNICEF, New York, 88 pages drawing from CSE (1985) *The State of India's Environment: a Second Citizen's Report*, Centre for Science and Environment, Delhi; Kothari, Smithu (1983) 'There's blood on those matchsticks' *Economic and Political Weekly* vol. XVIII, pp. 11–91; and Lee-Wright, Peter (1990) *Child Slaves*, Earthscan Publications, London.

neighbourhood. But four problems are worth emphasizing within the neighbourhood environment – dangerous sites, no collection of household garbage, disease vectors, and inadequate provision for drainage and other forms of infrastructure.

House sites

Tens of millions of urban inhabitants in Africa, Asia and Latin America live on hazardous land sites, either because of natural hazards or risks from human activities, or a combination of the two.[54]

It is easy to see which areas are at risk from natural hazards in most cities – for instance, the clusters of illegal housing on steep hillsides, floodplains or desertland. Large concentrations of poor settlements can be seen on hills prone to landslides in Rio de Janeiro (Brazil), La Paz (Bolivia) and Caracas (Venezuela); or in deep ravines (Guatemala City); or in sandy desert as in Lima (Peru) and Khartoum (the Sudan); or on land prone to flooding or tidal inundation or under water as in Guayaquil (Ecuador), Recife (Brazil), Monrovia (Liberia), Lagos and Port Harcourt (Nigeria), Port Moresby (Papua New Guinea), Delhi (India), Bangkok (Thailand), Jakarta (Indonesia), Buenos Aires and Resistencia (Argentina), Accra (Ghana) and many others.

Densely populated residential areas also develop on sites which, as a result of human actions, are hazardous – for instance around solid-waste dumps, beside open drains and open sewers or close to quarries or particular factories with high levels of air pollution. Many settlements with a high proportion of low-income households develop on sites subject to high noise levels, close to major highways or airports for instance.

There is often a complex interaction between natural hazards and human actions – human actions can often greatly lessen or eliminate environmental hazards but they may also act to make them more frequent or increase the scale and severity of risk.[55] For instance, in Caracas, where close to 600,000 persons live on slopes with a high risk of landslide, most slope failures were associated with earthquakes until the 1960s.[56] From the 1970s onwards, they have been increasingly associated with rains and with areas where low-income barrios have developed; it is the changes introduced in the slopes through their development for housing which has increased the likelihood that rainfall can trigger the slope failure.[57]

The vast majority of those living on sites with such natural or human-induced environmental hazards are low-income groups. Rarely do they live here in ignorance of the dangers; such sites are chosen because their location and low monetary cost meet more immediate and pressing needs. Poorer groups need to minimize the cost and time taken getting to and from work (or to and from places where incomes can be earned); most also need to pay as little as possible for housing. Hazardous sites are often the only places where poorer groups can build their own house or rent accommodation. The sites are cheap or can be occupied without payment because the environmental hazards make them unattractive to alternative users. Such sites are often publicly owned and may have been designated as parks. Polluted sites next to industries or steep hillsides on outcrops of rock or valley slopes close to city centres are close to jobs. If the land is unsuitable for commercial developments, the possibility of avoiding eviction from such sites is much greater.

To the hazards inherent in the site are added those linked to a lack of investment in infrastructure and services. For instance, most new residential developments in most Third World cities do not include storm and surface water drains (nor provision for sanitation). The introduction of water supplies with no provision for draining away wastewater may add significantly to the risk of slope failure for houses on steep hillsides. There may also be a lack of knowledge among the settlers as to how to reduce risks – for instance minimizing the amount of vegetation cleared from a slope as it is developed for housing, which can reduce the risk of land/mudslides.[58] Or the knowledge may be there, but without the collective organization to permit its effective use. For instance, those who have settled on a slope may be powerless to prevent new housing developments or a new road development at the base of the slope which puts the whole hillside at risk.[59] However, it should also be noted that many illegal settlements located on steep slopes have developed cheap and effective ways of minimizing the risks, which may indeed be more cost-effective than those recommended by external specialists.

The impact on health of unsuitable sites is often the result of a mix of everyday risks, risks in particular seasons (for instance the rainy season for those on steep slopes or areas subject to flooding) and occasional but high risks from particular natural events. Sites subject to flooding are often damp with pools of stagnant water for large portions of the year and damp housing can contribute significantly to poor health. Poorer groups living up hillsides usually have to transport the goods they use (from groceries to building materials) up the hill, which can represent a major drain on their time and energies. Hillsides lacking drainage, steps and paved roads are also hazardous, especially when wet, and younger and older age groups may have particular difficulties avoiding accidental falls and subsequent injuries.

Accidents may occur regularly, although their scale and severity will vary. For instance, there were hundreds of people killed or seriously injured and thousands made homeless by mudslides in Rio de Janeiro in 1988, in Medellin in 1987 and in Caracas in 1989. These were sufficient in scale to attract news coverage, although each year there are many smaller scale disasters where several people are killed or injured which are hardly reported.

In most instances, there are relatively cheap and effective ways by which the public authorities can greatly reduce the risks in such sites (for instance by paving access roads, installing drains and other safeguards) and can reduce the loss of life, injury and damage to property through disaster preparedness. The conventional approach of seeking to evict all those living on hazardous sites is hardly realistic, unless the public authorities have the capacity to offer all those displaced safer sites which meet their own needs and priorities. A more realistic approach – and one very rarely seen in Third World cities – is for public authorities to work with those living in hazardous areas in mapping the sites and shelters most at risk. They might then implement household and community-level interventions to reduce the likelihood of a disaster or its severity when it happens, and ensure plans for rapid action, if or when it takes place.

Box 2.4 Landslides in Rio de Janeiro and Caracas

Rio de Janeiro (Brazil): In February 1988, after very heavy rainfall, landslides in Rio de Janeiro destroyed 500 homes and killed 94 people. 15,000 people lost their homes and found refuge in local public schools. Among the rain-induced damages were 300 complete and 150 partial building collapses, over 800 landslides and nearly 200 accidents from rock slides or falls. More than 600 emergency calls for assistance due to floods were recorded. Other rain-induced damage included disruptions to sewers, collapsed walls, fallen trees, damaged water reservoirs and electricity pylons. The city's Civil Defence Coordination body assists an average of 200 accident occurrences per year, 21 per cent of which are building collapses and 30 per cent are landslides. Forty per cent of the assistance in the *favelas* is for shacks which collapse as a result of a lack of technical or financial resources to construct safe, rain-resistant housing.

Early in 1992, there was a landslide in Terespolis, Rio de Janeiro: a Civil Defence worker warned a household about the risk at 17.30 hours the evening before, but they refused to abandon their home. The next morning, after a night of rain, the landslide occurred. The seven members of the family were reported dead.

Caracas (Venezuela): An estimated 574,000 people live in illegal settlements on slopes with a significant risk of landslides. The number of landslides has grown very rapidly in recent decades. Between 1800 and 1949, only 12 landslides were recorded. During the next 20 years, between 1949 and 1969, there were 23 landslides recorded. Between 1971 and 1979, there were 221 landslides and in the following nine years, between 1980 and 1989, a further 266. Most of the areas continuously affected by slope failures have been low-income settlements.

Sources: Costa Leite, L (1988), 'Urban disasters in the Third World: The poor first in line', *UN Development Forum*, vol. XVI, no.3, May-June; and *Jornal do Brasil*, 6 January, 1992; Jimenez Diaz, Virginia (1992) 'Landslides in the squatter settlements of Caracas; towards a better understanding of causative factors' *Environment and Urbanization* vol. 4, no. 2.

However, it is not only peripheral areas built on land subject to floods or droughts which present particular problems. So too can more central areas. Box 2.5 gives an example of how low-income groups living in certain central areas of Lima, Peru have become increasingly at risk from seismic activity. Once again, the issue is not so much a lack of land; most of the Third World's major cities and metropolitan areas have large areas of valuable land which are not prone to natural hazards and this is left undeveloped or only partially developed.[60] But poorer groups are denied access to such land.

Box 2.5 Seismic vulnerability in metropolitan Lima

Lima experiences periodic earthquakes due to its location on the Pacific coast of Peru where two tectonic plates come into contact. One estimate in 1980 suggested that, over a 100 year period, the probability of an 8.6 Richter earthquake occurring is 96 per cent. Quite apart from the physical characteristics of the area itself, there are many factors which affect the number of deaths and amount of destruction caused by an earthquake. In buildings, the materials used, the structure, the height and the level of deterioration are all important variables. How dangerous a particular neighbourhood is will depend on the availability of open space, the width of the streets, the number of access routes and the building density. Other factors include the population density and the ability of people to escape and deal with an emergency. Income and occupational structures also affect vulnerability. Seismic vulnerability is determined by a complex interplay of all the above factors.

In Lima, three broad patterns of seismic vulnerability can be identified. In residential areas developed by the private sector for government agencies for middle- and high-income groups, vulnerability is relatively low. Buildings are generally well constructed, complying with building regulations and incorporating antiseismic structures. Population densities are low. There are open spaces and broad streets. If affected by an earthquake, people's income gives them a better chance of recovery from disaster. In the new informal or illegal settlements (*pueblos jovenes*) on the city periphery, seismic vulnerability is also fairly low. Housing is either built from lightweight materials such as bamboo, or else has fairly solid brick construction with reinforced concrete columns. Populations densities are also generally low. If people are affected, their low incomes are a handicap but on the other hand possibilities of recovery are enhanced by a generally high level of organization.

It is in the inner-city slum areas that seismic vulnerability is highest. Houses are built from adobe, a material with little seismic resistance. Structures have been weakened by deterioration and the effects of earlier earthquakes. There is an absence of open spaces and escape routes and streets are narrow. Buildings have multiple occupation with severe overcrowding. Organization is almost non existent and most families have low and irregular incomes. People in these areas are most likely to suffer disaster and least able to recover. The situation in some inner city *pueblos jovenes* is also critical.

An understanding of the expansion of Lima since 1940 helps explain how the vulnerability of the poor has occurred. As industrial, commercial and service activities located in traditional high-income residential areas, families moved out to new middle-class suburbs. Some of these large houses were subdivided, offering cheap rented rooms for migrants needing to find work in the city. Empty lots were used to build workers housing for the rental market and some families built their own houses on vacant sites. Such housing was important in helping low-income families become established; it was cheap and offered good accessibility to work and services. The risk of earthquakes was well known – there is even an earthquake saint – but it was not an important factor to residents because they had so few options. In the 1950s, organized groups of families from the slums invaded desert sites and hills at the edge of the city to form new settlements. Some migrants moved to such areas to improve their housing prospects. But during the 1970s, such land became more scarce and the new settlements were located at increasing distances from the centre. As the economic crisis deepened, poorer groups' struggle for survival became more difficult and accessibility became more important for increasing numbers of people. Building costs rose faster than real incomes and the possibilities for self-build were reduced. The amount of cheap rental housing in the city actually decreased in some areas as residents were evicted to be replaced by more profitable activities and new blocks of flats, offices and shops. As a consequence, in some areas of Lima, the numbers living in old adobe and *quincha* buildings has increased 30- or 40-fold in this century giving rise to an unprecedented increase in vulnerability. The formation of such areas cannot be explained in isolation. It is characteristic of an urbanization process in which land, building materials and finance are under the control of a small, powerful group, within the context of a political and socioeconomic structure dominated by national and international market forces.

Source: Maskrey, Andrew (1989) *Disaster Mitigation: A Community Based Approach*, Oxfam Development Guidelines no. 3, Oxford.

In most cities, a high proportion of all children and young adolescents live in settlements with little or no provision for the public space and facilities they need for play, sport and social life. Roads, garbage tips and other hazardous places become their playgrounds, in the absence of any better alternative.[61] They are particularly at risk from road vehicles, pathogens and toxic substances – problems range from (say) that of contracting diarrhoea through ingesting pathogens from faecal matter which contaminates the land on which they play, or from coming into contact with some toxic chemical in a nearby stream or dumped on a land site nearby, to being hit by a car. Risks posed by road traffic are often particularly serious since many illegal settlements have developed next to major roads or highways. Worldwide, estimates suggest that accidents are ranked fifth among the leading causes of death.[62]

Children and young people also have physiological limitations (in terms of motor and sensory development, reaction capacity and experience) which make them particularly susceptible to accidents; they also take more risks as part of their need to explore, experiment and test themselves.[63] A survey of 599 slum children in Rio de Janeiro found that accidents accounted for 19 per cent of all health problems; most reported accidents were falls (66 per cent), cuts (17 per cent) and burns (10 per cent).[64] The age of the child was an important determinant of accidents; peaks in accidents were in the second or fifth year of life. The authors note that the hazardous physical environment is only one variable in this; another is the limited possibility for parental child care and supervision when all adult members work.[65]

Garbage

There is the additional problem of inadequate or non-collection of household garbage. It is estimated that 30–50 per cent of solid wastes generated within urban centres remains uncollected;[66] Box 2.6 gives some examples of this in specific cities. Such refuse accumulates on waste land and streets (sometimes to the point where it actually blocks roads).[67]

The resulting problems are obvious and almost always given too low a priority by government: the smells, disease vectors and pests attracted by garbage (rats, mosquitoes, flies etc), the overflowing drainage channels clogged with garbage. Since provision for sanitation is so often deficient, water from overflowing drains is frequently contaminated with excreta. Uncollected garbage can also be a serious fire hazard as well as a serious health hazard for children playing on the site.[68] It is often common practice for households to burn their wastes if there is no service to collect them, and this adds to air pollution.[69]

It is the poorer areas of the city which generally have the least adequate garbage collection service, or no service at all. Most poor households also have very limited space (especially in tenements and high-density illegal settlements) which makes waste storage or transporting garbage to a supervised dump site difficult.[70] Many poor settlements are also on land sites to which access by motor vehicles (especially large conventional garbage trucks) is difficult if not impossible.

The impact of burns, cuts, scalds and other injuries contracted in and around the home is further magnified by a lack of first aid provision within the neighbourhood. In addition, sick or injured people cannot be rapidly transported to hospitals. A lack of paved roads and the fact that the houses

Box 2.6 Inadequacies in household garbage collection in nations' largest cities

Accra (Ghana): The Metropolitan Authority has very limited capacity to collect garbage; a study in 1989 found that only 10 per cent of garbage was collected with 81 per cent dumped and 9 per cent burned. Although there were 130 official communal refuse dumps, some 100 unauthorised dumping sites have been created along with widespread dumping of refuse along water courses, channels, on waste ground and roadside verges.

Bangkok (Thailand): Although 80 per cent of the population is served by a refuse collection service, in 1987, 24 per cent of solid wastes were dumped, mostly onto vacant land or in canals and rivers.

Bogota (Colombia): Around half the 1.5 million tons of garbage generated every year is collected and disposed of by local authorities. Every day, some 2500 tons is left uncollected – some is partially recycled informally while the rest is simply left to rot in small tips or in canals, sewers or the streets.

Dar es Salaam (Tanzania): Some two thirds of all solid wastes from both residential areas and from commercial enterprises remains uncollected.

Guatemala City: Of the some 1100 tons of garbage produced each day, only some 750 tons are collected by private and municipal companies; the rest is thrown into clandestine garbage dumps or left to rot in the ravines that surround the city.

Jakarta (Indonesia): Around 40 per cent of the solid wastes generated within Jakarta are not collected; much of it ends up in canals and rivers and along the roadside where it clogs drainage channels and causes extensive flooding during the rainy season.

Karachi (Pakistan): Only one third of the solid waste produced by households in the city is being collected and transported to dump sites.

Kampala (Uganda): Less than 10 per cent of the city's population benefits from a regular collection of household wastes and less than 20 per cent of the solid wastes generated within the city are collected. Large volumes of organic wastes are evident in public spaces, backyards, lanes, pathways and vacant plots. A household survey in one district of Kampala found that 90 per cent of households had nowhere in which to dispose of household wastes. City Council collection bins, where they exist, are usually overflowing.

Kinshasa (Zaire): The collection of household waste is only undertaken in a few residential areas. In the rest of the city, household waste is put out on the road, on illegal dumps or in storm-water drains or buried on open sites.

Manila (Philippines): Less than half of the solid waste generated in metropolitan Manila is collected and transported to solid waste sites.

Nairobi (Kenya): Newly developed residential estates and the informal settlements (in which a high proportion of the total population live) are not served by the city's garbage collection service.

São Paulo (Brazil): One third of the population are living in areas with no service to collect solid wastes

NB: These are simply cities for which data was available and several of these cities seem relatively well served by garbage disposal services compared to many cities which could not be included for lack of accurate data.

Sources: Accra: Songsore 1992 and Tahal 1981. Bangkok: Sivaramakrishnan and Green 1986; Phantumvanit and Liengcharernsit 1989; and United Nations 1987. Bogota: Castaneda 1989. Dar es Salaam: Kulaba 1989 and Yhdego 1991. Guatemala City: Di Pace *et al* 1992. Jakarta: Sivaramakrishnan and Green 1986 and Clarke, Hadiwinoto and Leitmann 1991. Kampala: UNEP 1988. Karachi: Hasan 1990; Beg *et al* 1985; and United Nations 1988. Khartoum: El Sammani, El Hadi Abu Sin, Talha, El Hassan and Haywood 1989. Kinshasa: Mbuyi 1989. Manila: Douglass 1992. Nairobi: Bubba and Lamba 1991. São Paulo: Faria 1988. Full references given in the bibliography.

are on sites which are difficult to reach with motorized vehicles (such as steep hillsides, or waterlogged sites) also mean that in the event of fires, neither fire engines nor ambulances can reach the settlement, at least not without long delays.[71]

Disease vectors

A large range of disease vectors live, breed or feed within or around houses and settlements. The diseases they cause or carry include some of the major causes of ill health and premature death in many cities – especially malaria (anopheles mosquitoes) and diarrhoeal diseases (cockroaches, blowflies and houseflies). But there are also many other diseases caused or carried by insects, spiders or mites including bancroftian filariasis (culex mosquitoes), Chagas disease (triatomine bugs), dengue fever (Aedes mosquitoes), hepatitis A (houseflies, cockroaches), leishmaniasis (sand-fly), plague (certain fleas), relapsing fever (body lice and soft ticks), scabies (scabies mites), trachoma (face flies), typhus (body lice and fleas), yaws (face flies), and yellow fever (Aegypti mosquitoes).[72]

Although some of these remain predominantly rural, many have long been urban problems (for instance, malaria is among the most common causes of infant and child death in many low-income settlements). Others have become urban problems. For instance, Chagas disease with an estimated 18 million people infected in Latin America primarily affects poor rural households, as the insect vector rests and breeds in cracks in house walls. But it is increasingly an urban problem too, both through the migration of infected persons to urban areas (there is no effective treatment for the disease) and through the periurban informal settlements where the insect vectors are evident.[73] Leptospirosis outbreaks have been associated with flooding in São Paulo and Rio de Janeiro – the disease passing to humans through water contaminated with the urine of infected rats or certain domestic animals.[74]

Urban expansion may also change the local ecology in ways which favour the emergence or multiplication of particular disease vectors.[75] For instance, *Aedes aegypti*, the mosquito vector for dengue fever and yellow fever is often found to breed in polluted water sources such as soak-away pits and septic tanks. Anopheline mosquitoes generally shun polluted water but certain species have adapted to the urban environment and now breed in swamps and ditches in or close to urban areas. Box 2.7 gives more details.

Box 2.7 Some health implications of urban expansion

Urban expansion may be associated with new diseases. The expansion of the built-up area, the construction of roads, water reservoirs and drains together with land clearance and deforestation can effect drastic changes to the local ecology. Natural foci for disease vectors may become entrapped within the suburban extension and new ecological niches for animal reservoirs may be created. Within urban conurbations, disease vectors may adapt to new habitats and introduce new infections to spread among the urban population. For instance in India, where the vector of lymphatic filariasis is a peridomestic mosquito, there has been a rapid increase in the incidence of the disease and in the vector population associated with the steady growth of human populations in these endemic areas. Anopheline mosquitoes generally shun polluted water yet *A. stephensi*, the principal vector for urban malaria, is also reported in India and the Eastern Mediterranean Region to have adapted to survive in the urban environment and other species of anophelines have also adapted to breed in swamps and ditches surrounding urban areas in Nigeria and Turkey. *Aedes aegypti*, the vector of dengue and urban yellow fever proliferates in tropical urban settlements and has been frequently found to breed in polluted water sources such as soak-away pits, septic tanks and other breeding sites which have been found to contain a high amount of organic matter. *Aedes albopictus* was introduced to the Americas from Asia around 1986 and within five years, it had spread in the United States to 160 counties in 17 states. It was also introduced into Brazil where it is reported to be present in four states. This is a peridomestic species like *Aedes aegypti* and an excellent vector of dengue and other mosquito-borne viruses.

Source: WHO (1992) *Our Planet, Our Health*, the report of the World Commission on Health and Environment, Geneva.

Drainage

It is appropriate to consider problems arising from the lack of provision for drainage in urban neighbourhoods after considering environmental hazards from house sites and disease vectors. Improved drainage can also help control certain water-related or water-based diseases or disease vectors. Stagnant water in urban areas can provide the breeding place for schistosomiasis snails and may contaminate shallow water aquifers; malarial mosquitoes and mosquitoes which serve as the vector for dengue, yellow fever and bancroftian filariasis may breed in standing water.[76] In urban communities with inadequate provision for sanitation, surface water is often contaminated with human and animal excreta.

Drainage is simply the removal of unwanted water from urban communities; this includes stormwater, external floodwater (for instance from rivers which top their banks), marshwater, sullage, and toilet wastes.[77] Sewers may deal adequately with sullage and toilet wastes but most of the Third World's urban population do not possess the connection to a sewer system. Excreta may also be disposed of safely in other kinds of sanitation system but there are still the other liquid wastes noted above which must be disposed of. The need for drainage also increases, as water supplies improve. Many low-income communities in Third World cities consider drainage to be their most urgent need because they occupy land sites subject to flooding or steep hillsides subject to erosion and landslides.[78]

3

The city environment

THE RANGE OF PROBLEMS

The environmental problems most commonly associated with cities in Europe, Japan and North America such as high levels of air and water pollution and of solid wastes (including toxic or otherwise hazardous wastes) might be assumed to be less important in the Third World for two reasons. One reason is that a smaller proportion of the population lives in cities. A second is that the Third World is less industrialised and despite having more than three quarters of the world's population, it still has a relatively small proportion of its industrial production.[1] Rural and agricultural environmental problems such as deforestation, soil erosion, water pollution and deaths and disablement from pesticide use (and over-use) may seem more urgent even if, as described later, some of these have important linkages with cities.

But there are hundreds of Third World cities or city-regions with high concentrations of industries and significant industrial output. Nations such as China, India, Mexico, Brazil and South Korea figure prominently amongst the world's largest producers of many industrial goods. Not surprisingly, Third World cities or city-regions with high concentrations of industries (especially heavy industries) suffer comparable industrial pollution problems to those in Europe, Japan and North America. In many cities, environmental problems are far more serious. Industrial production has increased very rapidly in many Third World nations in the last 30 years in the absence of an effective planning and regulation system. More than 35 nations recorded annual average growth rates for industrial production of 5 per cent or more between 1965 and 1980; even during the 1980s, 20 Third World countries sustained growth rates for industrial production of five or more per cent a year – half of these being among the 35 nations with high industrial growth rates in the previous 15 years.[2] The more rapid the growth in industrial production, the more serious the environmental problems related to industrial pollution are likely to be since time is required to identify and act on problems and political circumstances may slow or halt such action. Until recently, very few governments have shown much interest in controlling industrial pollution. Governments' concern to create jobs usually meant that when a new factory was proposed – by local, national or international businesses – little attention was given to the likely environmental impacts.

A second reason why pollution can be particularly serious is the concentration of industry in relatively few locations; in most Third World nations, industrial production is heavily concentrated in one or two city regions or 'core regions' within each nation. For instance, the metropolitan areas of Bangkok, Dhaka, Lima, Mexico City, Manila and São Paulo include a high proportion of their nation's industrial output; the same is true in less industrialized countries – for instance Bissau, Nairobi and Port-au-Prince also contain a high proportion of their nation's total industrial output.[3] In Thailand, the metropolitan area of Bangkok and the neighbouring provinces contain three quarters of all factories dealing with hazardous chemicals. Within Bangkok and five satellite towns are five of Thailand's seven lead smelting plants and over 90 per cent of its chemical, dry-cell battery, paint, pharmaceutical and textile manufacturing plants.[4] While some governments have managed to support a decentralization of industry away from the largest cities, many new industrial plants have set up outside the main city but still within or close to its metropolitan area.

Industrial pollution is not the only cause of air and water pollution. The high proportions of households and businesses not served by sewers, drains and garbage collection add greatly to land and water pollution problems, while very congested traffic and inefficient and poorly maintained engines in most road vehicles add greatly to air pollution. Other factors may increase pollution in particular cities, for instance many households use inefficient heaters and cookers (especially those using solid fuel). Local conditions can also exacerbate the pollution. For instance, thermal inversions (where a mass of warm air well above the city helps trap pollutants in the cool air underneath it) are common in the winter for northern Chinese cities.[5] Many cities have long periods in the year with very little wind to help disperse air pollution; where there is also a high concentration of automobiles and an abundance of sunshine, photochemical smog has become an increasing problem.[6] One of the world's most populous metropolitan areas, that of Mexico City, has an environment ill-suited to the large concentration of industries and motor vehicles. The valley in which it developed is 2200 metres above sea level and is surrounded by mountains. These provide the conditions for thermal inversions which trap pollutants within the valley. In addition, the high altitude also means a lower concentration of oxygen in the air which causes higher emissions of hydrocarbons and carbon monoxide from motor vehicle engines.[7]

TOXIC/HAZARDOUS WASTES

In Third World cities, as in the North, one sees the familiar list of chemical pollutants: heavy metals (which include lead, mercury, cadmium and chromium and their compounds), oxides of nitrogen and sulphur, carbon monoxide, petroleum hydrocarbons, suspended particulates, polychlorinated biphenyls (PCBs), nitrates, cyanide and arsenic, as well as various organic solvents and asbestos. Some of these and certain other industrial and institutional wastes are categorized as 'hazardous' or 'toxic' because of the special care needed when handling, storing, transporting and disposing of them, to ensure they are isolated from contact with humans and the natural environment. Most come from chemical industries although others producing primary and fabricated metal and petroleum, pulp and paper, transport and electrical equipment and leather and tanned products also produce significant quantities of hazardous wastes.

There are many different kinds of hazardous wastes. Some are highly inflammable – as in many solvents used in the chemical industry. Some are highly reactive – and can explode or generate toxic gases when coming into contact with water or some other chemical. Some have disease-causing agents; sewage sludge or hospital wastes often contain bacteria, viruses and cysts from parasites. Some wastes are lethal poisons – for instance cyanide and arsenic and many heavy-metal compounds; many are carcinogenic (ie cancer inducing). Table 3.1 gives some examples of toxic chemicals, their use and their potential health impacts.

Only in the last 15 years has the scale of the problem of hazardous wastes and the potential risk to people's health been recognized.[8] The United States provides an example of the high costs which build up as industry expands in the absence of adequate controls on hazardous waste disposal or of their enforcement. The US industrialized rapidly, giving little consideration to the regulatory aspects of hazardous wastes. Now it is faced with the problem of some 50,000 land sites where hazardous wastes may have been dumped without control, and without provision to ensure the wastes do not pollute groundwater. The cost today of having to deal with the result of many years of inadequate control runs into tens of billions of dollars.[9] As more costs are charged to the polluters, the incentives for illegal evasions increases.

In the Third World, most toxic or otherwise hazardous wastes are either disposed of as liquid wastes which run untreated into sewers or drains or direct into rivers, streams or other nearby water bodies, or are placed on land sites with few safeguards to protect those living nearby or nearby water sources from contamination. Very few nations have effective government systems to control the disposal of hazardous wastes; in most,

Table 3.1 Examples of toxic chemicals, their use and their potential health impacts

Chemical	Use	Health problems
Arsenic	Pesticides; some medicines; glass	Toxic; dermatitis; muscular paralysis; damage to liver and kidney; possibly carcinogenic and teratogenic
Asbestos	Roofing insulation; air conditioning conduits; plastics; fibre; paper	Carcinogenic to workers and even to family members
Benzene	Manufacture of many chemicals; gasoline	Leukaemia; chromosomal damage in exposed workers
Beryllium	Aerospace industry; ceramic parts; household appliances	Fatal lung disease; lung and heart toxicity
Cadmium	Electroplating; plastics; pigments; some fertilizers	Kidney damage; emphysema; possibly carcinogenic, teratogenic & mutagenic
Chromates	Tanning; pigments; corrosion inhibitor; fungicides	Skin ulcers; kidney inflammation; possibly carcinogenic; toxic to fish
Lead	Pipes; some batteries and paints; printing; plastics; gasoline additive	Intoxicant; neurotoxin affects blood system
Mercury	Chloralkali cells; fungicides; pharmaceuticals	Damage to nervous system; kidney damage
PCBs	Electric transformers; insulator electric equipment	Possibly carcinogenic; nerve, skin and liver damage
Sulphur dioxide	Sugar; bleeding agent; emissions from coal/some oil combustion	Irritation to eyes and respiratory system; damage to plants and buildings
Vinyl chloride	Plastics; organic compound synthesis	Systemically toxic; carcinogenic

Source: Krishnamurthi, CR Toxic Chemicals in *State of the Environment: Some Aspects, National Committee on Environmental Planning*, New Delhi quoted in G Anandalingam and Mark Westfall (1987) 'Hazardous Waste Generation and Disposal: Options for Developing Countries', *Natural Resources Forum* vol. 11, no. 1.

there are no regulations dealing specifically with such wastes (or even the legal definition of toxic wastes), let alone a system to implement them. Such systems need a competent, well staffed regulatory authority with the ability to make regular checks on each industry likely to be using or generating toxic chemicals, and with the power to penalize offenders. This authority needs the backing of central government and the courts. For effective control of toxic wastes, industries must keep rigorous records of the kinds and quantities of waste and the dates and methods by which these are disposed of. Businesses which specialize in collecting and disposing of these wastes must be very carefully monitored; so too must the specialized facilities which need to be created to handle toxic wastes. Since the safe disposal or safe incineration of toxic wastes is extremely expensive, there are enormous incentives to cheat any regulatory system.

Reports of problems arising from the careless disposal of wastes with heavy metals are increasingly frequent. The problem of mercury-contaminated wastes being discharged into water bodies, which received such publicity through the hundreds of deaths and thousands of disablement it caused in Minamata, Japan and which has caused serious problems in many North American water bodies has also been noted in Bangkok, Perai, Bombay, Managua, Alexandria, Cartagena and some Chinese cities.[10] The Global Environment Monitoring System of the United Nations Environment Programme found heavy metal contamination in several rivers in Chile, China, Japan, Mexico, Panama, the Philippines and Turkey.[11] Significant build-ups of compounds of mercury, lead, cadmium, copper and chromium have been reported in recent years in almost every industrializing nation in Southeast Asia.[12] The Kalu river which runs through two of Bombay's industrial suburbs receives the liquid effluents of over 150 industrial units and these include heavy metals; this causes dangerously high levels of mercury and lead in the water near the village of Ambivali and villagers are slowly being poisoned as heavy metals enter the food chain through cattle browsing on the river bank vegetation.[13] On the Southeast Pacific coast of Latin America, heavy metals have been detected in practically all areas that receive industrial and municipal wastes and worryingly high concentrations of mercury, copper and cadmium have been found in some fish species.[14] Lead and cadmium concentrations in drinking water were found to exceed the guideline values in about a quarter of the 344 stations which monitor water pollution within the Global Environmental Monitoring System.[15] Thirteen children were reported to have died of mercury poisoning in Jakarta in 1981 after eating fish caught in the waters of Jakarta Bay tributary, while mercury concentrations in the water polluted by nearby factories were found to have reached dangerously high levels.[16] Jakarta Bay remains the source of much of the fish consumed in the city; it was recently reported that of a sample of fish and shellfish caught in the bay, 44 per cent exceeded the World Health Organization's guidelines for lead, 38 per cent those for mercury and 76 per cent those for cadmium.[17] Reports from China in 1980 and 1981 note 'some astonishingly high cadmium and mercury concentrations in rivers and underground waters'; concentrations in water and in fish have been found to be many times the level considered safe – in some rivers, the concentration is hundreds or even thousands of times the maximum recommended concentration within the European Commission.[18]

One kind of toxic waste which deserves special attention is radioactive waste. The problems are illustrated by an accident in Goiania, Brazil, where a scrap metal dealer broke up an abandoned cancer therapy machine and released the radioactive caesium-137 from inside it. Because the powder and some of the metal glowed in the dark, the scrap dealer and his family and friends handled it. Around 240 people were contaminated and several people have died; many of those that survive will probably develop cancer.[19] Even for nations with no nuclear power stations, radioactive chemicals are widely used in other activities. Wherever governments seek to develop waste-disposal sites for these or other toxic wastes, local citizens are likely to mount strong protests. For instance, there was a long battle in Papan, Malaysia between Asian Rare Earth Company (which was partly owned by the Japanese Mitsubishi Chemical Company) and local residents (aided by environmental groups) because this Company was disposing of radioactive thorium wastes on an open site, close to the town.[20] Citizen action against this took place not only in Malaysia but also in Japan where a coalition of citizen groups denounced the Mitsubishi Chemical Company.[21]

EXPORT OF TOXIC WASTES OR POLLUTING INDUSTRIES

There is also the transfer of dirty industries from the North to the Third World or the transfer of dangerous industrial equipment or of the toxic wastes themselves. To take first the transfer of production, there are examples of such a transfer in hazardous industries – for instance many industries manufacturing asbestos transferred from the United States to Latin America, with Brazil and Mexico as the most frequently noted recipients. Asbestos textile imports into the United States from Mexico, Taiwan and Brazil grew rapidly between 1969 and 1976 and Taiwan and South Korea have been displacing Japan as a source of asbestos textiles for the United States as new regulations for this industry have been introduced in Japan.[22] There has been a comparable transfer of production by Japanese and North American subsidiaries in other 'dirty industries' with Taiwan, South Korea, the Philippines and Thailand being among the recipients.[23]

In general, there is no evidence of a widespread relocation of industries from Europe and North America to the Third World because of costs saved through less stringent environmental and occupational health controls.[24] But there are particular industries in which relocation may increasingly take place; for instance, environmental and workplace regulations may have motivated relocation of certain US industries (those producing highly toxic products such as asbestos and certain pesticides and those processing copper, zinc and lead).[25] To meet demand for the products of certain 'dirty industries' in Japan, Western Europe or North America, multinational corporations may increasingly transfer production to Third World nations to avoid the costs of meeting workplace safety and pollution standards. Barry Castleman has documented a large number of instances of multinational corporations with industries in Third World nations which have serious problems of pollution or occupational health (or both).[26] Most of these cases arise in asbestos-related industries, pesticide industries or chemical industries.[27] Arsenic production, lead refining and battery manufacture, metal smelters and biocide production are among the industries where this transfer may increasingly take place. This transfer, allied to increasing 'dirty industry' production in certain Third World cities to meet local and regional demand, has serious implications for the health of city populations both now and in the future.

There is also the question of the export to Third World countries of outdated industrial technology which brings with it substantial environmental hazards. For instance, a recent report highlighted the case of an industry in Indonesia utilizing an outdated mercury cell process for the production of caustic soda which meant leaks of mercury to the environment per unit of output exceeding by several thousand times the acceptable standards.[28] The lessons learnt in the North on the enormous health costs associated with occupational exposures in particular industries and with uncontrolled disposal of toxic wastes by certain industries do not seem to be heeded by Third World governments and are often ignored by the industrial sector.

There is also the issue of the 'export' of hazardous wastes to the Third World. A number of European or North American businesses or municipal authorities have sought to transport toxic wastes to certain Third World nations with little or no consideration of the possible consequences for local populations. The local authorities at the disposal sites were often unaware of the composition of the wastes and of the hazards that they presented.[29] In the late 1980s, it also became evident that the volume of such exports was likely to grow very rapidly, unless steps were taken to curb this trade. The cost of transporting toxic wastes to Third World nations was only a fraction of the cost of safely incinerating or storing them in the West and meeting government regulations in doing so. In addition, both companies and public authorities in the North were also facing rising public opposition to the opening of new waste disposal sites. Box 3.1 gives some examples.

Box 3.1 The North's export of toxic wastes

Argentina: Towards the end of 1987, American Security International was reported to be negotiating with the government of Argentina (and of Peru, Paraguay and Uruguay) for the export of toxic wastes from the United States. The firm was proposing to export 100,000 barrels a month and was prepared to pay US$40 a barrel. The wastes included solvents and used lubricants.

Thailand: Large quantities of chemical wastes have been stored in Bangkok's main port, Klong Tuey. Most came from unknown shippers in Singapore although some also came from the United States, Japan, Germany and Taiwan. Officials from the government's National Environment Board have expressed fears that the barrels may contain PCBs or dioxin which can only be destroyed in high temperature incinerators which Thailand does not possess.

Benin: European firms were seeking a contract to send five million tons of wastes each year from Sesco, a company registered in Gibraltar. It was reported that Benin was to receive $2.50 for each ton received while Sesco would charge firms up to $1000 a ton or more to dispose of the wastes. Benin is one of the poorest nations in the world and lacks virtually all the infrastructure and the government system needed to handle and manage even a small fraction of the five million tons a year proposed.

Guinea Bissau: It was reported that Lindaco, a firm based in Detroit, applied to the US government to ship up to 6 million tons of chemical waste to Guinea Bissau, one of the world's poorest nations. Other contracts have been signed for importing chemical and industrial wastes from Western nations.

Nigeria: 3800 tons of European chemical wastes were dumped by Italian ships in the southern port of Koko on the Niger river with a payment to the landowner of the equivalent of around $100 a month; the cost of disposing of these in Europe would be of the order of $350-1750 a ton. The wastes were stored in 45 gallon (c 200 litre) drums, many of them leaking and most in poor condition. Many drums had volatile chemicals which, in a hot climate, present a serious risk of a spontaneous fire or explosion.

Venezuela: In October 1987, 11,000 barrels of chemical wastes were returned to Italy after a private Italian company had tried to store them in a warehouse in Puerto Cabello; local inhabitants claimed that some barrels leaked and caused various diseases

Sources: IIED-AL, CEA and GASE 1992, Consumer Information and Documentation Centre 1988, Kone 1988, MacKenzie and Mpinga 1988, Phantumvanit and Liengcharernsit 1989, Secrett 1988 – see Bibliography for full references.

Some reports suggest that this problem has existed for some years – especially in Northern Mexico with the illegal dumping of toxic wastes produced by US firms being shipped across the border.[30] However, an increasing concern about the growth in this international trade has prompted some action. It resulted in a number of countries prohibiting the export of hazardous wastes. The Italian government also took on the responsibility of addressing the problems caused by the dumping of toxic wastes described in Box 3.1 in Koko, Nigeria, even though the dumping had been carried out without their knowledge.[31] International measures have been taken to limit this problem – for instance through the Basel Convention on the Control of Transboundary Movements of Hazardous Wastes and their Disposal – although it is not clear whether this will prove effective. In addition, a lot more attention needs to be given to the disposal of hazardous wastes by branches of multinational firms or by domestic industries within Third World nations. In most nations, there is little or no control of the dumping of hazardous wastes and little or no provision for the special facilities needed to safely store or treat such wastes. Most hazardous wastes are currently dumped with other wastes on open land sites with no provision to ensure these remain isolated from contact with plants, animals and humans. Or they are simply dumped within liquid wastes into sewers, drains, wells or nearby water courses: rivers, lakes, and estuaries.

WATER POLLUTION

In terms of impact on human health in Third World cities, the dangers from most toxic industrial wastes are probably more localized and more open to swift and effective government control than those from other industrial pollutants. With regard to water pollution, there are usually four main sources: sewage, industrial effluents, storm and urban run-off and agricultural run-off.[32] Agricultural run-off is often an 'urban' problem since water sources from which an urban centre draws may be polluted with agricultural run-off and contain dangerous levels of toxic chemicals from fertilizer and biocides. Box 3.2 describes some of the most common kinds of pollution arising from these sources.

Virtually all Third World cities have much more serious 'nonpoint' sources of water pollution than cities in the North because of the lack of sewers and the inadequacies in garbage collection services. A comprehensive sewage and storm drainage system makes it much easier to control water pollution since the wastes collected by this system can be treated, before being returned to rivers, lakes, estuaries or the sea. A comprehensive solid-waste collection and disposal system greatly limits

Box 3.2 Water pollution

Most water pollution falls into one of three categories: liquid organic wastes; liquid inorganic wastes; and waterborne or water-based pathogens.

Liquid inorganic wastes: Most inorganic liquid wastes come from industry; these are not broken down in water in the same way as organic wastes but for most, their dilution in large water bodies renders them harmless. Many such wastes kill animal and plant life, unless diluted sufficiently. Some inorganic wastes can become concentrated up the food chain to fish or through other fresh- or salt-water products (shellfish, seaweed) to the point where they can kill or do severe damage to the health of humans who eat them. Wastes which include certain chemical elements known as heavy metals (which include cadmium, mercury and lead) or some of their compounds can be particularly dangerous. Many of the pollution incidents which have resulted in the largest number of deaths and serious injuries from water pollution have arisen from human ingestion of fish, or crops contaminated with heavy metals or their compounds.

Liquid organic wastes: These can be termed 'oxygen demanding' wastes since when disposed of into water, bacteria and other micro-organisms combine with oxygen dissolved in the water to break them down. The biochemical oxygen demand (BOD) of such wastes is a measure of how much oxygen dissolved in the water they will need to be broken down and as such, is one of the most widely used indicators of pollution. Liquid organic wastes include sewage, many wastes from industries (especially industries processing agricultural products) and run-off from rains and storms which picks up organic wastes from land, before flowing into streams, rivers, lakes or seas. Too great a volume of organic wastes can overload the capacity of the water's bacteria and other micro-organisms to the point where all dissolved oxygen becomes exhausted. As the concentration of dissolved oxygen decreases, so fish and aquatic plant life suffer or die. Some portions of rivers or lakes which receive large volumes of organic wastes can have all their dissolved oxygen used up. They then lose their ability to break down these kinds of wastes and become black and foul smelling.

Waterborne or related pathogens: Many pathogens (disease causing agents including bacteria, viruses and worms) are spread in water – either through human ingestion of contaminated water or because water provides the habitat for intermediate hosts. Much the most common and widespread problem is pathogens from human excreta which contaminate water supplies. Typhoid, diarrhoeal diseases and cholera are among the diseases spread in this way. Contaminated water also has a central role in the transmission of many intestinal worms. Table 2.1 gives more details.

the amount of solid waste that can be washed into water bodies. In the absence of such systems, much of the liquid wastes from households and businesses (and often industries) and a considerable proportion of the solid wastes end up washed into the nearby streams, rivers or lakes, greatly increasing the biochemical oxygen demand. The advantage of point sources is that treatment plants can be easily added – although in most Third World cities, in the absence of adequate treatment, most 'point' sources (liquid wastes coming from sewers and industrial waste pipes) with minimal or no treatment are also major sources of water pollution.

Most rivers in Third World cities are literally large open sewers. Take the case of India, as documented in two volumes on *The State of India's Environment: a Citizen's Report* produced by a network of Indian NGOs coordinated by the Centre for Science and Environment in Delhi. This points out that of India's 3119 towns and cities, only 209 have partial sewage and sewage treatment facilities and eight have full facilities. On the river Ganga alone, 114 cities each with 50,000 or more inhabitants dump untreated sewage into the river every day.

> DDT factories, tanneries, paper and pulp mills, petrochemical and fertilizer complexes, rubber factories and a host of others use the river to get rid of their wastes .... The Hooghly estuary is choked with the untreated industrial wastes from more than 150 major factories around Calcutta... raw sewage pours into the river continuously from 361 outfalls.[33]

Box 3.3 gives examples from other cities.

The Consumers Association of Penang is another Third World NGO which has helped highlight serious pollution problems in its own country. In peninsular Malaysia, many rivers are grossly polluted: the three principal sources being organic wastes from sewage, and discharges from oil palm and rubber factories. The range and complexity of water pollution problems caused by the discharge of other (non agro-based) industrial effluents has increased, especially in industrial centres such as Kuala Lumpur, Petaling Jaya and Penang. The main industrial sources of pollution come from electroplating industries, tanneries, textile mills, food processing industries, distilleries, chloro-alkali plants, sulphuric acid plants and electronic factories. Many of these industries discharge wastes containing different compounds, including heavy metals, into public water courses without prior treatment. Significant levels of toxic heavy metals, have been encountered in the Juru River Basin. Measurements in coastal waters and estuarine waters in various locations showed very high concentrations of coliform bacteria.[34]

Box 3.3 Examples of water pollution in Third World cities

Alexandria (Egypt): Industries in Alexandria account for around 40 per cent of all Egypt's industrial output and most discharge liquid wastes, untreated, into the sea or into lake Maryut. In the past decade, fish production in Lake Maryut has declined by some 80 per cent because of the direct discharge into it of industrial and domestic effluents. The Lake has also ceased to be a prime recreational site because of its poor condition. Similar environmental degradation is taking place along the seafront as a result of the discharge of untreated wastewaters from poorly located outfalls. Paper, textile and food industries contribute most to the organic load.

Bangkok (Thailand): Most of the canals in and around Bangkok are so severely polluted that they are anaerobic (ie all dissolved oxygen has been depleted by organic wastes). Most houses discharge wastewater direct into storm drains which in turn normally discharge into nearby canals. Of the 51,500 factories registered with the Department of Industrial Works, some 20,000 are classified as water polluting factories. Since the canals eventually discharge into the Chao Phraya river which runs through Bangkok, this too has dissolved oxygen levels well below the official standard in its middle section and has almost anaerobic conditions in its lower section.

Bogota (Colombia): There is a high degree of pollution in the Tunjuelito, a tributary of the Bogota river. Many tanneries and plastic processing plants pour untreated wastes into it and the dissolved oxygen in the water is almost depleted. The wastes include heavy metals such as lead and cadmium. Other rivers are not so heavily polluted with chemical wastes but receive large volumes of untreated sewage waters.

Jakarta (Indonesia): All the rivers crossing Jakarta are heavily polluted although some of the pollution arises from wastes entering the rivers upstream of the city. While passing through the city, the rivers receive discharges from drains and ditches carrying untreated wastewaters from households, commercial buildings and institutions and the discharges from industries, solid wastes and faecal wastes from overflowing or leaking septic tanks. Water-related diseases such as typhoid, diarrhoeal diseases and cholera increase in frequency, downstream across the metropolitan area. The seawater and sediment in Jakarta Bay are clearly affected by the pollution load carried by the rivers discharging there. Apart from sediment and high biochemical oxygen demand, high concentrations of certain heavy metals have been found in the sea sediment and seawater in the bay.

Karachi (Pakistan): The Lyari river which runs through Karachi (Pakistan's largest industrial city) is an open drain from both chemical and micro-biological points of view; a mixture of raw sewage and untreated industrial effluents. Most industrial effluents come from an industrial estate with some 300 major industries and almost three times as many small units.

Three fifths of the units are textile mills. Most other industries in Karachi also discharge untreated effluents into the nearest water body.

Shanghai (China): Some 3.4 million cubic metres of industrial and domestic waste pour mostly into the Suzhou Creek and the Huangpu river which flows through the heart of the city. These have become the main (open) sewers for the city. Most of the waste is industrial since few houses possess flush toilets. The Huangpu has been essentially dead since 1980. In all, less than five per cent of the city's wastewater is treated. The normally high water table also means that a variety of toxins from industrial plants and local rivers find their way back into groundwater and contaminate wells which provide the balance of water.

São Paulo (Brazil): The Tiete river, as it passes through Greater São Paulo, receives 300 tonnes of effluents each day from 1200 industries located in the region. Lead, cadmium and other heavy metals are among the main pollutants. It also receives 900 tonnes of sewage each day, of which only 12.5 per cent is treated by the five sewage treatment stations located in the area.

Sources: Alexandria: Ahmad 1986; and Hamza 1989. Bangkok: Phantumvanit and Liengcharernsis 1989 and Ard-Am, 1991. Bogota: Castaneda 1989. Karachi: Beg, Mahmood and Yousufzai 1984. Shanghai: Sahabat Alam 1986 and Green and Sivaramakrishnan and Green 1986. Jakarta: Clarke, Hadiwinoto and Leitmann 1991. São Paulo: SABESP/CNEC. See Bibliography for full references.

A shortage of water adds greatly to the problem of disposing of wastes – especially liquid wastes from industries and sewage. Large volumes of water dilute wastes and can render them much less dangerous; in addition, bacteria in the water break down organic wastes, as long as the volume of wastes relative to the volume of water is not too great. Mexico City, like most of the largest cities and many smaller cities, is facing the mounting cost of increasing the water supply. Over-exploitation of underground water sources has made the city sink – in some areas by up to nine metres.[35] New sources of water are at a considerable distance and these have to be pumped up 1000 metres or more which adds considerably both to costs and to fuel consumption.[36]

Mexico City is just one of many cities which developed in an area with limited water resources and which has now outgrown the capacity of the region to provide adequate, sustainable supplies. Dakar, the capital of Senegal, provides an example of a smaller city which is also facing serious problems of water supply. Water has to be drawn from ever more distant sources, as local groundwater supplies were fully used (and polluted) and local aquifers over-pumped, resulting in saltwater intrusion; a substantial part of the city's water has to be brought from the Lac de Guiers, 200 kilometres away.[37] Hundreds of urban centres which developed in relatively arid areas have grown beyond the point where adequate supplies can be tapped from local or even regional sources. Many of the coastal cities in Peru (including Lima), La Rioja and Catamarca in Argentina and various cities in Northern Mexico are among the many cities with severe constraints on expanding freshwater supplies. Many others are facing problems in financing the expansion of supplies to keep up with demand: Bangkok and Jakarta are two among many major coastal cities with serious problems of subsidence from drawing too much from underground aquifers and from saline intrusion into such ground-waters; in Jakarta, many shops, houses and offices can no longer drink the water from the wells they use because of saline intrusion.[38]

AIR POLLUTION

Most outdoor air pollution in urban areas comes from the combustion of fossil fuels – in industrial processes, for heating and electricity generation, and by motor vehicles.[39] The use of fossil fuels in each of these tends to expand with economic growth; so too does air pollution unless measures are taken to promote efficient fuel use; the use of the least polluting fuels (for instance natural gas rather than coal with a high sulphur content for domestic and industrial use, and unleaded petrol for motor vehicles); and the control of pollution at source.[40]

In many Third World cities, the concentrations and mixes of air pollutants are already high enough to cause illness in more susceptible individuals and premature death among the elderly, especially those with respiratory problems.[41] Air pollution may also be impairing the health of far more people but the links have not been proven. The (limited) data on air pollution in Third World cities also suggests that it is generally getting worse.

Table 3.2 outlines the effects on health of some of the most common urban air pollutants. Until relatively recently, most urban air pollution came from the combustion of coal or heavy oil by industry, power stations and households;[42] this produced a mix of sulphur dioxide, suspended particulates and inorganic compounds. These were the source of the infamous London 'smogs' of the 1950s and although in most cities in the North, sulphur dioxide concentrations have fallen considerably, they remain the main source of air pollution in many Third World cities. Sulphur dioxide reacts with gases in the air (including water vapour) to form sulphuric acid – a major contributor to acid rain. Most sulphur dioxide comes from power stations burning coal or oil which contains sulphur – although in some cities, the burning of coal with high sulphur content in domestic stoves and small-scale industries can be a major source. In many cities, open fires or inefficient solid fuel stoves are also

Table 3.2 Some urban air pollutants and their effects on health

Pollutant	Reaction to exposure	Effect
1. Traditional ('reducing') pollutants from coal/heavy oil combustion		
Smoke/suspended particulates (some contribution from diesel traffic too)	Can penetrate lungs; some retained: possible long-term effects. May also irritate bronchi.	LONDON SMOG COMPLEX *Short term effects:* sudden increases in deaths, in hospital admissions and in illness among bronchitic patients. Temporary reductions in lung function (patients and some others). *Long term effects:* increased frequency of respiratory infections (children). Increased prevalence of respiratory symptoms (adults and children) Higher death rates from bronchitis in polluted areas.
Sulphur dioxide	Readily absorbed on inhalation: irritation of bronchi, with possibility of bronchospasm.	
Sulphuric acid (mainly a secondary pollutant formed from sulphur dioxide in air)	Hygroscopic; highly irritant if impacted in upper respiratory tract. Acid absorbed on other fine particles may penetrate further to promote bronchospasm.	
Polycyclic aromatic hydrocarbons (small contribution from traffic also)	Mainly absorbed on to smoke; can penetrate with it to lungs.	*Possible carcinogenic effects:* may take some part in the higher incidence of lung cancer in urban areas.
2. Photochemical ('oxidizing') pollutants from traffic or other hydrocarbon emissions		
Hydrocarbons (volatile: petrol etc.)	Non-toxic at moderate concentrations	LOS ANGELES SMOG COMPLEX *Short term effects:* primarily eye irritation. Reduced athletic performance. Possibly small changes in deaths, hospital admissions *Longer term effects:* Increased onsets of respiratory illnesses (children), increased asthma attacks (adults). No clear indication of increased bronchitis.
Nitric oxide	Capable of combining with haemoglobin in blood but no apparent effect in humans	
Nitrogen dioxide and ozone (mainly secondary pollutants formed in photochemical reactions)	Neither gas is very soluble: some irritation of bronchi but can penetrate lungs to cause oedema at high concentrations. Urban concentrations too low for such effects, but evidence of reduced resistance to infections in animals	
Aldehydes, other partial oxidation products, peroxyacetylnitrate	Eye irritation, odour	
3. Others from traffic		
Carbon monoxide (other sources contribute – smoking an important one)	Combines with haemoglobin in blood, reducing oxygen-carrying capacity	Possible effects on central nervous system (reversible unless concentrations are very high). Some evidence of effects on perception and performance of fine tasks at moderate concentrations
Lead (some industrial sources contribute to air lead; human intake often dominated by lead in food and drink)	Taken up in blood, distributed to soft tissues and sometimes to bone	Possible effects on central nervous system (longer time scale than in case of CO and not necessarily reversible). Indications of neuropsychological effects on children within overall environmental exposure range, but role of traffic lead uncertain.

Source: Drawn from WHO, *Our Planet, Our Health*, Report of the WHO Commission on Health and Environment, WHO, Geneva, 1992, quoting Holland, WW *et al* (eds) (1991) *Oxford Textbook of Public Health* vol. 2: Methods of Public Health, Oxford University Press, Oxford.

major contributors. This is the case in many Indian cities; for instance, one estimate suggests that domestic fuel burning generates about half of Delhi's air pollution.[43] In China, although total fuel combustion by households is small by comparison to industry and power stations, 'the burning of raw coal in millions of small, inefficient stoves is a very burdensome air pollution source through the colder half of the nation'.[44] In Seoul, heavy oil burned in home heating units and power stations and anthracite briquettes used for domestic heating and cooking contribute to high levels of air pollution.[45]

More recently, largely as a result of growing automobile use, what are termed photochemical ('oxidizing') pollutants have become a major source of air pollution in many cities. Among these, the oxides of nitrogen are particularly important; these are also the result of fossil fuel combustion but in this instance, it is usually not stationary sources (industries, power stations, household stoves) but petrol-fuelled motor vehicles which are the major source. Hydrocarbons are another important pollutant, most of them come from petrol evaporation and possibly leaks in gas pipes and emissions from petroleum industries. Secondary reactions in the air between nitrogen dioxide, hydrocarbons and sunlight cause the formation of ozone which is present in photochemical smog along with other hazardous chemicals; ozone can have serious health impacts when in high concentrations in or close to cities – while by contrast, the ozone layer in the stratosphere has an essential role in maintaining health since it absorbs the fraction of ultraviolet rays coming from the sun which can damage human health and other living organisms.[46]

Carbon monoxide is also a common air pollutant, formed by the incomplete combustion of fossil fuels; the main danger in cities is high concentrations in particular areas, from motor vehicle emissions. Lead is also a common air pollutant in urban areas, with high concentrations often evident where lead compounds are still widely used as additives in petrol (as in most Third World cities and often with high levels of lead additives in the petrol[47]). Airborne lead can also contaminate the soil and dust near busy roads[48] – affecting crops grown in gardens or other open spaces. There may also be small concentrations of certain organic chemicals in the air – for instance aldehydes, benzene and polyaromatic hydrocarbons.[49]

An estimated 1.4 billion urban residents worldwide are exposed to annual averages for suspended particulate matter or sulphur dioxide (or both) which are higher than the minimum standards recommended by the World Health Organization.[50] The trend in many (if not most) cities in the North is towards declining sulphur dioxide concentration; the (limited) data available for Third World cities suggests the trend is towards increasing concentrations.[51] Box 3.4 gives some examples of cities with high levels of air pollution.

Box 3.4 Examples of air pollution in Third World cities

São Paulo: Suspended particulate matter routinely exceeds minimum levels in all 22 measuring stations in the metropolitan area; an official report recently noted that violations of standards occur in all observed stations. Observed values are well above the standard, showing a very serious suspended particulates problem in the entire region. Carbon monoxide levels routinely exceed air quality standards by a large margin at almost all sampling stations. Ozone concentrations have continuously exceeded the standard set by the US Environmental Protection Agency for the USA and are probably being underestimated. Lead and sulphur dioxide levels have declined with the increased use of alcohol fuel. A combined index of air quality shows that in 1988, 16 per cent of the days in São Paulo and 9 per cent in other municipalities in the metropolitan area had unacceptable air quality. Two of the three worst cases (25 per cent of days unacceptable) were at measuring stations in the city of São Paulo.

Santiago de Chile: In Santiago de Chile, a combination of high levels of polluting emissions from motor vehicle exhausts and industries, dust particles from severely eroding hills and a site surrounded by mountains on three sides often produces dangerous levels of air pollution. This is especially so during the winter months. Santiago had one of the highest annual averages for smoke and carbon monoxide for 1980–84 among the cities covered by the GEMs/Air network and some sites within the city had among the highest concentrations of nitrogen dioxide.

Bangkok: The annual average for total suspended particulates exceeded the official standards (and the WHO guideline level) at all ambient air quality monitoring stations in Bangkok city. Short-term, 24-hour averages near the main streets were also often far above official standards (and WHO guideline levels). Carbon monoxide concentrations were generally below standards although in certain locations (typically streets with heavy traffic, narrow streets and tall buildings on both sides), short-term (eight-hour average) concentrations sometimes exceed official standards. Airborne lead was not a city-wide problem but concentrations of lead in particular roadside stations exceeded WHO guidelines, in some instances by several times. Other air pollutants do not seem to be a problem.

Shanghai: Seven power stations, eight steel works, 8000 industrial boilers, 1000 kilns, 15,000 restaurant stoves and one million cooking stoves are the major source of air pollution; most use coal with a relatively high sulphur content. In 1991, the annual average concentration for sulphur dioxide in the urban core was more than twice the WHO recommended average with peak concentrations during the winter. The annual average for total suspended particulates was more than four times the WHO recommended average.

Other cities in Southern China: Some of the highest levels of sulphur dioxide concentration occur in cities in Southern China because of the widespread burning of coal with a high sulphur content, particularly in domestic stoves and small scale industries; annual average concentrations in the southern cities of Chongqing and Guiyang are 100–150 ppb which is several times the WHO guideline level. These averages even exceed the guidelines set for what level pollution should not exceed for more than seven days a year.

Sources: Shanghai: Zipei 1992. China: Zhao and Xiong 1988 and Conway and Pretty 1991; Santiago: WRI 1992; São Paulo Hogan 1992, drawing from official sources. Bangkok: Wangwongwatana 1992

The scale of the pollution, the relative importance of different pollutants and the relative contribution of different sources varies greatly from city to city and often from season to season.[52] Existing evidence suggests that city-wide air pollution problems are most serious in the larger industrial cities of the Third World, in cities where solid fuels are widely used for cooking and heating in homes and small scale industries, or in large cities where local conditions inhibit the dispersal of air pollutants. More localized problems with air pollution occur in and around particular industries or roads or particular hot spots created by particular combinations of emissions and weather conditions. The concentrations of air pollutants may vary greatly during a day.

For most air pollutants, different air quality standards are set which depend on the period of exposure. For instance, for sulphur dioxide and suspended particulates, standards may be set not only for the maximum permitted concentration for the annual average but also a less stringent standard which is permitted for less than seven days each year. For air pollutants such as carbon monoxide, ozone and nitrogen dioxide, with much more immediate health impacts, air quality standards are set for shorter exposures. For carbon monoxide, since the health effects are immediate (the reduction in oxygen carrying capacity of the blood with impacts on the central nervous system and the heart), different air quality guidelines are set for 15 minutes, 30 minutes, one hour and eight hour exposures.[53] Air quality guidelines for ozone and for nitrogen dioxide usually have a one hour average maximum permitted concentration.

In many of the largest cities in the more wealthy Third World nations, emissions from road vehicles and the secondary pollutants (such as ozone) to which they contribute may be more of a problem than the traditional (reducing) pollutants from coal/heavy oil combustion which are the main problem in cities such as Shanghai, Chongqing and Guiyang (see Box 3.4).

Among the (relatively few) Third World cities for which there is data on nitrogen dioxide levels, the highest averages are usually among the main cities in the wealthier nations (eg São Paulo and Singapore) while cities such as Bombay and New Delhi have relatively low averages.[54] Ozone concentrations are a particular problem in Mexico City and high ozone concentrations have been one reason for major restrictions on road traffic.[55]

The extent to which particular air pollutants (or a particular mix of pollutants) constitutes a threat to human health will depend much on the city site and on weather conditions. For instance, in cities such as Bangkok and Buenos Aires, the location on or close to the coast on a flat plain means that a prevailing wind helps disperse pollutants. A combination of topography, particular climates and weather conditions can help trap pollutants in or over a city. For cities in valleys (such as Mexico City and

Chongqing) or surrounded by mountains (as in Santiago de Chile), particular weather conditions help trap pollutants for substantial parts of the year. Box 3.5 shows the range of factors which influence the level of risk to the general public.

Box 3.5 Factors which influence the public's level of risk from exposure to air pollution

The extent to which air pollution poses a risk to the general public depends on a number of factors including:

- the hazard of the compound released or of derivatives formed by chemical processes occurring within the air (for instance the formation of secondary pollutants such as ozone and acid sulphates) – including the stability and persistence of the agent within the environment and its ability to penetrate indoors;
- the amount of pollutant released and the height at which it is released; tall chimney stacks tend to protect local people but disperse the pollutant over a wider area;
- the atmospheric conditions leading to dilution and dispersal of the pollutant, including worst-case inversion conditions and geographical considerations; local topographical and climatic conditions can exacerbate the situation as in Mexico City where thermal inversions trap pollutants within the valley in which the city is located
- the person's distance from the source
- the composition, activities and location of the general public in relation to the time of release (eg they might be exercising; children might be present)
- the presence of particularly susceptible individuals in the exposed groups

Source: WHO (1992) *Our Planet, Our Health*, Report of the Commission on Health and Environment, Geneva.

Airborne lead remains a particular concern, especially for children, since there is increasing evidence that relatively low concentrations of lead in the blood may have a damaging effect on their mental development with an effect which persists into adulthood.[56] Children's exposure to lead comes not only from the exhausts of petrol-engined motor vehicles where lead additives are still used in the petrol but also from lead water piping, (especially where water supplies are acidic), lead in paint and some industrial emissions.[57] A study of blood lead levels in adult volunteers in ten cities undertaken by the World Health Organization and the United Nations Environment Programme between 1979 and 1981 found the highest lead concentration in Mexico City residents; lead blood levels were above the WHO guideline, and also 2–4 times higher than in cities where low-lead or lead-free gasoline was used.[58] In Mexico City and in Bangalore (one of India's major metropolitan centres), 10 per cent of the sampled population had particularly high blood lead concentrations well above the WHO guideline, at a level above which biochemical changes in the blood begin to occur.[59] A more recent study in Mexico City in 1988 found that over a quarter of the newborn infants in Mexico City had lead levels in their blood high enough to impair neurological and motor-physical development.[60] A study in Bangkok which sought to rank urban environmental problems on the basis of their health risks suggested that lead should be ranked, with airborne particulates and biological pathogens (primarily acute diarrhoea, dengue fever, dysentery and intestinal worms), as the highest risk environmental problems.[61] Exposure to lead may also contribute significantly to higher risks of heart attacks and strokes in adults. One major reason for such high concentrations of lead is the high lead content in gasoline permitted by most Third World governments.[62] However, there does now seem to be a growing awareness that the concentration of lead additives can often be cut, and that a substantial proportion of petrol-engined vehicles can use unleaded petrol with little or no modification to their engine.

There is also increasing concern about suspended particulates, especially since the (limited) data available on Third World cities suggests that a high proportion of their population is already exposed to unacceptable concentrations and that the trend is towards increasing, not decreasing concentrations.[63] All the cities in Box 3.4 had annual averages for suspended particulates that were higher than the WHO guideline figure. In the early 1980s, Kuala Lumpur was reported as having a concentration of suspended particulates in the air 29 times the desirable goal recommended by the Malaysian Environmental Quality Standards Committee.[64] Bangkok, Beijing, Calcutta, Delhi and Tehran were also reported in the early 1980s to greatly exceed the WHO seven-day guideline (the concentration which should not be exceeded for more than seven days each year). These cities exceeded this guideline on more than 200 days a year.[65] The concern is not only about the health impact of the smoke but also about the potentially toxic pollutants present in much smaller concentrations – some of them bound to particles of smoke. For instance, high levels of suspended particulate matter are common in cities in China – one key factor being the high proportion of all energy production coming from coal combustion (power stations, small furnaces and domestic stoves) with inadequate or no control equipment for particulates.[66] Analyses of the chemical composition of particulate matter from Beijing and Tianjin shows the presence of relatively high levels of organic compounds, including the carcinogen benzo-pyrene.[67] Although much uncertainty remains as to the precise nature and scale of the health impacts, estimates suggest that between 300,000 and 700,000 premature deaths a year could be avoided in the Third World if all urban centres brought suspended particulate matter concentrations down to those considered safe by WHO; this is equivalent to between 2–5 per cent of all deaths in the urban centres in which this kind of pollution is a problem.[68] Chronic coughs in urban children would also be much reduced; so too would the chance that these children will face permanent respiratory damage.[69]

For nitrogen oxides and carbon monoxide, there is insufficient data to make any generalizations for Third World cities; too few cities monitor air pollution levels and of those that do, few have data showing trends over time. There are isolated examples of documentation on particular cities with problems – for instance high nitrogen dioxide concentrations in São Paulo in the early 1980s[70], while high concentrations of carbon monoxide (virtually all coming from motor vehicles) have been recorded in particular locations (usually alongside busy roads or in central areas) in Kuala Lumpur, Bangkok, Calcutta, Lagos and Rio de Janeiro.[71]

Motor vehicles are the major source of carbon monoxide in locations where short-term exposure levels routinely exceed accepted standards; they are also the major contributors to oxides of nitrogen, lead and hydrocarbons and contribute to suspended particulate matter. Air pollution from vehicles might be assumed to be less of a problem than in Europe, North America or Japan because poorer nations have fewer automobiles. This is no longer true for many major cities. Major cities in richer Third World nations have as many automobiles per capita as many cities in the North, although not as many as cities such as Los Angeles. Even where the ratio is lower, a combination of narrow congested streets and old and poorly maintained vehicles with higher levels of polluting emissions can result in serious air pollution problems.

However, it is difficult to identify the impact of the most common urban air pollutants on the health of the general public, both because of inadequate information on air quality and because direct evidence of adverse health effects is relatively limited. It is also difficult to identify the health impact of one particular air pollutant as distinct from others and to separate it from other social, economic and demographic factors which also affect health.[72]

In certain industrial centres, air pollution levels can be sufficiently high to show demonstrable health impairment for the population in general or for particular groups. For instance, in Cubatao (Brazil), air pollution levels have been linked to reduced lung functions in children[73] (see Box 3.6). Non-ferrous metal smelters are often major contributors to air pollution and although no well-documented example was found in the Third World, a recent study in the Katowice district in Upper Silesia (Poland) shows the links between high air pollution levels from non-ferrous metal industrial plants and elevated lead and cadmium concentrations in the blood of 20 per cent of children. Some of those tested were also found to exhibit the early detectable symptoms of toxic lead effects, especially the children.[74]

A more common indicator of the health impacts of air pollution comes from comparisons between the health of people in highly polluted areas within cities against those in less polluted areas. These generally show a strong association between the incidence of respiratory infections and pollution levels and may also show possible links with certain kinds of cancers. If the incidence of (say) cancers and respiratory diseases is drawn on a city map, this often pinpoints certain areas where residents suffer most from air pollution – directly linked to one industry or one industrial complex.

Bombay, with its concentration of population and heavy industry probably suffers more than India's other cities. There is a large concentration of industries in the Trombay-Chembur area along the eastern coast of the island which is the core of the city and in the Lalbaug area which includes a thermal power station, a chemicals and fertilizer plant, a gas company and numerous petrochemical plants, oil refineries and textile mills. In one study in 1977–78, the health of residents in Chembur and Lalbaug (with heavy concentrations of industry) was compared to that of residents in a cleaner suburb, Khar. People living in the congested industrial areas suffered from a much higher incidence of diseases such as chronic bronchitis, TB, skin allergies, anaemia and eye irritations. The rate of absenteeism by workers was much higher, particularly in Lalbaug's textile mills, and there was a notable rise in the number of deaths from cancer in Lalbaug.[75] However, causal relationships between urban air pollution levels and lung cancer rates are difficult to establish, because of the difficulties in separating the contribution of ambient air pollution as distinct from (say) occupational exposures, tobacco smoking, or socioeconomic status.[76]

In cities where acute air pollution episodes occur at particular times (for instance when high emissions coincide with particular meteorological conditions), the link between air pollution and health can often be seen in increased mortality among particular vulnerable groups, for instance the elderly.[77] One of the best known examples of an acute air pollution episode is the smog in London (UK) in the winter of 1952 which hastened the death of at least 4000 people. Acute air pollution episodes occur regularly in cities such as Mexico City, Santiago de Chile and many cities in Southern China.

A few studies have sought to link air pollution with health outcomes. A survey by the Bombay Municipal Corporation states that TB and respiratory diseases are the major killers in the city; between 1971 and 1979, deaths from TB went up from 83 to 101 per 100,000 people although deaths from breathing impairments came down from 170 to 143, largely due to the use of low sulphur gas in the most polluting industries.[78] Others have sought to estimate the health impact. One estimate for Latin America suggests that over two million children suffer from chronic coughs as a result of urban air pollution and that air pollution means an excess of 24,300 deaths a year in Latin America. This same source estimated that some 65 million person days of workers' activities were lost to respiratory-related problems caused by air pollution. While the authors emphasise that these are rough estimates, they give an idea of the size of the problem.[79]

A report on Bangkok estimated up to 1400 deaths a year and between nine and 51 million days per year of restricted activity for respiratory reasons as a result of particulate matter.[80] A report in Calcutta estimated that 60 per cent of its residents suffer from respiratory diseases related to air pollution.[81] In Mexico City's metropolitan zone, emissions of sulphur dioxide, nitrogen oxides and carbon monoxide all increased substantially between 1972 and 1983 and air pollution is a likely cause or contributor to most respiratory illnesses and infections[82] (although the extent to which chemical air pollutants can reduce people's resistance to acute respiratory infections is not well understood). Sulphur dioxide emissions from oil refineries and thermal-electric industries, and carbon monoxide from car exhausts are a particular problem. In addition, the thermal inversion helps trap pollutants in the valley within which the city is located; it was recently reported that schools were shut down because air pollution levels had reached such high concentrations and major restrictions on road traffic and on industrial activities have become commonplace.[83]

Cubatao in Brazil remains one of the most dramatic examples of unchecked industrial pollution and its impact on human health (Box 3.6). What is difficult to assess is whether the levels of industrial pollution permitted in Cubatao during the 1970s and early 1980s are an extreme example, or representative of what has happened and what continues to happen in many industrial complexes in the Third World. It is perhaps revealing that only with the return to democracy in Brazil has the scale and nature of the pollution in Cubatao (and elsewhere) become widely known and action taken to address it. It was local citizen organizations who helped document and publicize the problem – and set up a system to monitor emissions from certain factories. Under the military government, there were restrictions on all press reports on Cubatao. Public pressure and a government more responsive to environmental issues and citizen concerns have produced sufficient improvement for Cubatao to be held up as a success story for what can be achieved by citizen pressure, rather than a cautionary story of what may be hidden under repressive political systems.

Box 3.6 Cubatao

The city of Cubatao in Brazil, close to São Paulo and to the major port of Santos, was long known as the 'Valley of Death'. The city contains a high concentration of heavy industry which developed rapidly under Brazil's military government from 1964 – including 23 large industrial plants and dozens of smaller ones. These included a steel plant, a pulp and paper plant, a rubber plant and several metallurgical, chemical and petrochemical industries. Most were Brazilian owned (including five owned by the Federal Government) although they included some multinational plants, for instance a Union Carbide fertilizer factory and the French Rhodia company.

There was little or no attempt on the part of government or companies to control pollution. High levels of tuberculosis, pneumonia, bronchitis, emphysema and asthma, and a high infant mortality rate were all associated with the very high levels of air pollution. At certain times, it also became common for young children to go, almost daily, to a hospital to breathe medicated air. The Cubatao river was once an important source of fish but industrial pollution severely damaged this. Local crabs began to contain too high a level of toxic chemicals to be safe to eat. Toxic industrial wastes were also dumped in the surrounding forests, contaminating surface and groundwater which was used for drinking and cooking. Vegetation in and around Cubatao suffered substantially from air pollution and from acid precipitation arising from locally generated air pollution, to the point where landslides occurred on certain slopes as vegetation died and no longer helped retain the soil. Many of those who came to work in the rapidly growing city lived in illegal settlements built on stilts above swamps; by building their homes on swamps, the inhabitants had a better chance of avoiding eviction, since the land had little commercial value. Hundreds of the inhabitants of one such settlement were killed in late February 1984 after a pipeline carrying gasoline leaked into the swamp under the settlement and then caught fire. In September 1984, an atmospheric inversion combined with the high level of polluting emissions led to the state governor declaring an emergency; the state's environmental agency ordered nine industries to close down and also an evacuation. Some months later, the release of ammonia from a ruptured pipe at a fertilizer factory led to the evacuation of 6000 residents.

For many years, there was little or no protection for the workers in many of the industries and many came to suffer from serious occupational diseases or disabilities arising from their exposure to chemicals or waste products while at work.

Conditions in Cubatao have improved. In 1983, the State of São Paulo's environmental body began to impose environmental controls and fined many industries while closing down others because they contravened the environmental regulations. The volume of industrial effluents disposed of in local rivers, and solid wastes placed in local landfills was cut substantially. Total emissions of particulates were reduced by some 70 per cent between 1984 and 1988 while sulphur dioxide emissions were reduced by some 37 per cent. The number of 'air pollution alerts' decreased from an average of 15 per year in 1984–5 to four per year from 1986 to 1988. Emissions of other industrial air pollutants such as hydrocarbons, ammonia and hydrogen sulphide were also reduced by the large petrochemical and fertilizer industries.

Some companies in Cubatao have publicly committed themselves to a more responsible attitude to the local environment, as they substantially reduced emissions and supported local initiatives to improve conditions in and around the city. The local authorities have sponsored a project to help poorer households move to more healthy sites and to build good quality housing for themselves. But for many people, this is too late, since they are already permanently disabled. The longer-term impact on health of pollutants already in the local rivers or leaking into groundwater is also uncertain.

Studies which measured the lung functions of children in 1983 and 1985 demonstrated the improvement in air quality, except in eight schools. In these schools, there was no improvement or lung function showed further deterioration. These were schools near the industries where air pollution levels were still high. In addition, a study which has monitored changes in children's lung function has shown a steady decrease in lung function over time.

Sources: The World Bank (1989) 'Adult health in Brazil: adjusting to new challenges', Report No 7808-BR, Brazil Department, Washington DC, quoted in Bartone, Carl R (1990) 'Sustainable responses to growing urban environmental crises', (mimeo) Urban Development Division, the World Bank; Hofmaier, VA (1991) *Efeitos de poluicao do ar sobre a funcao pulmonar: un estudo de cohorte em criancas de Cubatao*, (Doctoral Thesis) São Paulo School of Public Health, quoted in WHO (1992) *Our Planet, Our Health*, report of the WHO Commission on Health and Environment, Geneva; Pimenta, JCP (1987) 'Multinational corporations and industrial pollution control in São Paulo, Brazil' in Charles S Pearson (ed.), *Multinational Corporations, Environment and the Third World: Business Matters*, Duke University Press, Durham; Leonard, H Jeffrey (1984) 'Confronting Industrial Pollution in Rapidly Expanding Industrializing Countries – Myths, Pitfalls and Opportunities', Conservation Foundation, USA; a film on air pollution by Bo Landin produced in 1987 by the Television Trust for the Environment as part of the series 'Battle for the Planet'; Macklin, Debbie, *South Magazine*, March 1989; and the World Bank (1992) *World Development Report 1992*, Oxford University Press, Oxford.

NATURAL AND HUMAN INDUCED HAZARDS

An earlier section described how in particular neighbourhoods or districts of the city, many urban dwellers live on sites prone to natural hazards – and how rare it is for governments to help reduce the risks or to respond rapidly and effectively, if a disaster happens. It also noted how the physical expansion of cities often takes place over dangerous sites, as the city outgrows the site or as poorer groups occupy sites at constant risk of flood, landslide or some other natural hazard because of the locational advantages they offer and their low price (if purchased or rented). Hazardous sites are often occupied illegally; the risk of eviction from such sites is small because of their low commercial value or because they are publicly owned and governments will not force their eviction for political reasons.

But there are also natural or human-induced hazards which pose threats to a much larger proportion of the city's population and which are less linked to specific sites – for instance severe storms, earthquakes, floods, heat waves and industrial accidents. To consider first the natural hazards, many cities either developed on sites subject to floods, earthquakes, landslides or other natural hazards, or their sites or buildings became hazardous because of the way in which the city developed. Ian Douglas has described in detail the ways in which city developments involve massive modifications to the natural site and to the circulation of energy, water and materials; hillslopes may be cut, dug, bulldozed into new shapes; valleys and swamps may be filled with rock and waste material; water and minerals may be extracted from under the city; and the regimes of soil and groundwater may be modified.[84] The extraction of groundwater, perhaps combined with the compaction of soil (for instance through the weight of buildings or from vibrations from earthquakes), often causes serious subsidence and damage to buildings; this may also increase the risk of floods and seriously interfere with natural or human-made drainage systems. The exposure of soil during the development of roads or new residential, industrial or commercial developments allows rapid weathering and subsequent erosion of surface soil, increasing silt loads of streams by as much as 50–100 times, which can block drains and raise the beds of rivers and streams – greatly exacerbating the scale of floods.[85]

It has also become common for cities to outgrow their sites. Many cities were founded in what were considered safe and convenient sites centuries ago. Most of the world's largest cities and metropolitan areas are relatively ancient foundations. For instance, in Latin America, virtually all the capital cities, and cities with 500,000 or more inhabitants, were founded by the Spaniards and Portuguese during the sixteenth and seventeenth centuries – while a few had pre-Columbian precedents.[86] Most major cities in India, Indonesia, Pakistan and China (which contain a high proportion of all the Third World's largest cities) have even longer histories. The same is true for many of the largest cities in Northern Africa and in Nigeria, the most populous country in sub-Saharan Africa.

The many cities which owe their foundation and early development to indigenous civilizations were often developed by cultures with great experience in the ecological advantages and disadvantages of different sites. But city locations then as now are also influenced by economic and political factors. Sites with major advantages for defence, transport and political considerations have often been developed as cities, despite the fact that the site (or certain locations within the site) are at risk from natural hazards.

For most cities, population growth was slow for much of their history. When relatively small, there was no need for urban development to take place on steep hillsides or over floodplains or in areas with unstable soil conditions. It is the vast expansion of the urban population and the subsequent demand for space which has done more to increase the scale and severity of risk. Most major cities had sites which served them well until recent decades; they were either relatively free from natural hazards, within their national context, or measures were taken to limit the risks. But city sites which can ensure relatively safe sites for tens of thousands or even hundreds of thousands of people often cannot do so when populations expand to millions. Large cities today have long since reached a size far beyond what their founders could have imagined as possible.

Thus, as these cities grew rapidly, so they exceeded the availability of safe sites – or at least the price of safe sites became such that poorer groups would no longer find accommodation there. For instance, for most of Caracas's history, the entire population was easily accommodated in the valley surrounded by hills. In recent decades, with the large expansion in the population and highly commercialized land markets which exclude poorer groups from good quality sites, poorer groups have been pushed in increasing numbers into settlements on steep hillsides with high risks of landslides.[87] Many cities which grew beside rivers, lakes or estuaries where once the urbanized area was confined to sites with little risk of flooding, have now expanded in population manyfold. Once again, highly commercialised land markets exclude poorer groups from all possibility of developing housing on safe, legal sites. Thus, illegal settlements built on land subject to flooding, represent the best possibility for housing that is easily accessible to jobs.

The question arises as to why, if a particular city outgrows its site, does it not stop growing, with new urban investments going elsewhere. One reason is the scale and influence of the city, by the time the environmental hazards become apparent. When countries (and their economies) began to urbanize rapidly, the economic and political power concentrates in the major cities ensuring a high concentration of population there, whether or not local physical and climatic conditions were well suited to the vast expansion of population and production. The scale of investments and the multiplicity of vested interests within any major city means an inertia against change which at best ensures a slow response. And even with severe environmental problems, the economies of scale in concentration for powerful groups may still exceed the costs.

A second reason why city populations continue to grow over hazardous sites is simply that it is often the poorer groups who bear most of the environmental costs. Even where they have sufficient political power to influence choices, their concern is more to limit the risk rather than consider moving to another site.

Many of the Third World's largest cities now find they are in sites ill-suited to the scale and concentration of pollutants generated there; the high levels of air pollution in Mexico City, Santiago de Chile and Chongqing and the particular characteristics of their site (and weather patterns) which inhibit their dispersal, have already been described. Other cities have developed on sites at risk from flooding, but the combination of the much increased numbers concentrated there and a failure to limit the negative impacts of human-induced changes in the hydrological cycle, have greatly increased both the number of people at risk, and the risk of flooding. Others have developed on seismic zones where again, the combination of much increased numbers and a failure to implement measures to limit the impact of an earthquake when it occurs, has also meant a large increase in the number of people at risk. Box 3.7 gives some examples of recent natural disasters and their impacts. In the earthquake in San Salvador, most of the damaged houses were those used by poorer groups – in illegal sub-divisions, tenements or squatter settlement. In the floods in Resistencia, most of the 15,000 people who lost their homes were low-income families.

Certain disease epidemics may be associated with natural disasters – especially floods which can contaminate all available water supplies and may be associated with epidemics of dysentery or other waterborne and water-washed diseases. Outbreaks of leptospirosis (usually caused by drinking water infected by rat urine) have been associated with floods in Rio de Janeiro and São Paulo and those living in poor quality settlements at risk of flooding, with high levels of overcrowding and inadequate provision for garbage collection (or living close to garbage dumps), are particularly at risk.[88]

Box 3.7 Major natural disasters in third world cities

Earthquake in San Salvador: The October 1986 earthquake with an intensity of 5.4 on the Richter scale caused 2000 deaths and injured 10,000 people; total damage was estimated at US $2 billion. A high proportion of the victims were squatters who, prior to the earthquake, were residing on marginal sites, such as the banks of steep ravines, along railroad tracks, and on public lands and on other sites that had been occupied illegally. Most of the houses were made of light-weight materials such as corrugated iron sheeting, cardboard, and wooden timbers. Much of the damage was caused not by the collapse of housing, but from landslides. A large number of the victims were displaced persons who had moved to the city to escape the violence of the civil war in the countryside. An El Salvadorean NGO, FUNDASAL, estimates that out of 60,000 damaged housing units, 16,382 were in illegal urbanizations (*colonias ilegales*), 28,924 were in tenements (*mesones*), 8860 were in squatter settlements (*tugurios*) and 1434 in improvised settlements (*campamentos*).

Floods in Resistencia (Argentina): The 1982–3 floods led to the evacuation of around 350,000 inhabitants and the cost in the Argentine section of the Paraguay–Parana basin was estimated at some US $1.5 billion. Fifty per cent of the urbanized area of Resistencia and 70 per cent of its population were directly or indirectly affected by the floods. Two hundred and fifty eight schools in the province of Chaco, representing 27 per cent of all schools, were flooded; 72 additional schools built on safe sites were used for emergency housing. Forty six per cent of the children enrolled in schools had to abandon school temporarily. As a result of the floods, some 15,000 people lost their homes; most were low-income families who dedicate a very high percentage (sometimes over 80 per cent) of the family income to the purchase of food. As entire households had to be evacuated and housed in distant places (in army barracks, schools, or improvised tents, for instance) they lost their informal sources of income which are located in the central district of the city.

Earthquakes in Mexico City: The earthquakes which hit Mexico City in September 1985 and their aftershocks are estimated to have killed at least 10,000 people, injured 50,000 and made 250,000 homeless. Damage was estimated at around US $4 billion. Around two thirds of the structures which suffered total or partial collapse were housing – although there were also great losses to health services (4260 hospital beds lost) and education (761 public school buildings affected). Fractures in the water network affected services to over 400,000 inhabitants. A high proportion of those who died or were seriously injured and who lost their homes were from low-income groups who lived in public housing or in *vecindades*, densely occupied, multifamily rental housing. Over 1000 people were killed in the collapse of four buildings which were densely occupied public housing units.

Sources: Davis, Ian (1987) 'Safe shelter within unsafe cities: disaster vulnerability and rapid urbanization' *Open House International* vol. 12, no. 3, pp. 5–15; Cuny, Frederick C (1987) 'Sheltering the urban poor: lessons and strategies of the Mexico City and San Salvador earthquakes' *Open House International* vol. 12, no. 3, pp. 16–20; Barraza, Ernesto, *'Effectos del terremoto en la infraestructura de vivienda'* and Lungo Ucles, Mario '*El terremoto de octubre de 1986 y la situacion habitacional de los sectores populares*' in '*El terremoto del 10 de octubre de 1986*', a special issue of *La Universidad*, Nino CXII no. 5, San Salvador, January–March, 1987; Lungo Ucles, Mario, (1988) 'San Salvador: el habitat despues del terremoto', *Medio Ambiente y Urbanizacion* no. 24, pp. 46–52; and Degg, Martin R (1989) 'Earthquake hazard assessment after Mexico' *Disasters* vol. 13, no. 3, pp. 237–246.

There are also many disasters which have an impact which goes far beyond a particular house or neighbourhood, as a result of industrial or other accidents. Recent examples include: the industrial accident at Bhopal in 1984 where the release of methyl iso-cyanate caused the death of over 3000 with perhaps 100,000 or more seriously injured (and 200,000 people evacuated); the natural gas explosion in Mexico City in 1984 (over 1000 dead, 4200 injured, over 200,000 evacuated); and the explosion in Islamabad (Pakistan) in 1988 (over 100 dead, some 3000 injured).[89] More recently, there are the deaths, injuries and vast damage to property in Guadalajara (Mexico) as a result of explosions of gas which had accumulated in the sewers; reports suggest that the illegal disposal of industrial wastes into the sewers was one major cause.

What is rarely documented is the social impact of disasters, especially the long-term impact. It is almost always poorer groups who suffer most. After counting the number of people killed and injured and moving the injured, evaluations of disasters usually reveal the vulnerability of the thousands of people who were affected. For instance, in many natural disasters, most of those who lost their homes are relatively poor households who had developed the site and built the shelter themselves. They have lost their homes and belongings because the design and technology used in constructing the house could not resist an earth-tremor or because the site where the people built their shelter was flooded or destroyed by a landslide. They may lose their source of income because they are relocated, usually under the direction of some public or international agency, to a place distant from their job or where they had previously earned an income. They lose most or all of their 'capital'; the physical improvements they made in the house and in the infrastructure within their settlement, such as an improvement in the water system or in the collection of garbage, a nursery, a health centre or sidewalks. And in some cases, they are forced to move to a new site, which means a large disruption to their social networks (family, friends and contacts important to finding paid work).

NOISE POLLUTION

The health impacts of noise on city inhabitants is now being given more serious attention, even if the precise health and environmental effects are not fully known.[90] Temporary or permanent hearing loss is the best known health impact, although high noise levels are also known to be one of the critical stress factors which influence mental disorders and social pathologies.[91] The most intense, continuous and frequent exposure to high noise levels are generally within particular jobs in particular industries.[92] In the wider urban environment, there are usually four principal sources of noise: aircraft, industrial operations, construction activities and highway traffic.[93]

Large areas of many Third World cities have high levels of noise from aircraft landing and taking off in nearby airports; for instance, in Latin America, many major airports are in the middle of densely populated areas (the international airport of Mexico City and airports in Lima, Bogota, Quito, Guayaquil, Buenos Aires, Port-au-Prince and Santiago de Chile).

Noise from major roads or highways is a major problem – especially since few Third World governments have instituted effective noise-control programmes on road vehicles, as in Europe and North America. In Shanghai, the average noise volume was reported as being as high as 62 decibels, with noise levels reaching an average of 75 decibels at rush hour, and 90 decibels in certain locations.[94] In Bangkok, noise pollution is considered a serious problem. Noise from trucks, buses and motor-cycles mean noise levels greater than 70 decibels in many locations; findings from Western nations suggest that outdoor noise levels should be kept under 65 decibels to comply with desirable limits indoors.[95] Motorboats, which are widely used in Bangkok, frequently exceed the noise standard of 85 decibels at a distance of 7.5 metres set by the Harbour Department and an examination of motorboat operators found that 80 per cent had hearing loss.[96] While noise pollution remains a major problem in Western nations, at least there are regulations, institutions to enforce them and democratic procedures through which protests can be organized; one or more of these is lacking in virtually all Third World nations.

ENVIRONMENT AND WELL-BEING

There are a large and complex range of environmental factors, other than those discussed already, which make cities, neighbourhoods and shelters more pleasant, safe and valued by their inhabitants, and thus more healthy. Good quality housing and living environments reduce stress and make life more pleasant; factors include sufficient indoor and outdoor space, location close to family and friends, easy access to desired services and facilities for safe play for children, and for recreation, minimum noise and few personal hazards.[97] Within the wider neighbourhood or district within which the shelter is located, it is clear that a sense of security, good quality infrastructure (eg roads, pavements, drains, street lights), services such as street cleaning, the availability of emergency services and easy access to educational, health and other social services, as well as cultural and other amenities, also contribute to good mental health/well-being.[98] It is difficult to be precise about what is needed – both because the interaction between environmental factors and human well-being is poorly understood, and because needs will differ between different cultures and, of course, age groups.

Our understanding of the importance of these kinds of environmental factors has been enhanced by the fact that so many psychosocial disorders are associated with poor quality housing and living environments. Among the most serious are depression, drug and alcohol abuse, suicide, and violence of different kinds such as child and spouse mistreatment and abuse, and target violence – such as teacher assault and rape.[99] Households constantly at risk from floods, landslides or other natural hazards are also more at risk from psychosocial disorders; the dislocation to their lives in the event of a disaster will also have health impacts. Of course, psychosocial disorders are also associated with non-environmental factors – for instance insecure tenure for the inhabitants (if they are squatters or tenants) and inadequate or insecure incomes.

Psychosocial and chronic diseases are becoming a major cause of death and morbidity among adolescents and young adults in many urban areas or in particular districts within urban areas. For instance, psychosocial and chronic diseases are among the most important causes of death in cities as diverse as Shenyang and Rio de Janeiro.[100] Homicides were responsible for 5 per cent of all deaths in São Paulo City in 1986.[101] It is clear that poor quality living environments can contribute to the stress which underlies many diseases. Many physical characteristics of the housing and living environment can influence the incidence and severity of psychosocial disorders through stressors such as noise, over-crowding, inappropriate design, poor sanitation and garbage collection, and inadequate maintenance.[102]

A recent study suggests the need to focus on three aspects of the physical environment when considering its possible impact on people's psychosocial health:

- the dweller's level of satisfaction with the house and its neighbourhood and its location within the urban area;
- the dwelling's physical structure (eg the amount of space, state of repair, facilities – which may influence the level of privacy, the

possibilities for meeting relatives and friends and child-rearing practices); and

- the neighbourhood (including the quality of services and facilities, and the level of security).[103]

Many characteristics of urban neighbourhoods which are not easily identified or defined may have important influences on each individual's level of satisfaction and on the incidence of crime, vandalism and interpersonal violence.[104]

It is also clear that the extent to which any individual or household has the possibility of modifying or changing their housing environment, and working with others in the locality to effect change in the wider neighbourhood, is also an important influence on their health (including their sense of well-being). Many critiques of public housing and of urban planning in Third World cities (especially 'slum' and squatter clearance and redevelopment) have centred on the loss of individual, household and community control that they entail.[105] There is also the importance for the physical and mental health of individuals and 'communities' of being able to command events which control their lives.[106] Medical doctors and psychiatrists are increasingly recognizing the importance of such a link.[107]

There are also the influences of the built environment on child development. Poor physical environments can inhibit or permanently damage a child's physical and mental development.[108] Children are especially vulnerable to deficiencies in provision for play and for informal learning from their peers – with particular needs also varying considerably at different ages. In most poor districts in cities, there is little or no formal provision for playgrounds for young children which are both safe (eg free from faecal contamination), and stimulating. The needs of older children and adolescents for easily accessible indoor and outdoor space for games, sports and socializing are also rarely met. Yet the importance of safe and stimulating play in, for instance, the evolution of a child's motor skills and communication skills, problem solving, logical thinking, emotional development and social and socialized behaviour is increasingly recognized.[109]

Infants and children often suffer not only from a poor physical environment in the sense of overcrowded and hazardous housing and inadequate provision for play (including dangerous and unsuitable play sites), but also from the psychosocial disorders which deficiencies in the physical environment and the stressors associated with them promote in their parents or carers. Among the key psychological and social development needs of children are a need for interaction (to provide stimulation and reaction to the child), the need for consistency and predictability in their caregiving environment, and a need to explore and discover.[110] It is easy to see how a poor physical environment makes these more difficult to provide although perhaps a more important (non-environmental) factor is that in many low-income households, all adults work long hours to obtain sufficient income to survive and providing child supervision, care and stimulation are very difficult.

The precise linkages between different elements of the physical environment, and people's health and sense of well-being are difficult to ascertain, and to separate from other influences. There are also other influences which can promote or prevent the process that might lead to disease[111] – for instance 'strong social networks and a sense of community organization in many rundown inner city districts . . . and squatter settlements . . . might help explain the remarkably low level of psychosocial problems.'[112] The importance of such networks can also be seen in the increase in physical and mental ill health among populations relocated from inner city tenements or illegal settlements to 'better quality' housing, partly because such networks became disrupted.[113] One key conclusion seems to be that it is people's capacity to choose housing and neighbourhoods whose built and natural environment meets their environmental and non-environmental needs that is important.

ENVIRONMENTAL PROBLEMS IN SMALLER CITIES

Given that in most Third World countries a significant proportion of urban dwellers live in relatively small urban centres, there is a remarkable lack of documentation on environmental problems in these centres. Virtually all the examples given of environmental problems so far in this book are for urban centres with more than one million inhabitants, yet two thirds of the Third World's urban population lives in cities or urban centres which have less than one million inhabitants. We also noted earlier how close to 50 independent nations had no city which had reached 500,000 inhabitants. All urban centres (whether large or small cities or urban centres too small to be called cities[114]) need water supply systems which ensure uncontaminated water is easily available to all households and provision for the disposal of household and human wastes (including excreta, household wastewaters, storm and surface run-off and solid wastes). All need preventative and curative health services and basic environmental management (for instance to protect water sources and to minimize breeding and feeding grounds for disease vectors). All need local authorities with the competence and capacity to ensure that these are provided.

Most small cities and urban centres have environmental problems arising from a lack of piped water supplies, or water sources used for human consumption being contaminated, lack of provision for drainage and for the safe disposal of excreta and lack of provision for garbage collection and disposal. Box 3.8 gives some examples from selected African urban centres. What is often clear in smaller cities is the local authorities' lack of investment capacity for installing or expanding basic infrastructure, and the inadequacy in the basic capital equipment. For instance, in the example of Kabale in Uganda given in Box 3.8, the entire population of some 28,000 people relies on one working tractor and trailer to collect wastes.

In most nations, smaller urban centres are likely to have a much lower proportion of their populations served by piped water systems and by sewage systems than larger cities. For instance in Argentina, the smaller the urban centre, the higher the proportion of households lacking piped water and connections to sewers. The average for urban centres with between 200,000 and 500,000 inhabitants is around 18 per cent lacking piped water and 60 per cent lacking connection to sewers. The average for urban centres with between 5000 and 10,000 inhabitants is over 40 per cent of households lacking piped water and more than 90 per cent lacking connection to sewers.[115] For instance, in Noetinger, a small agricultural town in the Pampas, there is no piped water system and no sewer system. The inhabitants get their water from tanks and individual wells from which water is pumped – and many draw water from the first aquifer from which there is a growing risk of contamination from excreta, much of it disposed of through septic tanks or simply holes.[116]

Although most small urban centres have little or no industry, there are still many small cities which have developed as centres for particular industries where there are serious problems from industrial pollution. Cubatao, whose environmental problems were described earlier in this chapter, is one example. Cubatao is one of many small cities which have developed because of a concentration of industries there, close to major metropolitan centres. Most of the Third World's largest metropolitan centres have one or more small city close by with high concentrations of industries. Other small cities develop as industrial centres because of some particular resource based there (for instance coal or large quantities of freshwater) or because of economic incentives (for instance duty-free export processing zones) or because of some political advantage (such as powerful politicians steering public industries there).[117]

Small cities usually have even less effective pollution control and land use planning (for instance to ensure polluting industries are downwind and downstream of the inhabitants) than larger cities. It also does not need a heavy concentration of industry to bring serious pollution problems.

Box 3.8 Water, sanitation and garbage services in small African urban centres

Jinja (Uganda): With 61,000 inhabitants in 1991, this is the second largest urban centre in Uganda. The water supply coverage in 1990 was 54 per cent of dwellings which is much higher than in most Ugandan urban centres (including Kampala, the capital). It is estimated that only 50 per cent of the waste generated within the municipality is collected; an assessment in 1990 found that the entire solid-waste collection and disposal system relied on three vehicles with skips but because two are of one make and the third of another, they cannot use each other's skips. Lack of spare parts and of tools to maintain them meant that they were working far below their capacity. There is no treatment of the solid waste, it is simply deposited on a land site on the outskirts of the town.

Kabale (Uganda): With 27,905 inhabitants in 1991, this is a market town in an extremely fertile and high density rural area. For water supply, there were just 217 connections to the piped water system and on average, water was supplied for four hours in the morning and two hours in the evening. Estimates suggest that less than 16 per cent of the population had access to water from this system. Provision for sanitation was also very deficient. Refuse collection relies on one working tractor and trailer which collects wastes from 20 areas marked with signposts where refuse may be deposited by the public. It is estimated that around 10–20 per cent of the daily refuse is collected.

Aliade, Igugh and Ugba (Nigeria): Each of these urban centres had a population estimated at between 6000–8000 in 1980. Two of them have no piped water system and in the third, only a small number of households have access to treated water (from the state rural water supply scheme). Most households obtain water from compound wells which are the responsibility of the compound owner; the next most common sources of water are streams, ponds and rivers. The State Water Boards in Nigeria are responsible for providing water supplies to urban centres but piped water schemes are rarely available to small urban centres. There is no public provision for sanitation; most households use pit latrines although some households have no access to a latrine. About half of the households using such latrines share them. Refuse collection and disposal is in theory a local government responsibility but 67 per cent of households dump refuse in their backyard while most of the rest burn or bury it. Only in one of the three urban centres was there neighbourhood collection and disposal and this was organized on a small scale.

Sources: Meekyaa, Ude James and Rakodi, Carole (1990) 'The neglected small towns of Nigeria', *Third World Planning Review* vol. 12, no. 1, pp. 21–40; and Amis, Philip (1992) *Urban Management in Uganda: Survival Under Stress*, The Institutional Framework of Urban Government: Case Study no. 5, Development Administration Group, INLOGOV, University of Birmingham, Birmingham.

Just one or two agricultural processing factories or chemical, pulp and paper or beverage factories can seriously pollute a river. Just one cement plant can create serious air pollution problems.

One example of industrial pollution in and around a small city comes from Dindigul in Tamil Nadu, India, as a result of the tanneries located there, as recently documented by J Paul Baskar.[118] There are 76 tanneries in Dindigul district and these employ some 3000 workers, more than half of them low paid child labourers. Each tannery uses large volumes of water and is thought to contaminate groundwater within a radius of six kilometres. Agricultural production in the region has been progressively cut, largely as a result of the accumulation of salts from tannery effluents, and most wells in the region have become unusable. There are also many illnesses locally which may be linked to tannery pollution. In 1990, the state government announced approval for a common effluent treatment plant and contributed towards its cost. Since this would treat effluents from the tanneries, contamination of soil and groundwater would be minimized. But one year after this announcement, work on the plant had not begun. Nor had a scheme to provide potable water to the affected villages.

One final example of the scale and range of environmental problems in urban centres other than the largest cities come from the two main urban centres in Cameroon, Douala and Yaounde. These may be the largest and most important cities in the Cameroon but both are on a much smaller scale than cities such as Shanghai or Bombay, São Paulo, Manila or Lagos and as such provide useful examples; the information presented here is drawn from a series of papers presented in a seminar about their environmental problems in 1983.[119] These show the range of environmental problems which exist even in relatively small cities; recent estimates put the population of both cities at over half a million inhabitants.[120] Yaounde is the national capital and Douala the chief port and main industrial centre. Both cities' populations have grown rapidly over the last three decades; in 1950 neither had reached 100,000 inhabitants.

Their environmental problems centre on emissions and effluents from industries; inadequate provision for the removal of household and human wastes; the concentration of motor vehicles; the many low-income people who have no alternative but to squat on house sites ill-suited to safe, healthy housing; and lack of planning to provide some separation between polluting industries and people (and the water they drink) and to control low-density sprawl.

Industries cause serious problems of air and water pollution in both cities[121] and were built in locations which best served the needs of that industry, with no logic or plan guiding this location in the wider public interest. There has been little concern for regulations to control industrial emissions.[122] Household and human wastes are disposed of with little regard to potential health hazards. The company responsible for emptying and cleaning septic tanks and latrines disposes of some of this untreated sewage into Yaounde's waterways or on waste ground. In both cities, these problems are made more acute by the fact that garbage collection is only provided for certain neighbourhoods. In those with no such collections, rubbish heaps build up on streets and sidewalks, providing breeding grounds for rodents and disease vectors. While rain might eventually wash them away, such garbage frequently gets stuck in bottleneck spots and causes flooding. Richer households tend to live 'upstream' on higher ground with the poorer quarters 'downstream' on lower ground. The waterways polluted by sewage and industrial effluents and the run-off from higher ground comes through some of the poorest residential areas.[123] There are also problems of air pollution – from factory dust and ash and the burning of household wastes, to the various oxides of nitrogen, carbon and sulphur emitted by internal combustion engines or industries.

In Yaounde and Douala, as in other Third World cities, it is usually lower income groups who suffer most from air and water pollution and from floods and other 'natural hazards'.[124] If many (or indeed most) city households cannot afford to buy or rent even the cheapest legal house, apartment or room where the most basic environmental standards are met, they have to resort to some form of housing with one or more major defect to bring down the price. One common solution is to live in shelters illegally built on sites subject to flooding or landslides or continual contamination from industrial emissions; or on (or close to) city garbage tips or right next to railways or major highways. One example is a large shanty town which has grown up around a quarry on the outskirts of Yaounde with the residents having to live with the problems of dust, explosions damaging houses, noise, air pollution from tar production and lack of piped water.[125] Other 'spontaneous settlements' in both Yaounde and Douala have grown up on valley bottoms and marshy sites infested with mosquitoes.

WHO BEARS THE ENVIRONMENTAL COSTS IN THIRD WORLD CITIES?

Perhaps the least surprising point arising from the review of environmental problems in this and the preceding chapter is that it is poorer groups who bear most of the ill-health and other costs of environmental problems. They are the least able to afford good quality housing in neighbourhoods with piped water, and adequate provision for sanitation, garbage collection, paved roads and drains. When water consumption per person in cities averages 20–40 litres per person per day (well below the minimum required for good health), most poorer groups' consumption is likely to be less than half the average.[126] Poorer groups' capacity to live at considerable distances from the main economic centres, where land prices are cheaper, are constrained by poor public transport and the costs in time and money of going to and from the places where they earn an income.

The scale of the differentials between richer and poorer groups in their access to natural resources (from adequate supplies of freshwater to safe land sites for their housing and open spaces suitable for children's play, recreation and sport) is a revealing indicator of the level of equality within that society. So too are the differentials in the scale and type of waste generation by households from different income groups; households in poorer city-districts often generate half the amount of waste per person as the city average and perhaps a third or a quarter of the per capita average in wealthy districts.[127] Poorer households often separate glass, metals, and paper from their wastes since these can be sold. Their vegetable wastes may go to feeding livestock; they may also go to making compost (also combined with ashes, if they use coal or woodfuel) where they have access to land on which food can be grown,

If there was sufficient information available to construct a map of each Third World city, showing the level of risk from all environmental hazards in each neighbourhood, the areas with the highest risks would coincide with the areas with a predominance of low-income groups. The correlations between income levels and environmental hazards would be particularly strong in such aspects as the quality and quantity of water, sanitation, solid-waste collection and risk from floods, landslides and other natural hazards; the reasons for this have been dealt with in some detail but they centre on the fact that housing and land markets price poorer groups out of safe, well-located, well-serviced housing and land sites. In many cities, there will be a strong correlation between indoor air quality and income because poorer groups use more polluting fuels and more inefficient stoves (or open fires) which ensure a much worse air quality indoors. The fact that poorer groups also live in much more cramped and overcrowded conditions obviously exacerbates this – and the transmission of infectious diseases. A high proportion of poor groups live in shacks made of flammable material, with higher risks of accidents. Poorer groups will generally have the least access to playgrounds, parks and other open spaces managed for public use.

The correlations between income level and level of air pollution may not be so precise. In certain 'hot-spots' such as close to quarries, cement works and industries with high levels of air pollution in their immediate surrounds, the correlation is likely to be strong. But the correlations are less clear when an entire city suffers from air pollution. In addition, particular 'hot spots' for air pollution have often developed relatively recently, and if they persist and are well defined, they will eventually be reflected in housing and land prices (as richer groups move out and poorer groups move in).

Many studies of the differentials in health status or infant mortality rates between city districts (or boroughs or municipalities) show conditions in poorer areas being much worse than the more wealthy areas or the city-average.[128] Infant mortality rates are often four or more times higher in poorer areas than in richer areas, with much higher differentials often apparent if the poorest district is compared to the richest district. Large differentials between rich and poor districts are also common in the incidence of many environment-related diseases – for instance tuberculosis and typhoid. Differentials in the number of people dying from certain environment-related diseases are often very large; for instance many more deaths in poorer communities are likely to come from diarrhoeal diseases and acute respiratory infections such as pneumonia and influenza. Earlier sections also noted how most of the people living in the districts and settlements most at risk from floods and landslides are low-income groups. Box 3.9 gives some examples of differentials between different areas within a city in terms of pollution levels, access to public services and health indicators

There are also inequalities not revealed by these statistics, however. Poorer groups generally have the least possibility of medical treatment if they are injured at work or fall ill from pollution. They have the least resources on which to call when floods or landslides damage or destroy their housing. They will have the least possibility of taking time off to recover from sickness or injury because the loss of income from doing so would press heavily on their survival and because they are unable to afford health insurance – or obtain the jobs for which health insurance is paid by the firm.

Among those with lower incomes, there is also likely to be considerable differentiation in the scale and nature of environmental hazards to which they are exposed. For instance, there are particular groups which face greater environmental risks because of their work. There are those who are particularly susceptible to infection or poisoning by toxic substances as a result of their age – for instance foetuses during pregnancy, infants and children. The elderly are particularly vulnerable to certain environmental hazards. There is also a differentiation by gender, some of it related to biological differences (for instance pregnant women are particularly vulnerable to certain environmental hazards), some related to the particular roles for which men and women take responsibility.[129]

Box 3.9 Intra-city differentials in environmental hazards, access to public services and health indicators

- **Differentials in environmental hazards**

Mexico City: The highest concentrations of particulate matter in the air are found in the south-east and the north-east areas which are predominantly low-income areas.

Bombay (India): A study in 1977 compared the health of residents in two districts with heavy concentrations of industries, with those in a district with very little industry. People in the industrialized districts suffered a much higher incidence of diseases such as bronchitis, tuberculosis, skin allergies, anaemia and eye irritation and there was a notable rise in deaths from cancer in one of the industrialized districts.

Caracas (Venezuela): An estimated 574,000 people live in illegal settlements on slopes with a significant risk of landslides; most of the areas continuously affected by slope failures are low-income settlements.

- **Differentials in access to public services**

Buenos Aires (Argentina): Of the 11 million or so inhabitants of the Buenos Aires metropolitan area, only 57 per cent have running water and only 45 per cent have connections to the sewer system. Virtually all of those in the Federal District (the centre of the metropolitan area with some three million inhabitants) have piped water and connection to sewers. It is in the poorer, peripheral municipalities outside this central area but within the metropolitan area that a high proportion of the population lack either running water or connection to sewers. For instance, in the municipalities of General Sarmiento, Merlo and Moreno, less than 5 per cent of the population have running water and less than 4 per cent have connections to sewers. Three other municipalities have less than 12 per cent of their population with running water and less than 10 per cent with connections to sewers.

Accra (Ghana): In the high class residential areas with water piped to the home and water closets for sanitation, water consumption per capita is likely to be well in excess of the recommended figure of 200 litres per person per day. In slum neighbourhoods such as Nima-Maamobi and Ashiaman where buying water from vendors is common, the water consumption is about 60 litres per capita per day.

Surabaya (Indonesia): The wealthiest 20 per cent of the population are reported to consume 80 per cent of the public services, including those essential to a healthy environment.

Mexico City: Residents in high-income Chapultepec consume on average some 450 litres of water per person per day; the average in Nezahualcoyotl is only 50 litres per day. Overall, nine per cent of consumers account for 75 per cent of the freshwater consumption while two million people have very inadequate access to safe water supplies.

Santiago de Chile: In some of the richest districts, per capita water consumption per day is between 300 and 450 litres per day. In many of the poorer districts, it is 100 litres a day or less (for instance just 80 litres a day in La Pintana on the periphery).

- **Differentials in health indicators**

  Jakarta (Indonesia): Official estimates suggest an infant mortality rate for the whole city at 33 per 1000 live births while estimates for some of the poorer areas suggest rates of four to five times the city average.

  Karachi (Pakistan): In three low-income areas, between 95 and 152 infants per 1000 live births died before the age of one; in a middle class area, only 32 per 1000 died.

  Manila (Philippines): In Tondo (one of the largest squatter settlements), the infant mortality rate was 210 per 1000 live births in the mid 1970s compared to 76 for non-squatter areas in Manila. The proportion of people with tuberculosis in Tondo was nine times the average for non squatter areas; typhoid was also four times as common.

  Port-au-Prince (Haiti): In the 'slums', one in five infants die before their first birthday while another one in ten die between their first and second birthday; this is almost three times the mortality rates in rural areas and many times the rate in the richer areas of Port-au-Prince where infant and child mortality rates were similar to those in urban areas of the USA.

  Porto Alegre (Brazil): Infant mortality rates among residents of 'shanty towns' were three times as high as among the 'non-shanty-town' residents. Neo-natal mortality rates were twice as high and post-neonatal mortality more than five times as high. Mortality from pneumonia and influenza was six times higher in 'shanty towns' and from septicaemia eight times higher.

  São Paulo (Brazil): Infant mortality rates can vary by a factor of four, depending on the district. In the core area, it is 42 infants per 1000 live births while in one of the predominantly poor peri-urban municipalities, the rate was 175 per 1000 live births. Infant death rates from enteritis, diarrhoea and pneumonia on the city's periphery were twice as high as in the core area.

  Tianjin (China): A study of environment-related morbidity and mortality in the different sub-districts of the city found large variations. For instance, the average for sub-districts' infant mortality rate was 13 but it reached as high as 31 in one district. TB prevalence in the sub-districts averaged 172 per 100,000 people with the highest sub-district figure being 347 and the lowest just 54. There were also major differences in mortality rates for lung cancer and cervical cancer.

Sources: Accra: Songsore 1992. Bombay: Centre for Science and Environment 1983. Buenos Aires: Zorrilla and Guaresti 1986. Caracas: Jiminez Diaz (1992) Jakarta: Harpham, Garner and Surjadi 1990. Karachi: Aga Khan University students 1986 (unpublished) quoted in Harpham, Lusty and Vaughan. Manila: Basta 1977. Mexico City: Schteingart 1989. Port-au-Prince: Rohde 1983. Porto Alegre: Guimaraes and Fischmann 1985. Santiago: Espinoza 1988. São Paulo: World Bank 1984. Surabaya: Silas, Johan quoted in Douglass 1992. Tianjin: Bertaud and Young 1990 quoted in Leitmann 1991. See Bibliography for full references.

Chapter 2 noted the vulnerability of pregnant women and their unborn children (and of the mother's ova and the father's sperm prior to conception) to certain chemical pollutants. Environmental factors also exert a strong influence on the child in the womb, for instance, through the mother's exposure to toxic chemicals in the workplace.[130] The influence may be less direct through environmental factors which influence the health and nutritional status of the mother – for instance malaria contracted by pregnant mothers is often associated with low birth weights and maternal mortality.

Infants and young children are at greater risk of dying from many environment-related diseases – for instance diarrhoeal diseases, malaria, pneumonia or measles.[131] Infants are also more at risk than adults from various chemical pollutants such as lead (in food, water and air) and high nitrate concentrations in water. The transfer of infants and young children from exclusive reliance on breast milk to formula milk and semi-solid and solid foods is often particularly hazardous in housing lacking safe water and the facilities needed for hygienic food preparation and storage.

Children are particularly at risk from various hazards commonly found in low-income areas: for instance, housing made of flammable materials combined with overcrowding and widespread use of open fires or stoves or kerosene heaters/cookers means a high risk of accidental fires. Open sites used by children for play and sport are often contaminated with faecal matter and with household wastes also attracting rats and other disease vectors. The increasing mobility of children and their natural curiosity and desire to explore can also expose them to many environmental hazards, where space and facilities are lacking both indoors and outdoors. For instance, in poor and overcrowded dwellings, it is difficult to keep chemicals used in the home out of their reach. Where provision for safe playsites is deficient, children will play on roads and garbage tips and other hazardous places.

Certain occupations are associated with particular environmental risks – for instance, those who make a living from picking through garbage or those working in particularly hazardous industries. Many industries in Asia and Latin America make widespread use of child labour with such children exposed to high levels of risk from dangerous machinery, heat, toxic chemicals and dust.[132] Street children who have been abandoned by their families (or have run away from home)[133] generally face a whole range of environmental hazards: the work they undertake may be particularly hazardous (for instance dodging traffic on major highways, selling goods to passing motorists) and they often have no adult to whom to turn when sick or injured. They generally have very poor quality accommodation (often sleeping in the open or in public places), have great difficulty finding places to wash and defecate, and obtaining drinking water and health services.[134] They are also exposed to child abuse – not least when child prostitution turns out to be one of the more dependable ways of ensuring sufficient income for survival. In addition, many children and youths imprisoned for crimes or vagrancy or simply placed in corrective institutions may not only have to live in a very poor quality environment but also be deprived of the child-adult relationships and stimulation which are so important for child development.[135] There are also other children in especially difficult circumstances who face particular environmental risks. For instance, a study by the Indian NGO, SPARC, in Bombay identified children of pavement dwellers and construction workers and 'hotel boys' as particularly vulnerable, along with street children.[136] For instance, the children of construction workers who live on site lack access to schools, day care, health facilities, water and sanitation, and life on construction sites also poses particular hazards for children.[137]

Women are often more at risk than men because of the particular tasks they undertake – for instance from their role in caring for the sick and laundering and cleaning soiled clothes where water supplies and sanitation facilities are inadequate.[138] The people within a household who are responsible for water collection and its use for laundry, cooking and domestic hygiene suffer most if supplies are contaminated and difficult to obtain – and these people are generally women. Poorer urban households more often use biomass fuels or coal for cooking and/or heating on open fires or poorly ventilated stoves and it is generally women (or girls) who take responsibility for tending the fire and cooking who inhale larger concentrations of pollutants over longer periods of time.[139]

In the regions around cities, it is generally the poorer households who suffer as their cheap or free sources of wood and land for grazing are pre-empted by commercial concerns, while their air and water suffer from wastes originating in the cities.[140] It is possible to envisage governments in the more prosperous nations or cities taking actions to meet the demands of richer households and businesses for more water, better drains and a cleaner environment, and still ignore the more pressing problems of poorer groups both within the city and within the surrounding region.

In most Third World cities, poor people have very little chance of obtaining a healthy legal house within a neighbourhood where environmental risks are minimized – that is, one with sufficient space, security of tenure, services and facilities, and on a site not prone to flooding, waterlogging or landslides. Many also have the constant fear of eviction from their homes; this is a permanent worry for most tenants, temporary boarders in cheap rooming houses, those in illegal settlements and 'land' renters.

The insecurity, and the environmental hazards evident within their homes and neighbourhoods, are in effect a direct result of their low incomes and of the refusal of government to intervene to guarantee their access to adequate living conditions, or to the resources to permit them to build these themselves. Ironically, dangerous land sites or polluted land sites located close to downtown or to other locations where poorer groups find some income sources often serve poorer groups well. For these are the only sites well-located with regard to income earning opportunities on which they have some possibility of living (illegally) because the environmental hazards make the sites unattractive for other potential users.

If an individual or household finds 'minimum standard' accommodation too costly, they have to make certain sacrifices in the accommodation they choose, to bring down the price. They usually make sacrifices in environmental quality. Although this means health risks and much inconvenience, these are less important for their survival than other items. For instance, expenditure on food or children's education or on (say) purchasing a second-hand sewing machine to allow a member of the family to earn additional income are more important than 'minimum standard' accommodation. Each low-income individual or household will have their own preferred trade-offs in terms of the size of accommodation, terms under which it is occupied, suitability of site, housing quality, location and access to infrastructure and services. For example, to bring down housing costs, a household of five persons might sacrifice space and live in one room, or sacrifice secure tenure and access to piped water and live in a self-constructed house on illegally occupied land. To understand the possibilities for improving the housing environment of such people, one must understand their very diverse needs and priorities. Complex questions have to be explored, including legality of site or house occupation, legality of the housing structure, and the terms under which the occupants live there (for instance, as guests, legal tenants, illegal tenants, sub-tenants or owners).

Poorer groups may even choose particular locations where pollution levels are highest because these are the only locations where they can find land for their housing close to sources of employment without fear of eviction. It was the high concentration of low-income residents around the Union Carbide Factory in Bhopal which caused so many people to be killed or permanently injured. In Manila, some 20,000 people live around a garbage dump known as Smokey Mountain where the decomposition of organic wastes produces a permanent haze and a powerful, rank smell affecting the whole area. Some of these people have lived there 40 years or more. Moving to a cleaner, safer location is beyond their means and many of them make a living scavenging on the dump, often sorting it with their bare hands.[141]

The dangerous living and working environments of low-income people reflect the failure of government in a number of tasks. The first is a failure to invest in basic services and infrastructure which can only be undertaken cost-effectively either by government or with their support. The second is the failure to implement pollution control. The third is the failure to enforce occupational health standards. The fourth is the failure to support increased supplies of legal land sites for housing – on a scale to have a downward pressure on land prices – within a planning framework which guarantees sufficient open space and minimizes infrastructure costs. The social costs of environmental degradation can be enormous, and much larger than the cost incurred by the individual or company responsible for the damage. Governments have also failed to collect the taxes and user-charges from those who benefit from publicly funded infrastructure and services. The costs of these failures fall most heavily on poorer groups.

In most cities, the environmental health of many poorer communities would be improved if governments simply enforced existing environmental legislation. Government measures to increase the supply and reduce the cost of stable, serviced land for housing would also have a positive impact on environmental health.

4

Cities' rural, regional and global impacts

CITIES' REGIONAL IMPACTS AND RURAL-URBAN INTERACTIONS

Important environmental considerations of relevance to cities occur outside the built-up areas themselves, and often outside city or metropolitan boundaries. These include environmental considerations in the surrounding region which usually comprises large areas defined as (or considered) rural. The inhabitants and the natural resource base of this wider region are usually affected by a series of environmental impacts coming from or influenced by city-based activities or city-generated wastes.

Cities demand a high input of resources – water, fossil fuels, land and all the goods and materials that their populations and enterprises require. The more populous the city and the richer its inhabitants, the greater its demand on resources and, in general, the larger the area from which these are drawn – although at any one time, each particular type of natural resource will have its own particular area of supply.[1] The more expensive and lighter commodities such as fruit and vegetables, wood and metals may be drawn from areas hundreds of kilometres away or imported from other countries. So may some lower-value foods, if these are not easily produced locally. But the more bulky, low-value materials will usually come from close by; as Ian Douglas notes, 'the physical structure of fabric of the city, the buildings, the roads, railways, airports, docks, pipe and conduit systems require large quantities of materials for their construction' and 'the bulk of the structures are derived from locally available clay, sand, gravel and crushed rock'.[2] This can be seen in the brick works, quarries, claypits, sand and gravel pits in and around most cities,[3] all of which have environmental impacts.

Cities are also major centres for resource degradation. Water needed for industrial processes, for supplying residential and commercial buildings, for transporting sewage and for other uses is returned to rivers, lakes or the sea at a far lower quality than that originally supplied. Solid wastes collected from city households and businesses are usually disposed of on land sites in the region around the city while much of the uncollected solid waste finds its way into water bodies, adding to the pollution. These can be termed regional impacts. We look first at the environmental impact of cities drawing resources from the wider region and then at the impact of city-based activities (especially waste disposal) on the wider region.

The demand for rural resources from city-based enterprises and households may limit their availability for rural households. For instance, in cities where wood and charcoal are still widely used for cooking and heating (mostly by lower-income households), city-based demand often pre-empts supplies formerly used by rural inhabitants. Where once poor rural inhabitants gathered wood from what was regarded as common land, now they may be barred from doing so, as the wood is harvested for sale. Common land once used for gathering wild produce and grazing is taken over by mono-culture tree plantations where such gathering or grazing is no longer permitted.[4] High demand for fuelwood from cities may be a prime cause of deforestation (and the soil erosion which usually accompanies it) and this may be taking place at considerable distances from the city (see Box 4.1).

Box 4.1 Firewood in the cities

To meet demand for firewood in Delhi, 12,423 railway wagons of firewood arrived at Tughlakabad railway siding during 1981–82, some 612 tons a day. Most of this wood comes from Madhya Pradesh, nearly 700 kilometres away. The Shahdara railway siding also receives firewood daily from the forests in the Himalayan foothills in Assam and Bihar – although in smaller quantities. In addition, the forested area and trees within Delhi yield thousands of tons annually. Yet Delhi has a relatively low per capita consumption of firewood, because of the ready availability of kerosene, coal and liquid petroleum gas (which are much preferred as fuel if they can be afforded). In Bangalore, an estimated 440,000 tonnes of commercial firewood are consumed each year, far more than Delhi, even though Bangalore has around half the population of Delhi. Most of it arrives by road – an average of 114 trucks a day. Most firewood comes from private farms and forests within 150 kilometres of Bangalore but 15 per cent comes from government forests, 300 to 700 kilometres away.

Source: CSE (1986) *The State of India's Environment 1984-5: The Second Citizens' Report*, Centre for Science and Environment, New Delhi.

A study of the long-term impact that Jakarta may have on its wider region provides an example of the complex rural-urban interactions taking place between a city and its surrounding areas and the serious environmental consequences.[5] The expansion of the urban area and urban activities pushes farmers from agricultural land; productive agriculture is replaced by urban developments or by commercial ventures for tourism and recreation. Agriculture is pushed onto land less suited to such use in hill and upland areas. Soil erosion there lowers agricultural productivity and causes siltation of water reservoirs, flooding after heavy rains plus reduced flows in rivers during dry periods. Meanwhile, the government must seek new sources of water to supply Jakarta since over-pumping of groundwater has already resulted in serious salt water intrusion into what were previously sweet water aquifers; the supply of water may need to multiply fourfold between 1983 and 2000, especially if the supply of piped water to city households is to improve; in 1980, only 26 per cent of the population were served with piped water. But many of the lowland river and water courses nearby have high concentrations of non-degradable organic chemicals and heavy metals from agricultural biocides which limit their use for human consumption (see Box 4.2 for more details).

Box 4.2 Regional impacts of Jakarta

The Jakarta metropolis now ranks as the eighth largest urban agglomeration in the world. By 1980, most of the growth in population was taking place on the periphery of the metropolis with the population in previously low density areas such as Depok and Cibinong growing at rates of 10 per cent a year. A significant proportion of population growth has occurred through the arrival of migrants from other regions of Java.

The first major planning study to deal solely with the spatial dimension of environmental degradation in the Jakarta metropolitan region was documented in a report by the United Nations Environment Programme in 1983. Among the problems identified were severe water pollution from both urban and agricultural uses, unnecessary loss and degradation of prime agricultural land through urban expansion, potentially serious erosion problems developing in the uplands, extensive loss of natural habitation and severe threats to the remaining areas of natural forest, coastland and marine ecosystems. Other studies of environmental conditions in Jakarta have noted the existence of mercury poisoning in Jakarta Bay and the absence of firm government measures to deal with the mounting levels of toxic wastes. These problems are not simply the result of either a unidirectional spread of urbanization into agricultural lands or the movement of rural households into ecologically critical uplands. Rather, they are the outcome of negatively reinforcing impacts of both rapid urbanization and the rapid expansion of rural land use in coastal, upland and forest areas in the region reaching beyond the Jakarta agglomeration, and along the Jakarta-Bandung corridor.

As the metropolis has expanded, the negative environmental impacts of one activity have been magnified by those of another. Industrial pollution of water systems has occurred alongside that caused by the excessive use of fertilisers, pesticides and herbicides in agriculture which feed into the same water system. Added to these impacts is a situation in which the vast majority of the population continues to depend upon natural river flows for daily water consumption and waste disposal.

In a region such as Jakarta, environmental problems go beyond the categories of simple negative externalities and threaten the very sustainability of development. One example is the extraction of groundwater at an accelerating rate by a multiplicity of users. The result has been that seawater has now intruded 15 kilometres inland, creating a zone of salinized groundwater reaching to the centre of the city.

The expanding population and economic activities have brought about land use changes within the region. As the zone of urban land expands, agriculture is pushed outward and upward toward less suitable agricultural land in hill and upland areas. In upland areas, soil erosion is a particular concern; besides lowering agricultural productivity, it also has potentially severe downstream impacts such as: the siltation of reservoirs; flooding through loss of upland capacity to retain water after heavy rains; and a reduced flow in other seasons which would exacerbate downstream pollution and create 'desertification-like' conditions of rural land in the region.

There is a major dilemma to be faced by efforts to improve the quality of life in metropolitan core regions in Asia. This centres on the fact that the major parameters which need to be guided are neither contained within Jakarta nor are subject to substantial manipulation by the spatial allocation of infrastructure in the capital city region. The major factors propelling the accelerated growth of the Jakarta metropolitan region are mechanization of agriculture and a decline in public spending on rural construction (both working to accelerate rural-metropolitan migration); the fall in the prices of outer-island exports, (which has reduced the economic pull to direct migration away from Java); import-substitution and, more recently, export-oriented manufacturing policies which have worked to polarise manufacturing employment within the Jakarta agglomeration.

It is already evident that land use management within the region must be dramatically improved if the negative impacts of land use changes and conflicts are to be reduced to allow for an environmentally sustainable development process. At present there are three main obstacles to land use policy implementation: the failure to effectively coordinate the programmes of government bureaux responsible for various aspects of land use control; the absence of sufficient incentives to guide land use changes by the private sector away from environmentally sensitive areas; and the absence of a clear political will to implement existing policies and regulations.

Source: Douglass, Mike (1989) 'The environmental sustainability of development: coordination, incentives and political will in land use planning for the Jakarta metropolis', *Third World Planning Review*, vol. 11, no. 2.

There are also many complex linkages between a city and the surrounding region which include flows of people, goods, income and capital. Such movements can have a major impact on cities' population growth and demographic structure and thus on the city environment. Migration to cities can be promoted by high population densities in rural areas, shortage of cultivable land, declining soil fertility, increasing commercialization of agriculture and agricultural land markets, inequitable land ownership patterns and exploitative landlord–tenant relations as well as government support for cash crops. Such processes are likely to be cumulative and mutually reinforcing. Cities not only feel the effects of these changes but their growing market for rural produce can in turn cause increasing commercialisation of agricultural land markets which may push peasants off the land. The livelihood of rural-based artisans has frequently been destroyed or damaged by the increasing availability of mass-produced goods made or distributed by city-based enterprises. Factors such as these, allied to the concentration of public and private productive investment in relatively few cities has meant rapid net in-migration to most cities in the Third World, at least for certain periods in their physical and demographic growth. Although a detailed discussion of these regional factors and their contribution to cities' environmental problems is beyond the scope of this chapter, their importance must not be underestimated.

In many cities – perhaps more often in those with rapidly expanding economies – there is no clear boundary which separates urban from rural. Many new factories and businesses develop in surrounding 'rural' areas although their functioning and markets are intimately tied to the city.[6] Many poorer groups who live in rural areas around cities and are considered rural inhabitants (and rural workers) will work part-time in the city. There is also growing evidence in some of the less industrialized Third World nations of the importance of food production by poorer groups within city boundaries – especially where city or metropolitan area boundaries encompass a significantly larger area than the built up area.[7]

These are some among many possible examples to show the difficulty in considering 'urban' and 'rural' problems separately. The impoverishment of rural people in a region and their movement to cities may be considered a rural problem – but it may be largely the result of the commercialization of agricultural land markets and crop production because of city-based demand. Deforestation may be considered a rural problem but it may be intimately linked to the demand for fuelwood or charcoal from city inhabitants and enterprises. The soil erosion linked to deforestation may be destroying rural inhabitants' livelihoods with the result that they migrate to the city. The environmental impacts of large hydro-electric dams (such as the loss of agricultural land and the introduction or exacerbation of waterborne or water-related diseases) are usually considered rural even if most of the electricity will be consumed in urban areas. Other examples include the environmental effects of agricultural or mining operations which produce raw materials for city-based activities or poorly designed and located bridges, highways and roads linking smaller settlements with cities which might contribute to problems of flooding.

Three particular kinds of city impact on their region deserve special attention:

- uncontrolled physical expansions;
- solid and liquid waste disposal; and
- air pollution.

Uncontrolled physical growth impacts most on what might be termed an immediate hinterland around a city; this cannot be described as urban or suburban and yet much of it is no longer rural. If the city has been designated a 'metropolitan centre', much or all of this hinterland may fall within the metropolitan boundaries.

Within this area, agriculture may disappear or decline as land is bought up by people or companies in anticipation of its change from agricultural to urban use, as the city's built-up area expands. There is a lack of effective public control of such changes in land use or on the profits which can be made from them. In many nations, it is also encouraged by a lack of other domestic high return investment opportunities.

There are usually many legal sub-divisions in this hinterland for houses or commercial and industrial buildings which have been approved without reference to any city-wide plan. There are usually many unauthorised sub-divisions as well. As the built-up city area expands towards this land, development occurs through legal and illegal action by various land-owners, builders, and real estate firms in an ad hoc way, producing an incoherent urban sprawl. Illegal squatter communities have often been forced out to this hinterland as well. In many cities (including Buenos Aires, Delhi, Santiago, Seoul and Manila), this hinterland also contains settlements formed when their inhabitants were dumped there, after being evicted from their homes by slum or squatter clearance.[8]

Unplanned and uncontrolled city expansion produces a patchwork of different developments, including many high-density residential settlements, interspersed with vacant land. This expansion usually has serious social and environmental consequences, including the segregation of the poor in the worst located and most dangerous areas and the greatly increased costs of providing basic infrastructure (such as roads and pavements, water mains and sewage pipes), public transport and social services. In 1980, the Governor of Lagos State, Nigeria, commented that many of the popular towns and districts in his state, especially those in and around Lagos Metropolis, had sprung up in contravention of official regulations and that in most, there were no services and infrastructure and those which did exist were grossly inadequate.[9] In these, as in so many other Third World cities and their hinterlands, one sees the paradox of extreme overcrowding and chronic housing shortages and acute shortages of infrastructure and services – and yet vast amounts of land left vacant or only partially developed with all that this implies in terms of increasing the cost of providing infrastructure and services.

The loss of agricultural land is another consequence of uncontrolled city growth. Cities often expand over the nation's most fertile land since so many cities grew up within highly fertile areas. Most Third World cities were important urban centres before the development of motorized transport, and at that time, no major city could develop too far from the land which produced its inhabitants' daily food and fuel requirements. In addition, many cities first developed as market centres to serve the prosperous farms and farming households around them. For example, almost all the large cities in the nations around the Pacific were established on lowland delta regions and continue to expand into their nation's most fertile agricultural land.[10]

This loss of agricultural land can usually be avoided if government guides the physical expansion and ensures that vacant or under-utilized land is fully used. In most cities, the problem is not a lack of vacant land but a lack of government action to guide new developments on land other than the best farmland. A report from Colombia notes that a lack of government regulation of the private market in this area

> 'has led in urban issues to the supply of a hardly satisfactory, and in many cases chaotic, product. Vast extensions of utility networks and buildings are under-used or deteriorating while the urbanisation process, guided by the incentive of private profit, proceeds with no control to the confines of the country's most productive land'.[11]

In Egypt, more than 10 per cent of the nation's most productive farmland has been lost to urban encroachment in the last three decades, much of it through illegal squatting or sub-division while at the same time prime sites within cities remain undeveloped.[12] The urban area of Delhi (including New Delhi) has grown nearly 13-fold since 1900, eating into surrounding agricultural areas and absorbing more than 100 villages. This unplanned and uncontrolled expansion has been accompanied by the expansion of brick-making kilns with fertile topsoil being used to make bricks.[13]

Uncontrolled physical expansion also destroys natural landscapes in or close to cities which should be preserved as parks, nature reserves, historic sites or simply areas of open space for recreation and children's play. The need to preserve or develop such areas might seem less urgent than, say, land for housing. But once an area is built-up, it is almost impossible (and very expensive) to remedy a lack of open space. The richer groups suffer much less. Their residential areas usually have plenty of open space. And they can afford to become members of the 'country clubs' which have become common on the outskirts of many cities and so can enjoy walks, playgrounds and facilities for sport.

Liquid, gaseous and solid wastes generated by city-based enterprises and consumers often have significant impacts in the region surrounding the city. The contamination of rivers, lakes and seashores is an example both of the impact of city-generated wastes on the wider region and of government's negligent attitude to protecting open areas. In cities on or close to coasts, untreated sewage and industrial effluents often flow into the sea with little or no provision to pipe them far enough out to sea to protect the beaches and inshore waters. Most coastal cities have serious problems with dirty, contaminated beaches and water, and there is a major health risk to bathers. Oil pollution often adds to existing problems of sewage and industrial effluents. Pollution may be so severe that many beaches have to be closed to the public. It is also worth noting that it is usually the most accessible beaches which suffer most and these are among the most widely used recreational areas by lower-income groups. Richer households suffer much less; those with automobiles can reach more distant, less accessible beaches.

Liquid wastes from city activities have environmental impacts stretching beyond the immediate hinterland. It is increasingly common for fisheries to be damaged or destroyed by liquid effluents from city-based industries with hundreds or even thousands of people losing their livelihood as a result; among the places where major declines in fish catches have been documented are many rivers, estuaries or coastal waters in India, China and Malaysia, Lake Maryut in Alexandria, the Gulf of Paria between Venezuela and Trinidad, Manila Bay, Rio de Janeiro's Guanabara Bay, the Bay of Dakar and the Indus delta near Karachi.[14] The fish may also be contaminated; in a sample of fish and shellfish caught in Jakarta Bay, Indonesia, 44 per cent exceeded WHO guidelines for lead while 38 per cent exceeded the mercury guidelines and 76 per cent exceeded the cadmium guidelines.[15] Perhaps the best known and most dramatic example of water contamination is that of Minamata in Japan; although Japan has long been the only Asian nation not to be classified as Third World, the example has relevance first because it illustrates the scale of damage that can be done (in this case by a single industry) and secondly because it shows the enormous cost in human life and health from the reluctance of the government to take prompt action.

River pollution from city-based industries and untreated sewage can lead to serious health problems in settlements downstream. One example is the Bogota river flowing through Bogota, the national capital, which is contaminated by effluents from Colombia's largest concentration of industries and by sewage and run-off from a city with close to five million inhabitants. At the town of Tocaima, 120 kilometres downstream, the river was found to have an average fecal bacteria coliform count of 7.3 million, making it totally unfit for drinking or cooking.[16] Paper and rayon factories in India are notorious water polluters and such pollution causes diseases in villagers who live downstream; it often means declining fish catches and declining water volumes as well.[17] Rivers which are heavily contaminated as they pass through cities may become unusable for agriculture downstream or particular contaminants in the water may damage crops or pose risks to human health. For instance, cadmium and lead concentrations in rivers cause particular problems downstream from certain industries and if the water is used for growing crops like rice, those regularly eating that rice can easily exceed the WHO defined acceptable daily cadmium and lead intake.[18]

This regional impact of water pollution can even extend to international water bodies. For instance, in the Persian/Arabian Gulf (a small, shallow, salty and almost landlocked sea) rapid urban and industrial growth on its shores is threatening its fragile ecosystem. While the major danger of marine pollution comes from oil, especially from tanker deballasting and tank washing, raw sewage from the rapidly expanding coastal cities and untreated industrial liquid wastes are also having a considerable impact, as are the concentration of desalination plants along the coast.[19] The Caribbean also faces comparable problems with large quantities of untreated sewage discharged directly into bays, estuaries, coastal lagoons and rivers and 'highly toxic effluents from rapidly developing light and heavy industries . . . also often discharged directly into adjacent bays'.[20]

Consideration must be given to the impact of *air pollutants* from city-based activities on the wider region. The air pollutants which cause the most damage to forests, soils and agriculture are sulphur dioxide, oxides of nitrogen and ozone (and other photochemical oxidants) and in certain instances fluorides;[21] Box 4.3 gives more details.

Box 4.3 The impact of air pollution on agriculture

Air pollution can cause serious losses to crops and animal husbandry, although the levels of loss under different circumstances are difficult to assess experimentally.

Acid pollution: Sulphur dioxide and the oxides of nitrogen coming from fossil fuel combustion in cities can be deposited directly from the air on farmers' fields (dry deposition) or from rain, clouds/fog or snow acidified by these chemicals. Both can damage plants at high concentrations (causing acute damage, especially to certain species of plants which are particularly sensitive to exposure) although the concentrations needed to achieve this are rare, except in the immediate vicinity of intense sources of emissions (for instance metal smelters with no pollution controls and lacking high chimneys). At lower concentrations, both sulphur dioxide and the oxides of nitrogen are associated with reductions in yields and growth for many crops, although there are many other factors which can influence this. For acid rain, experimental reports of foliar injury are for pH values of less than 3.5, a level of acidity which rarely occurs. Soils are also at risk since in many tropical and subtropical countries, the soils are already acidic and unable to buffer any further additions in acidity. Further acidification can bring into solution potentially toxic trace elements; for instance, aluminium in acid soils disrupts the metabolic processes of roots and inhibits their growth.

Ozone: Ozone is produced by complex photochemical reactions involving air pollutants which are common over cities (oxides of nitrogen, carbon monoxide and hydrocarbons) reacting in sunlight. Temperature inversions over cities can keep the reactive chemicals in touch, by inhibiting the dispersion of pollutants. Ozone continues to be generated in plumes of contaminated air originating in cities but often at a considerable distance from the source, which can make the concentration of ozone in rural areas downwind of cities higher than in the city itself. Plumes downwind of large North American cities produce ozone concentrations of between 130 and 200 parts per billion, often over distances of 100–300 km;[22] ozone concentrations of only 60–100 ppb are sufficient to cause significant loss of yield in a wide variety of crops. The most direct impact on plants is the reduction in the amount of light caused by the photochemical smog. In many cities, ozone also causes visible leaf damage while ozone concentrations well below that needed to cause visible injury (and also below that of most air quality standards) are also known to significantly reduce crop growth and yields for a wide range of plants, including oranges, lemons, grapes, wheat and rice.

Fluorides: These are typically emitted as hydrogen fluoride from brick, glass and tile works, steel works, potteries, aluminium smelters, phosphate factorys and some other industries. Particular industries can cause acute damage over considerable distances, if no measures are taken to limit emissions. For vegetation far from the emission source, the hazard arises from long-term exposure to very low levels, so trees and perennial plants are more likely to suffer damage than annuals. Fluoride may directly damage fruits or accumulate in forage and so present a particular risk to grazing livestock.

Other air pollutants and their interactions: Soot or dust may affect plant growth by reducing the rate of photosynthesis or damaging the plant. Mixtures of pollutants may produce synergistic or antagonistic effects, or one gas may predispose or desensitize a plant to the effect of another. Gaseous pollutants may also stimulate more serious attack by pests such as aphids and white fly.

Sources: Text drawn from Conway, Gordon R and Pretty, Jules N (1991), *Unwelcome Harvest*, Earthscan Publications, London.

The most dramatic examples of damage to crops (and other flora) come in the immediate vicinity of industries with very high sulphur dioxide emissions. Metal smelters without pollution controls and tall smokestacks can cause severe damage to vegetation over areas of several hundred square kilometres. The emissions from cities do not produce such high concentrations, although a combination of high emissions and a lack of winds to disperse them can mean evidence of damage to vegetation or falling crop yields. The problem is particularly acute in Southwestern China – for instance around cities which have high levels of sulphur dioxide emissions such as Guiyang and Chongqing.[23] In the provinces of Guizhou and Sichuan, some 40,000 square kilometres now receives rainfall of a pH less than 4.5.[24] At Guiyang itself, the pH of rainfall is less than 4.0 from September to January. Around Chongqing, large areas of (rice) paddy have turned yellow, following rainfall with a pH of 4.5 while in Chongqing itself, vegetation has been damaged by rain with a pH of 4.1.[25] Reports in 1978 noted heavy industrial air pollution in a district in Lanzhou (a major city and industrial centre) which had destroyed the fruit trees in nearby villages. Furthermore, dates flowered but did not bear fruit, pumpkins failed to mature, and livestock contracted oral cavities which ulcerated, perforated and kept them from eating, causing high death rates.[26] Professor Vaclav Smil in his review of environmental problems in China suggests that such cases are 'most certainly just the proverbial tip of the iceberg' and that regional damage to plants and livestock must also be quite considerable near coal-fired power stations, refineries and chemical works with no (or only rudimentary) controls.[27]

There are few other reports which suggest such serious damage – although in South Korea, considerable damage was reported in the early 1980s to the Samsoon plains; this was once an important rice-producing area but became seriously damaged from air pollution arising from power, petrochemical and fertiliser plants, copper and zinc smelters and oil refineries.[28] There may be other city-regions where damage to agriculture is visible, although the need for a high concentration of emissions combined with particular meteorological conditions will make this unusual. However, acid precipitation sufficient to result in declining or disappearing fish populations and serious damage to forests (and tree deaths) is likely to be much more common.[29] Toxic metals may also be leached from the soil into water used for animal or human consumption or copper, lead, cadmium or copper mobilized by acidic drinking water supplies from piped water systems.[30] Acid precipitation, which has become such a major issue in Europe and North America, is also causing concern in the areas surrounding many Third World cities including the areas around São Paulo, Petaling Jaya (Malaysia), several Indian cities and Cubatao (Brazil).[31]

Emissions of fluorides, particulate matter and chemicals which react in sunlight to produce ozone from urban areas can also damage flora in the surrounding regions. Ozone concentrations may not reach a maximum until the urban plume of pollutants is well away from the city.[32] For fluorides, although the damage to crops, pasture and livestock is well known, there are few reports on this outside the North; one exception is the serious damage reported to sericulture from fluoride emissions from small rural industries in China.[33]

CITIES' ECOLOGICAL FOOTPRINTS

Two issues inhibit more effective measures to limit cities' ecological impacts. One was highlighted by Mike Douglass in his discussion of Jakarta's environmental impact on its region – the fact that there are so many different influences on land use from local concerns (for instance the competition between agriculture and urban development for land), to regional and national concerns (the promotion of industrialization, much of which is in Jakarta), to international concerns (the fall in the prices of export crops for outer islands, reducing the attraction for migrants of areas outside Java and Jakarta). The second is the difficulty in coordinating actions in different places by different agencies and different levels of government because cities' environmental impacts are so diverse and often happening over such distances (as in the example of Delhi described in Box 4.1 with much of the firewood coming from a region nearly 700 kilometres away).

One concept which helps an understanding of such issues – ie the impact of a city on natural resources and ecosystems – is to consider what William Rees has termed a city's 'ecological footprint': the land area and the natural capital on which it draws to sustain its population and production structure.[34] Box 4.4 outlines this concept. Considering such ecological footprints can highlight how a wealthy city can greatly exceed the ecological carrying capacity of its region, because natural resources can be imported from distant regions or from other nations. But this does not become evident in environmental deterioration in that city's surrounds, because city-based activities rely so much on natural resources brought from other regions (whose production draws on the carrying capacity of these regions). The consideration of a city's ecological footprint can also reveal the extent to which it draws on the carrying capacities of other nations (as in imported goods) or on the whole biosphere (as in emissions of greenhouse gases and stratospheric ozone-depleting chemicals). These are considered in the next section.

Box 4.4 The ecological footprint of cities

All cities draw on natural resources produced on land outside their built up areas (eg agricultural crops, wood products, fuel); the total area of land required to sustain a city (which can be termed its ecological footprint) is typically at least ten times or more greater than that contained within the city boundaries or the associated built-up area. In effect, through trade and natural flows of ecological goods and services, all cities appropriate the carrying capacity of other areas. All cities draw on the material resources and productivity of a vast and scattered hinterland.

Ecologists define 'carrying capacity' as the population of a given species that be supported indefinitely in a given habitat without permanently damaging the ecosystem upon which it is dependent. For human beings, carrying capacity can be interpreted as the maximum rate of resource consumption and waste discharge that can be sustained indefinitely in a given region without progressively impairing the functional integrity and productivity of relevant ecosystems.

Preliminary data for industrial cities suggest that per capita primary consumption of such things as food, wood products, fuel, and waste-processing capacity co-opts on a continuous basis several hectares of productive ecosystem, the exact amount depending on individual material standards of living. This average per capita index can be used to estimate the land area functionally required to support any given population. The resultant aggregate area can be called the relevant community's total 'ecological footprint' on the Earth.

The lower Fraser Valley of British Columbia, Canada (Vancouver to Hope) serves as an example. For simplicity's sake consider the ecological use of forested and arable land alone: assuming an average Canadian diet, the per capita land requirement for food production is 1.9 hectares, while forest products and fossil fuel consumption require an additional 3.0 to 4.0 hectares of forested land (2.0–3.0 hectares of this is required to absorb per capita carbon dioxide production and/or to produce the bioenergy equivalent of per capita fossil energy use). Thus, to support only the food and fossil fuel demands of their present consumer lifestyle, the region's 1.7 million people require, conservatively, 8.3 million hectares of land in continuous production. The valley, however, is only about 400,000 hectares. So, the regional population 'imports' about 20 times as much land for these functions as it actually occupies.

Regional ecological deficits do not necessarily pose a problem if import-dependent regions are drawing on true ecological surpluses in the exporting regions. A group of trading regions remains within net carrying capacity as long as total consumption does not exceed aggregate sustainable production. The problem is that prevailing economic logic and trade agreements ignore carrying capacity and sustainability considerations. In these circumstances, the terms of trade may actually accelerate the depletion of essential natural capital thereby undermining global carrying capacity.

Because the products of nature can so readily be imported, the population of any given region can exceed its local carrying capacity unknowingly and with apparent impunity. In the absence of negative feedback from the land on their economy or lifestyles, there is no direct incentive for such populations to maintain adequate local stocks of productive natural capital. For example, the ability to import food makes people less averse to the risks associated with urban growth spreading over locally limited agricultural land. Even without accelerated capital depletion, trade enables a region's population and material consumption to rise beyond levels to which they might otherwise be restricted by some locally limiting factor. Ironically then, the free exchange of ecological goods and services without constraints on population or consumption, ensures the absorption of global surpluses (the safety net) and encourages all regions to exceed local carrying capacity. The net effect is increased long-range risk to all.

This situation applies not only to commercial trade but also to the unmonitored flows of goods and services provided by nature. For example, northern urbanites, wherever they are, are now dependent on the carbon sink, global heat transfer, and climate stabilization functions of tropical forests. There are many variations on this theme touching on everything from drift-net fishing to ozone depletion, each involving open access to, or shared dependency on, some form of threatened natural capital.

Source: Rees, William E (1992) 'Ecological footprints and appropriated carrying capacity: what urban economics leaves out', *Environment and Urbanization* vol. 4, no. 2.

CITIES AND THE GLOBAL COMMONS

No overview of environmental problems in Third World cities would be complete without some consideration of the impacts of city-based activities on the global commons. These include the depletion of non-renewable resources and emissions of greenhouse gases and of gases which contribute to the depletion of the stratospheric ozone layer. They also include the environmental degradation to which city-based demand for goods and city-generated wastes contribute, which do not arise only within the city boundaries or the surrounding region. There is also the issue of impacts on Third World cities arising from global climate change.

The main contribution of city-based production and consumption to greenhouse gases is carbon dioxide emissions from fossil fuel combustion by industry, power stations, motor vehicles and domestic and commercial energy use. City-based activities also contribute to emissions of other greenhouse gases – for instance of chlorofluorocarbons by certain industries or industrial products, of nitrous oxide by motor vehicle engines and of methane by city-generated solid and liquid wastes. City-based demand for fuelwood, pulp and timber also contributes to deforestation in most countries. A considerable proportion of the greenhouse gas emissions arising from rural food production (for instance methane emissions from livestock and rice cultivation) can be attributed to city-based consumption of such food.

There are few figures available for cities on greenhouse gas emissions – although those that do exist suggest relatively low levels of per capita emissions for carbon dioxide (the main greenhouse gas) when compared to cities in the North.[35] Figures available for different nations' per capita consumption of non-renewable resources and greenhouse gas emissions show much higher consumption and emission levels in the North when compared to the South.[36] This suggests that cities in the North have in aggregate a much higher draw, per capita, on the global commons both in terms of resource consumption and in terms of using the atmosphere and seas as sinks for wastes. Among other evidence which would support this would be: the much lower levels of fossil fuel consumption per capita in Third World cities; the small proportion of world industrial production located there;[37] the lower numbers of automobiles per inhabitants;[38] and the much lower levels of waste generation per capita.[39]

However, the phenomenal diversity within Third World cities suggests an enormous variation between different cities. Cities such as São Paulo with its high concentration of industry and of middle- and upper-income groups with high levels of fuel use, resource use and waste generation are likely to put their per capita resource use and greenhouse gas emissions far above the average for Third World cities. In terms of greenhouse gas emissions, this may also be true for some of China's centres of heavy industry, but here the greenhouse gas emissions derive mostly from the widespread use of coal in industry and for domestic and commercial heating, and not as a result of high consumption levels.

By contrast, most cities and smaller urban centres in the poorer Third World nations and many others (for instance market towns in richer nations which are essentially service centres with few industries and few automobiles per inhabitant) are likely to have per capita greenhouse gas emissions far below the average. The very low incomes on which such a high proportion of the Third World's urban population survive is one reason for this. From the point of view of the global commons, the rich nations are fortunate indeed that the urban (and rural) poor make such a minimal call on the world's non-renewable resources and contribute so little to greenhouse gas emissions. Among the 600 million or so poor urban dwellers in the Third World, most housing construction makes widespread use of recycled or reclaimed materials and little use of cement and other materials with a high energy input. Such households have too few capital goods to represent much of a draw on metals and other finite non-renewable resources. They also generate very low volumes of household waste and in most instances, metal, glass, paper and often rags and other items are re-used or recycled. Most rely on public transport (or walk or bicycle) which ensures low averages for oil consumption per person.[40] City averages for electricity consumption per person are often low – perhaps not surprisingly when a considerable proportion of the population do not have homes connected to electricity supplies.

A wealthy city can export many of its environmental problems. Good environmental quality can be maintained in its own region by appropriating the ecological resources of other cities or societies by drawing natural resources from distant producer regions (including those in other continents) where their production or extraction causes serious problems of environmental degradation.[41] Most cities in Europe, North America and Japan can only have forests, parks and nature reserves nearby because such land need not be utilized to meet the demand for food and other natural resources arising from city-consumers and enterprises; such food and natural resources are imported. Here, as in many other city-based environmental problems, the separation of 'urban' and 'rural' often obscures a detailed understanding of causes and of the options available for addressing the problems. As William Rees emphasises, a consideration of each city's 'ecological footprint' requires 'formal recognition of the dependency of cities on distant landscapes (productive natural capital) and their simultaneous negative impact on the very land that feeds their inhabitants.'[42]

What are termed 'green trade' issues have considerable relevance to environmental problems in many cities; the environmental implications of free trade worldwide will have to be addressed if, within nations, this is leading to serious and sustained ecological deterioration and, within the world system, to ever increasing greenhouse gas emissions. But such green trade issues at present have more relevance when considering rural environmental degradation in the Third World, linked to urban-based demand for goods in the North.

Cities' ecological footprints in terms of the scale of greenhouse gas emissions which derive from city-based production and consumption also need consideration. While the average contribution of each urban citizen in Africa, Asia and Latin America to greenhouse gases may be relatively low, with the urban population growing rapidly and an increasing share of the world's urban population located there, the future form and content of urban development both in its built form and in its spatial organization in these continents has major implications for atmospheric warming worldwide.

IMPACTS OF GLOBAL WARMING ON THIRD WORLD CITIES

There are very serious environmental consequences for most Third World cities if global warming and stratospheric ozone depletion continue (as is likely, at least in the foreseeable future). For stratospheric ozone depletion, the most direct health consequence will be a rise in skin cancers and damage to eyes; indirect effects may include a suppression of people's immune system and reduced productivity in crops and marine plankton.[43]

For global warming, the main environmental implications are higher global mean temperatures, sea level rises and changes to both the function and the structure of ecosystems.[44] Changes in climate (a poleward shift in the thermal and moisture limits) are likely to result in changes in the structure of ecosystems as favoured species displace others. Displaced species will be forced to migrate and local or global extinction may occur. But much uncertainty remains as to the exact nature of the different impacts on particular cities and their relative importance.[45] There will be many different impacts on cities from global warming arising from environmental changes such as:

- the increase in average temperature;
- the rise in sea level;
- changes in precipitation;
- changes in river flow resulting both from the increase in temperature (and the melting of snow and ice) and changes in precipitation;
- the movement of the permafrost zone;
- changes in evaporation rates;
- changes in plant growth rates and favoured species; and
- changes in insect populations including pests and disease vectors.

Their scale and the nature of the consequences will certainly differ, depending on the city location and site characteristics and on the particular changes in that region in (for instance) precipitation and humidity.

A recent WHO report on the links between health and environment noted various direct and indirect consequences of atmospheric warming, with significant impacts on cities.[46] The direct consequences will include increased human exposure to exceptional heat waves – from which the elderly, the very young and those with incapacitating diseases are likely to suffer most. There may also be an increase in respiratory diseases as a consequence of accelerated photochemical reaction rates among chemical pollutants.[47] For most cities, the indirect impacts are likely to be much greater. This is especially so for cities on the coast – and for historic reasons linked to their colonial past, most of the Third World's largest cities are ports. Box 4.5 draws on a recent publication describing cities at risk from global warming. It outlines some of the environmental impacts of sea level rise on Alexandria in Egypt and how other human-induced changes such as reducing sediment flow and floodwater flows in the Nile have also helped increase the risk of flooding in the city.[48]

Box 4.5 The impact of sea level rise and other human induced changes on Alexandria, Egypt

Alexandria is on the north-east fringe of the Nile delta, on the Mediterranean sea. The Nile delta has a rare set of fossilized sand dunes along its coastal fringe which provide a stable foundation for the city above the low delta plain. The Old City is as much as 12 metres above sea level and is safe from the direct effects of sea level rise. However, the port area and newer suburbs which have been built on low land with the aid of flood defences are definitely at risk. The low marshes and lagoons which surround the city could be lost or seriously contaminated with saltwater due to sea level rise. Ultimately, the city could become a peninsula, surrounded by the Mediterranean, only reached by bridges and causeways.

Both subsidence and coastal erosion have been enhanced by development projects – which have also increased the city's vulnerability to climate change. The control of floods on the Nile (the most important being through the Aswan High Dam completed in 1964) have produced major benefits for irrigated farming and tourism but have stopped sediment previously brought down to the coast – which has meant some dramatic erosion around the mouths of the Damietta and Rosetta river mouths. Sediment starvation may eventually erode the already fragile beaches protecting Alexandria. The control of floodwaters in the Nile has also reduced the volume of water that recharges the aquifers below the delta. This has led to increased rates of groundwater withdrawal which in turn increased subsidence and saltwater intrusion into freshwater aquifers. The net result is deeper extraction and even more subsidence.

A sea level rise of just 10–20 centimetres would accelerate significantly the retreat of the coastline. Rises of 30–50 centimetres would probably require expensive and extensive protection measures to reduce the risk to Alexandria (and also to Port Said). Plans to boost beach tourism would certainly be jeopardized. A relative rise of one metre could submerge lowlands to within 30 kilometres of the coast; engineering solutions could mitigate the flooding problem but the capital costs would be high.

Source: Turner, R K, Kelly, P M and Kay, R C (1990) *Cities at Risk*, BNA International, London, drawing on El Raey 1990, El Sayed 1990, Meith 1989, Sestini *et al* 1989, see bibliography for full references.

Port cities are particularly vulnerable because of the rise in sea level and the increased frequency and severity of storms. The risk of flooding will increase substantially for large areas in or close to many coastal cities, including some highly developed city areas (especially those developed on reclaimed land) and many ports, oil refineries and thermal power stations which are concentrated on the coast.[49] Many of the Third World's most densely populated areas are river deltas and low-lying coastal regions. Shanghai is one among many major cities built on a low-lying delta; sections of the central city have been reclaimed from the sea and already lie below the normal level of high tide.[50] Saltwater intrusion also threatens the Yangtze delta within which Shanghai and several other major cities are located, along with some of the most productive agricultural areas in the world.[51] The Nile delta which is so critical to agricultural production in Egypt is also under threat from sea level rise. As noted already, it is also common in Third World cities for a considerable proportion of the poorest groups to have developed their settlements on low-lying lands which are at greatest risk from floods.

Rising sea levels and increased scale and frequency of floods also implies disruption to sewers and drains and undermining of buildings.[52] One particular problem for many coastal cities will be the increasing frequency and severity of storm-induced tidal surges.[53] Coastal cities whose economies benefit from tourism may have considerable difficulties protecting tourist attractions such as beaches and nearby wetlands.[54] There are also the impacts of changes in the availability of freshwater resources – for instance shortfalls because of reduced precipitation levels and the difficulties in protecting groundwater resources from contamination by seawater. For instance, Dhaka's drinking water supply is threatened by a landward shift in the interface between saltwater and freshwater.[55]

There will also be serious impacts for many inland cities. One example is an increased intensity of flooding as a result of the changes predicted in rainfall regimes in South America, which will pose serious threats to thousands of city dwellers in Lima, Santiago, Quito and Bogota, all in the foothills of the Andes.[56] Increasing rainfall or changes in its distribution over the year in many areas may seriously affect many cities built by rivers – for instance cities such as Formosa, Clorinda, Resistencia and Goya which lie on reclaimed land beside the middle Parana and lower Paraguay rivers.[57] There is also the impact on cities of disruptions to rural production – both in disruptions to rural production destined for cities, and to rural incomes spent in cities. Many cities will have increased in-migration of people who have lost their homes and livelihoods as a result of the direct or indirect effects of global warming.

Many of the environmental changes associated with global warming may increase the number of people at risk from disease vectors, natural disasters and extreme weather conditions. For example, global warming may permit an expansion in the area in which mosquitoes (vectors for malaria, dengue fever and filariasis) can survive and breed; the same is true for the vectors of schistosomiasis, leishmaniasis and Japanese encephalitis.[58] Flooding, landslides and mudslips may increase dangers for some residential sites as changes in precipitation result in increased groundwater.[59] Storms and other extreme weather conditions may become more frequent in a number of areas. In such conditions, new building regulations may be required, investments needed in disaster preparedness, and an effective emergency response prepared. The impacts of disasters often fall particularly heavily on the poor, both because they are often forced to live in more vulnerable areas and because they lack the resources to minimize the risk and the damage, cope in the event of a disaster and rebuild their lives afterwards.

Some of the most profound effects of global warming will be the result of the changes such warming induces in the intensity and spatial distribution of economic activity. The economic base of many villages, towns and cities will be altered, affecting existing patterns of regional, national and continental urban development. The agricultural productivity of many areas will be affected by changes in temperature and precipitation; in some cities and regions, opportunities will increase and incomes rise while other areas will experience economic decline. Reduced rainfall in the Sahel has already considerably increased population growth in urban centres such as Nouakchott, as pastoralists deprived of their livelihood move there. One estimate of the additional cost of meeting global food demand has been estimated to be up to ten per cent of world GDP.[60] A considerable range of manufacturing and service industries will also be affected. For example, reductions in the availability of water will jeopardise those industries which use large volumes of water, while changes in agricultural production will affect food processing industries, and changes in the weather will impact on the tourist industry.

The uncertainty surrounding all such changes means that planning is difficult and expensive. There are three areas which are unknown: first, the future level of emissions of greenhouse gases; second the climate effects of any future level of emissions; and thirdly, how a global change in climate will impact on regional and seasonal climates. For example, the lower land mass in the Southern Hemisphere means that warming may be delayed relative to the Northern Hemisphere. Whether this is the case and, if so, by how much, is not clear.

5

Addressing environmental problems

TACKLING ENVIRONMENTAL HEALTH PROBLEMS

The idea that environmental quality and pollution control are expensive luxuries to be pursued when a country is rich enough is slowly being eroded, at least with regard to industrial pollution. Attitudes concerning the cost of safe and hygienic collection and disposal of household and human wastes and the provision of safe water supplies are not so enlightened. It has taken 30 years or more for many governments to accept that illegal settlements and land invasions are not a threat to established institutions but a growing movement that emerges out of poor people having no other way to secure a house site. Most new urban housing and urban neighbourhoods in the Third World are developed in this informal way. While some governments still seek to prevent or inhibit such processes, most have accepted them, or at least do not bulldoze the settlements out of existence. Let us hope that it does not take another 30 years for governments to accept the need to work with the inhabitants of these informal settlements to tackle the environmental health problems – and also to understand how much improvement can be made to water, sanitation and drainage and to health in general at relatively low cost.

One reason for so little government action is that the health impacts of the most serious environmental problems are largely confined to poorer groups as described in Chapter 3. It is common for the residential areas of middle- and upper-income groups and the main commercial and industrial concerns in a city to receive good quality water supplies, sewers, drains, electricity supplies and regular services to remove solid wastes while 30 per cent or more of the city population in the poorer residential areas receive little or nothing.[1] The middle- and upper-income households are often subsidized in the publicly provided infrastructure and services they receive, since they are not charged a price which reflects the total costs of supply.[2]

National and city governments frequently claim that extending piped water, sewers, drains and garbage collection services to poorer areas is too expensive. But this assessment is based on the cost of systems in Europe and North America. Such systems are expensive and also bring with them major disadvantages from the point of view of resource use. In cities in the North, there is a very large throughput of resources with the used resources becoming wastes which then have to be collected and disposed of. Large volumes of solid wastes have to be collected from households and businesses and are usually disposed of in landfills. Large volumes of liquid wastes are collected by sewers and drains and dumped in the nearest convenient water body, generally after some treatment. These systems may be convenient for households and businesses – and they have certainly contributed to much better health. But they are expensive in financial and resource terms and result in an enormous throughput of resources. They also require sophisticated management to keep them functioning effectively. Two key questions remain:

- are there alternative ways of addressing the environmental health problems associated with contaminated and insufficient water, and inadequate or no provision for sanitation, drainage and garbage collection, which are cheaper, less wasteful of resources, and better matched to the institutional constraints evident in most Third World cities?
- and is there a sufficient range of alternatives so their diversity matches the diversity within Third World cities in terms of need, preference and capacity to pay?

IMPROVING WATER AND SANITATION

For excreta disposal, there is a wide range of alternatives far cheaper than conventional sewers and sewage treatment plants, but far more effective and hygienic than pit latrines, bucket latrines or simply defecating in open space. World Bank research involving field studies in 39 communities in 14 nations found a wide range of household and community systems which could greatly improve the hygienic disposal of human wastes. Within this range were options which could be implemented to match the particular physical conditions and economic resources in each locality and the social preferences of the inhabitants. Several options had a total annual cost per household of between one tenth and one twentieth that of conventional sewerage systems. Most needed far lower volumes of water while some demanded no water at all (although of course household water needs for drinking, cooking and washing still have to be met). It is also possible to install one of the lowest cost technologies initially and then upgrade it in a series of steps.[3]

The last ten years has brought a wealth of experience in implementing these alternatives and a better understanding of the necessity of involving low-income households and their community or neighbourhood organizations in decisions about the most appropriate design and how new facilities can be maintained and repaired.[4] Many countries have large-scale programmes already implemented in urban areas for pour-flush latrines and ventilated improved pit latrines and a knowledge of where these are or are not appropriate. There is a growing number of case studies of shallow sewer or small bore sewer schemes which proved much cheaper than conventional sewers.[5] On occasion, significant improvements have been achieved at low cost; for instance, a simple ventilation pipe used with the Ventilated Improved Pit Latrine can greatly reduce the smells associated with pit latrines while covering the vent pipe with a gauze screen can greatly reduce the number of flies.[6] What is needed in each city is the knowledge and experience to permit appropriate choices to be made within each settlement or district – including provision for maintenance and repair. Most household or community systems for excreta also need a regular and reliable system to empty them. Changes in national or municipal rules and regulations may also be needed since these will be contravened by many of the most effective and appropriate sanitation systems.

Improvements in the quality of water and its availability are also often possible at relatively low cost and with good possibilities of cost recovery, especially if optimal use is made of local resources and knowledge.[7] In many cities, largely self-financing water supply systems can reach poorer groups with much improved levels of service. A piped-water system can often be installed to replace water vendors and provide the water vendors' customers with a larger, safer and more convenient supply for the same price that they previously paid to vendors.[8] A thriving informal market for water is evidence of a demand unsatisfied by the formal sector. It is also evidence of the money value that poorer groups give to the time they would have to spend obtaining water from the nearest available public source if they did not buy from vendors and is therefore indicative of how much they would be willing to pay for an adequate conventional water supply, were it made available to them.[9] Involving residents in decisions about the level of service and payment often surprises professionals as to what 'poor people' would be prepared to pay; widely used guidelines often underestimate the value they place on the saving in time and energy provided by water piped to their home or yard in comparison to collecting water from a public standpipe.

Where there are shortages of freshwater supplies, better management and maintenance of existing water systems may increase available supplies more cheaply and quickly than increasing capacity. Many water supply systems lose 60 per cent of their water to leaks in the pipes. Reducing the leakage rate from 60 per cent to 12 per cent (the typical figure for systems in Britain or the United States) would more than double the amount of water available for use.[10] Often, just 20 per cent of the leaks account for 80 per cent of the water losses.[11] In São Paulo, the proportion of water leaking out of the system has been reduced by some 50 per cent over a ten year period.[12] There is also a large range of techniques and technologies which reduce the volume of water that large water consumers need, for which consumers can rapidly repay the additional capital cost through lower water bills.[13] In many regions where cities are running out of new, cheap freshwater resources, a combination of improved water management, better maintenance of water supply systems and encouragement to larger users to use water more efficiently, can often enormously increase the volume of available freshwater.[14] Many commercial, industrial and recreational water uses can be served by wastewater from urban sewers or drains, with some minimal treatment within the city area.[15]

The approach needed is one which analyses local problems and assesses which combination of actions best utilizes local resources. Sandy Cairncross has pointed out that various approaches considered 'unconventional' by western trained engineers may be the cheapest and most effective in certain localities.[16] For instance, where capital to extend piped water systems is lacking, a government programme to make water vendors more efficient and their water of better quality might be the most cost-effective option. In others, making use of local water sources for small independent networks for particular city areas may be more cost effective than extending the water mains system. In areas with sufficient rainfall, grants to households to install guttering and rainwater tanks may be a cheap way of improving supplies. Where piped systems are installed, modifications to official standards can often produce major cost savings with little or no reduction in performance; the minimum depth set for laying sewage pipes hardly needs to be to a depth to protect it from 40 ton trucks if the pipe is being installed in a high density, low-income settlement.[17] Standards appropriate to local circumstances do not always mean lower standards; higher standards may be appropriate in some cases to compensate for lower levels of maintenance.[18]

A BETTER USE OF EACH CITY'S NATURAL RESOURCES

One of the most revealing environmental audits of any city is how efficiently its inhabitants and businesses make use of the city's natural resources and how and in what form and scale the wastes are generated, recycled, re-used or treated (if at all) and disposed of. In wealthy societies, solid waste generation per capita is generally between 0.7 and 1.8

kilograms per day; in low-income countries, it is generally between 0.4 and 0.6 kilograms per day (although it may be as low as 0.1–0.25).[19]

One characteristic of most Third World cities is the remarkable scale and complexity of waste minimization, recovery of materials from wastes for re-use or recycling and the intensity with which limited resources are used. This can be seen in the use of small ponds for fish-rearing, the use of road verges, wasteland or other open spaces for crops, trees or livestock, the low volumes of wastes generated by poor households, the use of waste materials by low-income households for the construction of their shelters and by small-scale industries and workshops as raw material in their production. All this activity keeps down waste levels and reduces consumption levels for non-renewable natural resources. It brings substantial economic benefits; the livelihoods of several million urban dwellers in Asia depends on wastes – including workers in small industries which use plastics, tin cans, bottles, bones, feathers, intestines, hair, leather and textile scraps.[20] Numerous businesses are part of the waste economy – itinerant buyers who collect or purchase certain kinds of wastes direct from households or businesses, waste pickers who recover materials from the streets to sell, dump pickers who recover materials from city dumps, small waste shops, second-hand markets, dealers, transporters and the various recycling industries.[21] In Calcutta, an estimated 40,000 people make a living from recovering and using (or selling) resources picked from wastes – and many thousands more make a living from intensive farming using composted household wastes, and fish-rearing in ponds fertilized by city sewage.[22] But it is not only in the poorer Asian cities where the reclamation and recycling of wastes are important sources of employment; in Bogota, the capital of Colombia, this is how an estimated 30,000–50,000 people earn a living including cart drivers, small-scale waste dealers, people reclaiming materials from street waste and the employees of the municipal waste disposal and street-cleaning department.[23]

The intensive use of city resources and wastes can bring major environmental benefits and cost savings. For instance, Margarita Pacheco has highlighted the major savings to Colombia from the energy saved in the recycling of glass, cardboard, paper and plastics.[24] Recycling cardboard and paper reduces demand for trees and thus alleviates deforestation. Food production in or near cities is generally less energy-intensive since transport and storage costs are cut;[25] where city-wastes are used to fertilize it, energy savings are also made since fertilizers are energy-intensive. In many cities, municipal budgets benefit greatly from the individuals, households and informal groups who separate recyclables from their own wastes and collect them from other waste streams (for example paper, metals and glass). This reduces waste volumes and in large cities, the cost of collecting and transporting solid wastes to landfill sites and the development of new landfill sites are a major part of total solid waste management costs.

SOLID WASTES; RECLAMATION, RE-USE, RECYCLING AND DISPOSAL

The typical European or North American garbage collection and disposal service is relatively expensive and may be beyond the means of most existing urban/municipal government budgets. As noted earlier, it is also wasteful of resources. There are sufficient examples of alternative approaches to suggest that major improvements in service provision can be made (including regular garbage collection from poor and peripheral districts) at much lower costs than the conventional 'western' approach with the added advantages of greater support for employment generation and waste reduction. Cities need solid-waste management strategies that have such broad goals and which build on existing informal waste recovery and recycling.[26]

Professional attitudes are beginning to change in regard to the collection and processing of garbage.[27] There is a greater recognition of the need to develop local solutions which match local needs and possibilities. One reason for this is that conditions vary so much from city to city in (among other factors): the scale and type of refuse generation; the amount residents can afford and are prepared to pay for this; the type of vehicles needed to get to each building in different settlements; local possibilities for recycling or reclaiming part of the refuse; local traffic conditions; the availability of land sites for city dumps; and the resources at the disposal of local authorities for the collection and management of garbage disposal. Approaches based on matching waste management with local needs and resources and on maximizing resource recovery imply solutions very different from those taught to engineers whose training is overwhelmingly based on western models and precedents.[28]

Christine Furedy at the University of York (Toronto) has documented the many and varied ways in which the recovery, recycling or re-use of materials from city wastes provides livelihoods for poorer individuals, households and informal groups. She has shown how city and municipal governments can make such activities a central part of their waste management programme with cost advantages to themselves, better returns and working conditions for those who make a living from the waste and the retention, by the city, of the environmental advantages. This section draws heavily from her work. Dr Furedy has demonstrated that alternative approaches can also include social goals since this large and complex process of resource utilization and waste recovery in Third

World cities is usually driven by poverty; her observation for Asian cities that the poorer or less equal the society, the greater the range and volume of wastes which have value and are re-used or recycled, has validity for cities in other regions.[29] The individuals or households who use or collect resources rarely obtain an adequate return relative to number of hours worked. They undertake this work since, in the absence of a better alternative, it provides a livelihood. It is common for some of the poorest and most disadvantaged groups to be involved in this work – for instance particular castes or outcaste groups or street children. During an economic recession, more people seek incomes from picking through wastes to recover goods for sale.[30] Such work is often unpleasant and has many health risks – for instance injuries from broken glass and the sharp edges of cans for those sorting by hand and exposure to excreta-related diseases from excreta-contaminated wastes (which are so common in cities where households do not have convenient sanitation). They are also at risk from disease vectors which may feed or breed in garbage or garbage dumps. In many cities, hazardous wastes become mixed with household wastes – for instance toxic wastes from industries and hospital wastes.[31] A critical consideration is how the great environmental advantages of informal resource recovery and utilization can be kept (and enhanced) while income levels and working conditions are improved and health risks reduced for the individuals, households and enterprises engaged in this process.

There are sufficient examples of innovative 'waste-minimization' or resource recovery projects to show that new approaches are feasible. Most innovative examples appear to be the result of initiatives taken by local NGOs or community based organizations and these suffer from the difficulties which most small, voluntary initiatives face.[32] The scheme outlined in Box 5.1 is unusual in that it was initiated by the municipal government.

Box 5.1 Composting and recycling in Triangulo de Peixinhos, Olinda (Brazil)

In 1983, the municipality of Olinda selected a *favela* (low-income settlement) with 450 low-income families covering an area of 3.5 hectares known as 'Triangulo de Peixinhos' for a pilot project in upgrading. The origins of the *favela* date back to 1945 but in 1983, only a handful of the occupants held legal titles to the land they occupied. The settlement had no sanitation facilities, and provision for drainage was inadequate or non-existent. There was no municipal garbage collection service and none of the roads were paved. Water supply was also inadequate although most dwellings were connected to the electricity network. Triangulo de Peixinhos is built in a swampy area which had previously been used as a rubbish dump. Prior to the project, houses were often flooded in the rainy season, because there was no system to drain away storm and surface water, and the settlement's streets became mud-baths. The groundwater from which many inhabitants obtained water was often contaminated with water draining from pit latrines and from the rubbish dump.

Faced with such problems, the project team realised the need for a solution which would involve the local community and provide simple but effective basic infrastructure. First, the team installed a drainage system for the whole settlement and then tackled other areas in need of urgent action such as latrines, individual house upgrading and the paving of roads and access paths.

Before the project, only part of the household refuse was placed in a skip set aside for waste collection nearby. The rest would usually be left in the streets to rot or would be dispersed by the wind and rain. A municipal engineer designed a small composting and recycling plant which was built with the help of the inhabitants. This offered clear advantages over a centralised system of rubbish collection for the whole city: first, a large number of unskilled labourers were given employment during construction; and second, running costs were comparatively low, partly because the community was involved in the everyday running of the plant.

Before building the composting plant, there had been a general 'spring clean' of the whole settlement, with all the rubbish which had accumulated in different parts of the *favela* collected, along with any other wastes that households wanted to get rid of; altogether, some 50 tonnes of rubbish were collected. A daily collection of refuse was begun using a simple hand-pushed cart designed and constructed by a local firm, with the support of the municipality. This cart could be operated by one person – and it was narrow enough to fit through even the narrowest allies and thus reach all houses.

The operational capacity of the composting plant was one ton per day. As the rubbish arrived, the recyclable matter was separated and sold. Most of the rest was compostable – and the composting process typically reduced the volume to a quarter of that of the garbage prior to processing. The municipal authorities in Olinda have also developed other composting plants, and also seek to design and implement rubbish collection and street cleaning systems which match local conditions and possibilities.

Source: Case study by Stenio de Coura Cuentro in Cuentro, Stenio de Coura and Gadji, Dji Malla, 'The collection and management of household garbage' in Jorge E Hardoy *et al* (eds) (1990) *The Poor Die Young: Housing and Health in Third World Cities*, Earthscan Publications, London, pp. 169–188.

As in actions on water and sanitation, the kinds of actions needed from government will vary greatly, depending on local circumstances. They may include providing health care for waste pickers and washing and sanitation facilities for their use at city dumps. Or, as in a project in Kathmandu, people picking items from garbage at a city dump were provided with a platform to allow the sorting of waste as it was unloaded from trucks, and land was allocated for housing for the pickers.[33]

It may be appropriate to have district-level transfer points for solid wastes where re-usable or recyclable materials can be separated before the wastes are taken to the city dump.[34] The less mixed and compacted the wastes, the easier and safer this separation is; items which can be re-used are also less damaged. Such district level separation can also guard against the mixing of toxic and hazardous wastes with conventional garbage.

City authorities might consider support for decentralized centres where recyclable material can be collected and compost made as in Olinda in Brazil (Box 5.1). In many peripheral low-income settlements, the cost to the city authorities of a regular garbage collection service is often high, especially if access roads to the site are poor. Support for a neighbourhood based composting plant with glass, cans and paper also separated for sale might be a more appropriate response. This would enormously reduce the volume of waste that had to be collected. The necessary form of support may simply be a guarantee by the municipal authorities of a price for the compost and its use in city parks, together with its collection – and the collection of wastes that were neither recyclable nor compostable. Another approach has been tried in Curitiba where the public authorities had a programme to 'purchase' garbage from the inhabitants of squatter settlements. Squatters received tickets for use on the public transport system and agricultural and dairy produce in return for garbage brought to a central collection point. Conventional garbage collection services were often impossible for such settlements because the garbage trucks could not reach them. In this experiment, the cost to the public authorities was equivalent to the cost of paying a private company to collect the garbage.[35]

Urban Agriculture

The scale and diversity of food and fuel production within many Third World cities is greatly under-estimated by public authorities. So, too, is its importance for poorer households as a source of income or food. A recent review of urban agriculture by Jac Smit and Joe Nasr highlighted its importance and the great variety of food and fuel items that it includes:

- aquaculture in tanks, ponds, rivers and coastal bays;
- livestock raised in backyards, along roadsides, within rights of way for railways or underneath electric pylons, in poultry sheds and piggeries;
- orchards, including vineyards, street trees and backyard trees; and
- vegetables and other crops grown on rooftops, in backyards, in vacant lots or industrial estates, alongside canals, on the grounds of institutions, on roadsides and in many suburban farms.[36]

This review also noted the extent to which rooftops, balconies and small backyards can be used and gave examples of medicinal herbs grown on rooftops in Santiago de Chile, silkworms on balconies in Delhi, pigeons in Cairo, rabbits in illegal settlements in Mexico City, orchids in houses in Bangkok and fruit and vegetables on rooftops and other spaces in a squatter area in Bogota.[37] Box 5.2 provides some examples of intensive household and 'backyard' farming in urban areas in China.

Box 5.2 Household and courtyard farming in urban areas in China

Fish and livestock, vegetables and fruit can be grown or raised together in small urban courtyards. One example comes from the courtyard of Yang Puzhong, located on the outskirts of Bozhou in Hebei Province. This courtyard is only 200 square metres in size. At the centre is a fish pool, 20 square metres in size and two metres deep where carp, black carp, grass carp, loach and turtle are raised. Around the pool is a grape trellis which produces more than 1000 kilograms of grapes a year. On one side of the pool is a pigeon house and a pigsty with about 40 pigeons and eight pigs. Above the pigsty is a chicken house with 20 chickens and on top of the chicken house, a solar waterheater. Below the pigsty is a methane generating pit. On the other side of the pool is a small vegetable garden which supplies the family with vegetables all year round. Chicken droppings are used to feed pigs, nightsoil is used to generate methane for cooking and liquid from the methane pit is used to feed the fish – with the remainder used as manure for farmland or as a culture medium for mushrooms.

Intensive cultivation is also evident in many other cities. For instance, in Shanghai, China's most populous city, there are increasing numbers of backyards, roofs, balconies, walls and vacant spaces near houses being used to develop such agroforestry systems as orange tree-vegetable-leguminous plant, grapevine–gourd and melon–leguminous plant and Chinese tallow tree–vegetable–leguminous plant.

Source: Honghai, Deng (1992) 'Urban agriculture as urban food supply and environmental protection subsystems in China' Paper presented to the international workshop on 'Planning for Sustainable Urban Development', University of Wales, 1992. This drew from Li Ping (1991) 'Eco-farming on Huaibei Plain, *Beijing Review* vol 34, no. 28, pp. 8–16.

The particular form that urban agriculture takes and the scope for its development obviously varies greatly, depending on, among other things, the nature of the city and its surrounds, the formal and informal rules governing who can use open land or water (and on what terms) and the natural resource base available for its support. Economic circumstances, the time constraints on potential farmers and fish-rearers and their knowledge of how to profitably engage in such activities also influence their extent. In some African and Asian cities, one influential factor is related to the colonial heritage;[38] the lack of planning and infrastructure provision in the 'indigenous quarters' of colonial cities (usually kept strictly segregated from the residential areas of the colonial elite) permitted newly arrived rural settlers to develop urban settlements with house forms and plans similar to their rural settlements. Low incomes also encouraged indigenous food production.

In certain cities, perhaps most especially in China, the policies and attitudes of public authorities have greatly enhanced the role of urban agriculture. In China, this builds on an ancient tradition of urban agriculture which has long used sophisticated methods of crop rotation, inter-planting, inter-sowing and use of human and animal wastes as organic fertilizer – and which has been developed and encouraged since 1949.[39] For instance, within the boundaries of Shanghai city region, there is some of China's most productive agriculture; this includes a belt of vegetable farms around the city which supply approximately 80 per cent of all vegetables shipped to Shanghai's core, while further out, cotton, food-crops and oilseeds are the major crops.[40] The remarkable scale and value of food production so often reported in Chinese cities may owe much to the fact that such production is considered within large administrative boundaries for city regions, which happens to include large amounts of rural area rather than just the boundaries of the built-up area.[41] Nonetheless, the public authorities have encouraged this synergy whereas its potential in other countries is often lost or diminished, as agricultural land on city peripheries is purchased as speculative investments (and no longer farmed), or developed illegally for housing. There are also examples of public entities who have leased urban land for agriculture – for instance hospitals in Lima and the University of Manila.[42]

In many cities in Africa, the scale of urban agriculture owes less to government policy (which may actively discourage it) and more to a combination of relatively low-density cities with open spaces suited to urban agriculture and the high proportion of households with low incomes for whom returns from urban agriculture are attractive. For many urban dwellers in Africa, access to land on which crops can be grown is an essential part of their livelihood and food so produced an important part of their nutritional intake. Box 5.3 describes the scale and range of urban agriculture in Nairobi and other Kenyan urban centres.

There are important city-wide benefits from urban agriculture, in addition to the obvious benefits to those people (many of them poor) involved in urban agriculture in terms of food, fuel or income. They include the relatively low energy intensity of the food produced, compared to conventional commercial food production systems; they often include

Box 5.3 Urban food production in Kenya

The importance of urban food production was shown by a study of six Kenyan towns completed between October 1984 and July 1985. In a survey of over 1500 urban households, almost two thirds of respondents grew some of their own food or fuel and about half kept livestock.

Nearly three quarters of urban households had access to land on which they could grow food. As might be expected, this proportion was highest in the smaller towns. Twenty-nine per cent of the urban population had access to local land and grew crops in the area in which they lived. Just under half of those with access to urban land farmed in their own backyards. Roadsides (used by 17 per cent of households with urban land) and riversides (13 per cent) were other sites which were farmed. The average farm was just 500 square metres in size. Maize and beans were the most popular crops, both grown by over 50 per cent of urban farmers. Ninety-five per cent of these producers grew only for domestic consumption. Average household production for the season prior to the survey was 155 kilograms. Land productivity equalled 3200 kilograms/hectare and was highest in Nairobi (9000 kilograms/hectare). Few urban farmers bought commercial fertilizer although 30 per cent used farmyard manure obtained from their own farms or those of friends and relatives. Women did most of the work growing crops in urban areas except where such work was paid.

Just over half of urban households kept livestock in urban or rural areas. Seventeen per cent kept livestock in the urban area in which they lived. The main reason why more families did not keep animals was lack of land. Of households with livestock, the largest number kept poultry (75 per cent) and/or goats (26 per cent). Just over half (52 per cent) kept livestock only for subsistence purposes; a further 39 per cent kept livestock for both subsistence and sale. In addition to the sale of livestock products, animals are an important form of saving. Prices are relatively low at the beginning of the year when many families sell in order to raise the money for school fees, and high at the end of the year when national and religious holidays increase the demand for meat. Small numbers of households kept more unusual livestock such as fish and bees.

The importance of urban subsistence farming is in part due to poverty. Fifty-seven per cent of the households interviewed were in the 'very low income' category. It was estimated that these households were unable to feed themselves on what they earned. Even among the poorest households, a majority were successful in obtaining access to urban land which could be used for farming. However, urban farming is not an activity confined to the poor; many richer households also undertake significant farming activities.

Existing planning policies take no account of urban farming. According to most by-laws, the activity is illegal although it is tolerated in most towns. Government could do much more to support such activities. For example, low density residential areas favour farming practices as households can use backyard areas. Productivity might also be improved with a crop extension service designed to help the urban poor.

Source: Lee-Smith, Diana *et al* (1987) *Urban Food Production and the Cooking Fuel Situation in Urban Kenya*, Mazingira Institute, Kenya.

the intensive use of organic wastes from household garbage which reduces waste volumes and reduces (or eliminates) the need for artificial fertilizers. For instance, in Calcutta, vegetable farms developed on refuse dumps where the mixture of organic refuse, coal ash, street sweepings and animal dung allowed intensive production, and these farms combined with farms in adjacent villages which use garbage as fertilizer provide some 150 tonnes of vegetables each day to the city.[43] In many cities, peri-urban agriculture also serves as a cheap and effective means of providing primary treatment to sewage.[44] Again, in Calcutta, fish-farms have long been functioning in the wetlands to the east of the city which are fed by the city's sewers and storm drains; the large, shallow ponds are fringed with water hyacinth (on which cows graze) and sustain several types of carp and tilapia.[45] In Mexico City, water borne sewage is used to irrigate over 100,000 hectares for growing livestock feed.[46] The potential costs – for instance the health risks in fertilizing fields and crops with sewage – can be minimized.[47] In addition, a combination of provision for urban agriculture and for parks, playgrounds and other areas of open space can have beneficial environmental impacts, providing shade and modifying the climate.[48]

The role of privatization

Low-income groups need safe and sufficient supplies of water. Drains are needed to take away wastewater and, where possible, sewers to take away excreta. Where sewers are too expensive, regular services are needed to empty pit latrines or septic tanks. Low-income groups also need health care services, all-weather roads and regular collection of garbage. Many governments and aid agencies are promoting privatization to improve provision for such basic needs. The idea that privatization alone can improve provision to low-income groups and solve the problems already outlined is greatly overstated.

A frequent justification for privatization given by its proponents is usually that the government is short of capital. Their hope is that the private sector will provide the capital needed to expand and improve services, if offered the opportunity. In this instance, the private sector would be taking over some of the responsibilities of local government.

In most Third World cities, many of the poorer inhabitants already use the 'private' sector to obtain land for housing, rented accommodation and certain services. Private enterprises are often the main supplier of water through water vendors. In most cities, they are the main providers of rental accommodation; the extent to which low-income groups depend on rental accommodation and the extent to which such accommodation is located in illegal or informal settlements is rarely appreciated in the

North.[49] Private enterprises often provide a range of services such as waste collection, childcare, and transport, some of which are wholly or partially provided by the public sector in the North. In these three instances of water, land for housing and rental accommodation, the private sector can hardly be said to provide good quality goods and services in many Southern cities. The lack of infrastructure and services supplied by the enterprises which develop illegal sub-divisions for sale, the level of tenant exploitation and the very poor conditions in most rental housing do not support the idea that privatization will necessarily improve standards for poorer groups. The high price and the often poor quality of the water sold by water vendors also suggests problems with 'privatization'.

The increased enthusiasm for 'privatization' of public companies or public assets may also pose threats to many squatter settlements. In many cities, a considerable proportion of the population live in illegal settlements which developed on publicly owned land – or on land belonging to public companies (for instance land belonging to railway companies). Although many governments have undertaken large-scale eviction programmes or suppressed any attempts by squatters to use public land, it has been common for governments to tolerate this process – especially since squatters are careful to avoid prime sites or sites whose occupation is likely to provoke strong public or government hostility. Such a process can serve government interests; it houses a high proportion of relatively poor households (in some cities more than half the population live in squatter settlements) with no direct costs for government. Governments can and often do use the fact that these people live on publicly owned land to gain the squatters' political support. But if land on which squatters live is now sold to private companies, there will be a much increased pressure to evict them. Similarly, poorer groups which have developed livestock rearing or agricultural production on public lands may lose this possibility if the land is sold; the study of food production in urban areas in Kenya (Box 5.3) noted the importance for poor urban households of access to public land.

The privatization of public water and electricity services – or other public utilities – may also pose special threats for squatter settlements. Governments have often tolerated illegal water connections or electricity connections in squatter settlements – or non-payment for water and electricity where this is publicly provided. From a societal perspective, the fact that the squatters get these free or cheap is very inadequate compensation for the lack of public provision in other areas. But it is unlikely that any private company taking over water or electricity supplies will tolerate this with the result that many low-income households will lose these services.

There is also the problem that not all infrastructure and service provision is an attractive investment for private companies. Some may not be provided at all – for example street lighting, site drainage and access roads – unless the companies are paid to do so by the government. In other cases, the lowest cost method of providing the service may require a large capital investment which the private sector is reluctant to undertake without the government providing some guarantee of continued demand. Private companies may be reluctant to extend services to poorer areas especially if this requires a large investment and they are uncertain of the willingness of residents to pay for their product. It does not cost much for a private company to see if a new bus service to a squatter community is profitable. If the venture loses money, a different route can be tried or the bus sold. But laying water pipes or sewers to a squatter community is a much greater risk, since it is far more expensive and the capital investment cannot easily be transferred.

Important cost savings may be lost if different forms of infrastructure are installed by different companies at different times. For instance, water supplies piped to each house require drains connected to each house – and preferably sewers. Sewers need sufficient water to keep them unblocked. House sites usually need drains for rain-water. Roads and other paved areas need drains. Drains need efficient garbage collection otherwise they become blocked with garbage; so too, on occasion, do sewers.

The public good is best served when water, sewage and drainage are installed simultaneously. First, this brings the greatest improvement in health; if only water supply is improved, this may increase health problems as wastewater forms stagnant pools which then serve as breeding grounds for insects which spread diseases. Second, there are large cost savings if piped water, drains and sewers are installed together, along with the paving of roads and footpaths. But private companies are unlikely to want to take on the operation of water, sanitation, drainage and garbage disposal services and the paving of roads and paths. Water supply is probably the most attractive for them because people pay as they consume and often pay for the initial cost of connection. Enforcing payment is easier because supplies can be cut off. Garbage collection may also be attractive since the capital costs to set up the service need not be high and again, services can be stopped if households do not pay. But private enterprises will not generally be attracted to the supply of site drains, roads and paths since it is difficult to penalize households for non-payment.

Many of the basic service and infrastructure industries are 'natural monopolies' and, once the investment has been made and the supplier established, customers may be vulnerable to exploitation by a single supplier. Piped water, sewers, drains and road systems present governments with special problems, since there are no competitive pressures to keep down prices and encourage improved quality. Such natural monopolies require large capital investments to set up the supply but once in place, the cost of extending them to more people within a city is relatively low. Once a piped-water supply, sewer system or road network is built, it is virtually impossible for another business to compete by building another water, sewer or road system. Customers who are dissatisfied with prices or quality cannot transfer and use the roads or pipes of another supplier.

When such a public service which is a natural monopoly is privatized, it has to be carefully regulated both in regard to prices and to quality of service. If a private firm runs a city's water supply, residents have no other piped supply they can turn to, if prices get too high or quality too low. But if water supplies are privatized because local government is so weak, how can this same local government regulate the private firms? How can it fulfil its responsibility to ensure that water quality is guaranteed and that prices are controlled?[50] Privatization does not remove the need for government intervention; it simply changes the nature of this intervention. Government remains responsible for ensuring an adequate quality of service is maintained and that the public are not over-charged.

In the case of certain goods and services, a lack of information means that consumers cannot easily determine the quality of the product regardless of whether the market is competitive. Domestic water supply is the most important example because households cannot necessarily judge whether the water they use is safe to consume. If private enterprises provide water supplies, local government must not only control prices but also monitor water quality and have in place an effective deterrent system to penalize companies who fail to maintain adequate standards. Likewise transport services will also require monitoring to ensure that the vehicles are safe to ride in and adequately maintained.

There are instances where the argument for privatization of certain services appears particularly convincing. In particular cities (or parts of cities), government weakness or inefficiency may provide a strong case for the private supply of certain services or certain kinds of infrastructure. Public companies which fail to provide adequate services to businesses who can afford such services also constrain the growth in production and employment. As Kyu Sik Lee has pointed out in his study of deficiencies in infrastructure provision in Nigeria, the failure of government to provide businesses with adequate standards of water supply, electricity, telephones and drains means that these businesses make very large investments to guarantee their own supplies – through their own electricity generators, wells for water and microwave telephone systems. The costs to each business are enormous and any larger-scale supplier (public or private) could meet their demands far more cheaply.[51]

In other services, especially those which are not a natural monopoly, private enterprises can help improve quality and choice for the public. In city transport, private enterprises often provide a cheaper, more flexible service than public sector bus companies; private buses, mini-buses, shared taxis, powered rickshaws and a whole host of other kinds of 'paratransit' either replace or supplement public sector buses in virtually all Third World cities. Large companies, whether private or public, may be poorly suited to running such services because they find it difficult to provide sufficient flexibility. In some cases, the public and private sectors can cooperate effectively together, with the government establishing the network and conditions for quality and cost of services with the private sector operating individual routes; this has been done in Curitiba within a public transport system which has been highly praised for being efficient and which does not lose money.[52] Private companies might also improve garbage collection at an affordable cost to customers with appropriate encouragement and regulation by local government. This might be particularly attractive for local governments which cannot obtain investment funds.

Where household water comes mainly from water vendors and where the combination of very low household incomes and poor local government makes the installation of piped supplies impossible, water supplies should be cheaper and of better quality if different vendors compete with each other and information is available about the quality of the water they sell. Here, one option for local government would be to assist water vendors to improve services as well as regulating quality.[53]

One reason why private companies may operate more profitably than public enterprises is their greater efficiency in collecting payments for services provided. Through the non-collection of payments, public companies often subsidize richer groups. For instance, a public water company's failure to collect payments for piped water or to increase tariffs to reflect rising costs has the effect of subsidizing those with piped water (often not among the poorer households). This penalizes those with no piped supply since it lowers the returns to the company and thus inhibits new investment to expand the service. Improving cost recovery – in terms of reducing the proportion of households who do not pay the full cost of some service – is one important way to pay for better maintenance of the system and its expansion to reach new households. If the poorest households are unable to meet the cost of services, then separate support may be required. However, improved cost recovery may penalize the poorest households and it may not result in improved services but in higher profits for the owners.

Allowing private enterprises to provide certain services now inadequately provided (or not provided at all) by local government can be useful and worth considering, especially in the services which are not natural monopolies. But in the services which are the main concern of this section, there will be problems with quality and with reaching poorer households if there is no strong and competent local government to supervise levels of private service and charges. If local government *is* strong and competent, it may be able to provide such services more cheaply and effectively itself. And if private provision is preferred, the government will still have an important regulatory role to play. The aim is to seek a compromise between guaranteeing a basic level of service to everyone and to maximizing cost recovery. New technologies and innovative institutional arrangements can greatly cheapen the cost of supplying a basic level of services – and greatly narrow the gap between a basic service cost and what poorer households can afford. They can also make it easy for households to obtain better services, once they can afford to pay more, by for instance bringing piped water into the house rather than into the yard outside. Privatization is only valid if considered within the more important long-term goal of developing strong, competent and representative local government.

ANOTHER ROLE FOR NGOs

A more relevant debate about privatization and improving environmental health for lower-income groups has to do not with private commercial enterprises but with non-profit organizations and with organizations set up by residents of particular areas. Local NGOs can not only match (or exceed) private enterprise's record in cost recovery but there are many examples of them providing cheaper services (since no profit is made) in ways which are more immediately accountable to their customers. This could be regarded as privatization in another form but where control of the infrastructure and services rests largely with representatives of the 'consumers' of that service. There is tremendous potential in new partnerships between local governments, local community organizations and local NGOs. The work of Orangi Pilot Project with low-income households and community organizations in the largest unauthorised settlement in Karachi shows what can be achieved with minimal external funding and with most of the investments made by the poor households themselves (see Box 5.4). There are many other examples of innovative water and sanitation projects involving partnerships between residents and local NGOs.[54]

Box 5.4 The Orangi Pilot Project in Karachi, Pakistan

Orangi is a unauthorized settlement with some 700,000 inhabitants; most inhabitants built their own houses and none received official help in doing so. There was no public provision for sanitation; most people used bucket latrines which were emptied every few days, usually onto the unpaved lanes running between houses. More affluent households constructed soakpits but these filled up after a few years. Some households living near creeks constructed sewage pipes which emptied into the creeks. The cost of getting local government agencies to lay sewage pipes in Orangi was too much for local residents – who also felt that these should be provided free.

A local organization called the Orangi Pilot Project (OPP) was sure that if local residents were fully involved, a cheaper, more appropriate sanitation system could be installed. OPP staff organized meetings for those living in 10–15 adjacent houses each side of a lane and explained the benefits of improved sanitation and offered technical assistance. Where agreement was reached among the households of a lane, they elected their own leader who formally applied for technical help. Their site was surveyed with plans drawn up and cost estimates prepared. Local leaders kept their group informed and collected money to pay for the work. Sewers were then installed with maintenance organized by local groups. The scope of the sewer construction programme grew as more local groups approached OPP for help and the local authorities began to provide some financial support. Over the last eight years, households in Orangi have constructed close to 69,000 sanitary pour-flush latrines in their homes plus 4459 sewerage lines and 345 secondary drains – using their own funds and under their own management.

OPP's research concentrated on the extent to which the cost of sanitary latrines and sewerage lines could be lowered to the point where poor households could afford to pay for them. Simplified designs and the use of standardized steel moulds reduced the cost of sanitary latrines and manholes to less than one quarter of the contractors' rates. The cost of the sewerage line was also greatly reduced by eliminating the profits of the contractor. The average cost of the small bore sewer system is no more than US$66 per house.

Women were very active in local groups; many were elected group leaders and it was often women who found the funds to pay for the sewers out of household budgets. But women had difficulty visiting health centres since custom dictates that they should stay at home. OPP developed a health programme, working through women's groups, also at the level of the lane, with advice provided on hygiene, nutrition, disease prevention, family planning and kitchen gardens. There is also an income generation programme which provides credit and advice to small businesses and a project to help upgrade physical conditions and academic standards in schools in Orangi.

Sources: Hasan, Arif (1989) 'A low cost sewer system by low-income Pakistanis' in Bertha Turner (ed.), *Building Community: a Third World Case Book,* Habitat International Coalition; Hasan, Arif (1990) 'Community organizations and non-government organizations in the urban field in Pakistan' *Environment and Urbanization* vol. 2, no. 1, pp. 74–86; and Khan, Akhter Hameed (1991), *Orangi Pilot Project Programmes*, Orangi Pilot Project, Karachi.

There are also many NGOs involved in the collection and disposal of garbage – either seeking to provide (or improve) services in low-income settlements which are not served through public provision or seeking to provide better livelihoods and/or living conditions for people who make a living from garbage.[55] For instance, the Waste Wise project in Bangalore (India) is seeking to combine an innovative waste separation and recycling programme (with composting of organic wastes and collection of recyclables) with income generation for street children.[56] Another example is from Manila in the Philippines where the San Luis 'Linis-Ganda' ('clean-beautiful') project is providing work for 60 boys and is collecting some 50 tonnes of recyclable materials each month for most parts of the year.[57]

The possibility of tackling the most serious environmental health problems with limited resources needs cooperation between local government and community-based citizen groups. Joint programmes can be set up to drain stagnant pools; to reblock existing settlements so pipes, drains and access roads can be installed and space made for schools and clinics; to locate and destroy disease vectors within homes and their surrounds; to design educational programmes on health prevention and personal hygiene; and to set up emergency life saving systems through which first aid can be provided in each neighbourhood and through which seriously ill or injured persons can be rapidly transported to a hospital.

Box 5.5 illustrates the impact that such an approach can have. It outlines three different ways of spending US$20 million to improve poorer groups' housing and living conditions. Option 1 was the most common approach during the 1960s and part of the 1970s; its high cost and low impact is evident. Option 2 represents one of the most common 'new' approaches of the last 20 years; its limitations are also all too evident. Option 3 represents a far more effective model; its effectiveness has been proven by hundreds of small projects implemented by community organizations with the help of NGOs or church groups over the last 30 years. What makes Option 3 unusual is that it is local government which supports it and does so on a scale which allows a real impact on the problem.

Box 5.5 Different options for government spending US$20 million on improving housing and living environments

Option 1: $20 million spent on the construction of two bedroom 'low cost' housing units 'for low income groups'. The cost of each unit is some $10,000, once the land has been purchased, the site prepared, the contractor paid for building the units and the infrastructure and the units allocated. Thus, 2000 households or 12,000 people receive a good quality house – if we assume that, on average, there are six persons per household. Cost recovery would be difficult if these were from among the poorer households.

Option 2: $20 million is spent on a serviced site project, so that more households can be reached than in public housing projects. Knowing that poorer households need to live close to the main centres of employment, a relatively central site was purchased for $12 million with the other $8 million spent on site preparation and installing infrastructure and services. At a cost of $2000 per plot, 10,000 households (or 60,000 people) could benefit. It would be easier to recover some costs than in the public housing project but for the poorer households, $2000 for a site on top of the cost of having to construct their own house would be too much.

Option 3: Local government makes available to any residents' organization formed by the majority of the inhabitants of an area the sum of $100,000 for site improvements. These residents' organizations have considerable flexibility as to how they choose to spend these funds and who they turn to for technical advice. For instance, they can use local NGOs for technical advice, as long as certain basic standards are met. Although what can be achieved with such a sum will vary greatly depending on site characteristics, local costs and the extent to which residents contribute their skills and labour free, within an area with 500 households, it should be possible to 'reblock' the site to allow better access roads and to pave them and also to greatly improve site drainage, water supply and sanitation. Support could be given to local artisans to fabricate the materials, fixtures and fittings which are most cheaply and effectively made on site – for instance, a carpenter's cooperative to make doors and windows or for cheap building block fabrication. Of the $100,000, an average of $150 is spent per household on improved infrastructure and services with $10,000 spent on technical advice and $15,000 on support for local businesses. The 'reblocking' of the site also frees up sufficient land to allow 50 more housing plots to be developed within the existing site or on adjacent land as yet undeveloped and the cost of providing these with infrastructure and services and of building a community health centre was paid for by selling them.

With $100,000 provided to 150 community organizations with an average of 500 households (3000 people) the total cost was $15 million and the whole programme reached 150 × 3000 people, ie 450,000 people. Since an average of 50 new housing plots was produced in each reblocking, not only did 450,000 people benefit from improved housing, infrastructure and services but 7,500 new plots with services were developed and new health centres constructed in each site. The possibility of cost recovery was much better than for Options 1 and 2 since most households could afford to pay $200 – or take out a loan which allowed repayment over a few years. Spending $15 million in this way still left $5 million from the original $20 million which could be used to improve some city-wide service – for instance, providing medical personnel to run health clinics and health campaigns in each settlement.

Source: Hardoy, Jorge E and Satterthwaite, David (1989) *Squatter Citizen: Life in the Urban Third World,* Earthscan Publications, London.

Consider these options in the context of a city of one million inhabitants, growing at 5 per cent a year. Each would take several years to implement. Options 1 and 2 would do nothing to improve conditions in existing settlements. Option 1 would not produce sufficient new housing for one year's growth in population and Option 2's 12,000 units would only just do so. Option 3 would reach half the city's population with improved infrastructure and services and contribute much more than the other options to employment creation. It would support the development of local NGOs as centres of advice and support for low-income organizations and would create almost as many new units as Option 2. Furthermore, US$5 million would be left for investment in improving some city-wide services and prospects for cost recovery would be much better than for the other two options.

Approaches like those outlined in Option 3 do not simply save money because local residents contribute labour free (many poor households lack 'free time' because of long working hours). There are also major savings in the time of architects, planners, surveyors and other expensive professionals as community consultations work out and resolve such issues as moving certain houses which stand in the way of access roads, and collect funds from households to pay for the improvements. There are also major savings as specialized equipment and materials are used to install not only piped water but also provision for sanitation, drainage and all-weather roads and paths. The match between what is provided and capacity to pay is much improved when local community organizations are fully involved in such decisions. Perhaps the most critical need is to ensure that there are *local* institutions from which community organizations can obtain loans and credits for these kinds of programmes and funds to pay for technical advice; external funding from national agencies or foreign sources could never fund the tens of thousands of such community initiatives which are needed since even if they had the commitment, they lack the institutional structure to allow them to do so. Here too, the role of local NGOs can be important. These could serve not only as technical advisors to community organizations but also as supervisors of loans or credits.

Table 5.1 sketches the actions needed to tackle the most pressing environmental health problems in the residential areas of Third World cities. The column on the left lists the most pressing health risks with the other columns summarising the actions needed at different levels: individual and household; neighbourhood or community; district and city. It also outlines the actions needed at national level, most of which are to support or empower action at district or at neighbourhood level.

The cost of the actions summarized in this table are not beyond the means of most Third World governments. But they do imply a change in the nature of governance. In discussing the political economy of urban poverty and environmental management in Asia, Mike Douglass stresses the need, above all, to increase poorer groups' access to key economic and environmental resources and to empower households and communities to participate as active decision makers in the use and management of resources. But, as he states, this implies significant changes in the institutional arrangements, and the practices underlying government-community relations;[58] most governments in Asia (and in Latin America and Africa) remain highly centralized. Many are also working actively to deny the legitimacy of political associations emerging from civil society[59] – and as such are actively disempowering the kinds of actions summarized in Table 5.1.

In addition, few city or municipal governments can address environmental problems with the necessary integration between the different policies and financial investments. In most Third World countries, the institutional structure for addressing environmental problems is not only weak and ineffective but also divided into different technical departments with little coordination.[60] Ironically, the fact that resources are so scarce actually requires municipal governments in the Third World to be more sophisticated, innovative and flexible than those in the First World. Ideally, each house should be provided with piped water and sewers and each residential area with paved roads, electricity and storm- or rain-water drainage. There should be regular collection of household wastes, nutrition programmes for vulnerable groups and health care and emergency life saving services. But this may be too expensive and local governments in consultation with citizen organizations must make pragmatic choices as to where limited funds should be spent. They need considerable sophistication and sensibility to detect the major health problems and to design and implement appropriate interventions.

To conclude this section, the issue is certainly about making the suppliers of services more responsive to consumer demands. It is about local government giving the private sector a greater role in both decision making, and in service provision and increasing their influence in determining priorities. But this private sector is made up of low-income citizens and their community organizations – and the non-profit professional groups who pioneer new ways of working with them.

TACKLING CITY-WIDE POLLUTION

The last 20 years experience has shown that polluting emissions can be controlled and solid and liquid wastes managed (and reduced), with resources and political will, allied to appropriate legislation and its

Table 5.1: Government-community partnerships in addressing health risks

Health risks	Action at individual and household level	Public action at neighbourhood or community level	Action at district or city level	Action at national level
Contaminated water – typhoid, hepatitis, dysenteries, diarrhoea, cholera etc.	Protected water supply to house; promote knowledge of hygienic water storage.	Provision of water supply infrastructure; knowledge and motivation in the community.	Plans and resources to undertake or support action at lower levels.	Ensure that local and city governments have the power, funding base and trained personnel to implement actions at the household, neighbourhood, district and city levels. Review and, where appropriate, change legislative framework and norms and codes to allow and encourage actions at lower levels and ensure that infrastructure standards are appropriate to the needs and the resources available. Support for training courses and seminars for architects, planners, engineers etc on the health aspects of their work.
Inadequate disposal of human wastes – pathogens from excreta contaminating food, water or fingers leading to faecal–oral diseases or intestinal worms (eg hookworm, roundworm, tapeworm, schistosomiasis).	Support for construction of easily maintained WC or latrine which matches physical conditions, social preferences and economic resources. Washing facilities to promote hand washing.	Mix of technical advice, equipment installation and its servicing and maintenance (the mix is dependent on the technology used).	Plans and resources to undertake or support action at lower levels. Trained personnel and finances to service and maintain them.	
Wastewater and garbage – waterlogged soil ideal to transmit diseases like hookworm; pools of contaminated standing water, conveying enteric diseases and providing breeding ground for mosquitoes spreading filariasis, malaria and other diseases. Garbage attracting disease vectors.	Provision of storm and surface water drains on house plot and spaces for storing garbage that are rat, cat, dog and child proof.	Design and provision of storm and surface water drains. Advice to households on materials and construction techniques to make houses less damp. Consider feasibility of community-level garbage recycling/reclamation.	Regular removal or provision for safe disposal of household wastes (including support for community schemes) and plan framework and resources for improving drainage.	
Insufficient water for domestic hygiene – diarrhoeal diseases, eye infections (including trachoma), skin diseases, scabies, lice, fleas.	Adequate water supply for washing and bathing. Provision for doing laundry at household or community level.	Health and personal hygiene education for children and adults. Facilities for laundry at this level, if not within individual houses.	Support for health education and public facilities for laundry.	Technical and financial support for educational campaigns. Coordination of housing, health and education ministries.
Disease vectors or parasites in house structure with access to occupants, food or water eg rats, cockroaches, mosquitoes or other insects (including Chagas disease vector).	Support for improved house structure – eg tiled floors, protected food storage areas, roofs, walls and floors protected from disease vectors.	Technical advice and information – part of adult and child education programme.	Loans for households to upgrade shelters. Guarantee supply of cheap and easily available building materials, fixtures and fittings.	Ensure building codes and official procedures to approve house construction or improvement are not inhibiting individual, household and local government actions. Support for nationwide availability of building loans, cheap materials (where possible based on local resources) and building advice centres. Produce technical and educational material to support this.
Inadequate size house and poor ventilation – helps transmission of diseases such as TB, influenza and meningitis (aerosol drops) especially when many households share premises. Risks of household accidents increased with overcrowding; impossible to safeguard children from poisons, open fires and stoves.	Technical and financial support for house improvement or extension and provision of cheap sites with basic services in different parts of city to offer poorer groups alternatives to their current shelters.	Technical advice on improving ventilation and lessening indoor fumes and smoke. Education on overcrowding-related diseases and accidents.	Loans for upgrading (including small ones with flexible repayment terms); support for building advice centres in each neighbourhood.	

Children playing in and around house site constantly exposed to hazards from traffic, unsafe sites (eg on slopes or with open drains) or sites contaminated with pollutants or faeces.	Child care services to allow care and supervision for children in households where all adults work.	Provision within each neighbourhood of well drained site, separated from traffic, kept clean and free from garbage and easily supervised for children's play. Ensure first aid services are to hand.	Support given to neighbourhood level play, sport and recreation facilities.	Support for city/local governments with information and advice on recreation and play provision for child development.
Indoor air pollution because of open fires or poorly designed stoves – exacerbate respiratory illness, especially in women and children.	Posters/booklets on improved stove design and improving ventilation.	Ensure availability of designs and materials to build improved designs.	Consider extent to which promotion of alternative fuels would lessen problem.	
House sites subject to landslides or floods as a result of no other land being affordable to lower-income groups.	Regularize each household's tenure if danger can be lessened; relocation through offer of alternative sites as last resort.	Action to reduce risks of floods/ landslides or to reduce potential impact; community based contingency plan for emergency. Encourage upgrading or offer alternative sites.	Ensure availability of safe housing sites that lower-income groups can afford in locations accessible to work.	National legislation, and financial and technical support for interventions by local and city governments in land markets to support action at lower level. Training institutions to provide needed personnel at each level.
Illegal occupation of house site or illegal subdivision with disincentive to upgrade, lack of services and mental stress from fear of eviction.	Regularization of each household's tenure and provision for piped water, sanitation and storm and surface drains.	Local government working with community to provide basic infrastructure and services and incorporation into 'official city'.	Support for incorporating illegal subdivisions and for providing tenure to squatter households.	
Nutritional deficiencies and low income.	Reduce intestinal worm burden and worm transmission. Support for income generating work within the house.	Food supplements/meals or community kitchens. If land is available, support food production.	Support for local enterprises and appropriate nutrition programmes.	Structural reforms, funds for nutrition programmes and other measures to improve poorer groups' real incomes.
No or inadequate access to curative/ preventive health care and advice.	Widespread availability of simple primer on first aid and health in the home plus home visits to promote its use.	Primary health care centre; emphasis on child and maternal health, preventive health and support for community action and for community volunteers.	Small hospital (first referral level) and resources and training to support lower level services and volunteers.	Technical and financial support for nationwide system of hospitals and health care centres. Preventive health campaigns (eg immunization) and nationwide availability of drugs and equipment. Set up training system for paramedics and community health workers. Provide guidelines for setting up emergency services and planning and risk minimization in risk prone areas to minimize injuries and damage if disaster occurs.
No provision for emergency life saving services in event of injury or serious illness.	As above, backed by educational programmes on minimizing risks.	Basic equipment (eg stretchers, first aid) available at all times. Community volunteers with basic training on call and arrangements for rapid transfer of sick/injured person to hospital. Equipment to rescue/treat those saved from burning houses.	Support for neighbourhood equipment plus organization of training programs for community volunteers. Fire fighting equipment. Contingency plans for emergencies.	
		Discussions with individuals and community organizations about some minimum changes to site layouts to improve emergency vehicle access and create fire breaks.		

Source: Developed from Hardoy, Jorge E and Satterthwaite, David (1987) 'Housing and health', *Cities* vol. 4, no. 3.

enforcement. Major improvements in the quality of many city environments are possible, simply through implementing existing pollution control and occupational health legislation, and giving more attention to making better use of existing infrastructure and equipment – for instance minimizing water losses in piped systems, and giving more attention to repair and maintenance in public service vehicles (whether buses or trucks collecting solid wastes, or trucks which empty latrines and septic tanks). In many cities, air pollution levels can be substantially reduced by ensuring that a few of the largest polluters (a few large industries and thermal power stations) reduce their emissions.

Measures promoting the use of cleaner fuels in households, industries and road vehicles can, over time, reduce concentrations of lead, suspended particulates and sulphur dioxide in the air. Measures taken now to ensure that new industrial and power station investments use, wherever possible, new plant designs which eliminate or minimize wastes also cumulatively build a less polluting industrial sector.

Industrial wastes

Numerous new industrial plant designs eliminate or reduce polluting wastes or recover and re-use process chemicals which were formerly dumped.[61] It is now common knowledge that for most industrial operations, a substantial reduction in pollution is possible for a small fraction of production costs. There are many examples of industries actually reducing costs or increasing profits at the same time as reducing solid and liquid wastes and the emission of air pollutants. Those wastes not amenable to elimination through changes in plant design and operation can often be used as inputs into other industries. Box 5.6 illustrates the benefits which can come from active government involvement in promoting the re-use or recycling of material or its reclamation from wastes. Quite apart from the environmental benefits, the Shanghai Resource Recovery and Utilization Company also generates some 29,000 full-time and many more part-time jobs. Since a large part of reducing resource use and waste is a substitution of labour and skill for capital, conservation can be strongly linked to job creation.

Organic residues from industries are usually among the most bulky of solid wastes and the most serious sources of water pollution (largely through their depletion of water's dissolved oxygen). However, they can be used as feedstock for the manufacture of animal feed, packing material, chemicals and pharmaceuticals, fertilizers, fuel, food and construction materials.[62] Wastes from many agro-processing industries can be valuable feedstock for other industrial operations. For instance, 'bagasse' (sugar cane waste) is commonly used as fuel for the sugar cane mill or an

Box 5.6: Resource recovery and utilization in Shanghai

The Shanghai Municipal Environmental Sanitation Administration serves a 150 square kilometre city (Shanghai) plus 6035 square kilometres of suburbs and rural areas around the city core, with a total population of some 12 million. Since 1957, it has developed into a state complex retrieving materials and marketing the reclaimed products, and now has some 29,000 full-time and many more part-time employees. A network of 502 purchasing stations and 1500 purchasing agents in rural areas acquires material for reclamation or recycling. These agents are paid on commission. Twenty-six integrated recycling centres reclaim or recycle material from industrial and consumer wastes and a network of sales departments and retail shops sell reclaimed products. Among the materials recovered are ferrous and non-ferrous metals, rubber, plastics, paper, rags, cotton, chemical fibre, animal bones, human hair, broken glass, glass bottles, old machine parts, chemical residues and waste oil. The company has subsidiaries specialising in copper refining, precious metal recovery and refining, iron and steel scrap recycling, plastics production, ferrous metal production and oil wastes recycling. Over 3600 people are employed to work directly with factories – for instance advising them on setting up containers for wastes and establishing systems by which the company can collect them.

Source: Gunnerson, C G (1987) *Resource Recovery and Utilization in Shanghai,* UNDP/World Bank Global Programme of Resource Recovery.

ingredient in animal feed or building materials. It can also be used as a feedstock in paper production. The Cuban Research Institute for Sugar Cane By-Products has developed a process which allows bagasse to be turned into high-quality newsprint at a reasonable production cost. This can replace newsprint which many Third World nations import at high cost.[63] A recently developed process allows rice straw to be used as feedstock for a pulp and paper mill without the continuous dumping of polluting 'black liquor' into rivers and streams. The process allows the recovery and re-use of process chemicals, thus reducing operating costs as well as polluting emissions.[64] Central waste treatment plants can often serve many medium sized and small companies which cannot individually afford waste treatment; for instance, a central waste treatment facility has established in Vaniambaddi (near Madras) in India to serve a few dozen tanneries and to recover and properly dispose of chromium salts from tannery wastewaters; the industries pay 75 per cent of the costs with government paying the rest.[65]

AIR POLLUTION

In most cities, much of the air pollution from industries comes from relatively few (and often old) factories or power stations; substantial reductions are possible by improving equipment or adding on pollution-control equipment, or by moving or closing the worst offenders.[66] For instance, in Mexico City's Metropolitan Zone, among the 35,000 industrial emission points, just the paint factories and one oil refinery were responsible for most industrial hydrocarbon emissions while four thermal power stations were responsible for around 30 per cent of sulphur dioxide emissions and cement plants were responsible for most total particulates.[67] New designs for power stations burning coal or heavy oil can greatly reduce the problem of sulphur dioxide emissions and increase the efficiency with which the fuel is converted into useful energy. Some Third World nations might benefit from the use of 'cleaner' technologies as they build or expand their industrial base.

Reducing air pollution from road vehicles is also possible; more efficient engines, mandatory annual checks for all vehicles (so engines are kept properly tuned) and a move to lead-free petrol can reduce the volume of polluting emissions. There may also be scope for promoting better quality fuels which reduce emissions for diesel and two-stroke engines.[68] Increasing taxes on gasoline can promote more fuel-efficient vehicles while providing a valuable revenue source; differential tax rates can be used to promote the use of lead-free petrol by making it cheaper. The widespread availability of lead-free petrol is also essential for vehicles with catalytic converters (which can reduce up to 90 per cent of the emissions of oxides of nitrogen, hydrocarbons and carbon monoxide from automobile exhausts) since these cannot use leaded petrol. Combine such measures with regulations on the use of private vehicles and efficient public transport, and problems of pollution and traffic congestion can be tackled at the same time. This can be achieved without resorting to such expensive measures as new subway systems. A judicious mix of taxes and physical restrictions on private automobiles, improved facilities for the most commonly used forms of transportation (from trains and buses to communal taxis and rickshaws, to bicycles and feet) and better traffic management can reduce congestion and greatly increase the efficiency of the whole transport system at relatively little cost. The Brazilian city of Curitiba greatly improved its transport system by relying on a bus system with exclusive bus lanes on the main transport arteries – and this brought other environmental benefits, including low levels of air pollution, substantially lower levels of per capita fossil fuel use, lower accident rates and a low average for citizens' expenditures on transport (see Box 5.7).

Box 5.7 Public transport and other environmental initiatives in Curitiba, Brazil

Curitiba is best known for its innovative public transport system but this is only one among several initiatives to improve environmental quality and reduce resource use. The improvements in public transport also depended on complementary initiatives in planning and land use management which are rarely included in descriptions of Curitiba's achievements.

The public transport system which has been developed over the last 20 years began with the use of express buses on exclusive bus lanes on axes radiating out of the city centre. These proved much cheaper and less disruptive than conventional metro or light railway systems. Over the years, these axes have been further developed and urban growth has been encouraged along them. There are five main axes, each with a 'trinary' road system. The central road has two exclusive bus lanes in the centre for express buses and is flanked by two local roads. Each side of this central road, one block away, are high capacity, free-flowing, one way roads – one for traffic flowing into the city, the other for traffic out. In the areas adjacent to each axis, land use legislation has encouraged high density residential developments, along with services and commerce. The express buses running along these axes are served by inter-district buses and conventional feeder buses with connections between different buses organized in a series of bus terminals.

With a more decentralized pattern of employment, the central city areas could be pedestrianized and the historic buildings protected from redevelopment. Several main thoroughfares have been closed to traffic and converted into tree-lined walkways. One important complementary action was the municipal government's acquisition of land along or close to the new transport axes, prior to their construction. This allowed the government to organize high density housing programmes close to the transport axes; in all, some 17,000 lower-income families were located close to these.

At present there are 53 kilometres of express lines, 294 kilometres of feeder lines and 167 kilometres of inter-district lines. Buses are colour coded: the express buses are red, inter-district buses are green and the conventional (feeder) buses are yellow. There is full integration between express buses, inter-district buses and conventional (feeder) buses. There are large bus terminals at the end of each of the five express bus lanes where people can transfer to inter-district or feeder buses. One single fare is valid for all buses. Along each express route, smaller bus terminals are located approximately every 1400 metres and are equipped with newspaper stands, public telephones and post office facilities. Here passengers arrive on feeder buses and transfer to the express buses. The latest innovation is the introduction of the 'direct' express bus system, where there are fewer stops and where passengers pay before boarding the buses in special raised tubular stations. These new stations (with platforms at the same height as bus floors) cut boarding and deboarding times; a rapid bus system with 'boarding tubes' can take twice as many passengers per hour. They also take three times as many passengers per hour when compared to a conventional bus operating in a normal street. The boarding tubes also eliminate the need for a crew on the bus to collect fares, which frees up space for more passengers.

Curitiba's public transportation system is used by more than 1.3 million passengers each day. Twenty eight per cent of express bus users previously travelled in their cars. This has meant savings of up to 25 per cent of fuel consumption city-wide. Curitiba's public transportation system is a major reason for the city having one of the lowest levels of ambient air pollution in Brazil. Two further effects of Curitiba's transport policy are also worth noting: one of the lowest accident rates per vehicle in the country; and the savings for inhabitants in expenditure on transport (on average, residents spend only about 10 per cent of their income on transport which is relatively low for Brazil).

Other environmental initiatives in Curitiba include innovative garbage recycling programmes and sewage treatment facilities, a large expansion in parks and green spaces (integrated into a flood prevention and control programme) and the combination of environmental education and day care provision in the low-income *favelas* (squatter settlements). The 'garbage that is not garbage' recycling programme encourages city residents to separate organic and inorganic garbage. Once a week, a 'garbage that is not garbage' lorry collects the materials which households have sorted. Over 70 per cent of the community now participates in the programme and its success is largely due to a city-wide environmental education programme which highlights the benefits of recycling. Since its inception, some 13,000 tonnes of garbage have been recycled; just its paper recycling saves the equivalent of 1200 trees a day. Apart from the environmental benefits, this recycling programme has generated other positive side effects, including support for social programmes since the income earned through the sale of the recyclable garbage is reinvested in local social programmes.

The 'purchase of garbage' programme is run in the *favela*. Since there was no service to collect household garbage (and very often the settlements lack access roads to permit garbage trucks to enter), the residents would simply dump their garbage in open air pits or vacant plots. *Favelas* residents can now 'sell' their bags of garbage for bus fares and agricultural and dairy produce. This programme has led to a considerable decrease in city litter and has helped to improve the quality of life of the urban poor. The payment to the communities through bus fares and food for garbage is equivalent to the municipality paying a private company to collect the garbage. More than 22,000 families are involved in 52 communities.

Source: Rabinovitch, Jonas (1992) 'Curitiba: towards sustainable urban development', *Environment and Urbanization* vol. 4, no. 2.

Many of the more modern and rapidly expanding industries such as electronics do not require the large consumption of natural resources and lack the potential contribution to air, water and land pollution of, say, the steel or pulp and paper industry;[69] this has helped cut industrial emissions in Europe and North America and may also do so in the more wealthy and industrialized Third World nations. In addition, in many Third World cities, a large and increasing proportion of the labour force work in service jobs which also imply fewer problems with pollution and heavy resource consumption.

THE INSTITUTIONAL CONSTRAINTS

National level

The initiatives outlined earlier in this chapter represent a very incomplete list; many more techniques could be described which also cut pollution and wastes and reduce resource use. But it is not the technical capacity to greatly reduce pollution that is in doubt but the political will and institutional capacity to act effectively.

Various political and institutional factors inhibit appropriate environmental action. On industrial pollution control, perhaps the most serious is governments' over-riding concern to expand industrial production and increase the exploitation of natural resources (which includes building the infrastructure that both need). Pressing problems with debt repayment makes increased exports a high priority. In many nations, this means increasing the export of natural resources, since either their industry cannot compete on world markets or the largest potential markets (Europe, North America, Japan) have protectionist barriers around them. The pressure on governments to increase exports and create more jobs inhibits longer-term considerations about the environmental consequences of the developments they sanction.

If a government's main concerns are the survival of the national economy and, no doubt, its own survival, and its priority is avoiding additional unemployment, new environmental legislation or implementing existing legislation will not be a high priority. The fear that enforcing pollution controls creates unemployment is still strong even if it has been overstated. In the long term, government policies to promote waste minimization and the recovery and re-use or recycling of wastes from domestic, commercial and industrial wastes are likely to lead to a net gain in employment. But many nations do have problems with a few 'dirty' industries whose survival may be threatened by more stringent pollution standards or the enforcement of existing standards.

There is also the problem of generating foreign exchange to pay for the import of new 'clean' technologies – whether for industrial production, water purification, power generation or engines for motor vehicles. Few Third World nations have sufficiently sophisticated or diverse capital goods industries to produce many of these new technologies so most new 'add-on' pollution control equipment or 'clean' technologies will have to be imported. Foreign exchange is usually very limited and in most nations, machinery and equipment already account for between a quarter and a third of all merchandise imports.[70] In virtually all nations, numerous commodities will be judged to be higher priority than such equipment.

Another set of problems arise because of cumbersome or inappropriate regulatory structures. Many governments in the Third World have drawn on examples from Northern nations which are rarely the most appropriate to their own particular circumstances. For instance, a review of US waste management technology and its relevance to the Third World noted that the main priorities for waste management should be waste reduction, then ways of recovering materials or using them (ie waste separation and concentration, waste exchange and energy and material recovery), *then* waste treatment or incineration and, as the last resort, secure landfill disposal.[71] Most regulatory structures promote the reverse. This review also noted the difficulties in developing a regulatory framework which promoted waste reduction.[72]

In theory, where power stations, mines and industries are owned and run by public agencies, good environmental performance should be easy to achieve. In practice, publicly owned factories and power stations are often among the worst polluters. In many Latin American and some Asian countries, some of the potentially most polluting industries such as basic metal or petroleum refining industries are either in government hands or in the hands of quasi-government entities.[73] Government agencies or parastatals own many polluting industries in sub-Saharan Africa. Government owned sewage and drainage systems and solid waste sites are often serious polluters and contravene environmental legislation.[74]

Finally, there is again the problem of so many unrepresentative governments. Improving urban environments and protecting rural resources (and rural inhabitants) from city-generated pollutants requires governments to identify, define and allocate costs and ensure their collection among different producers and consumers. This means charging producers and consumers for the cost of providing basic services and facilities (like water, drains, and disposal sites), strongly penalizing individuals or companies who dispose of their wastes in ways that affect others or damage the environment, and enforcing occupational health standards. At present, in many Third World nations, most of the benefits of government investment in basic services and facilities go to richer households and businesses who are often paying well below real costs. Meanwhile, as described in an earlier section, most of the costs fall on poorer groups in the form of polluted water, air and land sites, and inadequate or no public provision of basic services.[75]

The most effective check on this misallocation of resources is a representative form of government which includes sufficient power, resources and trained personnel at city/municipal level to ensure basic services are provided, environmental legislation enforced and a legal system exists which allows rapid redress for those who lose out. The last 15 years have seen most Third World governments set up national environmental agencies. An increasing number of examples can be given where major industries were fined for contravening government pollution standards. But few governments have set up the institutional structure to implement a sustained and effective environmental policy. While over 100 nations have national environmental agencies of one kind or another, many are small, weak institutions – one-person offices or inter-agency coordinating committees with no independent authority.[76] Others are better staffed but find that law courts are not prepared to back their actions, or that penalties for industries contravening regulations are so small as to provide little deterrent. Ten years ago, two specialists commented that the enforcement of environmental regulations in the Third World

> 'is a relatively haphazard process, depending heavily on the political power of those who violate the regulations and on the extent to which the government is under pressure to take action to stop pollution and environmental degradation. Enforcement is arbitrary at times, in ways which appear to have more to do with political considerations than concern with the environment'.[77]

There is little evidence of much change in this, over the last decade. A report in 1991 noted that most existing environmental regulations in Third World countries are usually replicas of past regulations in the North and 'have little grounding in local realities and cultures and therefore are largely unenforceable', and that 'the agencies responsible for their enforcement are rarely given the authority and the means for enforcement'.[78]

Many examples of governments acting on environmental problems in Third World nations (as in the North) owe much to well-organized citizen pressure and usually occur in societies with representative forms of government. But government action usually consists of *ad hoc* responses to specific local pressures such as a group of fishermen complaining about industrial effluent damaging their livelihood, or a group of farmers or citizens complaining about the damage to their homes or farms from pollution coming from one particular plant or industrial complex. This is more common than coherent, sustained programmes of incentives, regulations and enforcement. One example of this *ad hoc* response comes from Taiwan where villagers living near an industrial zone in the south forced local companies to pay around US$35 million compensation for the damage caused by petrochemical plants' wastewaters to coastal areas and fishing grounds. But the residents had to invade the industrial zone and force the plants to close down. They had also threatened to cut the supplies of coal to local power plants which would have meant power cuts in the heavily industrialized south.[79]

City level

Virtually all the measures outlined to improve environmental health conditions and to tackle city-wide pollution depend on forms of 'better local practice'. These in turn depend on competent city and (for large cities or metropolitan areas) sub-city (municipal/borough/district) government. One returns to the fact that most governments at these levels lack the trained personnel and the financial base and autonomy to provide necessary investments, services and pollution control. This weakness of city governments also makes other changes difficult to implement – from the enforcement of environmental legislation to the efficient collection of garbage, management of solid waste sites and improvement of traffic management. As Carl Bartone at the World Bank has commented, 'the most urgent need is to strengthen (Third World) waste management institutions at the municipal level, to improve their financial base, and then to introduce appropriate waste management technologies – in that order of priority.'[80]

City governments in Africa, Asia and Latin America often have one hundredth or (at their most extreme) one thousandth of the revenue per capita available to most city or municipal governments in Europe. Yet their range of responsibilities is often comparable. The range of tasks for which city or sub-city levels of government are responsible vary considerably from nation to nation. But in virtually all, they include many tasks which are central to a healthy environment: the regulation of building and land use and of production (including pollution control); the provision and maintenance of systems to supply water, sanitation and garbage collection and its disposal. Most have major responsibilities for traffic management, emergency services, streets and street lighting. Health care and schools are usually local responsibilities. Where some of these are the responsibility of central government agencies or contracted to private companies, local governments usually have important supervisory roles. Most of these responsibilities are met inadequately, if at all. It is common for local government budgets to have the equivalent of US$20–50 per person per year with virtually all of it being spent on recurrent expenditures; in some of the poorer Third World nations, municipal governments have the equivalent of only a few US dollars per capita per year. It is rare for local government to have any significant capacity for investment in expanding or extending infrastructure and services.

In addition, in many cities, rapid population growth means that the already large deficits in terms of the number of people lacking piped water, sanitation, garbage collection, schools, health care and emergency services also grow rapidly. In cities made up of different local government areas, it is generally the poorest and weakest local governments on the urban periphery which have the most rapid growth in population. In most cities, there are few (if any) mechanisms to channel funding from richer to poorer local government units.

One of the most critical roles of city and municipal government is providing the institutional means to ensure that the combination of all sectoral policies and actions achieves a balance between social, economic and environmental goals. To take only one example, the attitudes and policies of governments on the use of city resources and wastes is probably the most important factor in achieving such a balance. Dr Furedy has noted that

> 'those who make decisions about formal recycling projects are usually not well informed about existing informal practices of waste recovery and recycling in their city and the possible implications of new interventions. Those directly involved (waste gatherers, traders and manufacturers) and those concerned about their health (community workers and informal groups) are rarely listened to.'[81]

Most urban authorities regard waste pickers and many other waste-related activities as illegal or unhygienic. Some actively seek to suppress and control such activities. Many tolerate it (within limits) since they have little alternative to offer those whose livelihoods depend on this work. Some have recognized that such informal processes can be part of their overall waste management and waste minimization policy. But rarely do they appreciate the extent of the economic, social and environmental advantages – or the kinds of public provision and support which retain the economic and resource advantages while reducing health risks and improving incomes for the poorer groups engaged in it. The extent of recycling within an city is also more driven by sectoral concerns than by a broader consensus of what is best done.[82]

This obstacle of weak, ineffective and unrepresentative city governments is not easily overcome. The acquisition by local governments of the power to raise substantial funding, the authority to direct private investments (and control pollution) and the financial base to meet their responsibilities for the provision of infrastructure and services are intensely political issues. Powerful and usually well-organized vested interests oppose such changes – as they did in Europe and North America little more than a century ago – although other interests favour change. Indeed, in New York (among other cities) it took repeated cholera epidemics and new powers for municipal authorities before opposition to such basic investments could be overcome.[83] In London, the proponents of piped water supplies and improved sanitation and garbage collection in the early nineteenth century were ridiculed by many people in government and by the most influential newspapers.[84]

The current role of aid agencies

Few aid agencies give much attention to cities' environmental problems – especially the problems which impact most on the health and livelihoods of poorer groups. Table 5.2 shows the low priority given by the major multilateral agencies to those interventions which are likely to have the largest impact on improving the environment for the poor majority – water supply and sanitation, the improvement of shelter for poorer groups, primary health care (including the control of disease vectors) and basic education. Only in one of the multilateral programmes listed in Table 5.2 did these receive more than 20 per cent of total commitments and in many, they received less than 10 per cent. Among multilateral agencies, UNICEF is an exception since most of its funds to urban projects either seek to improve environmental health (water, sanitation and other basic services), or protect poorer groups from biological pathogens (for instance immunization programmes), or provide the possibility of treatment for illnesses and injuries (community/family based health services and increasing the availability of oral rehydration salts to treat diarrhoeal diseases).

Most of the bilateral agencies give a low priority in urban (and rural) areas to water supply, sanitation, the control of disease vectors, primary health care and improving shelter conditions for poorer groups. The low priority given to primary health care among both multilateral and bilateral agencies is puzzling, given most agencies' endorsement in the late 1970s of its importance.

Most aid agencies also give little or no support to enhancing the capacity of city or municipal governments in the Third World in the implementation of other interventions which could help improve city environments such as: improved solid waste collection and disposal; more effective pollution control; and land management programmes which ensure a better match between urban needs (especially for children's play and recreation) and the protection of ecological resources.

Table 5.2 Proportion of multilateral agencies' total commitments to environmental health-related projects 1980–1989

Agency	Proportion of total project commitments to: Shelter related	Water and sanitation	Primary health care	Basic education	% of total commitment
Aid (concessional loans)					
International Development					
Association • Africa	1.5	2.8	1.9	3.5	9.7
• Asia	1.8	4.3	2.6	1.7	10.4
• Latin America	3.0	3.9	–	2.6	9.6
African Development Bank+	0.7	10.5	2.2	2.4	15.9
Asian Development Fund+	1.4	1.3	1.3	0.5	4.4
Inter-American Development Bank	3.9	15.0	1.2	3.1	23.1
Non concessional loans					
International Bank for					
Reconstruction and Development					
• Africa	2.6	8.4	0.7	1.0	12.7
• Asia	2.8	2.7	0.6	0.5	6.6
• Latin America	3.7	4.9	0.9	0.8	10.3
African Development Bank+	0.3	7.5	0.3	0.3	5.5
Asian Development Bank+	2.4	6.4	1.4	–	10.3
Inter-American Development Bank	1.8	5.1	1.7	0.4	7.5

+ Figures for 1980–88, not 1980–89.

NB: Water and sanitation are part of primary health care so the column here headed primary health care includes components other than water and sanitation. Basic education is taken to include primary education and literacy programmes. Shelter related commitments include slum and squatter upgrading, serviced site schemes, core housing schemes, housing finance and community development projects which include housing improvement. Water and sanitation includes drainage projects which were to improve drainage in low-income residential areas but does not include water projects whose primary goal was improved water supply for industry.

Source: IIED Human Settlements Programme aid flows and aid project database[85]

Most aid agencies and development banks give a higher proportion of their funds to large urban infrastructure projects such as ports, power stations (and electrification), public transport, hospitals and secondary or higher education institutions (virtually all of which are located in urban areas). For many bilateral agency projects, this is as much to do with promoting their exports and contracts for their own companies as to any explicit policy to improve conditions in urban areas. For instance, public transport systems have received substantial support in some of the larger cities but those sponsored by bilateral agencies tend to mean large civil construction contracts for companies from the donor nation. Third World cities are littered with projects or capital goods which proved ineffective or inappropriate: buses, garbage trucks and water treatment plants which could not be maintained; waste incineration or composting plants which do not work or which never produced the anticipated cost-savings; and sophisticated metro systems which do not serve most of the poor areas of the city and whose revenues from fares do not even cover their operating costs, let alone the bill for their construction.[86] An analysis of donor funded urban projects in the late 1980s found that many were to rehabilitate infrastructure or replace capital goods which had fallen into disrepair – and which had been funded by donor agencies, some years previously.[87]

Few aid agencies have a coherent policy for the support they provide to urban development. Decisions about urban projects are made on an *ad hoc* basis with little attention as to how particular projects or investments fit within a long-term programme of developing the capacity and competence of recipient governments to address environmental problems. There is little coordination between donors to ensure coherence between all the projects funded by different donors – although this may reflect many Third World governments' reluctance to set up the administrative and managerial structure to promote a more coherent policy. It is rare for donor agencies to support projects or programmes to build urban governments' institutional capacity so that they can identify and act on environmental problems. Over the last three decades, as most Third World countries urbanized rapidly, very little attention was given by donor agencies (or by Third World governments) to ensuring that city and municipal authorities acquired the power, skills and resources to manage this rapid growth.

There is some evidence of a change in attitude among many donors and a change in emphasis by some. One example is the World Bank which began a programme of support to urban projects in 1972 and, although it never represented a large percentage of total lending, it came to represent the largest single programme of donor support for urban projects. But it became evident that the funds available to the World Bank and to other development assistance agencies prepared to support urban development, were small in relation to need. For instance, despite the fact that during the 1980s, the World Bank's loan commitments to urban shelter, infrastructure and services projects in Latin America were much the largest commitments of any agency to the region, these were estimated to represent little more than 2 per cent of the total capital investments by sub-national governments in the region[88] – and despite this, urban investments in the region still failed to keep up with urban growth.

The fact that funds made available by donor agencies are so small in relation to needs has encouraged some of the largest agencies to move away from supporting urban projects to supporting a strengthening in the capacity of city and municipal governments to invest in and manage urban development. This is most evident in the urban lending of the World Bank over the last decade when a high proportion of its loans to urban development went to help strengthen the institutional and financial capacity of specific city governments, or to institutions which support this level of government (for instance municipal banks or development funds or infrastructure funds). Although the World Bank, the Inter-American Development Bank and a few other agencies have long given some support to building institutional capacity, only in the last few years has it become common for support to be provided specifically to institution building, training in urban management, local government finance and urban planning. The Urban Management Programme, a joint initiative of UNDP, the World Bank and the United Nations Centre for Human Settlements, is also intended to complement this by providing technical assistance.

But building the capacity, competence and representative nature of urban government is only one part of an effective environmental agenda. The other is support for community and/or neighbourhood initiatives in low-income settlements to address their most pressing environmental problems. There are hundreds of small, innovative urban projects run or funded by international private voluntary organizations to improve water supplies, sanitation, drainage and housing conditions and to provide preventive and curative health care in low-income urban communities – for instance by MISEREOR (Germany), by the British, Dutch and Norwegian Save the Children Funds, the World Council of Churches, Homeless International and SELAVIP. Many private voluntary organizations now have annual budgets exceeding US$10 million a year and also receive funding from official government bilateral aid programmes. Some channel much of their support, whenever possible, through local or national NGOs. So, on occasion, have the large official donors – for instance, the World Bank support to FUNDASAL in El Salvador and the support of the Swedish International Development Authority to FUPROVI in Costa Rica – both innovative NGOs working to improve housing conditions and basic services for low-income households with a strong emphasis on participatory working methods. UNICEF has also channelled support through local NGOs in many of its urban basic services projects.[89]

It is not possible to assess precisely the scale of such support and its impact but in most major cities it is certainly too small to make a significant impact; at best, there are successful programmes in a few of the hundreds of low-income settlements in a large city. There are also many large cities and thousands of smaller urban centres where no international agency is working. But the last 30 years have produced many precedents which show effective, local solutions in which local NGOs had a central role. There are numerous examples of innovative, participatory interventions[90] – often more cost effective and more able to reach the poorest groups than official government projects.[91] What is lacking, both among the private voluntary organizations and the larger official aid programmes is any realistic idea of how to *multiply* tenfold or a hundredfold the number of communities or neighbourhoods in which participatory action programmes are receiving support. It is no longer adequate for international agencies to hold up a few examples of successful projects when there are hundreds of thousands of neighbourhoods or districts lacking basic infrastructure and services.

In many of the larger Third World cities, there are hundreds of squatter settlements; in the absence of government capacity to deliver and maintain improved infrastructure and services, and support other actions to improve environmental health, support is needed in each for neighbourhood level actions.

No official bilateral or multilateral aid agency that we know has begun to explore how it can channel technical and financial support to hundreds of neighbourhood level actions where the inhabitants and their organizations have any significant influence over what is funded. Most decisions about what is funded remain centralized in the international agency. Most international agencies retain cumbersome procedures through which applications for (even minimal) funding has to go; this means long delays before a particular neighbourhood knows whether it can go ahead with an initiative it has planned. Each international agency also has its own particular criteria for what can be funded, which may not match the priorities in different neighbourhoods. In addition, few funding agencies are prepared to fund the salaries of community organizers and of the staff of local NGOs to whom they turn for support.

Most international funding agencies also fail to appreciate the need to support a constant process in most low-income neighbourhoods. It is not so much that large amounts of funding are needed in each low income settlement but that a constant flow of support is needed, so that each action can build on the experience of the previous one. Initiating a neighbourhood programme in which the inhabitants are fully involved and which works in ways which best suit local circumstances (which have to respect, for instance, the very limited amounts of free time that most poor people have) often takes a long time. But once a momentum has been built up, one successful community-based action (for instance the construction and running of a mother and child centre) often leads to another and then another. Most poor neighbourhoods have a multiplicity of environmental problems which have to be addressed. In addition, their capacity to work together develops which also allows more complex and ambitious actions to be undertaken. Support is much needed for this continuous process by which the inhabitants of a particular neighbourhood develop their capacity to work together and to negotiate with other agents (for instance the municipal authorities and state or national government agencies). But most international funding agencies impose time limits on their support to a particular community – or will only support one project (or one particular type of project) – and assume that their role ceases when the project is completed. Almost none have understood that building effective community responses to a lack of piped water, sanitation, drainage, paved roads, street lighting, schools, health care, child care, play facilities... is a long-term process over which the inhabitants themselves must have influence and which involves recurrent costs. Virtually all aid agencies seek to be participatory. But in most instances, there is very little possibility for those who are meant to receive aid to influence these agencies' priorities, not only in terms of what funds they might receive and for what activities, but also the way funds are provided (including the conditions attached to them). New channels must be found, if aid is to be effective in supporting a vast diversity of initiatives at neighbourhood level, to permit low-income groups and the community, or neighbourhood associations they form, to address their environmental priorities.

6

Sustainable development and cities

INTRODUCTION

Previous chapters have concentrated on environmental problems in Third World cities in terms of their impact on human health (including well-being) and on natural resources. This chapter considers how these environmental problems and the policies to address them fit within a more general debate about sustainable development. In doing so, it must also consider resource use and waste generation in cities in the North.

Although there is a large, diverse and rapidly growing body of literature about 'sustainable development', only a small proportion of this literature considers sustainable development with regard to cities (or to urban systems).[1] This is perhaps surprising, given that it is within cities that a considerable (and growing) proportion of the world's population live, and a much higher proportion of all resource use and waste generation is concentrated. Worldwide, urban-based producers and consumers account for most fossil fuel and other non-renewable resource consumption, and most greenhouse gas emissions, because of the concentration of the world's industries and of middle- and upper-income households in urban centres. Urban plans, building and planning norms, and codes and regulations in use (and the extent to which they are implemented) influence the energy and resource intensity of both production and consumption in cities. Urban policies and plans and the influence of official rules and regulations on buildings and land developments will have a central role in any national strategy which promotes sustainable development, and city and municipal governments will be important agents in any successful strategy.

It is clear that many current global trends (including those associated with cities) are neither sustainable nor contributing to development. In the South, widespread poverty exists and four decades of 'development planning' have failed to substantially lessen the proportion of the population living with their basic needs unmet – and there are worrying trends in terms of unsustainable levels of use for some resources too (for instance through deforestation and soil erosion). In the North, the problem centres on the scale of resource use, waste, pollution and greenhouse gas emission – although even in richer countries, there are also millions of people whose development needs are not met. While meeting the needs of poorer groups in both the North and the South need not imply an unsustainable level of resource use, it is clear that extending the levels of resource consumption and waste generation currently enjoyed by the rich minority to an increasing proportion of the world's population almost certainly does.[2]

SUSTAINABLE DEVELOPMENT

The term 'sustainable development' brings together two strands of thought about the management of human activities – one concentrating on development goals, the other on controlling or limiting the harmful impacts of human activities on the environment. Although the origins of a concern for both the environment and development go back several decades, this concern was made more explicit, and the use of the term 'sustainable development' promoted, by *Our Common Future*, the Report of the World Commission on Environment and Development (also known as the Brundtland Commission), published in 1987. In one of the most widely quoted definitions of the goal of sustainable development, the report states that we must meet 'the needs of the present generation without compromising the ability of future generations to meet their own needs'.[3]

In the broadest sense, most discussions about sustainable development fall within this definition, although different groups chose to emphasise different aspects. The literature on sustainable development has grown so rapidly that already there are at least 80 different definitions of sustainable development or some part of it.[4] Within these definitions are many different understandings of what is meant by the words development and sustainable.

Most discussions on sustainable development (and most literature on the subject) concentrate on ecological sustainability. Indeed, the objections of many governments and NGOs from the South to the agenda for the Earth Summit (the UN Conference on Environment and Development) in Rio de Janeiro in June 1992 centred on the low priority given to meeting social and economic development goals; discussions which centred on biodiversity, control over deforestation and limits to greenhouse gas emissions had sustainability, not development, as their central goal.

Similarly, many authors who discuss what they term 'sustainable development' do not include a discussion of 'development goals' at all.

Their concerns are with sustainability, not sustainable development. Understanding the roots of this stress on sustainability over development is central to a concern for sustainable development and cities, since it has important implications for all urban policies. For cities, a stress only on sustainability would imply large investments in reducing the use of fossil fuels (especially coal), decreasing the throughput of freshwater and non-renewable resources, and controlling air and water pollution. It might include draconian measures to prevent people moving to urban centres. Such policies would, in general, do little for poorer groups and in many instances may exacerbate their problems.

Before discussing sustainable development and cities, it is worth considering the different interpretations given to sustainability and how these arose.

HOW A CONCERN FOR SUSTAINABILITY AROSE

It is in mapping the growth in concern for 'sustainability' over the last 20 years that the widely diverging opinions as to what it means and how it should be applied become evident. Among the first considerations of the possible links between global economic growth and natural resource scarcity was the report *Limits to Growth* published by the Club of Rome in 1972.[5] Deriving from a research project initiated in 1968, a group of scientists explored a 'world model' looking in particular at the viability of continued growth. Concluding that capital investment must at some point be restricted, they argue that continuing development can concentrate on 'the most satisfying activities...education, art, music, religion, basic scientific research, athletics, and social interactions..'(p.175). The importance of the links between environment and development was stressed in the book *Only One Earth* by Barbara Ward and Rene Dubos[6] also published in 1972. Written for a popular audience, the book describes the concerns that had led to the 1972 United Nations Conference on the Human Environment in Stockholm. This is one of the first books in which discussions about natural resource use and pollution are linked to those on development. It drew together care for the environment and a concern for meeting human needs and eliminating poverty. The book considers the possibilities for, and the problems associated with, economic growth, and was also one of the first works to stress that present human needs must be met without compromising the needs of future generations. The definition of sustainable development used by *Our Common Future* in 1987 certainly draws from this much earlier book which states that the 'charge of the United Nations to the (Stockholm) Conference was to clearly define what should be done to maintain the earth as a place suitable for human life not only now, but also for future generations' (p. 25).

The second half of the 1970s and first half of the 1980s saw an increased awareness of the finite nature of certain non-renewable resources worldwide and the vulnerability of global life support systems to pollution arising from human activities.[7] Although these had been identified as potential problems some years previously, they were perceived as uncertain threats. If the concerns about environment and development in the late 1980s and early 1990s are compared to those in the mid-1970s, there are at least three changes in emphasis. The first is the much increased concern about damage arising from human activities to global natural systems; the depletion of the stratospheric ozone layer and atmospheric warming are now perceived as far more serious threats to sustainability than was the case in the early 1970s. The second is the concern about the depletion of non-renewable mineral resources which has to some extent receded, while the concern about the finite nature of many renewable resources (especially fertile soil and freshwater resources) has increased. The third is the wider acceptance among many environmentalists of the need for economic growth within many nations and regions (especially the poorest ones) to provide the economic base to allow needs to be met. Rather than recommending 'no growth', it has become more common to hear reference to 'green growth', that is economic growth which also seeks to minimize ecological damage.

The increasing interest in sustainable development shown by governments and inter-governmental bodies was fuelled by the growing popular concern about the environmental implications of human activities. Such concerns first became important political issues in the 1960s, for example, in the protests by citizens and consumer groups in the North as to the environmental damage done by intensive farming, industrial production and high-consumption lifestyles. The potential dangers arising from the accidental release of radioactive materials by nuclear (fission) power stations and activities associated with nuclear power (for instance the wastes generated, the facilities needed for producing and reprocessing the fuel and the links between the nuclear industry and nuclear weapons) also spurred the growth of the environment movement. Oil price rises in the 1970s made the public (and governments) aware of the possible impact of global natural resource scarcity, even if the price rises were not a result of scarcity. The 'environment movement' gradually widened its focus and its initial concentration on risks to the human environment in the richer industrialized nations and began to look at associated problems in the South.

The concern for the environment in the South soon developed clear links with the concern for development – for instance in identifying the link between soil erosion and the inadequate size of poorer groups' land holdings, and the link between community impoverishment and the appropriation by powerful vested interests of land and forest resources which had previously been common (or open access) property.[8] In the Third World, NGOs and local community based organizations became more active on environmental issues both at project level (for instance organizing opposition to a dam or to indiscriminate logging) and at national level (lobbying their governments for changes in legislation and its enforcement).[9] Concern for the environment also helped forge links between groups in the North and South. International networks are bringing political pressures to bear on multinational companies, industrial concerns and inter-governmental agencies (including the largest development assistance agencies and development banks) to give more consideration to the environmental impacts of their activities.

THE MEANING OF 'SUSTAINABILITY'

As with the term 'sustainable development', sustainability has been given many different meanings. Sustainability is generally used to contrast with a lack of sustainability which is seen as something which breaks down or does not continue. In some cases, sustainability is used simply to mean that the long-term result of some action or set of actions is consistent with desired outcomes.

There is also some confusion as to what is to be sustained, that is, to what the criteria of 'sustainability' should be applied. This is particularly apparent in respect of two areas: first, to what sectors does it apply (ecological, social or economic?); and second, at what scale (local projects, cities, nations, or the sum of all activities globally?). In so far as these areas can be discussed separately, the paragraphs below focus primarily on the first of these areas – although some consideration is given to the issue of scale.

The term 'sustainable' is most widely used in reference to ecological sustainability, that is in terms of the natural resources used either in a specific project or broader programme of human activities. The use of the term is premised on the understanding that natural resources are necessary to economic development but there are finite limits in their supply. Overstepping these finite limits may result in one of three kinds of environmental degradation:

- depletion, a reduction in the quality and/or quantity of a resource used in consumption/production activities;
- pollution, or overuse of the waste-absorbing capacity of the environment which may limit its value in breaking down such waste; and
- reduction in biodiversity, ie a loss of some types of resource all together.[10]

Projects or other activities which are judged to be sustainable in this ecological sense generally meet one or more of any three criteria:

- The activity does not damage natural resources significantly so that the same quantity and quality of such resources are available for further use as if the project had never happened.
- The activity does damage some natural resources but it has positive impacts on other natural resources such that the net effect (when assessed on some common scale) is judged to be resource neutral.
- The activity does not damage the natural resources required for completing the activity itself.

In the preparations for the Earth Summit, as an increasing number of UN agencies, bilateral aid agencies and other international organizations began to discuss 'sustainable development' the ambiguity in the term became increasingly apparent. Among many aid/development assistance agencies, achieving sustainability is about making their projects continue to operate and meet development objectives when these agencies' external support is cut off at the 'end of the project'. In this sense, 'sustainability' is far more about operation and maintenance (or 'institutional and managerial sustainability') than about any concept of ecological sustainability. It also gives little or no consideration as to whether the sum of all the 'sustainable' projects would prove sustainable in an ecological sense. In some cases, project sustainability and project success are used almost interchangeably.[11] Thus, at the level of aid-funded projects, the term sustainable development has come to have two different meanings – a project which secures development objectives with a sustainable use of natural resources both for productive inputs and waste assimilation; *and* a project which secures development objectives which will continue without outside support once the initial project finishes. In some cases, these judgements are applied to sets of projects (or other activities) rather than to each specific case. In many cases, these conditions are theoretical rather than practically applied. Examples of some different definitions are given in Box 6.1

A further extension of the term 'sustainability' has been its use in relation to social relations and customs. Some of the literature about sustainable development discusses 'social sustainability', 'cultural sustainability' and 'political sustainability'. There is no consensus as to what these terms mean. For instance, some consider social sustainability as the social pre-conditions for sustainable development while others imply that it is the need to sustain specific social structures.

We choose to use the concept of sustainability *only* in regard to ecological sustainability, both because of the lack of consensus as to what

Box 6.1 Definitions of sustainability

The *World Conservation Strategy* (published in 1980) outlines what might be characterised as the ecological approach to sustainable development. It outlines three objectives regarded as necessary for living resource conservation: the maintenance of essential ecological processes and life-support systems; the preservation of genetic diversity; and the sustainable utilisation of species and ecosystems.[12] The achievement of sustainable development requires the adoption of these objectives.

The authors of *Blueprint for a Green Economy* considers that 'future generations should be compensated for reductions in the endowments of resources brought about by the actions of present generations.'[13] The book suggests that one generation should leave the next generation a stock of assets at least as great as that they inherited themselves. The authors note that there are two possible interpretations of this condition; the first aggregates all types of assets, the second differentiates between assets which are 'natural' and those which are not, arguing that it is environmental (or natural) assets which are critical in securing sustainability. In general, the authors favour the latter interpretation.

Safe minimum standards stress that the degree of diversity within the total stock of environmental assets is important as well as total quantity of resources.[14] However, the safe minimum standard for any particular aspect of the environment is difficult to define and it is not always clear to what the criteria should be applied. For instance, does sustainability require the conservation of a specific type of forest and/or forest landscape, a capacity to sustain biomass production, or simply a continuing ability to grow trees?[15]

The concept of 'sustainability' is also used in reference to specific kinds of human activity – for instance for discussions of 'sustainable industrial development' or 'sustainable agricultural development'. Conway suggests that agricultural sustainability should be defined as the ability to maintain agricultural productivity, whether of a field or farm or nation, in the face of stress or shock.[16] There are several aspects to this definition which need highlighting. First, sustainability is no longer considered only in an environmental or ecological context; there may be other threats to sustainability. Second, sustainability is only one of four criteria used to judge agricultural development – the others being productivity, stability and equity. A third point to note is a new emphasis on possible trade-offs between the different objectives.[17]

sustainability might mean in other contexts and because we believe the term has been inappropriately applied. Meeting economic, social and political goals obviously has to be sustainable in an ecological sense since human life and well-being depend on this. Sustaining societies or cultures is more ambiguous. Indeed, the achievement of many social, economic and political development goals requires fundamental changes to social structures including changes to government institutions and, in many instances, to the distribution of assets and income. This can hardly be equated with 'social sustainability'.

Social sustainability suggests that institutions, customary behaviour, and relationships should be sustained. Such structures are fundamentally different from the species and ecosystems which are the concern of sustainability when used in an ecological sense. An examination of history shows both the diversity of culture and the transient or changing nature of social structures. There are many different ways through which the human species meets its emotional, physiological and social needs. It is in this ecological sense that the Brundtland definition can be interpreted, the constraint through which present generations can endanger future generations is through their use of environmental resources. 'Sustainable global development requires...lifestyles within the planet's ecological means', but equally 'sustainable development is not a fixed state of harmony but rather a process of change...'. Indeed, the human species is remarkable for its ability to adapt to changing (often stressful) circumstances. The impact of human activities on other species and ecosystems has been so damaging just because they have a limited ability to adapt.

Sustainability is in danger of being used in a pejorative sense as it moves from being a term used in an ecological context to a general measure of 'successfulness'. Many characteristics of modern society which are judged as social evils (high crime rates, widespread drug and alcohol abuse and violence, rising homelessness...) do not threaten the sustainability of the human species. Indeed, it is the poverty of such a high proportion of the world's population which has helped *limit* the threat to ecological unsustainability; if the two billion poorest people in the world (the vast majority of whom are in the Third World) acquire levels of consumption comparable to those which are common in the North, the scale of resource use, waste generation and greenhouse gas emissions worldwide would increase manyfold. It may even be that some of the reluctance of the nations in the North to address structural issues which limit economic growth in the South is linked to the fact that keeping the South poor also keeps down greenhouse gas emissions.

There is no justification in seeking to impose a set of sustainability criteria inappropriately transferred from ecological systems to social systems. When judged by the length of time for which they sustained, some of the most 'successful' societies were also among the most exploitative, where the abuse of human rights was greatest. These are not societies we would want to 'sustain'. Within the goals of development are strong and explicit social objectives but most demand social change, not 'sustainability' in the sense of 'keeping them going continuously'.

Discussions on 'social sustainability' when defined as the social conditions necessary to support environmental sustainability are valuable in so far as they stress that natural resources are used within a social context and it is the rules and values associated with this context that determine both the distribution of resources within the present generation, and between the future generations and the present. Our avoidance of the term is both because it can invite confusion with other interpretations and because it can imply that there is only one way to achieve ecological sustainability, whereas there are generally a range of possible options.

The social and ecological aspects of human society come together through an understanding that the environment is also a social construct; the way in which we perceive the environment is through a set of social relations and values which influences our actions to the environment.[18] As such, it is also subject to change. Much of what is written about sustainable development is actively trying to change the collective perception of the environment, and our use of it, to favour the sustainable use of natural resources and systems.

The population debate is often one of those areas in which simplistic comparisons are made between the human species and other parts of the ecosystem. A perception of the human race as a species growing out of control is sometimes promoted. But in this area, as in all other aspects of the human species, a broad set of social, political and economic factors must also be considered. Humans are unique both in the scale of the ecological damage they have caused and in the scale of the differentials within their own species in terms of natural resource use and waste generation. It is this scale of resource use, and additional impacts due to the inequality in income and asset distribution within and between nations, which are now threatening the sustainability of many ecosystems, including global life support systems. Limiting population growth may be one factor in achieving sustainable natural resource use but it cannot be considered in isolation from other influences which determine access to, and use of, natural resources.

Within the discussion about sustainability (or sustainable development), there is an important theme relating to the need to develop within human society shared values, perceptions and attitudes which help to contribute to the achievement of sustainable development. This has also led to some discussion of 'cultural sustainability'. The question arises as to whether this is a valid goal within sustainable development. It is clear that development should include as a critical component a respect for cultural patrimony. Culture implies knowledge, and a vast wealth of traditional knowledge of relevance to sustainable natural resource use (and to development) is ignored or given scant attention in development plans. But the term 'cultural sustainability' seems a rather imprecise term for the need to recognize the importance of culture and respect it within development. Culture is never static; to argue that it should be sustained is to deny an important aspect, its changing and developing nature.

DEFINING SUSTAINABLE DEVELOPMENT

The ambiguities inherent in discussions of economic, social or cultural sustainability lead us to suggest that the 'sustainable' component of 'sustainable development' be used only in terms of ecological sustainability, that is, in terms of modes of natural resource use and use of local and global sinks which can be sustained without compromising the ability of future generations to meet their own needs. The 'development' component includes all economic, social, political and cultural goals. The implications of the term 'sustainable development' for governments and international agencies are more easily understood if divided into these two components.

The combination of a range of development goals and the achievement of sustainable levels of resource use requires the simultaneous achievement of social, economic, political and ecological goals; although there are powerful synergies between many of these, overall, their combination will require trade offs.[19]

Figure 6.1 seeks to illustrate the multiple goals of sustainable development. The development goals can be taken as those contained in the United Nations Universal Declaration of Human Rights – which are, meeting each person's right to a standard of living adequate for health and well-being including food, clothing, housing and medical care and necessary social services. It is clear that urban policies and institutions have a central role in ensuring the fulfilment of, for instance, people's needs for water, sanitation, safe and secure shelter, transport and an environment safe from life or health threatening pollutants, pathogens or other hazards. This same Declaration, subsequent United Nations documents, and *Our Common Future* also stress that development goals should include the right to vote within representative government structures.

The 'sustainable' component requires no depletion of environmental capital. Environmental capital can be divided into three broad types:

- The 'natural sink' capacity of local and global systems to absorb or break down human wastes – from the capacity of a particular water body to break down organic wastes to the capacity of global systems to absorb greenhouse gases without adverse effects on climate and gases which threaten to deplete the stratospheric ozone layer.

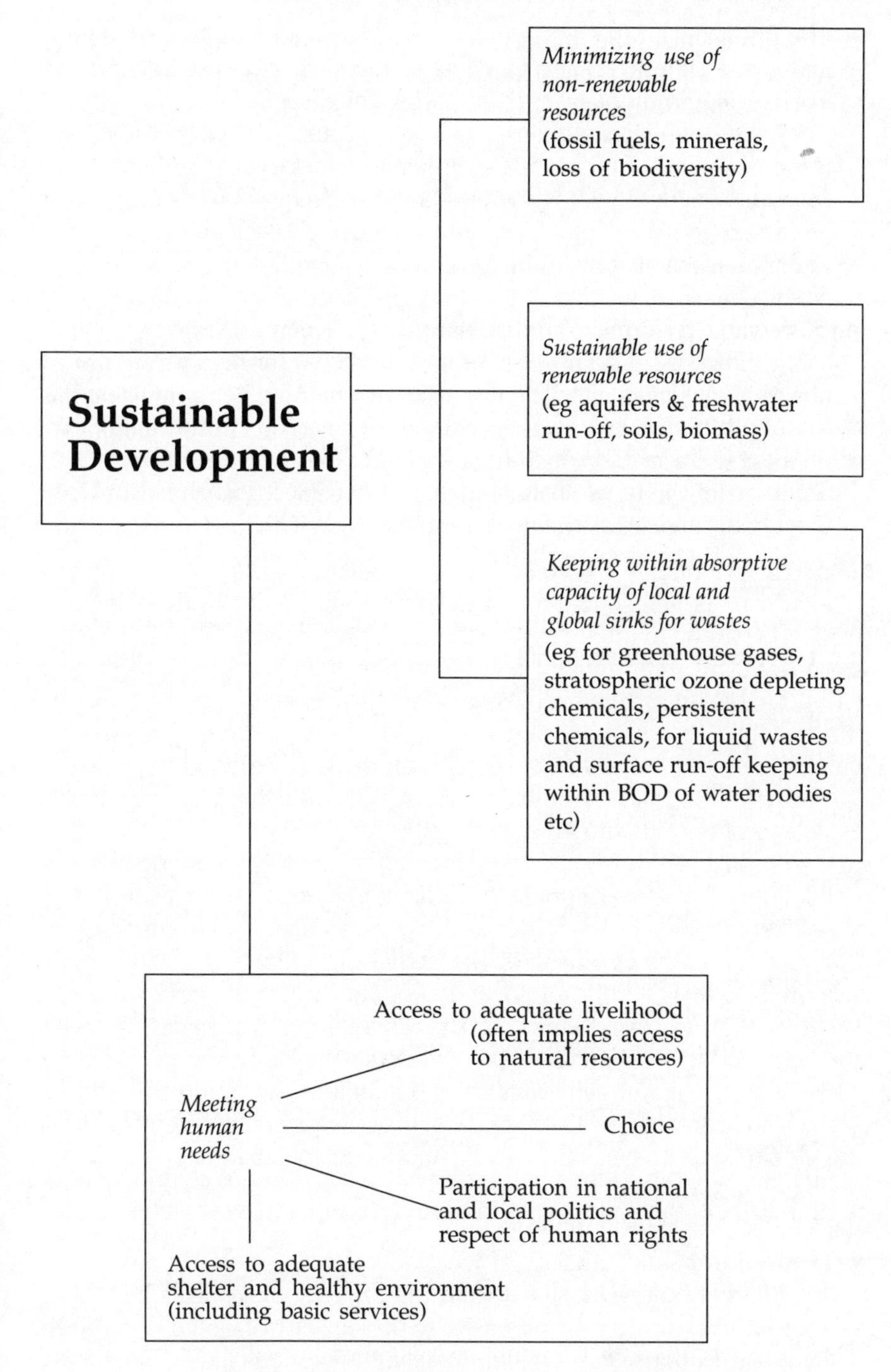

Figure 6.1 Components of sustainable development

- The finite stock of non-renewable resources – for instance fossil fuels and other mineral resources. Most of these resources (especially the fossil fuels burnt for heat and power) are consumed when used, so finite stocks are depleted with use. Others are not 'consumed' since the resource remains in the waste – for instance metals used in capital and consumer goods – and to an extent, these are 'renewable' if materials in discarded goods are reclaimed and recycled. Biological diversity, one key part of environmental capital, might also be considered a non-renewable resource.
- 'Renewable resources'. Human use of some renewable resources (such as the direct use of solar power or its indirect use through wind or wave power) does not deplete the resource. But many renewable resources (especially crops and trees) are renewable only within finite limits set by the ecosystem within which they grow. Fresh water resources are also finite; in the case of aquifers, human use often exceeds their natural rate of recharge and as such is unsustainable.

The term sustainable is used both for particular projects/activities and in reference to larger systems (perhaps city-wide, nation-wide or world-wide). It is useful to differentiate between the two applications of the term since both are important in considering sustainable development and cities. Simple inter-relationships between specific development activities (for instance, expanding a piped-water supply or developing a sanitary landfill site) and natural resource-use can be assessed and judged using the criterion of sustainability. Alternatively, the focus can be much broader, concerned with large aggregates and systems of activities. The first approach is concerned with making a single part of the system sustainable. The second approach has a different focus, recognising that it is difficult to make all activities sustainable, and that what is important is that the sum (or net effect) of the activities within a specific area is sustainable. In general, our focus is on the second of these contexts, ensuring that urban systems (and the economies and societies of which they are part) are sustainable, rather than specific urban projects, or even cities. The successful achievement of sustainable development requires society to establish institutions which are capable of ensuring that individual projects add up to an acceptable aggregate outcome without demanding such stringent conditions on individual projects that they inhibit the achievement of development goals.

CITIES AND ECOLOGICAL SUSTAINABILITY

This disaggregation of sustainable development into its two components simplifies its discussion in regard to cities. The sustainability component is the impact of each city (or rather of the producers and consumers located within the city) on environmental capital: local and global sinks, renewable resources, and non-renewable resources. The development component is the performance of each city and its institutions in meeting its inhabitants' development needs; as previous chapters have stressed, this also has an important environmental component since the quality of the home, work, neighbourhood and city environment, and the extent to which the inhabitants are protected from biological pathogens and chemical pollutants in the water, air, soil or food or other environmental hazards has a major influence on the health and well-being of the population.[20]

It is also useful to distinguish between two aspects of the discussion about cities and sustainable development. The first is the implications *for* cities and *for* urban policies of not achieving 'sustainable development' in sectors which are the main users of natural resources. The second is the contribution of urban policies (and urban management) to the *achievement* of sustainable development, including the sustainable use of environmental capital.

Renewable resources

Some natural resources are essential to the existence of any city – fresh water, food and fuel supplies. Many of the economic activities on which a city's prosperity depend require regular supplies of renewable resources; without a continuing supply of fresh water, agricultural goods and forest products, many cities would rapidly decline in size and in employment opportunities offered to their residents. Many other formal and informal economic activities, although not directly linked to resource exploitation, are dependent on the exploitation of natural resources to generate income to support their own activities.

In their role as the main centres of industrial production and of resource consumption, urban centres are also the location for the generation of most wastes.[21] If provision is not made to control the level of wastes or to remove them and ensure their safe disposal, acid precipitation and the pollution of land and water bodies can cause serious ecological damage in the surrounding region, as described in Chapter 4.

But there are also many examples of less ecologically damaging interactions between city wastes and surrounding areas. Some were mentioned in Chapter 5 – for instance organic solid and liquid wastes which originate from city-based consumers or industries being returned to soils – which demonstrate alternatives to the heavy use of artificial fertilizers and to the disregard of nutrients within city wastes. An examination of any large city's use of resources reveals a scale and complexity of linkages with rural producers and ecosystems which implies that 'sustainable urban development' and 'sustainable rural development' cannot be separated.

Rural-urban linkages can be positive in both developmental and environmental terms. For instance, demand for rural produce from city-based enterprises and households has often provided the basis for prosperous farmers and rural settlements, where environmental capital is not being depleted. Few governments in the South appear to appreciate the extent to which productive, intensive agriculture can support development goals in both rural and urban areas.[22] Increasing agricultural production can support rising prosperity for rural populations and rapid urban development within or close to the main farming areas – the two supporting each other. Many of the most rapidly growing urban centres in Africa and Latin America in recent years have been those within or close to the agricultural areas growing high-value crops (for instance fruit, tea or coffee). For instance, in the Upper Valley of the Rio Negro in Argentina, there has been very rapid net in-migration for many decades, with most new jobs being in agriculture or in enterprises with forward and backward linkages with agriculture, or in enterprises meeting the demand of consumers whose incomes derive from agriculture-related activities.[23] Such rural-urban links can also have negative aspects. For instance, agricultural land can be lost as built up areas expand without control, and land speculation on urban fringes drives out cultivators; this appears to be more common in most Third World nations.[24]

There is also the need to consider the sustainability of each city within the broader context of the ecosystem within which it is located. The relationship between human populations and ecosystems' carrying capacity may receive increasing attention in the next decade. Latin American specialists have suggested that most of the areas in South and Central America experiencing rapid population growth in recent decades are within the more fragile eco-zones, where sustainable exploitation of natural resources is more problematic.[25]

However, the rapid movement of rural population into urban centres is more likely to be the result of economic, social and political factors than environmental factors – including inequitable land owning structures and changes in crops grown and technologies used which diminish the demand for labour.[26] Even where pastoralists, shifting cultivators or small farmers reach ecological limits which force their migration (or that of part of their household) to urban areas, it is usually the inequitable land owning structure, rather than an overall lack of land, which is the underlying cause. Drought and famine continue to have a major impact on population movements in many of the poorest nations but this, too, is rarely the result only of environmental change, and is likely to involve a complex set of other factors.[27]

There is also the environmental damage arising from deforestation to meet urban (and rural) based demands for timber and other forest products. A great variety of products are obtained from forests but only a tiny proportion of the world's natural forests is being managed in ways which allow current yields to be sustained.[28] Fuelwood is one important forestry product; many urban households in the poorest and driest African countries are dependent on wood for energy.[29] Other important forest derivatives include 'a variety of foods including bushmeat ... fuelwood and charcoal, framing, panelling and thatching materials, and a range of other goods including berries, nuts, fruit, wild animals, honey, resins, oils, rattan and medical products.'[30] The rich ecological diversity of tropical forests may include important sources of new plants, potentially useful as a source of drugs. Forests are often important in maintaining the ecological balance in a region, preventing soil erosion and consequent problems of flooding.

Deforestation or forest depletion is likely to have a number of effects on urban centres. Perhaps the most serious impact will be the loss of employment, income and consumption goods for urban centres in areas where forest exploitation is a major part of the local economy. There is also the increasing difficulty experienced by those living in such settlements in obtaining fuel. The ecological effects of deforestation, including changes in run-off and subsequent erosion, may add to the risk of small floods, reduce the capacity of hydro-electric stations (whose electricity is usually destined for urban consumers or enterprises) and reduce the productivity of agriculture. Deforestation of river catchment areas and associated soil erosion may be a contributory factor in floods which devastate large areas downstream, including cities or city-districts built alongside rivers.[31]

Consideration of a city's sustainability must also take into account the ecological impacts of its demand for resources in distant regions. Chapter 4 described how many cities now draw on the fresh water resources of distant ecosystems, as their demand for fresh water exceeded local capacities. It also described the concept developed by William Rees of cities' 'ecological footprints' to examine this phenomenon.[32] City-based consumers and producers in a rich nation may appropriate the carrying capacity of a city or a rural region in a poor nation – for instance, demand for wood products in the North could be the major factor in deforestation and soil erosion in one particular region in the South. The attempt by businesses and municipal authorities in the North to export hazardous wastes to the South or by multinational corporations to move their dirtier industries there, are other examples of ways in which the ecological 'sustainability' of the rich world is achieved through the transfer of ecological costs to Third World nations.

Non-renewable resources

Per capita consumption of non-renewable resources such as metals and fossil fuels in the richest nations and cities of the world has reached unprecedented levels. In 1988, average energy consumption per capita in sub-Saharan Africa was 95 kilograms of oil equivalent; in many of the richest nations, per capita figures exceeded 5000 kilograms of oil equivalent, more than 50 times the sub-Saharan African average.[33] The average per capita consumption of steel within OECD nations is 450 kilograms compared to 43 kilograms in the South.[34] Comparable contrasts exist between per capita consumption in rich and poor nations for most other non-renewable resources.

There are fewer figures comparing city populations' non-renewable resource consumption but those that do exist also reveal an enormous disparity between North and South. Gasoline use per capita in cities such as Houston, Detroit and Los Angeles in 1980 was between four and eight times that in most European cities and likely to be between 100 and 1000 times that of most Third World cities.[35] By the late 1980s, the average waste generation for each urban citizen in North America was 826 kilograms compared to 394 kilograms for Japan and 336 kilograms for the European OECD nations; the average for low-income countries is between 150 and 200 kilograms a year and in many cities (or poor city districts) in the South the average can be as low as 50 kilograms per person per year.[36] The disparities in terms of the amount of non-renewable resources thrown away in the garbage (especially metals) are much higher because of the higher proportion of metals discarded in city waste in the North.

In one sense, comparisons of per capita non-renewable resource consumption between nations or between cities are misleading. Worldwide, it is the middle- and upper-income groups which account for most resource use and most generation of household wastes; this only becomes a North:South issue because most of the world's middle- and upper-income people with high-consumption lifestyles live in Europe, North America and Japan. High-income households in Third World cities such as Lagos, São Paulo and Bangkok may have levels of non-renewable resource use comparable to high-income households in Los Angeles or Houston; it is the fact that there are so much fewer of them within the city population which keeps city averages much lower.

But levels of household wealth alone are insufficient to explain the disparities between cities in terms of per capita resource use. In 1980, gasoline use per capita in cities such as Houston, Detroit and Los Angeles was five to seven times that of three of Europe's most prosperous and attractive cities: Amsterdam, Vienna and Copenhagen.[37] A study of the differences in gasoline use between cities suggested that larger vehicles, greater wealth and cheaper gasoline in the United States explains only between 40 and 50 per cent of the variation; other key factors were urban density and the pattern of land use which in turn were linked to public transport performance and level of traffic restraint.[38] The influence of density on per capita gasoline use can also be seen in the comparisons made between the core, inner suburbs and outer suburbs of Toronto; on average, each person in the outer suburbs had twice the gasoline consumption of each person in the core because of greater use of automobiles (and less use of public transport) and greater number of automobiles per head of population.[39] The disparities are even larger in New York, those in the outer area averaged five times the gasoline use per person of those in the central city (mainly Manhattan).

The dates at which the price of non-renewable resources will begin to rise rapidly, reflecting depletion of their stocks, may have been over-stated in the various reports produced during the 1970s, but the finite nature of non-renewable resource stocks is not in doubt. There may be sufficient non-renewable resources to ensure that 9–10 billion people on earth, late in the next century, have their needs met. But it is unlikely that the world's resources and ecosystems could sustain a world population of 9 or 10 billion with a per capita consumption of non-renewable resources similar to those enjoyed by the richest households today, or even the average figure for cities such as Houston and Los Angeles.

Cities and global systems

Discussions in regard to the impact of human activities on global life support systems centre on their contribution to reducing the stratospheric ozone layer and to atmospheric warming.[40] The disparities in terms of greenhouse gas emissions per capita or emissions of stratospheric ozone depleting chemicals between countries or cities in the North and South are as striking as those outlined earlier in terms of non-renewable resource use. Cities such as Canberra, Chicago and Los Angeles have between six and nine times the per capita carbon dioxide emissions of the world's average and 25 or more times that of cities such as Dhaka.[41] The per capita disparities for the consumption of chlorofluorocarbons and halons (the main cause of stratospheric ozone depletion) are just as striking; figures for 1986 show that most countries in the North have per capita consumptions of one or more kilograms per year with Switzerland having 1.30 and the USA 1.37; most Third World countries for which data was available have per capita consumptions below 0.1 kilograms per year while many have figures far below this. For instance, per capita figures for India and Indonesia were for 0.01 (around one hundredth the average figure for wealthy Northern nations) while for China it was 0.2.[42]

Chapter 4 outlined some of the consequences. It is clear that urban planning and management has three important roles in regard to climate change: limiting global warming by contributing to lower levels of greenhouse gas emissions; building defences and incorporating additional safety features within the built environment; and developing disaster preparedness.

LINKS BETWEEN URBAN POLICIES AND SUSTAINABLE DEVELOPMENT

Given the diversity of cities in terms of their size and population growth rates, and of their economic, social, political, cultural and ecological underpinnings, it is difficult to consider 'urban policy and management' for sustainable development in general terms. In most cities there are contradictions between sustainability and development: most of the cities which can be judged positively by development criteria (where social, economic and political goals are met) have among the highest per capita draws on environmental capital (in terms of use of non-renewable resources, draw on watersheds, forests, and agricultural systems, ecosystems' waste absorption capacities and per capita emissions of greenhouse gases and stratospheric ozone depleting gases). Most of the world's cities with the least draw on environmental capital are the ones which perform worst in development terms, with high proportions of their population lacking safe and sufficient water, sanitation, good quality housing, access to health care, secure livelihoods and – in many – basic civil and political rights.

Priorities in a move towards sustainable development are going to differ greatly for each city. For cities (or urban systems) with high levels of non-renewable resource use, the priority must be increasingly lower levels of fossil fuel use and waste generation (through reducing waste levels and through more recycling) – while maintaining a productive, stable and innovative economy, and a better record in reaching disadvantaged groups. Some clues as to how this can be achieved might be found in the cities which currently have among the world's best quality living standards but a relatively small draw on environmental capital which is not simply the result of a less energy intensive economic base. Examples of cities such as Copenhagen and Amsterdam with one seventh of the per capita consumption of petrol of Detroit and Houston were cited earlier. There are also several studies which show how major reductions in resource use and waste generation are possible in the North without a decline in the quality of life.[43]

For cities with low levels of non-renewable resource use and waste generation (which usually implies a relatively poor city), the priority is the achievement of social, economic and political goals, but within a commitment to minimizing the call on environmental capital. In terms of non-renewable resource use, many cities in the South are among the most resource conserving cities in the world. Per capita consumption levels are much lower and every item of waste from households or businesses which has some value is reclaimed for re-use or recycled. As described in Chapter 4, this process is generally driven by the poverty of so many citizens; thousands of households can depend for their survival on a meagre income derived from selling materials obtained by sifting through garbage at the local/city dump or on industrial sites or other places where wastes are aggregated.[44]

In the longer term, if poorer nations in the South do develop more stable and prosperous economies, they will make increased use of non-renewable resources and their greenhouse gas emissions per capita are also likely to increase – especially if they expand their heavy industry. The extent of this growth in the use of environmental capital will depend not only on the level of wealth created and its distribution but also on the extent to which provisions are made now and in the immediate future to promote the efficient use of resources and the minimization of wastes. For example, in rapidly growing cities, measures to encourage fuel-efficient buildings and land use patterns which *respond* to citizens' priorities for easy access to employment and services within fuel efficient transport systems can, over time, bring increasingly large savings in the use of fossil fuels (and thus also in the emissions of greenhouse gases) relative to wealth.[45] For instance, the bus-centred public transport system in Curitiba, Brazil has succeeded in keeping petrol consumption per capita well below that expected, with its relatively high per capita income and high ratio of automobiles per inhabitant.[46] Similarly, there are cities in the South where development goals are met without high levels of resource use and waste generation.

LINKING GLOBAL AND LOCAL SUSTAINABILITY

There may be contradictions between global sustainability and local ecological sustainability. At a global level, the world's cities cannot remain prosperous if the aggregate impact of their economy's production and their inhabitants' consumption draws on global resources at unsustainable rates and deposits wastes in global sinks at levels which ensure rapid climatic change. As noted earlier, many cities in the North achieve sustainable development goals within their own region (such as high-quality living environments and protection of local ecosystems) by drawing heavily on the environmental capital of other regions or nations, and on the global sink. This implies the need for international agreements which set limits for each national society's consumption of resources, and use of the global sink for their wastes. But it is also clear that most action to achieve sustainable development has to be formulated and implemented locally. The fact that each city and its place within local and regional ecosystems is unique implies the need for optimal use of local resources, knowledge and skills for the achievement of development goals within a detailed knowledge of the local and regional ecological carrying capacity. This demands a considerable degree of local self-determination, since centralized decision making structures have great difficulty in implementing decisions which respond appropriately to such diversity. Nevertheless, some new international institutions are required to ensure that individual cities or countries do not take advantage of others' restraint.

National governments inevitably have the key role in linking local and global sustainability. Internationally, they have the responsibility for reaching agreements to limit each nation's call on the world's environmental capital. Nationally, they are responsible for providing the framework to ensure local actions can meet development goals without compromising local and global sustainability.

At the level of city and municipal government, there are at least four key policy areas, to secure both development and sustainability:

- respond to citizen demands for a safe and healthy living and working environment which includes ensuring the availability of shelter and the provision of basic infrastructure and services; and ensure there is an effective legislative and regulatory system to protect citizens from exploitation by landlords and employers;
- penalize polluters (establish appropriate mechanisms and enforce them), give further incentives to encourage innovative ways to reduce pollution and conserve resources (especially reductions in air pollution and fuel consumption of road vehicles), and encourage recycling, re-use and reclamation of both non-renewable and renewable resources and waste materials;
- manage urban growth to promote minimal use of environmental capital while meeting social and economic goals – for example provide for city generated wastes (especially toxic wastes and point source water pollution) to be handled effectively; and
- identify and support the development of new economic activities which enhance both the urban centre's economic base and its environment.

But city and municipal governments may well fulfil these four roles while no modifications are made to ensure that the consumers and producers within their boundaries contribute to regional or global sustainable development. While meeting development goals must remain the priority in most cities in the South, this does not mean that 'sustainable' goals should be excluded. Their most obvious role is in planning, guiding and regulating the built environment – building-material production, construction, building design and performance, site and settlement planning and so on. Goals relating to local or global ecological sustainability can be incorporated into the norms, codes and regulations which influence the built environment and whose aim is (in theory) to promote development goals.

But city and municipal government cannot be expected to take the lead in addressing such issues as reduction of greenhouse gas emissions, a steady increase in fuel efficiency among road vehicles and domestic appliances, the promotion of more sustainable international trade practices and other essential elements of sustainable development. This has to come from national or state government which must provide the legislative, regulatory and fiscal framework within which competent, representative urban government can operate and meet its own local and regional sustainable development agenda – and at the same time contribute to national and international goals. It also remains the task of national government to consider the social and environmental impacts of their macro-economic and sectoral policies which may be contributing to the very problems their sustainable development policies are seeking to avoid.

THE NATIONAL FRAMEWORK FOR CITY ACTION ON SUSTAINABLE DEVELOPMENT

No national government has set up the regulatory and incentive structure to ensure that the aggregate impact of their economic activities and citizens' consumption is in accordance with global sustainability – although a few in Europe have taken some tentative steps towards some aspects. In most nations in the South, national governments have also denied city and municipal governments the power and resources they need to promote development. Weak national economies and highly centralized political structures are among key reasons why; so, too, in much of Africa and Asia is a colonial heritage which for decades denied powers to local ('native') authorities and introduced norms, codes and regulations which ill-matched local needs and cultures.

The achievement of urban development goals which also seek to promote ecological sustainability (or at least minimize the contribution of city-based activities to unsustainability) requires both supportive and regulatory structures. The first are needed to encourage the private sector and community initiatives to contribute to sustainable development. For instance, promoting a greater commitment among companies to recycling and waste minimization generally needs national action. The second are needed so that the workings of the market are not such that the weak and vulnerable are exploited (so development goals are not met) and air and water quality damaged, natural capital depleted and global systems disrupted (so sustainability goals are not met).

The policy options can be subdivided into three broad areas: regulatory controls which use penalties enforceable by sanctions; market incentives (either taxes or subsidies) to influence choices made; and the allocation of property rights, such that externalities are 'internalised' becoming one of the set of market decisions. In practice no one single method is used by governments in their attempt to promote environmental quality for the local population and less waste. Each method has particular advantages and disadvantages associated with it and so is useful in different circumstances.

There is much discussion as to the relative advantages and disadvantages of regulatory controls and market incentives. Traditionally, OECD countries have used regulation as the basic tool for carrying out environmental policy.[47] Legislation exists to enforce controls and whatever pollution remains after its enforcement is dealt with by local authorities. One weakness of this approach in regard to the Third World is the scale of the task allocated to local authorities. To be effective, the controls have to be enforced; a high proportion of air and water pollution in Third World cities is illegal and the problems arise not from a lack of legislation but from inadequate or no enforcement.[48] Third World countries rarely have city and municipal governments with sufficient power and resources to enforce controls and with a sufficient tax base to cover the costs of an effective enforcement agency and pay for the facilities needed to dispose of residual pollution. In the last decade, regulation has been viewed less favourably, and government intervention has often been criticised for being costly and inefficient, and new methods of using market incentives have become more popular.

There are several different ways in which market incentives can be used. One of the most popular is through the use of taxes on activities which are polluting or which are costly in their use of natural resources. In some cases such charges are intended to have a major effect on behaviour, in other cases they are merely seen as an additional source of revenue (perhaps to pay for compensating measures). Such charges are justified because the market does not operate to include all social and environmental costs incurred in producing or consuming a product and therefore an efficient market requires some price adjustment. For example, local governments may decide to charge motorists according to how often they choose to drive in busy locations during peak periods. In other cases, governments may choose to subsidise certain kinds of behaviour in order to encourage people to act in a environment-friendly way. It is common for city governments in Europe to subsidise their public transport networks.

One advantage of market incentives is the flexibility with which such intervention can be applied. For example, taxes dependent on the level of polluting emissions means that companies with a more limited ability to change to cleaner processes may continue to pollute the area (and pay the charge) but those for which alternatives are available will switch to other processes. But such schemes may be hard to operate in certain markets in the Third World, particularly those made up of many small buyers and sellers. In such circumstances, the cost of enforcing a charge would exceed several times the amount collected. Leach and Mearns consider the feasibility of a tax on wood to ensure that forest resources are not exploited as a free good, leaving future generations to bear the costs of replanting. They noted that

> 'as long as taxes on urban traders are small, they are likely to have little effect on curbing forest use....If, on the other hand, taxes are large, there will be even stronger incentives than now for the transporters and traders to evade them.'[49]

Neither regulation nor market incentives can offer an alternative to efficient and effective local government.[50] Regulations and incentives require that local government has the resources to identify environmental damage that occurs and to develop an understanding of local conditions such that it can intervene effectively. Governments need the resources to monitor and enforce whatever environmental policies are chosen, with the necessary powers and penalties for effective prosecutions. Policy makers also need to consider the broader impacts of such policies. Charges imposed through market intervention policies and additional costs incurred by regulations which discourage certain types of behaviour may increase inflation. Charges which increase the cost of basic necessities may impact particularly heavily on low-income groups and have undesirable redistributional implications. More stringent pollution control may simply encourage polluting enterprises to set up elsewhere – outside the municipality, region or nation where the controls are being implemented.

A third option open to governments is the allocation or reallocation of property rights. This can result in the creation of new markets, for example a market in the right to pollute, with companies being allocated pollution rights which they can trade with other companies. This may have radical impacts on the distribution of resources. For example, if pollution rights are retained by companies, then pollution will continue if it is poorer groups living or working nearby who suffer, since they cannot afford to pay to prevent or reduce such pollution. If alternatively, pollution rights are owned by the poor, then the industrialist can afford to pay them to allow some pollution. Even if – the worst eventuality from the environmental perspective – the industrialist pays so that pollution continues at the previous level, the poor are considerably better off because they have the income generated by the sale of their environmental asset.[51] Pezzey argues that the

> 'allocative effects of redistributing environmental property rights from rich to poor people...might be an effective way of simultaneously improving the lot of the poor and improving the environment. But the political difficulties of such redistribution should never be underestimated, since they will certainly limit the pace at which redistribution can proceed.'[52]

ENABLING LOCAL ACTION

Much of what has been discussed above stresses the concept of central government as an enabler, developing the laws, institutions and policies that support and encourage individuals, communities, enterprises and local governments to undertake economic or social activities with a high proportion of government plans, policies and actions determined and implemented at local level.

The discussion of government as 'an enabler' has a long history. Within the evolution of development theory, it is perhaps through discussions of appropriate housing policies that the importance of an enabling policy has been stressed and its form made more explicit. The origins of the idea that government actions with regard to housing should concentrate on 'enabling' and supporting the efforts of citizens and their community organizations to develop their own housing goes back at least to the 1950s and perhaps earlier. The concept of enablement has also spread to many other sectors – for instance in the supply and maintenance of water systems and in the organization of agricultural extension services.

The concept of enablement is based on the understanding that most human investments, activities and choices which influence the achievement of development and sustainability goals take place outside 'government'. Most are beyond the control of governments (or at least of democratic governments) even where governments seek some control. In Third World cities, the point is particularly valid since most homes, neighbourhoods, jobs and incomes are created outside of government and often in contravention of official rules and regulations.[53] There is the understanding – expressed so clearly by Adam Smith some 200 years ago – that inappropriate government controls and regulations discourage and distort the scale and vitality of individual, family and community investments and activities. But there is also recognition that, without controls and regulations which are scrupulously enforced, individuals, communities and enterprises can impose their externalities on others. The 'environmental health' centred reforms of city and municipal governments in the North in the late nineteenth and early twentieth centuries developed systems of urban governance to regulate and control the supply of water and the disposal of liquid and solid wastes. Environmental legislation in the second half of the twentieth century has centred on government control of air and water pollution and solid waste generation and disposal, which imposed costs on urban citizens and on the citizens and ecosystems beyond the city boundaries. In each instance, central government had to provide the framework for action, and city and municipal governments had to act; successful government enablement is always a careful balance between encouragement and control.

The application on 'enabling policies' has received considerable support from the growing recognition that democratic and participatory government structures are not only important goals of development but also important means for achieving development goals. Participation and enablement are inseparable since popular priorities and demands will be a major influence on the development of effective and flexible enablement. The concept of government policies, actions and institutions as rooted in enablement has a much wider relevance since it is important to the promotion of sustainability as well as development. It would be politically unacceptable in most societies for governments to substantially restrict individual consumption levels, but sustainable development worldwide is impossible without national frameworks which promote substantially lower levels of demand by wealthy households on the world's environmental capital.

IMPLEMENTING SUSTAINABLE DEVELOPMENT IN CITIES

The broad regulatory and incentive structure needed to support the achievement of development goals, within a framework which promotes local and global ecological sustainability, is relatively easy to conceive as an abstract exercise. The poverty suffered by the minority of urban dwellers in richer nations and the majority in poorer nations can be drastically reduced without a large expansion in resource use. The social and ecological costs of providing safe and sufficient water supplies, provision for sanitation, garbage removal and health care and ensuring safe, secure shelters are often over-stated.[54] The quality of life of the wealthy, high-consumption individuals and households need not diminish, and in certain aspects may indeed improve within a long term programme to cut their draw on the world's environmental capital. The prosperity and economic stability that poorer nations need to underpin secure livelihoods for their populations, and the competence necessary at national and local government could be achieved without a much increased call on environmental capital.

But translating this into reality both within nations and globally is another issue. Powerful vested interests oppose most if not all necessary policies and priorities. The likely levels of reduction needed in the use of non-renewable resources (especially fossil fuels) will impinge most on richer groups' lifestyles. Richer groups are unlikely to willingly forsake the comfort and mobility that they currently enjoy. Technological change can help to a limited extent – for instance, moderating the impact of rising gasoline prices through the relatively rapid introduction of increasingly fuel-efficient automobiles, and introducing alternative fuels derived from renewable energy sources. But if combatting atmospheric warming does demand a rapid reduction in greenhouse gas emissions, this will imply changes in people's right to use private automobiles which cannot be met by new technologies and alternative ('renewable') fuels – at least at costs which will prove politically acceptable. So many existing commercial, industrial and residential buildings and urban forms (for instance low-density suburban developments and out-of-town shopping malls) have high levels of energy use built into them and these are not easily or rapidly changed.[55]

At the same time, in the South, the achievement of development goals which minimize the call on local and global environmental capital, demands a competence and capacity to act by city and municipal government which is currently very rarely present. The achievement of key development goals is also unlikely without strong democratic pressures and processes to influence decisions about the use of public resources.

One of the most important policy issues in implementing sustainable development (and, within this, sustainable patterns of natural resource use) is building the institutional framework within each city, district and region which can develop and implement sustainable development strategies which are acceptable to the majority of people living there. Adding a concern for sustainability onto existing development concerns further strengthens the rationale for institution-building at local level. Development goals cannot be met without effective 'developmental' institutions within each nation. Such institutions are also important in any move towards more sustainable levels of resource use.

The capacity of local governments to plan and manage the area under their jurisdiction, to promote more sustainable patterns of resource use and urban form, to invest in needed infrastructure and services, to enhance the locality's attraction for new productive investment while guided by the needs and priorities of its citizenry, is central to both development and sustainability. At local level, the priority is for each society to develop its own response to local environmental problems and resource limitations, using the tools most appropriate to its own unique situation. As a recent review of African cities stated:

> 'ultimately, solutions to problems of urban finance, housing, public transport, the siting and standards of urban infrastructure, public health and public cleansing services, water, electricity and numerous other urban amenities *must be formulated locally, by local people, on the basis of local experience and information*'.[56]

Local governments cannot take on these roles without a strong financial base, the support of national government and an appropriate legislative, regulatory and incentive structure. The laws, norms and regulations set by national government must have considerable flexibility, otherwise they inhibit rather than enable local action and the best use of local resources. There is also the need for mechanisms to allow inter-local government area resource transfers; otherwise, only local governments in more prosperous areas will have the resources to address development and sustainability goals.

The capacity of local government to work in partnership with community organizations, NGOs, non-profit foundations and private sector enterprises is also central to the achievement of development goals, and this is especially true where economic circumstances limit the investment capacity of local government. Many case studies have demonstrated the capacity of community organizations to improve low-income neighbourhoods and to set up and run basic services, with very limited resources. A stress on 'enablement' at local level is to provide the support and advice that will encourage community initiatives and multiply manyfold the number that start and succeed. Such policy directions imply the need for new kinds of 'enabling' institutions widely distributed within each nation to provide funding and technical advice.

AGENDA 21 AND THE GLOBAL CONTEXT FOR SUSTAINABILITY AND DEVELOPMENT

Citizen pressure can and often has pressured city and municipal governments into pursuing more sustainable patterns of resource-use and waste minimization, where the ecological impacts are local or regional or (on occasion) national. This can be seen in the environmental movements and in the role taken by environmental issues in election campaigns in the North. But these have been largely driven by citizen concern for their own health and quality of life. There is little citizen pressure on city and municipal governments to press for changes in production and consumption patterns which have their most serious ecological impacts overseas or on global cycles. Yet the achievement of sustainable development depends on cities responding to the ecological damage to which their enterprises and consumers contribute far beyond their boundaries.

Earlier sections have emphasised that the achievement of good environmental performance among all city and municipal governments requires an appropriate set of incentives and regulations at national (or, for large federal nations, state) level – as well as sufficient power, resources and accountability for city and municipal governments. Such a set of incentives and regulations has developed in most nations in the North, and some in the South, over the last 20 years. Given greater prosperity and economic stability among poorer nations in the South, it is also conceivable that comparable changes can occur there too. But national governments in both North and South are unlikely to set the incentives and regulations needed to promote sustainable development outside their national boundaries without international agreements. One of the key international issues for the next few decades will be attempts to resolve the pursuit of increased wealth and development by national societies (most of whose members have strong preferences for minimal constraints on their consumption levels) within a recognition of the material limits of the biosphere.

The technical *capacity* to achieve sustainable development is easier to envisage than the political *processes* within nations to accept international agreements, and the regulatory and incentive structures to ensure that this happens. This, sadly, was borne out at the Earth Summit (the United Nations Conference on Environment and Development, held in Brazil in June 1992) with the watering down of the Global Climate Change convention and the refusal of the United States government to even discuss limits on the right of US consumers and businesses to consume in ways which deplete environmental capital.[57]

Nevertheless, the Earth Summit is notable for its explicit recognition of many of the problems discussed in this book. In addition to the single issue negotiations, governments discussed and were invited to sign Agenda 21, one of several documents emerging from the Summit. In the words of its introduction, the document is intended as

> 'an action plan for the 1990s and well into the twenty-first century, elaborating strategies and integrated programme measures to halt

and reverse the effects of environmental degradation and to promote environmentally sound and sustainable development in all countries'.

Agenda 21 contains 40 chapters divided into four broad sections: social and economic dimensions; conservation and management of resources for development; strengthening the role of major groups; and means of

Box 6.2 Agenda 21 – environmental problems in Third World cities and global priorities

Agenda 21 considers many aspects relevant to identifying and acting on environmental problems in Third World cities. There are separate sections on urban health, health risks from environmental pollution and hazards, the provision of environmental infrastructure, and planning for human settlements in disaster prone areas. There are also individual chapters on promoting sustainable human settlement development and the environmentally sound management of toxic chemicals, hazardous wastes, and solid wastes and sewage-related issues. Some key points are highlighted below:

Urban health: Agenda 21 argues that urban growth has exposed people to serious environmental hazards and that the rate of growth has exceeded the capacity of municipal and local government to provide the environmental health services required. Environmental pollution in urban areas is associated with excess morbidity and mortality. One of the Agenda's objectives is to improve the health and well-being of all urban dwellers. Local authorities are identified as the key agents of change. Agenda 21 argues that better national and municipal statistics based on practical standardized indicators are required, as are methodologies to measure intra-urban and inter-urban district variations in health status and environmental conditions.

Human settlement management: In order to improve conditions for people living in urban centres, Agenda 21 recognises the need to improve the level of infrastructure and service provision in poorer areas. It argues that cities should: institutionalize a participatory approach; improve the urban environment by promoting social organization and environmental awareness; and strengthen the capacities of local governing bodies.

Environmental infrastructure: Residential densities in urban areas offer unique opportunities for the cost-effective provision of environmental infrastructure. The poor quality and quantity of investment in such areas is currently responsible for much of the ill health and preventable deaths. One objective of Agenda 21 is to secure the provision of adequate environmental infrastructure facilities in all settlements by the year 2025.

Waste management: Agenda 21 recognises the need to strengthen and expand national waste re-use and recycling systems. It argues that multinational and national government institutions and NGOs should actively promote and encourage waste re-use and recycling. There is also a need to establish environmentally sound waste disposal and treatment systems for waste which cannot be recycled or reused. It is estimated that, by the year 2000, over two billion people will be without access to basic sanitation and half the urban population will be without adequate solid waste disposal services; there is an obvious need to rapidly improve and extend such services

Who are the key actors? Agenda 21 recognises the critical contributions of both NGOs and local authorities, and includes separate chapters focusing on the work of these groups. The document stresses the importance of partnerships in improving social, economic and environmental quality in urban areas; partnerships between public, private and community sectors and participation in decision making processes by community groups and special interest groups.

implementation. In its discussion of all subjects related to sustainable development, Agenda 21 includes mention of urban environmental problems. Box 6.2 outlines some of Agenda 21's main points.

However, Agenda 21 can only encourage and persuade. While it includes many practical suggestions to assist in achieving sustainable development, it does not have the power or resources to ensure the implementation of these recommendations. The governments attending the Earth Summit did not agree to grant such power and resources to any international institution. National governments are increasingly willing to acknowledge the inter-dependence between nation states but are not yet willing to agree to the major political changes in global institutions needed to effectively manage this international inter-dependence.

The issue of global warming can be seen as a 'test case' in that this is likely to be the first global environmental problem whose resolution depends on significant changes in consumption patterns in the richest and most powerful nations. International agreements have been achieved which limit the call of each national society on global or other nation's environmental capital – for instance the reductions in the use of CFCs and the Basel Convention on the Control of Transboundary Movements of Hazardous Wastes and their Disposal. But these did not imply significant changes in the consumption patterns of the wealthy. Unless the earth's capacity to absorb increasing levels of greenhouse gas emissions without atmospheric warming has been greatly underestimated, greenhouse gas emissions will have to be controlled. This implies constraints on the richest nations' consumption levels.

There are conflicts between promoting global ecological sustainability and promoting development. A more prosperous and economically stable South does imply increases in per capita fossil-fuel use (and thus greenhouse gas emissions). An increasing concern in the North with global warming may mean aid budgets increasingly dominated by measures to minimize greenhouse gas emissions in the South. This implies an even lower priority than is evident today in helping to meet human needs for water, sanitation, health care, education and in strengthening Third World governments' own capacity to do so. It also implies an increasing concentration of aid in those nations in the South which are major net greenhouse gas emitters – and away from many of the poorest nations.

Thus, it is not only the achievement of the 'sustainable' component of sustainable development that requires international agreements; so too does the meeting of human needs in the South. Most nations in the South cannot meet development goals, and very few are likely to meet sustainability goals, without changes in the world market and the way that development assistance is provided. A government seeking to resolve a debt crisis and reliant for most foreign exchange on the export of natural resources cannot address longer-term sustainability issues. It is also difficult to see the moral basis for demanding that poorer nations whose economies have made very little demand on finite resources or contributed little to the pollution of the global commons, must now be denied the use of the cheapest energy sources because the First World made such a high demand on these same resources in the process of becoming rich. In addition, a more sustainable basis for trade in natural commodities is needed with changes in the relationships between the world's major consumer markets (Europe, North America, Japan) and nations in the South, which are the major producers of natural resources.

7
Conclusions

INTRODUCTION

There is a growing concern that large cities in the Third World will reach a size where the beneficence of nature will be surpassed in terms of providing freshwater, breaking down pollution loads (or through dilution, rendering them less hazardous), providing raw materials and yielding cheap and easily exploitable energy sources. The preceding pages have noted many examples of local ecosystems' carrying capacities being exceeded: freshwater withdrawals exceeding aquifers' natural rate of recharge; the level of organic pollutants from industries, sewers and urban run-off exceeding the capacities of rivers and estuaries to break them down; and city-based demands for fuel, timber and bricks exacerbating deforestation, soil erosion and loss of agricultural land. Urban areas often expand over prime agricultural land; so, too, do waste dumps to cope with the increasing volume of solid wastes generated by city-based producers and consumers. In many cities, there are problems of acid rain which damages soils, trees and crops in surrounding areas.

Ambient air pollution and greenhouse gas emissions in Third World cities are receiving increasing attention. In many cities or particular city districts, the combination of air pollutants from motor vehicles, industries, power stations and (in some instances) household stoves or fires has reached levels where potentially dangerous concentrations persist, especially when high emissions coincide with particular atmospheric conditions. There is growing concern about the increasing role of Third World, city-based production and consumption in greenhouse gas emissions. These concerns for ambient air quality, greenhouse gas emissions and natural resource consumption or degradation have much in common with city-concerns in the North.

But such a list of environmental problems is very incomplete and in some senses misleading. It concentrates on chemical pollution and damage to natural resources and ecosystems. It gives too little attention to two critical environmental problems: biological pathogens in the urban environment; and people's access to natural resources (especially freshwater and safe land sites for housing). The main reasons for biological pathogens being present are contaminated and inadequate quantities of water, inadequate provision for sanitation and the disposal of solid and liquid wastes; inadequate measures to control disease vectors (especially insects); poor quality, overcrowded housing; inadequate health services; and inadequate (or lax enforcement of) environmental and occupational health legislation. Such factors underlie millions of preventable deaths every year in urban areas of the Third World. They also contribute to serious ill health or disablement for hundreds of millions. Similarly, in most cities, between one third and two thirds of the population cannot afford safe and healthy housing. These are the environmental problems which deserve a high priority. Since there is a growing interest among governments in the problems of managing and disposing of 'toxic wastes', it would seem appropriate to put human excrement as the most serious 'toxic waste' – and, indeed, one whose safe disposal is relatively cheap. Below, we elaborate on points first raised in chapter 1 with regard to a new environmental agenda for cities.

ENVIRONMENTAL PROBLEMS; POLITICAL SOLUTIONS

It may be misleading to refer to many of the most pressing problems as 'environmental' since they arise not from some particular shortage of an environmental resource (such as land or freshwater) but from economic or political factors which prevent poorer groups from obtaining them and from organizing to demand them. The severe shortage of water supplies for much of the Third World's urban population is a serious environmental problem but rarely is its cause environmental; in most cities, it is not a shortage of freshwater resources but governments' refusal to give a higher priority to water supply (and the competent organizational structure its supply, maintenance and expansion requires). In some cities, there are serious constraints on expanding freshwater supplies, as the size of the city and its production base has grown to exceed the capacity of local freshwater resources to supply it on a sustainable basis – but even here, adequate supplies to poorer groups may demand *less* water than that saved by better maintenance of the existing system and more realistic charges for the largest industrial water users. The same is true for land; most cities or metropolitan areas in the Third World have sufficient unused or under-utilized land sites within the current built-up area to accommodate most, if not all, the low-income households currently living in very overcrowded conditions.[1] Perhaps not surprisingly, one recent paper discussing the linkages between poverty and the urban environment in Asia was subtitled 'access, empowerment and community-based management'.[2] Ensuring that low-income groups and their community organizations can obtain access to safe land sites and water supplies and to municipal services is central to an improved urban environment.

A failure of governance underlies most environmental problems – government failures to control industrial pollution and occupational exposure; to promote environmental health; to ensure that city-dwellers have the basic infrastructure and services essential for health and a decent living environment; to plan in advance so that sufficient land is available for housing developments for low-income groups; and to implement preventive measures. For many Third World countries, this can be partly explained by the national economy's weakness; effective governance in ensuring a healthy environment for citizens is almost impossible without a stable and reasonably prosperous economy.

It is remedying this failure of governance within Third World cities and city-districts, and addressing the reasons which underlie it, which should be central to any new urban environmental agenda. This may not parallel the contemporary urban agenda in Europe and North America – although it certainly parallels the urban agenda there less than a century ago when public provision of infrastructure and services, and public control of pollution and occupational health hazards were as inadequate as they are today in most Third World cities. In effect, Third World cities need the 'environmental health' revolution which most European and North American cities underwent in the last few decades of the nineteenth and first few decades of the twentieth centuries, as well as action on the environmental concerns raised in the 1960s and 1970s. Some Third World cities also underwent an 'environmental health' revolution in the first few decades of this century but the momentum was never maintained. Strengthening the capacity of city and municipal governments to address the lack of sewers, drains, piped-water supplies, garbage collection and health services is generally a precondition for building the institutional capacity to address air and water pollution, protect natural resources and reduce greenhouse gas emissions.

At present, the pressure for environmental action in urban areas of the Third World which comes from research and activist groups and donor agencies in Europe and North America is neglecting the 'environmental health' agenda. Measures to prevent or limit the transmission of diarrhoeal diseases, typhoid, cholera and other waterborne, water-washed or water-based diseases, or acute respiratory infections and tuberculosis, or vector-borne diseases such as malaria, dengue fever and yellow fever, have critical environmental components. These must remain at the centre of the urban environmental agenda, along with measures to ensure rapid treatment of environment-related diseases, where prevention is not possible.

Another example of the transfer of Northern perceptions to Third World cities is the stress on the loss of agricultural land to urban sprawl. Many recent reports on environmental problems in Third World cities suggest that this is one of the most serious problems. While this can be judged a serious problem in certain nations with very limited agricultural land, in most nations urban areas cover only 1 or 2 per cent of the national territory. In addition, urban planning can be made to minimize their encroachment on productive land (for instance by ensuring that vacant plots within the urbanized areas are developed). And as chapter 4 noted, there are also many examples of cities which have, within their boundaries, large areas with intensive production of crops and livestock. This is not to imply that agricultural land should not be protected from urban sprawl, where possible. But where it is given more attention than such critical environmental problems as waterborne and vector-borne diseases, this does imply an inappropriate set of priorities.

The growing pressure for action on environmental problems in Third World cities must press for action in all urban centres. Most of the literature on environmental problems in Third World cities is about a handful of large cities – typically Mexico City, São Paulo, Lagos, Bangkok, Calcutta, Cairo, Jakarta, Bombay, Delhi and Karachi. Yet only a small proportion of the Third World's urban population lives in large cities; as an earlier chapter noted, the 'megacities' of ten million plus inhabitants house less than 3 per cent of the Third World's total population and while this proportion will rise, it will never represent more than a small proportion of the Third World's urban population.[3] Improved water supplies, sanitation, solid and liquid waste management, control of disease vectors, capacity to plan and manage new commercial, industrial and residential developments and preventive-focused health services are needed in virtually all urban areas of the Third World – including the tens of thousands of small and intermediate sized urban centres in which a high proportion of the Third World's urban population lives.

Building the basis for a new environmental agenda for urban areas centres should centre on four aspects:

- institutional change within Third World governments and new roles of aid agencies;
- support for NGOs and citizen groups;
- an urban agenda which responds to the specifics of each society and culture; and
- new professional attitudes.

INSTITUTIONAL CHANGE AND THE ROLE OF AID AGENCIES

The long-term solution to any city's environmental problems depends on the development within that city of a competent, representative local government. Lessons drawn from 40 years experience of national or international agencies demonstrate that most local problems need local institutions. Outside agencies – whether national ministries or international agencies – often misunderstand the nature of the problem and the range of options from which to choose the most appropriate solutions.

The acquisition by city and municipal governments of the capacity and power to invest in, maintain and extend water supply, sanitation, drainage, garbage collection, health care and other essential elements of a good urban environment involves complex political changes. Powerful and well organized vested interests will oppose such changes – as was the case in Europe and North America little more than a century ago. It also implies substantial institutional changes in most countries – for instance, most governments in Asia remain highly centralized and approach planning as a political process – and these highly centralized power structures are least able to provide support to local institutions.[4]

Each Third World city must develop and implement an action programme, based on a careful evaluation of its own problems and resources. Even if current levels of aid to urban environmental problems were multiplied many times, most cities will still never receive substantial amounts of international aid and for those that do, the amounts will never be more than a useful supplement to their own resources. This book does not recommend a diversion of resources by governments and aid agencies from rural to urban areas; in most countries, far too little attention is given to the environmental problems which impact most on the health and livelihoods of poor rural dwellers – and to addressing their causes. What is recommended is a far higher priority for a better use of existing resources which includes increasing the capacity of city and local governments to tackle both short- and long-term environmental problems, and channelling more funds direct to community-based organizations and the local NGOs with whom they choose to work.

The political changes by which the capacities of city and municipal government are increased and made more accountable to the electorate are often opaque to outside agencies. Interventions by aid agencies and development banks who seek the efficient implementation of 'their' project may even inhibit this change. Innovative local solutions which are cheaper and more appropriate may be ignored in favour of far more expensive but less effective solutions funded and supported by external aid and designed by foreign consultants. In addition, international agencies can never stay in a city to guarantee the maintenance and expansion of the new water or sanitation or garbage collection system that they helped to fund. Table 7.1 contrasts the characteristics of many successful community-based projects aiming to improve environmental health with the characteristics which make implementation easier for external funding agencies; the difficulties in reconciling the two are obvious.

Table 7.1 The most important aid project characteristics from two different viewpoints

Characteristics of many successful projects	Project characteristics which make implementation easy for outside funding agency
Small scale and multi-sectoral – addressing multiple needs of poorer groups	Large scale and single sector
Implementation over many years – less of a project and more of a longer-term continous process to improve housing and living conditions	Rapid implementation (internal evaluations of staff performance in funding agencies often based on volume of funding supervised)
Substantial involvement of local people (and usually their own community organizations) in project design and implementation	Project designed by agency staff (usually in offices in Europe or North America) or by consultants from funding agency's own nation
Project implemented collaboratively with beneficiaries, their local government and certain national agencies	Project implemented by one construction company or government agency
High ratio of staff costs to total project cost	Low ratio of staff costs to total project cost
Difficult to evaluate using conventional cost–benefit analysis	Easy to evaluate
Little or no direct import of goods or services from abroad	High degree of import of goods or services from funding agency's own nation

Basic infrastructure and services – water, sanitation, garbage disposal, health care, drains – cannot be adequately provided to poorer groups without effective local institutions. Outside agencies may bring knowledge, expertise, capital and advice – but they cannot solve most environmental problems without effective local institutions. Most aid agencies and development banks also operate on a 'project by project' basis when what is needed is a long-term process within each city to strengthen institutional capacity, overseen by democratic governance. There may be potential for private sector enterprises to provide some necessary improvements in infrastructure and services, but most literature on privatization overstates this potential and may even forget that effective privatization needs strong, competent and representative local government to oversee quality and control prices charged, especially in those services which are a natural monopoly.

THE ROLE OF NGOs AND CITIZEN GROUPS

Given the limited capacity of most city and municipal governments and, for many, their lack of democratic structures (and transparency in decisions about resource-use), it would be a great mistake to continue channelling most external support through national governments. After all, it is the failure of these governments which underlies the most serious environmental problems. In addition, it is low-income individuals, households and communities working *outside* of government who have been responsible for building most new housing units in Third World cities, and for a large proportion of all investments in housing and infrastructure and services.[5]

More support should be channelled to help fund the choices made and actions taken by low-income individuals and households and the community organizations that they form to address their environmental problems. This can mean not only more cost-effective action than through the state; it can also strengthen citizen and community movements which in turn are central to building more democratic and accountable state structures. It is worth recalling that in Europe, North America and Japan, only through well organized citizen action and protest sustained over many years did governments begin to act on the environmental problems created by industries and motor vehicles. Citizen groups did much to document the scale and nature of the problems and to alert people to the dangers. Citizen groups, philanthropic societies, and what today we would call NGOs also had a major role in driving the political and institutional changes which so greatly improved the quality of the urban environment in the North in the late-nineteenth and early-twentieth centuries.[6]

This link between democracy and citizen action is illustrated by the literature on environmental problems in Third World cities. Our review of this literature produced numerous examples from India and Malaysia. This might be taken to imply that environmental problems were more serious there. We suspect a different reason – the fact that in both nations there are national and local non-government organizations active on environmental issues. They include some, such as the Centre for Science and Environment in Delhi, the Consumers Association of Penang and Sahabat Alam Malaysia, which have international reputations. If this is the reason, it gives a clue about how to mobilize action in the Third World. Outside agencies wanting to stimulate more action on environmental problems in cities might consider providing support direct to citizen groups and NGOs within these cities, not only to implement projects, but also to document the problems and to organize lobbies. There are fewer environmental NGOs in most Third World nations, especially NGOs which concentrate on the most pressing environmental problems (particularly those which affect poorer groups most) and their political underpinnings. Those that exist often work in much more difficult circumstances than their First World counterparts. For instance, funding is less easy to find and government legislation to control pollution is less clear. In many instances, such NGOs suffer from harassment or repression by government. The fact that so many examples in this report come from India reflects the fact that Indian NGOs are among the most active and well-organized – and among the first to identify the critical links between environmental issues and poverty. And as noted earlier, the scale of industrial pollution in Cubatao, and the Brazilian and multinational firms responsible for it, only came to light with the return to democracy in Brazil.

New channels of support must also be found for community-based action: for instance for squatter settlements whose inhabitants have no chance of public support for a piped-water supply, drains and a child health centre. Although there are many examples of highly cost-effective projects in squatter settlements funded by external agencies, the scale of support remains small and generally *ad hoc*. Decisions about what and who to fund remain firmly centralized in the North. The scale of funding and the conditions under which it is available remains more appropriate to the funding base and accounting procedures of northern institutions than the needs of southern groups. We need to develop new channels – for instance, funds to support community-level initiatives where decisions are made locally and where accountability is to local institutions. Even the most flexible institutional structure among external donors cannot support hundreds of community based initiatives, if all decisions about funding and all monitoring and evaluation is concentrated in the donor's office in the North. Box 7.1 outlines a possible form for a Fund for Community Initiatives to channel loans, technical advice and additional support to low-income households and their community organizations for income generation; improved infrastructure and services; shelter upgrading; and improved environmental health. Three critical features are worth highlighting:

- decisions about what is funded are made locally with a minimum gap between the request and its consideration;
- the decision-making process is completely transparent so all groups in a city know who applies for funds, who receives funds and why; and
- most funding is made available as a loan with further loans dependent on cost recovery.

Aid agencies wishing to support community level initiatives could channel their support through such funds.

A CITY-SPECIFIC ENVIRONMENTAL AGENDA

Each city has its own unique set of environmental problems which, with limited resources, can only be addressed with a knowledge of local resources, local constraints and the possibilities for innovative approaches which reduce capital requirements. The fact that capital is limited demands a more profound knowledge of the nature of environmental problems and their causes to allow limited resources to be used to best effect; only with large capital resources can conventional solutions be implemented, applying uniform standards to serve all citizens.[7] Solutions must be discussed locally and influenced by local citizens' own needs and priorities. Partnerships between municipal authorities, local NGOs and community organizations formed by low-income groups within particular neighbourhoods have often proved more cost effective than conventional approaches.[8]

This implies a different agenda to the path taken by European or North American governments towards environmental policies during the 1970s and 1980s. One obvious difference is the level of wealth and prosperity. But four other differences need stressing.

- Most Third World economies, employment patterns and foreign exchange earnings are more *dependent on natural resource* exploitation. In the North, a very small proportion of the labour force depends on farming or forestry so a decision to protect the beauty of a rural landscape by putting controls on farming or forestry hardly affects the balance of payments, the scale of economic activities or employment opportunities. The impact of comparable controls is much greater in nations where a substantial proportion of foreign exchange earnings and jobs depend on farming and forestry. In many Third World nations, the most profound environmental (and political) conflicts are centred on who has the right to own or use forests, freshwater resources and fertile land; worldwide, tens of millions of low-income rural households are losing the right to use natural resources which have long formed the basis of their livelihoods.[9]

Box 7.1 A fund for community initiatives

If the scale of funding to support community-level initiatives to improve environmental health is to increase substantially, new institutional channels are needed. Existing funding agencies cannot cope with a large increase in requests for small projects.

One possibility would be a Fund for Community Initiatives set up within each country, accepting funds from external donors but managed by a small board of representatives drawn from existing NGOs already working in that country with low-income groups and community organizations.

Kinds of projects to be supported:

- *health*: for example, support for the construction of sanitary latrines or improved water supplies; campaigns to promote personal and household hygiene and preventive health measures including mother and child immunization; the setting up or expansion of community based health centres;
- *education*: for example, special programmes for children or adolescents who left school early; literacy programmes;
- *housing*: building material banks, small loans for individual households to upgrade their housing;
- *environment*: site drainage, improved water supplies; or
- *employment*: support for micro-enterprises, local employment exchanges; skill training etc.

Funding: Between US$2000 and US$20,000 available to any group or community organization formed by low-income households. The first loan provided would generally be small, with further loans available if the project (and cost recovery) proceeds to plan. Some level of counterpart funding will be expected (although this might be in the form of labour contribution).
Terms: Total or close to total cost recovery sought for most kinds of projects – with allowance made for inflation and for the cost of borrowing funds. For most projects, a short grace period would be permitted before the loan repayment had to begin (typically three months to a year) so that income generated or savings made are partially realised before repayments begin. The Fund for Community Initiatives would also provide a range of support services – for instance, assistance to community organizations to develop proposals, and technical and managerial support in project implementation. Grants or soft loans could be made available for certain specific interventions where cost recovery is difficult to achieve (either because funding cannot easily be collected or because incomes are too low).
Administration: The administration of the Fund including application procedures and decision-making processes has to be kept simple, with a capacity to respond rapidly. It also has to be transparent, with information about all decisions made public to avoid possible misunderstandings. This transparency would include the setting of explicit loan conditions including repayment period, grace period (if any), interest rate and subsidy element.

- Virtually all Third World nations *lack the institutions* and the infrastructure on which to base effective actions to address urban environmental problems. In Europe and North America, when the 'environmental movement' began to grow and acquire increasing influence in the early 1960s, the basic infrastructure – water pipes, drains, sewers and treatment plans, and landfill sites – were already in place even if more investment was needed to improve the quality of sewage treatment and solid waste disposal. Perhaps more importantly, the institutional structure to implement it was also there, especially the local government structure and an established system to fund local government investments and expenditures. Most Third World governments cannot implement comparable environmental policies with their weak institutional structures (especially at local government level), very inadequate capital budgets, large backlogs in providing basic infrastructure and economies far less able to generate the capital needed to address the backlog.
- There are also obvious differences in the *nature of government*. In West Europe and North America, action on environmental problems was almost always citizen led; citizen groups and NGOs provided the lobby which eventually produced changes in government policy. This required representative government structures. Many Third World nations do not have representative governments; many of those which have returned to democratic rule at national level still retain relatively undemocratic structures at local level. These are unlikely to implement environmental policies, except those that benefit the richer and more powerful members of society, unless there are strong democratic pressures pushing them in these directions. There has been no shortage of citizen groups pressing strongly for water, sanitation, health care and the right to live in cities without the constant fear of eviction but this does not appear to have had much impact on the housing and health policies of most Third World governments. These causes have rarely been supported by middle-class professionals or indeed by unions and religious bodies.
- Much of the environmentalism in the North in recent decades has been driven by middle- and upper-income groups whose health or access to natural landscapes was being impaired. Most of the environmental problems they highlighted could be addressed without changes in the *distribution of income and assets*. This is not the case for many environmental problems in the Third World, since they are rooted in the current distribution of assets, income and rights to use resources.[10]

NEW PROFESSIONAL ATTITUDES

One reason for the lack of attention by professionals to the most pressing environmental problems can be attributed to the sectoral nature of government and of professional disciplines. As Richard Stren has pointed out, in the final chapter of his book *Sustainable Cities*, most environmental problems are multi-dimensional, interconnected, interactive and dynamic which makes appropriate actions difficult for conventional government structures. The architects, planners and engineers who work for departments of housing or public works know very little about the environmental health problems faced by those they are meant to serve. Their training may not even consider this as an issue – especially if the curriculum for their training is based on Western models. Where a Ministry or Department of the Environment is set up, these problems may also fall outside its brief. Peter Kolsky has illustrated the problems posed by professional and administrative boundaries in relation to drainage.[11] Sewerage, drainage and solid waste services (including street cleaning) are often the responsibility of different agencies – yet their design, implementation and management should be carefully coordinated. Drainage systems cannot work in most Third World cities without solid-waste management which keeps drains clean. Drainage networks need coordinated action at household, neighbourhood and city level – and beyond the city to maintain water quality for those living 'downstream' of the city – yet rarely do their design and operation take account of this fact. There is also the separation between those who design, and those who run, these systems; professionals who design sewerage, drainage and solid-waste management systems are rarely from the public agencies who are responsible for their operation and maintenance.

There is a need for new attitudes among professionals whose training also equips them to work cooperatively with low-income households and the community organizations they form. If, as many specialists have recommended, more support is to be channelled to citizen-directed community-level initiatives, professionals will need to learn how to work cooperatively at community level. As a recent report by a WHO Expert Committee on environmental health in urban development states, there is also a need for community-oriented environmental health workers who are analogous to primary healthcare workers who can serve as a bridge between public-sector services and community residents as promoters and organizers of community efforts.[12] New tools and methods are also needed for community-based actions which guide professionals in how to work with low-income groups and their community organizations in identifying problems and their underlying causes, and developing appropriate solutions. This will include a better understanding of the needs and priorities of women in low-income communities – which are so often ignored or misunderstood (see Box 7.2).

Box 7.2 Gender aspects of environmental improvement in cities

The provision of water supplies, sanitation, health care and other essential forms of infrastructure and services must be based on an understanding of the needs and priorities of those who, within households, are responsible for water collection, sanitation, laundry, disposing of household wastes, child rearing, caring for the sick and other daily necessities. In most instances, these are responsibilities which fall on women. For households engaged in urban agriculture, it is generally women who take on most of the responsibility for growing crops or raising livestock.

But women are rarely consulted about their needs when plans are drawn up for improving infrastructure and services in squatter settlements, or for new residential developments for poorer households. They are rarely consulted about their preferences for the form and content of services – for instance, health clinics and ante- and post-natal services are often open at times which working women cannot attend. Public transport provision is often timed to serve primary-income earners but rarely considers the transport needs of secondary-income earners or adults who work at home. Provision of water supply rarely considers the needs of those who are responsible for washing, household hygiene and laundry or the time it takes to collect water although this has important health implications. When such services are not provided, it is generally women who have to give extra time and effort. The low priority given to crèches and childcare centres is often a reflection of choices made with little or no involvement of those primarily responsible for childcare – women. Residential zoning may prohibit the kinds of informal productive activities in which women commonly engage within their homes.

Designs for housing and settlements must take into account the special needs and responsibilities of women. For instance, if women's needs are taken into account, the size and design of house plots in serviced-site schemes may be changed to take into account women's priorities for space for income earning activities within the home. Easy access to clinics, childcare centres, markets and schools would get a higher priority, if those responsible for childcare and housework were allowed more influence in settlement design.

Government programmes for low-cost housing, for housing finance and for skill training must ensure that they do not exclude women. To date, many such programmes have explicitly or implicitly excluded women – for instance through only accepting applications from 'male heads of household' or through 'proof of formal employment' when 40 per cent of more of all households are women headed households, most of whom cannot work in the formal sector. Application forms for low-cost housing,

housing finance or skill training are often complex and this discriminates against women, if women already suffer discrimination through lack of access to education. Self-help housing projects must also recognize the limitations faced by women-headed households in allocating time to self-help activities.

Policies and programmes to protect common lands or public lands must help protect the rights of the poorer groups who currently use such lands for foraging, firewood collection and livestock grazing. Since it is often poor women who are responsible for foraging and firewood collection, a failure to protect such common resources from appropriation by private interests or to protect their productivity often hits women hardest.

Government programmes to support community actions to improve housing and living conditions or encourage resource conservation must be framed with an understanding of the role of women and their own networks within communities. Women are likely to be more responsive than men since such programmes should bring direct benefits to those who are responsible for child rearing, maintaining the house and nursing the sick.

Sources: Drawn from various chapters in Moser, Caroline O N and Peake, Linda (eds) (1987) *Women, Human Settlements and Housing*, Tavistock Publications, New York and London; and from different papers in the special issue of *Environment and Urbanization* edited by Diana Lee-Smith and Ann Schlyter on 'Women in Environment and Urbanization' (vol. 3, no. 2, October 1991).

Some innovative work has been done on participatory tools and methods for developing community-based action programmes (for instance on Primary Environmental Care[13] and on participatory appraisals of health problems and their causes) but this remains an area where much work is still needed. In rural areas, 'participatory rural appraisal' is helping to transform professional attitudes about how to work with low-income groups and their own organizations in agriculture, natural resource management and social issues in villages; a comparable transformation is needed for professionals in urban areas.

Professional resistance to innovative local solutions is also a major constraint. There is no lack of case studies from around the Third World showing how the most pressing environmental problems can be greatly reduced at a relatively modest cost – especially where local groups and institutions take a central role in developing solutions. Major improvements can be made to poorer groups' living environments at relatively modest per capita costs through six interventions:

- water piped into or near to the home of each inhabitant;
- systems installed to remove and dispose of human excreta;
- a higher priority to the installation and maintenance of drains and services to collect garbage;

- primary health care systems available to all (including a strong health prevention component which is so central in any primary health care system);
- house sites made available to poorer groups which are not on land prone to flooding, landslides, mudslides or any other site-related hazard; and
- the implementation of existing environmental legislation.[14]

The cost constraints of applying these measures appear to be over-stated; work on alternatives to conventional water, sanitation and garbage collection systems have shown a range of cheap options[15] while poorer groups' willingness and ability to pay for improved services – if these match their own priorities – appears to have been under-estimated.[16] In many cities, it is not so much a lack of demand for water, sanitation, health care and garbage collection that is the problem, but a combination of an institutional incapacity to deliver cheap and effective services, and a reluctance of professionals to develop innovative local solutions.

CITY PROBLEMS WITHIN A GLOBAL PERSPECTIVE

The fact that the environmental issues which dominate discussions in Europe, Japan and North America are rarely the environmental issues which pose the most serious risks to most Third World citizens' health, threatens to exacerbate the divisions between North and South apparent 20 years ago. For instance, the concentration in the North on issues such as global warming, stratospheric ozone depletion and deforestation in the lead up to the 1992 United Nations Conference on Environment and Development, could be seen as a way through which the North might limit the competitiveness of Southern economies in the world market. It is not surprising that issues relating to the modification of global climate have come to the top of the agenda both of governments and of environmental groups in the North, given estimates of their cost to northern economies which could result from stratospheric ozone depletion and sustained atmospheric warming.[17] In the North, most regional, city, neighbourhood and housing-related environmental problems described in earlier sections have been addressed. Public memories there are too short to recall just how dangerous and unhealthy the city environments in the North were, only 100 years or so ago, because of damp and overcrowded housing, contaminated water, a lack of sewers, drains and provision for garbage collection and street cleaning, no pollution control and ineffective urban government. Diarrhoeal diseases, typhoid, pneumonia and tuberculosis were major causes of death in London just 100 years ago – while in poor, crowded districts, more than one child in five died before its first birthday,[18] as is common in poor districts in Third World cities today. What is also forgotten is the essential role that more effective, accountable and democratic urban governance took in transforming the quality of the urban environment.

The continued stress by groups in the North on the links between environmental degradation and 'over-population', where the South is seen as the guilty party, is also divisive. Such a stress is of questionable accuracy when it is the high-consumption life styles of the relatively well-off – most of them in the North – which accounts for most non-renewable resource consumption, most of the generation of toxic and hazardous wastes, most of the greenhouse gases currently in the atmosphere and a considerable proportion of the pressure on soils and forests. It can be argued that it is not over-population which underlies most of the deforestation and soil erosion caused by poorer groups, but the inequitable land owning structures which prevent poorer groups obtaining sufficient land to allow sustainable exploitation; in most nations with significant amounts of rural poverty, there is no absolute shortage of good-quality agricultural land.[19] This is even the case in particular regions long known for their scale of rural poverty.[20] According to the most obvious criteria for judging whether nations are 'over-populated' – per capita figures for land area, cultivable land area, natural resource consumption, waste generation and greenhouse gas emissions – most Third World nations and nearly all the poorest nations come out as among the world's least 'over-populated'.

If a growing proportion of a growing Third World population acquire levels of resource consumption comparable to those in the North, then the global environmental problems which preoccupy the North will be much exacerbated. But what is far more significant for 'sustainable development' is that high standards of health and good-quality environments in Third World cities (and rural areas) can be achieved without high levels of resource consumption and environmental degradation.[21] In addition, improved water supplies, sanitation, drainage, disease vector control and other elements of healthier living environments for poorer groups are likely to contribute significantly to lowering population growth rates.[22]

Most citizens in Africa, Asia and Latin America find it difficult to share the environmental concerns of the North. Questions of survival 20 or more years into the future have little relevance to those concerned with survival today. Attempts by the governments of the North (or the United Nations system) to obtain agreement on controls of greenhouse gas emissions should have as a precondition that support be available for Third World societies to develop their capacity to tackle the environmental problems which daily affect the health and livelihoods of poorer groups – and this includes the economic prosperity and stability on which effective governance may depend. The North should not hope to promote global agreements on important long-term perspectives for maintaining the integrity of global systems when such a high proportion of Third World citizens are suffering from such enormous short-term environmental health problems, and when so many Third World governments face seemingly insurmountable economic problems.

There is a danger that both governments and environmental groups in the Third World will dismiss the global concerns promoted by the North for two reasons. The first is the obvious question of who will pay; the measures needed to reduce greenhouse gas emissions will be expensive to implement, especially for countries which are industrializing rapidly, and have cheap coal. The second is that the North has shown little interest in helping Third World nations resolve the environmental problems which impact most directly on their citizens; indeed, certain multinational corporations with their headquarters in Europe, North America or Japan are seen as major contributors to the Third World's environmental problems.

Perhaps global concerns such as atmospheric warming provide Third World nations with a power in global negotiations which they have never enjoyed, except for OPEC's relatively short-lived power in regard to oil prices. No doubt the North will seek to avoid negotiations with 'the Third World' and will concentrate on individual negotiations with the largest potential Third World contributors to global warming. But it still remains an interesting prospect – whether Third World nations could once again raise demands for a more equal world market and for more aid (and new channels for it) to address their most pressing environmental problems, in return for joint agreement to reduce the threats to global warming.

A joint programme to address environmental problems must have the long-term goal of building the capacity within each society to identify, analyse and act on their own environmental problems. Building such a capacity in turn demands action on such issues as unrealistic debt repayment levels and the removal of protectionist barriers around the North's own markets. More prosperous, stable economies in the Third World with citizens no longer suffering constantly from environment-related (and usually easily preventable) diseases, disablement and premature deaths should be preconditions for global agreements. These also provide a more realistic basis from which to advance other important development goals – not least among these being stronger democracies and more effective, accountable local governments.

One special concern of this report has been the impact of urban environmental problems on the health and well being of poorer groups. This too is an aspect given inadequate attention in the North. Researchers there tend to focus too much on the presence of some pollutant or pathogen and too little on how and why they are there and on whom they impact most severely. In considering environmental problems, one must consider why certain groups of people are worst affected.

Third World cities' environmental problems are wider in scope that those conventionally considered by environmental groups in the North. The housing environments of lower-income groups in Third World cities rank as among the most life-threatening and unhealthy living environments which exist. When confronted with statistics such as one child in three dying before the age of five – as is the case in some of the worst served illegal settlements – the seriousness of the problem becomes apparent. The need for more documentation, monitoring and pressure for action is acute, and should be encouraged by the fact that an enormous reduction in these problems is relatively easy to achieve, even with limited investments.

The effectiveness of Third World environmental groups and citizen groups can be enhanced with support from the North. Northern environmental groups have considerable experience in organizing well-targeted lobbying and publicity campaigns. Working together on the most immediate and serious environmental problems, including those in cities, would lay an appropriate foundation for joint action on global concerns. Only through joint actions to tackle the environmental problems which impact most on poorer citizens of the Third World, are they able to share First World citizens' longer-term environmental concerns. Only through a redistribution of decision-making powers and resources in their favour, both within and between nations, will they be able to act effectively on both.

Notes and references

1 A NEW ENVIRONMENT AGENDA FOR CITIES

Unless otherwise stated, urban statistics have been drawn from United Nations (1991) *World Urbanization Prospects 1990; Estimates and Projections of Urban and Rural Populations and of Urban Agglomerations*, United Nations, New York, ST/ESA/SER.A/121.

1. Environmental capital is understood to include: local and global sinks, renewable resources, and non-renewable resources; see chapter 6 for more details.
2. Douglas, Ian (1983) *The Urban Environment*, Edward Arnold, London.
3. In general, the costs per household of installing most forms of infrastructure and supplying most kinds of service fall with increasing population density. Higher capital expenditures per person in infrastructure and service provision in urban areas is more a reflection of higher quality provision than higher costs; this only becomes a public expenditure bias towards urban areas if the beneficiaries do not pay the full costs. However, increasing population density can also demand higher investment – for instance, relatively low-cost ventilated improved pit latrines can often provide hygienic and convenient forms of sanitation in rural settlements and in urban areas where population densities are not too high – but more expensive systems are needed in higher density urban settlements. The costs of infrastructure and services may also rise with city size, if the costs of acquiring land for their provision is a significant part of the total cost. The need for more complex and sophisticated pollution controls may also rise with increasing population density. For instance, treatment for effluent from sewers and storm drains from a small urban centre may not need as complex and expensive a treatment as those from larger cities. There are also the costs to the public authorities of formulating and implementing environmental legislation which may rise with city size. See Linn, Johannes F (1982) 'The costs of urbanization in developing countries' *Economic Development and Cultural Change* vol. 30, no. 3 for a more detailed discussion. See also World Bank, (1991) *Urban Policy and Economic Development: An Agenda for the 1990s* Washington DC.
4. We use the term 'Third World' and 'South' interchangeably to refer to all countries in Africa, Latin America, and Asia (except Japan) and Micronesia,

Melanesia and Polynesia. The term 'the North' is used to refer to countries in Europe, Northern America and the former Soviet Union and to Japan. None of these terms are entirely satisfactory; 'North' and 'South' have the advantage of having no normative implications but they are not accurate geographically (for instance, Australia and New Zealand may be included in the 'North' politically and economically but are clearly part of the 'South' in geographic terms). With recent changes in the former Soviet Union and East Europe, the term 'Third World' has lost its relevance in delineating the non-aligned countries from those associated with the two main power blocs, within a world shaped by the cold war (the First and Second Worlds). But the 'Third World' and 'the North and the South' are less value laden and inaccurate than such terms as 'developing' and 'developed' countries or 'more developed' and 'less developed'. The use of the terms 'industrialized' and 'non-industrialized' nations has also lost its meaning, given the high level of industrialization evident in many Latin American and Asian nations, and some African nations. Although the term 'Third World' is sometimes interpreted as having pejorative implications, its original use (especially by the non-aligned nations themselves) never had this intention.

5. This is an issue discussed in more detail in Chapter 6. Some of the most populous Third World countries such as China, India, Indonesia, Brazil and Mexico are now among the largest contributors to greenhouse gas emissions but their contributions per capita remain much smaller than those of countries in the North (especially the USA, Canada, Australia and the wealthier European nations). See Agarwal, Anil and Sunita Narain (1991) *Global Warming in an Unequal World – a Case of Environmental Colonialism*, Centre for Science and Environment, Delhi and World Resources Institute, (1991) *World Resources 1991–92: a Guide to the Global Environment: Toward Sustainable Development*, Oxford University Press, Oxford.
6. Rabinovitch, Jonas (1992) 'Curitiba: towards sustainable urban development' *Environment and Urbanization* vol. 4, no. 2. See also Chapter 5 for more details.
7. Di Pace, Maria J, Federovisky, Sergio, Hardoy, Jorge E, Morello, Jorge H and Stein, Alfredo (1992) 'Human Settlements and Sustainable Development – the Latin American Case' in Stren, Richard E. and Rodney White (eds), *Sustainable Cities: Urbanization and the Environment in International Perspective*, Westview Press, Boulder, pp. 205–227.
8. Cairncross, Sandy *et al* (1990) 'The urban context' in Jorge E Hardoy, Sandy Cairncross and David Satterthwaite (eds), *The Poor Die Young: Housing and Health in Third World Cities*, Earthscan Publications, London 1990. More recently, this figure was endorsed by WHO (1992), *Our Planet, Our Health*. Report of the Commission on Health and Environment, Geneva, 1992.
9. Edgerton, Lynne (1990) 'Warmer temperatures, unhealthier air and sicker children', in James McCulloch (Editor), *Cities and Global Climate Change*, Climate Institute, Washington DC, pp. 145–148.
10. We have been using these geographic categories of home and workplace, district or neighbourhood, city, city-region, and global-level for some years to highlight the particular way in which an environmental agent impacts on

human populations. Ian Douglas has suggested four similar but slightly different scales through which to consider the interactions between cities' physical form and flows of energy, water and materials: the micro, meso, macro and mega-scale. See Douglas, Ian (1989) 'The rain on the roof: a geography of the urban environment' in Dick Gregory and Rex Walford (eds), *Horizons in Human Geography*, Barnes and Noble, New Jersey, pp. 217–238.

11. This figure is drawn from United Nations (1991) *World Urbanization Prospects 1990; Estimates and Projections of Urban and Rural Populations and of Urban Agglomerations*, United Nations, New York. ST/ESA/SER.A/121. This lists 172 urban agglomerations in the Third World which had one million or more inhabitants in 1990. However, the list included Naucalpan in Mexico as a separate urban agglomeration and since this is part of the Mexico City Metropolitan Area, the total number of urban agglomerations with one or more million inhabitants was adjusted to 171.
12. This is drawn from an analysis of data from a database on city populations which include all available figures for city populations historically, as well as those from recent censuses. This includes current and historic data for all urban centres in Latin America and the Caribbean, drawing on Jorge Hardoy's work on pre-Columbian, colonial and post-colonial urbanization in Latin America and on the compilation of all available data on urban populations for all urban centres with 10,000 or more inhabitants in the most recent census for Latin America and the Caribbean between 1850 and 1989 which IIED-América Latina and IIED recently completed. For Africa and Asia, the database relies mostly on United Nations (1991) *World Urbanization Prospects 1990; Estimates and Projections of Urban and Rural Populations and of Urban Agglomerations*, United Nations, New York, ST/ESA/SER.A/121, for city populations between 1950 and 1990, with new data from recent censuses incorporated into this, as this becomes available. For historic data for cities in Africa and Asia, the database drew on Showers, Victor (1979) *World Facts and Figures*, John Wiley and Sons, Chichester, and on Chandler, Tertius and Gerald Fox, (1974) *3000 Years of Urban Growth*, Academic Press, New York and London – with individual figures for particular cities up-dated or amended, as more detailed or accurate figures or estimates were found.
13. United Nations 1991, see note 11.
14. Since Japan is not classified as part of the Third World, this figure does not include Japanese cities.
15. Drawn from the database described in note 12.
16. Some care must be taken in making projections well into the future. It is impossible to produce an accurate description of recent urban trends because census data after 1980–82 is not yet available for most nations. We know little about the scale of urban change during the 1980s. Most of the urban population statistics given for 1985, 1990 and beyond in statistical compendia are simply projections based on older census data. Once sufficient census data comes available to show urban trends for the 1980s, it is likely to reveal a considerable slow-down in the rate at which urbanization levels have

increased in most Third World nations, and slower growth rates for most national urban populations and large cities. These will reflect slower economic growth or economic stagnation during the 1980s which in most instances implies a slower transfer of population from rural to urban areas. Slower rates of increase in the level of urbanization will also reflect the fact that such rates tend to slow as a society becomes more urban. Slower growth rates for the largest cities and for national urban populations will also reflect lower rates of natural increase.

17. During the 1970s, UN projections for the population of Mexico City by the year 2000 were generally over 30 million. Since then, the projections for 2000 have varied between 25.6 million and 27.6 million. If preliminary results from the 1990 census prove accurate, Mexico City may have less than 16 million people in 1990 and this implies less than 20 million people by 2000, unless there is a major change in prevailing trends. Similarly, Calcutta's population in 1991 according to preliminary census figures was 10.9 million and its population in the year 2000 is likely to be several million less than UN projections for 2000. Census data from Argentina and Nigeria which have become available during 1992 also show a slower growth in urban populations and in the population of most 'mega-cities' than UN projections had suggested. In regard to Mexico City's population, see Garza, Gustavo (April 1991) 'The metropolitan character of urbanization in Mexico, 1900–1988', (Mimeo), For more discussion on the validity of UN projections, see chapter 8 of Hardoy, Jorge E and David Satterthwaite (1989) *Squatter Citizen: Life in the Urban Third World*, Earthscan Publications, London.
18. Statistics drawn from the newsletter ANAWIM published by the Share and Care Apostolate for Poor Settlers vol. IV, no. 4, 1990.
19. Lamba, Davinder (1992), draft report on *Environmental Problems of Nairobi*, Mazingira Institute, Nairobi. (This report will be completed in early 1993 and available from Mazingira Institute, Box 14550, Nairobi, Kenya).
20. The question of whether Colombo has a high population density depends on whether this is calculated based on Colombo City (with some 600,000 inhabitants in 37 square kilometres), the urban core with 235 square kilometres, or the city region with some 1,800 square kilometres; see Sivaramakrishnan, K.C. and Leslie Green (1986), *Metropolitan Management – The Asian Experience*, Oxford University Press (for the World Bank) Oxford. Shanghai has a low population density; its population in 1990 was 12.8 million within an area of 6,340.5 square kilometres, giving an average density of around 20 persons per hectare. However, the average density in different administrative districts varied from more than 600 to less than 50 and in certain parts of the central city, it rises to over 1,500 per hectare. See Zipei, Zhao (1992) 'Air quality of Shanghai and strategies to control it' Paper presented at an international workshop on 'Planning for Sustainable Urban Development', University of Wales College of Cardiff, and Zhongmin, Yan (1988) 'Shanghai: the growth and shifting emphasis of China's largest city' in Victor FS Sit (ed.), *Chinese Cities: the Growth of the Metropolis since 1949*, Oxford University Press, Hong Kong, pp. 94–127.

21. Squatter settlements often appear densely populated, but this is usually due to so few of the buildings having more than one storey. In terms of the number of residents per hectare, they usually have a much lower density than high quality residential areas in central districts of European cities with 3–5 storey terraced housing. For instance, much of Chelsea in London, one of this city's most expensive and desirable residential areas, has more than 500 persons per hectare. If squatters can obtain legal tenure, it is usually possible to develop their shelters into two or three storey dwellings (which can greatly reduce overcrowding within the housing stock) while also making it easier to find space to improve access roads or paths.
22. Based on an analysis of Brazil's 1980 census.
23. Results of the 1984 census reported in Environmental Protection Council (1989), *Ghana Environmental Action Plan* vol. 1, Accra.

2 ENVIRONMENTAL PROBLEMS IN THE HOME, WORKPLACE AND NEIGHBOURHOOD

1. Definition based on that in chapter 1 of WHO (1992) *Our Planet, Our Health*, Report of the WHO Commission on Health and Environment, Geneva.
2. Cairncross, Sandy (1990) 'Water supply and the urban poor' in Jorge E Hardoy *et al* (eds), *The Poor Die Young: Housing and Health in Third World Cities*, Earthscan Publications, London.
3. WHO (1992) *Our Planet, Our Health*, Report of the WHO Commission on Health and Environment, Geneva.

4–5. Cairncross 1990, see note 2.

6. World Bank (1988) *World Development Report 1988*, Oxford University Press, Oxford, p 146.
7. Briscoe, John (1986) 'Selected primary health care revisited', in Joseph S Tulchin (ed.), *Health, Habitat and Development*, Lynne Reinner, Boulder.
8. Ngom, Thiecouta (1989) 'Appropriate standards for infrastructure in Dakar', in Richard E Stren and Rodney R White (eds), *African Cities in Crisis*, Westview Press, USA, pp. 176–202.
9. Sinnatamby, Gehan (1990), 'Low cost sanitation' in Jorge E Hardoy *et al* (eds) (1990), *The Poor Die Young: Housing and Health in Third World Cities*, Earthscan Publications, London.
10. Centre for Science and Environment (1983) *The State of India's Environment – a Citizen's Report*, Delhi, India.
11. Kulaba, Saitiel (1989), 'Local government and the management of urban services in Tanzania', in Richard E Stren and Rodney R White (eds), *African Cities in Crisis*, Westview Press, USA pp. 203–245.
12. Sivaramakrishnan, KC and Leslie Green (1986) *Metropolitan Management – The Asian Experience*, Oxford University Press (for the World Bank), Oxford.
13. Schteingart, Martha, (1989) 'The environmental problems associated with urban development in Mexico City', *Environment and Urbanization* vol. 1, no. 1, pp. 40–49.

14. Zorrilla, Silvia and Guaresti, Maria Elena, (1986) *Sector Agua Potables y Saneamiento: Lineamientos para una Estrategia Nacional*, PNUD (UN Development Programme), Buenos Aires. Most of the population within the central city (the Federal District) of Buenos Aires has piped water and sewer connections; it is the 8.4 million people living in the metropolitan area but outside this district (within the Province of Buenos Aires) which are so poorly served – roughly half lack piped water and two thirds lack sewer connections. The population figure of 11.3 million for Buenos Aires is a preliminary figure from the 1991 census.
15. For more details and discussion, see Hardoy, Jorge E and Satterthwaite, David (1981)*Shelter: Need and Response; Housing, Land and Settlement Policies in Seventeen Third World Nations*, John Wiley and Sons, Chichester, UK.
16. Cairncross 1990, see note 2.
17. WHO 1992, see note 3.
18. For detailed examples, see Aina, Tade Akin (1989) *Health, Habitat and Underdevelopment – with Special Reference to a Low-Income Settlement in Metropolitan Lagos*, IIED Technical Report, London; and Murphy, Denis (1990) *A Decent Place to Live – Urban Poor in Asia*, Asian Coalition for Housing Rights, Bangkok.
19. WHO 1992, see note 3.
20. Centre for Science and Environment 1983, see note 10.
21. Pio, A, (1986) 'Acute respiratory infections in children in developing countries: an international point of view', *Pediatric Infectious Disease Journal* vol. 5, no. 2, pp. 179–183.
22. WHO 1992, page 204, see note 3.
23. WHO 1992, see note 3.
24. McGranahan, Gordon (1991) *Environmental Problems and the Urban Household in Third World Countries*, The Stockholm Environment Institute, Stockholm.
25. McGranahan 1991, see note 24.
26. McGranahan, Gordon (1992) 'Household environmental problems' Paper presented at the International Workshop on 'Planning for Sustainable Urban Development', University of Wales College of Cardiff, July.
27. Esrey, SA and Feachem RG (1989), 'Interventions for the Control of Diarrhoeal Disease: Promotion of Food Hygiene', World Health Organization, Geneva, WHO/CDD/89.30, quoted in WHO 1992, see note 3.
28. WHO (1990) *Global Estimates for Health Situation Assessments and Projections 1990*, Division of Epidemiological Surveillance and Health Situation and Trend Analysis, World Health Organization, Geneva, WHO/HST/90.2, Geneva.
29. First draft of a report on *The Environmental Problems of Metropolitan Lagos*, Lagos Group for the Study of Human Settlements, to be published in 1993.
30. Auer, C (1989) *Health Problems (especially intestinal parasitoses) of Children Living in Smokey Mountain, a Squatter Area of Manila, Philippines*, Msc.

Thesis, Swiss Tropical Institute, Department of Public Health and Epidemiology, Basel.

31. Bundey, DAP, Kan SOP and Rose R (1988) 'Age related prevalence, intensity and frequency distribution of gastrointestinal helminth infection in urban slum childrem from Kuala Lumpur, Malaysia' *Transactions of the Royal Society of Tropical Medicine and Hygiene* vol. 82, pp. 289–294.
32. Misra, Harikesh (1990) 'Housing and health problems in three squatter settlements in Allahabad, India' in Jorge E Hardoy *et al* (eds), *The Poor Die Young: Housing and Health in Third World Cities*, Earthscan Publications, London.
33. This was a sample of countries for which reliable statistics were available – see Manciaux, M and Romer, CJ (1986) 'Accidents in children, adolescents and young adults: a major public health problem' *World Health Statistical Quarterly* vol. 39, no. 3, pp. 227–231.
34. Manciaux and Romer 1986, see note 33.
35. WHO 1992, see note 3.
36. SR Kamat, personal communication, in WHO 1992, see note 3.
37. WHO (1989) *Urbanization and its Implications for Child Health: Potential for Action*, World Health Organization, Geneva.
38. WHO 1990, see note 28.
39. WHO (1992) *Report of the Panel on Industry*, WHO Commission on Health and Environment, Geneva, WHO/EHE/92.4.
40. WHO 1990, see note 28.
41. Pepall, Jennifer (1992) 'Occupational poisoning' reporting on the work of Mohamad M Amr in *IDRC Reports* vol. 20, no. 1, Ottawa, p. 15.
42. Castonguay, Gilles (1992) 'Steeling themselves with knowledge' report on the work of Cristina Laurell, *IDRC Reports* vol. 20, no. 1, pp. 10–12.
43. Phantumvanit, Dhira and Liengcharernsit, Wanai (1989) 'Coming to terms with Bangkok's environmental problems', *Environment and Urbanization* vol. 1, no. 1, pp. 31–39.
44. See Centre for Science and Environment (1985) *The State of India's Environment: a Second Citizens' Report*, Delhi, India; and Centre for Science and Environment 1983 (see note 10) for many examples.
45. Centre for Science and Environment 1983, see note 10.
46. Centre for Science and Environment 1983, see note 10.
47. Matte, TD, Figueroa, JP, Ostrowski, S, Burr G, *et al* (1989), 'Lead poisoning among household members exposed to lead–acid battery repair shops in Kingston, Jamaica (West Indies)' *International Journal of Epidemiology* vol. 18, pp. 874–881.
48. Askoy, M *et al* (1976) 'Types of leukaemia in a chronic benzene poisoning', *Acta haematologica* vol. 55, pp. 67–72, quoted in WHO 1992, see note 3.
49. Michaels, David, Barrera, Clara and Gacharna, Manuel (1985) 'Economic development and occupational health in Latin America: new directions for public health in less developed countries' *American Journal of Public Health* vol. 85, no. 5, pp. 536–542.
50. UNICEF (1992) *Environment, Development and the Child*, Environment Section, Programme Division, UNICEF, New York.

51. UNICEF 1992, see note 50.
52. Lee-Wright, Peter (1990) *Child Slaves*, Earthscan Publications, London.
53. Lee-Wright 1990, see note 52.
54. Douglas, Ian (1983) *The Urban Environment*, Edward Arnold, London.
55. Douglas 1983, see note 54.
56. Jimenez Diaz, Virginia (1992) 'Landslides in the squatter settlements of Caracas; towards a better understanding of causative factors' *Environment and Urbanization* vol. 4, no. 2.
57. Jimenez Diaz 1992, see note 56.
58. See Greenway, DR (1987) 'Vegetation and slope instability' in ME Anderson and KS Richards (eds), *Slope Stability*, John Wiley and Sons, Chichester for a discussion on the different effects of vegetation on slope stability – both adverse and beneficial.
59. Douglas, Ian (1986) 'Urban Geomorphology' in PG Fookes and PR Vaughan (eds), *A Handbook of Engineering Geomorphology*, Surrey University Press (Blackie and Son) Glasgow, pp. 270–283.
60. Hardoy, Jorge E. and Satterthwaite, David (1989) *Squatter Citizen: Life in the Urban Third World*, Earthscan Publications, London. See also McAuslan, Patrick (1984) *Urban Land and Shelter for the Poor*, Earthscan Publications, London; van der Linden, Jan (1982) 'Squatting by organized invasion – a new reply to a failing housing policy?', *Third World Planning Review* vol. 4, no. 4, pp. 400–412; and Sarin, Mahdu (1983) 'The Rich, the Poor and the Land Question' in Angel, Shlomo, Raymon W Archer, Sidhijai Tanphiphat and Emiel A Wegelin (eds) *Land for Housing the Poor*, Select Books, Singapore, pp. 237–253.
61. Unicef 1992, see note 50.
62. Manciaux and Romer 1986, see note 33.
63. Hughes, Bob (1990) 'Children's play – a forgotten right' *Environment and Urbanization* vol. 2, no. 2, pp. 58–64.
64. Reichenheim, M and Harpham, T (1989) 'Child accidents and associated risk factors in a Brazilian squatter settlement' *Health Policy and Planning* vol. 4, no. 2, pp. 162–167.
65. Reichenheim and Harpham 1989, see note 64.
66. Cointreau, Sandra (1982) *Environmental Management of Urban Solid Waste in Developing Countries*, Urban Development Technical Paper no. 5, The World Bank, Washington DC; Lee, James A (1985) *The Environment, Public Health and Human Ecology*, The World Bank, Johns Hopkins University Press, Baltimore and London.
67. For one example, see Izeogu, CZ, (1989) 'Urban development and the environment in Port Harcourt', *Environment and Urbanization* vol. 1, no. 1, pp. 59–68.
68. Cairncross, Sandy and Feachem, Richard G (1983) *Environmental Health Engineering in the Tropics – An Introductory Text*, John Wiley and Sons, Chichester.
69. McGranahan 1991, see note 24. See also Yhdego, Michael (1991) 'Urban environmental degradation in Tanzania' *Environment and Urbanization* vol. 3, no. 1, pp. 147–152.

70. Cointreau 1982, see note 66.
71. Goldstein, Greg (1990) 'Access to life saving services in urban areas' in JE Hardoy *et al* (eds), *The Poor Die Young: Housing and Health in Third World Cities*, Earthscan Publications, London pp. 213–227.
72. WHO 1992, see note 3; Schofield, CJ, Briceno-Leon, R, Kolstrup, N, Webb, DJT, and White, GB (1990), 'The role of house design in limiting vector-borne disease' in Jorge E, Hardoy, *et al* (eds) *The Poor Die Young: Housing and Health in Third World Cities*, Earthscan Publications, London.
73. Gomes Pereira, M (1989) 'Characteristics of urban mortality from Chagas' disease in Brazil's Federal District' *Bulletin of the Pan American Health Organization* vol. 18, no. 1, 1990; and Briceno-Leon, Roberto *La Casa Enferma: Sociologia de la Enfermedad de Chagas*, Consorcio de Ediciones Capriles CA, Caracas.
74. WHO 1992, see note 3.
75. WHO 1992, see note 3.
76. Cairncross, Sandy and Ouano, EAR (1990) *Surface Water Drainage in Low-income Communities*, WHO, Geneva.
77. Kolsky, Peter J (1992) 'Water, health and cities: concepts and examples' Paper presented at the international workshop on Planning for Sustainable Urban Development, University of Wales, July.
78. Cairncross and Ouano 1990, see note 76.

3 THE CITY ENVIRONMENT

1. UNIDO (1981) *A Statistical Review of the World Industrial Situation in 1980.*
2. Calculated from tables in World Bank (1991) *World Development Report 1991*, Oxford University Press, Oxford.
3. Bissau – Davila, Julio D (1987) *Shelter, Poverty and African Revolutionary Socialism: Human Settlements in Guinea Bissau*, IIED, London. Dhaka – World Bank Urban Sector Memorandum quoted in ESCAP (1986) *Study and Review of the Human Settlements Situation in Asia and the Pacific*, vol. II, Country Monographs, United Nations, Bangkok. Lima – Richardson, Harry W (1984), 'Planning Strategies and policies for Metropolitan Lima' in *Third World Planning Review* vol. 6, No. 2. Manila – Apacible, MS and Yaxley, M, (1979) 'Manila through the eyes of the Malinenos and the Consultant' PTRC Summer Annual Meeting, and Jimenez, Rosario D and Velasquez, Sister Aida (1989) 'Metropolitan Manila: a framework for its sustained development', *Environment and Urbanization* vol.1, no. 1, pp. 51–58. Port-au-Prince – US AID (1980) *Haiti Shelter Sector Assessment*, Office of Housing and Urban Development. São Paulo – Hamer, Andrew M (1984) *Decentralized Urban Development and Industrial Location Behaviour in Sao Paulo, Brazil: A Synthesis of Research Issues and Conclusions*, Discussion Paper, Water Supply and Urban Development Department, World Bank, Washington DC.

4. Phantumvanit, Dhira and Liengcharernsit, Wanai (1989) 'Coming to terms with Bangkok's environmental problems', *Environment and Urbanization* vol. 1, no. 1, pp. 31–39.
5. Smil, Vaclav (1984) *The Bad Earth: Environmental Degradation in China*, ME Sharpe, New York, and Zed Press, London.
6. See for instance Sani, S (1987) 'Urbanization and the atmospheric environment in Southeast Asia', in *Environment, Development, Natural Resource Crisis in Asia and the Pacific*, Sahabat Alam, Malaysia.
7. SPP (1984) *Programa de Desarrollo de la ZMCM y de la Region Centrale*, Mexico, quoted in Nigel Harris (1990) *Environmental Issues in the Cities of the Developing World*, DPU Working Paper no. 20, University College London.
8. WHO (1992) *Our Planet, Our Health*, Report of the WHO Commission on Health and Environment, Geneva.
9. Anandalingam, G and Westfall, Mark (1987) 'Hazardous waste generation and disposal: Options for developing countries', *Natural Resources* vol. 11, no. 1, pp. 37–47.
10. For Bangkok, Phantumvanit and Liengcharernsit 1989, see note 4. For Perai, Ruddle, Kenneth (1983) 'Inshore marine pollution in Southeast Asia', *Mazingira* vol. 7, no. 2, pp. 32–44. For Bombay, Centre for Science and Environment, (1983) *The State of India's Environment – a Citizen's Report*, Delhi, India. For Managua, IRENA (1982) *Taller International de Salvamento y Aprovechamiento Integral del Lago de Managua*, vol. 2, no. 2, and Street, Annie (1981) 'Nicaraguans cite Pennwalt, US company has poisoned its workers and Lake Managua', *Multinational Monitor* vol. 2, no. 5, pp. 25–26. For Alexandria, Hamza, Ahmed (1983) 'Management of industrial hazardous wastes in Egypt', *Industry and Environment* Special Issue on Industrial Hazardous Waste Management, no. 4, UNEP-Paris Office, pp. 28–32. For Cartagena, Lopez, Jose Manuel (1988) 'The Caribbean and Gulf of Mexico', *The Siren* no. 36, pp. 30–31. For China, Smil 1984, see note 5.
11. UNEP (1991) *Environmental Data Report, 1991–2*, GEMS Monitoring and Assessment Research Centre, Blackwell, Oxford and Massachusetts.
12. Jimenez, Rosario D and Velasquez, Sister Aida (1989) 'Metropolitan Manila: a framework for its sustained development', *Environment and Urbanization* vol. 1, no. 1; and Leonard, H Jeffrey (1984) *Confronting Industrial Pollution in Rapidly Industrializing Countries – Myths, Pitfalls and Opportunities*, Conservation Foundation.
13. Centre for Science and Environment (1983) *The State of India's Environment – a Citizen's Report*, Delhi, India.
14. Escobar, Jairo (1988) 'The south-east Pacific', *The Siren* No. 36,, pp. 28–29.
15. UNEP/WHO, (1987)*Global Pollution and Health – results of health-related environmental monitoring,* Global Environment Monitoring System.
16. Leonard 1984, see note 12.
17. World Bank (1992) *World Development Report 1992*, Oxford University Press.

18. Smil 1984, see note 5. European standards from Haigh, Nigel (1984) *EEC Environmental Policy and Britain – an Essay and a Handbook*, ENDS, London.
19. Anderson, Ian (1987) 'Isotopes from machine imperil Brazilians', *New Scientist* 15th October 1987, p. 19; and Consumer Information and Documentation Centre (1988) *Consumer Currents*, International Organization of Consumers Unions, March, April, pp. 5–6.
20. Consumer Information and Documentation Centre 1988, see note 19 and Castleman, Barry I (1987) 'Workplace health standards and multinational corporations in developing countries' in Charles S Pearson (ed.), *Multinational Corporation, the Environment and the Third World*, pp. 149–172, Duke University Press, Durham, USA.
21. Castleman 1987, see note 20. The Indian journal *Down to Earth* vol. 1, no. 7, 31 August 1992 reported that a Malaysian court had ordered the shutdown of the chemical plant.
22. Castleman, BI (1979) 'The export of hazardous factories to developing countries', *International Journal of Health Sciences* vol. 9, no. 4, pp. 569–597.
23. Castleman 1979, see note 22; El-Hinnawi, Essam, (1981) 'Three environmental issues', *Mazingira* vol. 5, no. 4, pp. 26–35; and Nishikawa, Jun, (1982) 'The strategy of Japanese Multinationals and South-east Asia', *Development and the Environment Crisis – A Malaysian Case*, Consumers Association of Penang.
24. Pearson, Charles S (1987) 'Environmental standards, industrial relocation and pollution havens' in Pearson 1987, see note 20.
25. Duerksen, Christopher and Leonard, Jeffrey, (1980) 'Environmental regulations and the location of industries: an international perspective' *Columbia Journal of World Business*, Summer, pp. 52–58, quoted in Pearson 1987, see note 20.
26. Castleman 1987, see note 20.
27. Castleman 1987, see note 20.
28. Anderson, Ian (1992), 'Dangerous technology dumped on Third World', report of a paper by Nabiel Makarim presented at a conference in Melbourne, Australia on the trade in hazardous machinery or technologies, *New Scientist*, 7 March.
29. WHO 1992, see note 8.
30. Consumer Information and Documentation Centre (1988) *Consumer Currents*, August, International Organization of Consumers Unions, p. 6.
31. WHO 1992, see note 8.
32. Lee, James A (1985) *The Environment, Public Health and Human Ecology*, World Bank, Johns Hopkins University Press, Baltimore and London.
33. Centre for Science and Environment 1983, p. 23 and 25, see note 13.
34. Maheswaran, A (1982) 'Water pollution in Malaysia; problems, perspectives and control', *Development and the Environment Crisis – A Malaysian Case*, Consumers Association of Penang.

35. Schteingart, Martha (1989) 'The environmental problems associated with urban development in Mexico City', *Environment and Urbanization* vol. 1, no. 1, pp. 40–49.
36. Toksoz, Sadik (1983) 'Impacts of the growth of Mexico City through water supply and waste disposal', UNCHS (Habitat), Nairobi, Kenya, reported in *Habitat News* vol. 5.
37. White, Rodney R (1992) 'The international transfer of urban technology: does the North have anything to offer for the global environmental crisis?' *Environment and Urbanization* vol. 4, no. 2.
38. Douglass, Mike (1989) 'The environmental sustainability of development – coordination, incentives and political will in land use planning for the Jakarta Metropolis', *Third World Planning Review* vol. 11, no. 2, pp. 211–238.
39. WHO 1992, see note 8.
40. World Bank 1992, see note 17.
41. WHO 1992, see note 8.
42. Emissions from diesel engines also contribute to this. See Waller, Robert E (1991) 'Field investigations of air' in WW Holland, R Detels and G Knox (eds), *Oxford Textbook of Public Health* vol. 2 (second edition), Oxford University Press, Oxford and New York, pp. 435–450.
43. Centre for Science and Environment 1983, see note 13.
44. Smil 1984, see note 5.
45. Kim, Ik Ki (1991) 'The environmental problems of poor communities in Seoul', Paper presented at the workshop on 'Urban Community-based Environmental Management in Asia', Bangkok, Thailand.
46. WHO 1992, see note 8.
47. UNEP and WHO (1988) *Assessment of Urban Air Quality*, Global Environment Monitoring Service, United Nations Environment Programme and World Health Organization.
48. WHO 1992, see note 8.
49. UNEP 1991, see note 11.
50. UNEP and WHO 1988, see note 47. These figures are arrived at by extrapolating from assessments of air pollution in over 50 cities.
51. UNEP 1991, see note 11.
52. WHO 1992, see note 8.
53. WHO (1992) *Report of the Panel on Energy*, WHO/EHE/92.3, WHO Commission on Health and Environment, Geneva.
54. UNEP and WHO 1988, see note 47.
55. *'Emergencia ambiental en Mexico por el alto indice de contaminacion' El Clarin*, Buenos Aires, 24 March 1992.
56. Needleman, Herbert L, Schell, Alan, Bellinger, David, Leviton Alan and Allred, Elizabeth N (1991) 'The long-term effects of exposure to low doses on lead in childhood: an eleven year follow up report' *The New England Journal of Medicine* vol. 322. no. 2, pp. 83–88.
57. WHO 1992, see note 8.
58. UNEP and WHO 1988, see note 47.
59. UNEP and WHO 1987, see note 15. In both cities, 10 per cent of the population had lead concentrations in the blood of more than 300 μg/litre

when the WHO Environmental Health Criteria on lead is 200 μg/litre as the level at which biochemical changes in the blood begin to occur.

60. Rothenburg, Stephen J, Schnaas-Arrieta, Lourdes, Perez-Guerrero, Irving A *et al* (1989) 'Evaluacion del riesgo potencial de la exposition perinatal al plombo en el Valle de Mexico' *Perinatologia y Reproduccion Humana* vol. 3, no. 1, pp. 49–56, quoted in WRI (1992) *World Resources 1992–93*, Oxford University Press, Oxford.
61. US AID (1990) *Ranking Environmental Health Risks in Bangkok*, Office of Housing and Urban Programs, Washington DC.
62. McGranahan, Gordon (1991) *Environmental Problems and the Urban Household in Third World Countries*, The Stockholm Environment Institute, Stockholm.
63. UNEP and WHO 1988, see note 47.
64. Sahabat Alam Malaysia (1983) *The State of Malaysian Environment 1983–4* – Towards Greater Environmental Awareness, Malaysia.
65. World Bank 1992, see note 17.
66. UNEP and WHO 1988, see note 47.
67. Zhao, D and Sun, B 'Atmospheric pollution from coal combustion in China' quoted in UNEP and WHO 1988, see note 47.
68. World Bank 1992, see note 17.
69. World Bank 1992, see note 17.
70. WHO and UNEP 1988, see note 47.
71. For Kuala Lumpur, Sani 1987, see note 6. For Calcutta, Murthy, BS, (1979) 'India: environmental aspects of motor vehicles', *Industry and Environment*, UNEP-Paris, April–June pp. 6–7. For Lagos and Ibadan, Achayo Were, PT (1983), 'The development of road transport in Africa and its effect on land use and environment', *Industry and Environment*, UNEP-Paris, April–June, pp. 25–26. For Rio de Janeiro, Leonard 1984, see note 12. For Bangkok, Wangwongwatana, Supat (1992), 'Bangkok metropolis and its air pollution problems', Paper presented at the International Workshop on Planning for Sustainable Urban Development, Cardiff, July.
72. WHO 1992, see note 8.
73. Hofmaier, VA (1991) *Efeitos de Poluicao do ar sobre a Funcao Pulmonar: un Estodo de Cohorte em criancas de Cubatao*, São Paulo School of Public Health, quoted by the WHO 1992, see note 8.
74. Jarzebski, LS (1991), 'Case Study of the Environmental Impact of the Non-Ferrous Metals Industry in the Upper Silesian Area', Paper prepared for the WHO Commission on Health and the Environment and quoted WHO 1992, see note 8.
75. Centre for Science and Environment 1983, see note 13.
76. WHO 1992 see note 8.
77. WHO 1992, see note 8.
78. Centre for Science and Environment 1983, see note 13.
79. Romieu, Isabelle *et al* (1990) 'Urban air pollution in Latin America and the Caribbean: Health perspectives', *World Health Statistics Quarterly* vol. 23, no. 2, pp. 153–167.

80. US AID, (1990) *Ranking Environmental Health Risks in Bangkok*, Office of Housing and Urban Programs, Washington DC.
81. Centre for Science and Environment 1983, see note 13.
82. Marco del Ponte, Louis (1984) *'El crimen de la contaminacion'*, Universidad Autonoma Metropolitana-Atzcapotzaldo, Mexico, quoted in Martha Schteingart, Chapter on Mexico City in Mattei Dogon and John D Casada (eds) (1988) *The Metropolis Era Volume 2*, Sage Publications, Beverly Hills, London and New Delhi.
83. Report in *The Economist*, 18–24 February 1989, p. 69. Also report in *El Clarin*, see note 55.
84. Douglas, Ian (1983) *The Urban Environment*, Edward Arnold, London..
85. Douglas, Ian (1986) 'Urban Geomorphology' in P G Fookes and P R Vaughan (eds), *A Handbook of Engineering Geomorphology*, Surrey University Press (Blackie and Son) Glasgow, pp. 270–283.
86. Hardoy, Jorge E, (1975) 'Two thousand years of Latin American urbanization' in JE Hardoy (ed.), *Urbanization in Latin America: Approaches and Issues*, Anchor Books, New York.
87. Jimenez Diaz, Virginia, (1992) 'Landslides in the squatter settlements of Caracas; towards a better understanding of causative factors' *Environment and Urbanization* vol. 4, no. 2.
88. WHO 1992, see note 8.
89. UNEP 1991, see note 11.
90. Lee 1985, see note 32.
91. WHO 1992, see note 8.
92. WHO 1992, see note 8.
93. Lee 1985, see note 32.
94. Zhongmin, Yan (1988) 'Shanghai: the growth and shifting emphasis of China's largest city' in Victor FS Sit (ed.), *Chinese Cities: the Growth of the Metropolis since 1949*, Oxford University Press, Hong Kong, pp. 94–127.
95. Phantumvanit and Liengsharensit 1989, see note 4.
96. WHO 1992, see note 8.
97. Ekblad, Solvig *et al* (1991) *Stressors, Chinese City Dwellings and Quality of Life*, D12, Swedish Council for Building Research, Stockholm; and Schaeffer, B (1990) 'Home and health – on solid foundations?', *World Health Forum* vol. 11, pp. 38–45.
98. Ekblad *et al* 1991 and Schaeffer 1990, see note 97.
99. WHO 1992, see note 8.
100. Bradley, David, Stephens, Carolyn, Cairncross, Sandy and Harpham, Trudy (1991) *A Review of Environmental Health Impacts in Developing Country Cities*, Urban Management Program Discussion Paper no. 6, World Bank, UNDP and UNCHS (Habitat), Washington DC.
101. Fundacao SEADE 1990, quoted in Leitmann, Josef (1991) 'Environmental profile of São Paulo' Urban Management and the Environment: Discussion Paper Series, UNDP/World Bank/UNCHS.
102. WHO 1992, see note 8.
103. Ekblad *et al* 1991, see note 97.

104. See Jacobs, Jane (1965) *The Death and Life of Great American Cities*, Pelican, London; and Newman, Oscar (1972) *Defensible Space: Crime Prevention through Urban Design*, MacMillan, New York.
105. Turner, John FC (1976) *Housing By People – Towards Autonomy in Building Environments*, Ideas in Progress, Marion Boyars, London; and Turner, John FC and Fichter, Robert (eds) (1971) *Freedom to Build*, Macmillan, New York and London.
106. WHO 1992, see note 8. Also Duhl, Leonard J (1990) *The Social Entrepreneurship of Change*, Pace University Press, New York.
107. Duhl 1990 see note 106 and WHO 1992, see note 8.
108. Myers, Robert (1991) *The Twelve Who Survive: Strengthening Programmes of Early Child Development in the Third World*, Routledge, London and New York.
109. Hughes, Bob (1990) 'Children's play – a forgotten right', *Environment and Urbanization* vol. 2, no. 2, pp. 58–64.
110. Myers 1991, see note 108.
111. Kagan, AR and Levi, L (1975) 'Health and environment: psycho-social stimuli – a review', in L Levi (ed.), *Society, Stress and Disease – Childhood and Adolescence*, Oxford University Press, Oxford, pp. 241–260.
112. WHO 1992 page 215, see note 8.
113. Turner 1976, see note 105.
114. There is no agreed international definition as to what is a city, although the term city is not understood in the same way as 'urban centre'. Many nations include settlements with a few thousand (and in some a few hundred) inhabitants as 'urban', in their census definitions, and many of these have a high proportion of the economically active population working in agriculture. Such small urban centres do not fit with most people's idea of a city since the term 'city' implies a larger settlement with most of the inhabitants working in commerce, industry, services or some other non-agricultural occupation. The term city need not imply a very large urban agglomeration; there are many urban centres in Europe which are regarded as 'cities' which have less than 30,000 inhabitants.
115. Zorrilla, Silvia and Guaresti, Maria Elena (1986) *Sector Agua Potables y Saneamiento: Lineamientos para una Estrategia Nacional*, PNUD (UN Development Programme), Buenos Aires.
116. di Pace, Maria J, Federovisky, Sergio, Hardoy, Jorge E and Mazzucchelli, Sergio A (1992) *Medio Ambiente Urbano en la Argentina*, CEAL, Buenos Aires. See also Mazzucchelli, Sergio A (1991) 'San Carlos de Bariloche: La problematica ambiental urbana' *Medio Ambiente y Urbanizacion* no. 37, pp. 75–92 for a case study of environmental problems in a small city.
117. For various examples, see Misra, HN (1986) 'Rae Bareli, Sultanpur and Pratapgarh Districts, Uttar Pradesh, North India' in Jorge E Hardoy and David Satterthwaite (eds), *Small and Intermediate Urban Centres; their role in Regional and National Development in the Third World*, Hodder and Stoughton (UK) and Westview (USA).
118. Baskar, J Paul (1992) 'Devastation by leather tanneries in Tamil Nadu' *Development in Practice* vol. 2, no. 2, pp. 127–129.

119. The information on Douala and Yaounde is drawn from papers presented at a national seminar on '*La Gestion d l'Environnement*', Palais des Congres, Cameroun, November 1983; general information from Jeune Afrique (1979), *Republique Unie de Cameroun*, les Atlas Afrique, Editions j.a., Paris.
120. United Nations (1991) *World Urbanization Prospects 1990; Estimates and Projections of Urban and Rural Populations and of Urban Agglomerations*, ST/ESA/SER.A/121, United Nations, New York. 1950 populations – United Nations, (1980) *Urban, Rural and City Populations 1950–2000, as assessed in 1978*, ESA/P/WP.66, Population Division, Department of Economic and Social Affairs.
121. Onono, Ondja and Mebenga A (1983) '*Le probleme de la pollution au Cameroun*', Paper presented at Seminaire National sur la Gestion de l'Environnement, Cameroun, November.
122. Onono and Mebenga 1983, see note 121.
123. Ebwele, P (1983) 'Urbanisation et environnement', Paper presented at Seminaire National sur la Gestion de l'Environnement, Cameroun, November.
124. For discussions of this in different Latin American nations, see Caputo, Maria G, Hardoy, Jorge E and Herzer, Hilda (compilors) (1985) *Desastres Naturales y Sociedad en America Latina*, CLACSO, Buenos Aires.
125. Bopda, A (1983) 'Industrie, urbanisation et pollution', Paper presented at Seminaire National sur la Gestion de l'Environnement, Cameroun, November.
126. Schteingart 1989, see note 35.
127. UNCHS (1988) *Refuse Collection Vehicles for Developing Countries*, UNCHS (Habitat), Nairobi, Kenya.
128. For a discussion of these differentials and their causes and a review of studies which have examined such differentials, see Bradley *et al* (1991) see note 100. See also: Jacobi, Pedro (1990) 'Habitat and health in the municipality of Sao Paulo' *Environment and Urbanization* vol. 2, no. 2, pp. 33–45; and Harpham, Trudy, Vaughan, Patrick and Lusty, Tim (eds) (1988) *In the Shadow of the City: Community Health and the Urban Poor*, Oxford University Press, Oxford.
129. UNICEF (1992) *Environment, Development and the Child*, UNICEF, New York.
130. UNICEF 1992, see note 129.
131. UNICEF 1992, see note 129 and WHO 1992, see note 8.
132. For instance, see Lee-Wright, Peter (1990) *Child Slaves*, Earthscan Publications, London; and UNICEF 1992, see note 129.
133. It is useful to distinguish between children who work in the street but live in a stable home, usually with their parents, and children who live and work on the streets. UNICEF has suggested three categories. The first is 'children on the street' which is much the largest category of 'street children'; these are children who work on the streets but have strong family connections, may attend school and, in most cases, return home at the end of the day. The second category is 'children of the street'; these see the street as their home

and seek shelter, food and a sense of community among their companions there. But ties to their families exist, even if they are remote and they only visit their families infrequently. The third category is 'abandoned children'; these are difficult to distinguish from children of the street since they undertake similar activities and live in similar ways. However, these children have no ties with their families and are entirely on their own.

134. Patel, Sheela (1990) 'Street children, hotels boys and children of pavement dwellers and construction workers in Bombay: how they meet their daily needs', *Environment and Urbanization* vol. 2, no. 2, pp. 9–26.
135. UNICEF 1992, see note 129.
136. Patel 1990, see note 134.
137. Patel 1990, see note 134.
138. Sapir, D (1990) *Infectious Disease Epidemics and Urbanization: a Critical Review of the Issues*, Paper prepared for the WHO Commission on Health and Environment, Division of Environmental Health, WHO, Geneva.
139. WHO 1992, see note 8.
140. Agarwal, Anil and Narain, Sunita (1992) 'Towards green villages; a strategy for environmentally sound and participatory rural development in India' and Lee-Smith, Diana and Trujillo, Catalina Hinchey (1992) 'The struggle to legitimize subsistence: Women and sustainable development', *Environment and Urbanization* vol. 4, no. 1.
141. Jimenez and Velasquez 1989, see note 12.

4 CITIES' RURAL, REGIONAL AND GLOBAL IMPACTS

1. See chapter 3 of Douglas, Ian (1983) *The Urban Environment*, Edward Arnold, for more details and also examples of maps showing the locations for sources of food or materials for different cities.
2. Page 26 of Douglas 1983, see note 1.
3. Douglas 1983, see note 1. The environmental impact of a city on its surroundings in terms of its draw on soil for construction, timber, wood fuel and other resources is one of the aspects of urban environmental problems being researched in a study undertaken by a team at the Muslim University of Aligarh, in collaboration with the Centre for Science and Environment in Delhi; preliminary findings of this regional impact have been published in Singh, Abha Lakshmi (1992) 'Land degradation around Aligarh' Paper presented at the International Workshop on Planning for Sustainable Urban Development, Department of City and Regional Planning, University of Wales, Cardiff, July, 17 pages.
4. Agarwal, Anil and Narain, Sunita (1992) 'Towards green villages; a strategy for environmentally sound and participatory rural development in India', pp 53–64 and Lee-Smith, Diana and Trujillo, Catalina Hinchey (1992) 'The struggle to legitimize subsistence: Women and sustainable development' in *Environment and Urbanization* vol. 4, no. 1, pp 77–84.
5. Douglass, Mike (1989) 'The environmental sustainability of development – coordination, incentives and political will in land use planning for the Jakarta Metropolis', *Third World Planning Review* vol. 11, no. 2, pp. 211–238.

6. Jones, Gavin W (1983) 'Structural change and prospects for urbanization in Asian countries', Papers of the East–West Population Institute no. 88, East–West Centre, Honolulu; and McGee, TG (1987) 'Urbanization or Kotadesasi – the emergence of new regions of economic interaction in Asia', Working paper, East–West Center, Honolulu.
7. Stren, Richard E (1986) *The Ruralization of African Cities: Learning to Live with Poverty*, Project Ecoville working paper no. 34, University of Toronto; and Mazingira Institute (1987) *Urban Food and Fuel Study*, Nairobi, Kenya.
8. Asian Coalition for Housing Rights (1989) 'Evictions in Seoul, South Korea' *Environment and Urbanization* vol. 1, no. 1, pp. 89–94; Makil, Perla Q (1982) 'Slums and squatter settlements in the Philippines', *Concerned Citizens of the Urban Poor* Series no. 3, Manila; Shrivastav, PP (1982) 'City for the citizen or citizen for the city: the search for an appropriate strategy for slums and housing the urban poor in developing countries – the case of Delhi' *Habitat International* vol. 6, no. 1/2, pp. 197–207; and Hardoy, Jorge E and Satterthwaite, David (1989) *Squatter Citizen: Life in the Urban Third World*, Earthscan Publications, London.
9. UNFPA (1980) Presentation at the Conference on Population and the Urban Future, Rome.
10. Douglass, Mike (1987) 'The future of cities on the Pacific Rim', *Discussion Paper No 3*, Department of Urban and Regional Planning, University of Hawaii.
11. Soto Sierra, Javier, Pedro (1977) '*Transformacionen el sector urbano*', VI Congreso Interamericano de Vivienda, Interhabitat 77.
12. Kishk, MA (1986) 'Land degradation in the Nile Valley', *Ambio* vol. XV, no. 4, pp. 226–230; and Blitzer, Silvia *et al* (1981) 'Shelter: People's Needs and Government Response', *Ekistics* no. 286, pp. 4–13.
13. Chaturvedi, A (1983) 'Bricks versus food: Delhi's dilemma', *Earthscan Feature*, London.
14. For India, Agarwal, Anil (1983) 'The poverty of nature: environment, development, science and technology', *IDRC Report No 12*, no. 3, Ottawa, Canada, pp. 4–6. For China, Smil, Vaclav (1984) *The Bad Earth: Environmental Degradation in China*, ME Sharpe, New York and Zed Press, London For Malaysia, Consumers Association of Penang (1982) *Development and the Environment Crisis – A Malaysian Case*; and reports in Environmental News Digest, 1982. For Alexandria, Hamza, Ahmed (1989) 'An appraisal of environmental consequences of urban development in Alexandria, Egypt', *Environment and Urbanization* vol. 1, no. 1, pp. 22–30. For Gulf of Paria, Cover Story (October 1988) *The Siren* no. 38, UNEP, Nairobi. For Manila Bay, Jimenez, Rosario D and Velasquez, Sister Aida (1989) 'Metropolitan Manila: a framework for its sustained development', *Environment and Urbanization* vol. 1, no. 1. For the Bay of Dakar, Kebe, Moctar (1988) 'The West and Central African Action Plan', Interview in *The Siren* no. 37, July 1988, pp. 31–34. For Indus Delta, Sahil (1988) 'Marine pollution and the Indus Delta' , vol. 1 (House journal of National Institute of Oceanography, Karachi, Pakistan), pp. 57–61; and Beg, M, Arshad Ali S, Mahmood, Naeem, Sitwat and Yousufzai, AHK (1984) 'Land based pollution and the

marine environment of the Karachi coast', *Pakistan Journal of Science, Industry and Resources* vol. 27, no. 4, pp. 199–205.

15. World Bank (1992), *World Development Report 1992*, Oxford University Press, Oxford.
16. Moreno, Gloria (1980) 'Drinking water: black with foam on top', *Earthscan Feature*, London. A coliform count is a good indicator of water quality since faecal coliform bacteria are found in human and animal wastes. Although coliform bacteria themselves do not cause disease, their presence can indicate the presence of bacteria that cause typhoid, cholera, dysentery and other waterborne bacterial diseases. A faecal coliform bacteria count gives the number of bacterial colonies per 100 ml of water and a sample with less than 100 is considered safe to drink while a sample with less than 200 is considered safe for swimming.
17. Gadgil, Madhav and Guha, Ramachandra (1992) 'Interpreting Indian environmentalism', paper presented at the UNRISD Conference on the Social Dimensions of Environment and Sustainable Development, Valletta, Malta, April – to be published in a book *Ecology and Equity; India's Green Alternative*.
18. Conway, Gordon R and Pretty, Jules N (1991) *Unwelcome Harvest*, Earthscan Publications, London.
19. Earthscan (1980) *The Gulf: Pollution and Development*, Press Briefing Document, London.
20. Lopez, Jose Manuel (1988) 'The Caribbean and Gulf of Mexico', *The Siren* no. 36, pp. 30–31.
21. Conway and Pretty 1991, see note 18.
22. Krupa, SV and Manning WJ (1988) 'Atmospheric ozone: formation and effects on vegetation' *Environmental Pollution* vol. 50, pp. 101–137 quoted in Conway and Pretty 1991, see note 18.
23. Conway and Pretty 1991, see note 18.
24. The pH of any substance is a numeric value given to its relative acidity or alkalinity; the neutral point is 7.0 although for rain, a pH value of below 5.6 is generally considered 'acidic'. For figures from China, see Zhao, D and Xiong, J (1988) 'Acidification in southwestern China' in H Rohde and R Herrera (eds), *Acidification in Tropical Countries*, SCOPE report no. 36, John Wiley and Sons, Chichester.
25. Conway and Pretty 1991, see note 18.
26. Smil, Vaclav (1984) *The Bad Earth: Environmental Degradation in China*, ME Sharpe, New York and Zed Press, London.
27. Smil 1984 page 121, see note 26.
28. Gennino, Angela and Shorrock, Tim (1982) 'South Korea: paying a high price for an 'economic miracle'', *Not Man Apart*, pp. 10–11.
29. Lee, James A (1985) *The Environment, Public Health and Human Ecology*, World Bank, Johns Hopkins University Press, Baltimore and London.
30. WHO (1992) *Our Planet, Our Health*, Report of the Commission on Health and Environment, Geneva.
31. For China, Smil 1984, see note 26. For Malaysia, Sahabat Alam Malaysia (1983) *The State of Malaysian Environment 1983–84* – Towards Greater

Environmental Awareness. For India, Centre for Science and Environment (1983) *The State of India's Environment – a Citizen's Report*, Delhi, India. For Cubatao, Bo Landin (1987) *Air Pollution*, film produced as part of the Television Series 'Battle for the Planet', Television Trust for the Environment.

32. Conway and Pretty 1991, see note 18.
33. Wang, Jia-Xi and Bian, Yong-Mei (1985) 'Fluoride effects on the mulberry-silkworm system' *Environmental Pollution* vol. 52, pp. 11–18, quoted in Conway and Pretty 1991, see note 18.
34. Rees, William E (1992) 'Ecological footprints and appropriated carrying capacity: what urban economics leaves out', *Environment and Urbanization* vol. 4, no. 2. See also Rees, William E (1991) 'Conserving natural capital: the key to sustainable landscapes' *International Journal of Canadian Studies* vol. 4, pp. 7–27.
35. Nishioka, Shuzo, Noriguchi, Yuichi and Yamamura, Sombo (1990) 'Megalopolis and climate change: the case of Tokyo' in James McCulloch (ed.), *Cities and Global Climate Change*, Climate Institute, Washington DC, pp. 108–133.
36. WHO (1992) *Our Planet, Our Health*, Report of the WHO Commission on Health and Environment, Geneva; and Agarwal, Anil and Narain, Sunita (1991) *Global Warming in an Unequal World – a Case of Environmental Colonialism*, Centre for Science and Environment, Delhi.
37. The ratio of greenhouse gas emissions to unit value of output may be significantly higher, both because of old, inefficient equipment and, for some nations, a greater reliance on heavy industries within the industrial sector.
38. In some of the larger and wealthier Third World cities, the number of automobiles per inhabitant may be comparable to some of the major cities in Europe and North America.
39. WHO 1992, see note 36.
40. A small proportion of the urban centres in the Third World do have high levels of automobiles relative to populations; some have higher ratios of automobiles to population than many cities in the North. But an average figure for per capita fuel consumption taken across all urban centres would produce a much lower figure than that for urban centres in the North.
41. Rees 1991 and 1992, see note 34. See also White, Rodney and Whitney, Joseph (1992) 'Cities and the environment: an overview' in Richard Stren, Rodney White and Joseph Whitney (eds), *Sustainable Cities Urbanization and the Environment in International Perspective*, Westview Press, Boulder, pp. 8–52.
42. Rees 1991, see note 34.
43. World Bank 1992, see note 15.
44. This section draws heavily on a briefing document prepared on this subject by Gerald Leach of the Stockholm Environment Institute.
45. IPCC (1990) *Potential Impacts of Climate Change: Report to IPCC from Working Group II*, World Meteorological Organization and the United Nations Environment Programme
46. WHO 1992, see note 36.

47. Gupta, Joyeeta (1990) 'A partnership between countries and cities on the issue of climate change – with special reference to the Netherlands' in James McCulloch (ed), *Cities and Global Climate Change*, Climate Institute, Washington DC, pp. 66–89.
48. Turner, RK, Kelly, PM and Kay, RC (1990) *Cities at Risk*, BNA International, London.
49. Parry, Martin (1992) 'The urban economy', presentation at *Cities and Climate Change*, a conference at the Royal Geographical Society, 31 March.
50. Turner, Kelly and Kay 1990, see note 48.
51. Smit, Barrie (1990) 'Planning in a climate of uncertainty' in James McCulloch (ed.), *Cities and Global Climate Change*, Climate Institute, Washington DC, pp. 3–19 and Turner, Kelly and Kay 1990, see note 48.
52. Smit 1990 see note 51 and Turner, Kelly and Kay 1990, see note 48.
53. Smit 1990, see note 51 and Turner, Kelly and Kay 1990, see note 48.
54. Turner, Kelly and Kay 1990, see note 48.
55. Muhtab, FU (1989) *Effect of Climate Change and Sea level Rise on Bangladesh*, Report prepared for the Commonwealth Expert Group on Climate Change and Sea Level Rise, Commonwealth Secretariat, London, quoted in Turner, Kelly and Kay 1990, see note 48.
56. di Pace, Maria, Federovisky, Sergio, Hardoy, Jorge, E, Morello, Jorge, H and Stein, Alfredo (1992) 'Latin America' chapter 8 in Richard Stren, Rodney White and Joseph Whitney (eds), *Sustainable Cities: Urbanization and the Environment in International Perspective*, Westview Press, Boulder.
57. di Pace *et al* 1992, see note 56.
58. WHO 1992, see note 36.
59. di Pace *et al*, 1992, see note 56.
60. IPCC 1990, see note 45.

5 ADDRESSING ENVIRONMENTAL PROBLEMS

1. Where government capacity to provide infrastructure and services is very weak, it is common for wealthy households and businesses to have developed their own solutions either through private provision in particular districts or industrial sites (for instance for solid-waste collection and disposal and street cleaning) or through individual provision (for instance sinking their own well for water).

2. World Bank (1988) *World Development Report, 1988*, Oxford University Press, Oxford.
3. Kalbermatten, John M, DeAnne, Julius S and Gunnerson, Charles C (1980) *Appropriate Technology for Water Supply and Sanitation: Technical and Economic Options*, World Bank, Washington DC.
4. Warner, DB and Laugeri, L (1991) 'Health for all: the legacy of the water decade' *Water International* vol. 16, pp. 135–141.
5. Sinnatamby, Gehan (1990) 'Low cost sanitation' in Jorge E Hardoy *et al* (eds), *The Poor Die Young: Housing and Health in Third World Cities*, Earthscan, London.

6. Sinnatamby 1990, see note 5.
7–10. Cairncross, Sandy (1990) 'Water supply and the urban poor' in Jorge E Hardoy *et al* (eds) *The Poor Die Young: Housing and Health in Third World Cities*, Earthscan, London.
11. Bachmann, Gunter and Hammerer, Max (1984) '80 per cent of losses come from 20 per cent of leaks', *World Water*, October, pp. 48–50.
12. Cairncross 1990, see note 7.
13. Rocky Mountain Institute (1991) *Water Efficiency: A Resource for Utility Managers, Community Planners and other Decision Makers*, the Water Program, Snowmass.
14. Rocky Mountain Institute 1991, see note 13.
15. For an example of this in Mexico City, see World Bank (1992) *World Development Report 1992*, Oxford University Press, Oxford, p. 102. This describes an initiative by a group of companies which have formed a new firm to draw wastewater from the municipal trunk sewer, treat it in a rehabilitated municipal wastewater treatment plant and supply it to companies with a shareholding in it at three quarters of the price charged by the government.
16. Cairncross 1990, see note 7.
17. Sinnatamby 1990, see note 5.
18. For further discussion, see Gakenheimer, Ralph and Brando, CHJ (1987) 'Infrastructure Standards', in Lloyd Rodwin (ed.), *Shelter, Settlement and Development*, Allen and Unwin, Boston and London, pp. 133–150.
19. Cointreau, Sandra Johnson, Gunnerson, Charles G, Huls, John M and Seldman, Neil N (1984) *Recycling from Municipal Refuse: a State of the Art Review and Annotated Bibliography*, World Bank Technical Paper no. 30, UNDP Project Management Guide no. 1, World Bank, Washington DC.
20. Furedy, Christine (1990) 'Social aspects of solid waste recovery in Asian cities' *Environmental Sanitation Reviews* no. 30, Asian Institute of Technology, Bangkok, pp. 2–52.
21. Furedy, Christine (1992) 'Garbage: exploring non-conventional options in Asian cities' *Environment and Urbanization* vol. 4, no. 2.
22. Furedy, Christine (1990) 'Urban wastes and sustainable development: a comment on the Brundtland Report' in Nicolas Polunin and John H Burnett (eds), *Maintenance of the Biosphere*, Proceedings of the 3rd International Conference on Environmental Future, Edinburgh University Press, Edinburgh, pp. 213–218
23. Pacheco, Margarita (1992) 'Recycling in Bogota; developing a culture for urban sustainability' *Environment and Urbanization* vol. 4, no. 2.
24. Pacheco 1992, see note 23.
25. Smit, Jac and Nasr, Joe (1992) 'Urban agriculture for sustainable cities: using wastes and idle land and water bodies as resources' *Environment and Urbanization* vol. 4, no. 2.
26. Furedy 1992, see note 21.
27. Cointreau, Sandra (1982) *Environmental Management of Urban Solid Waste in Developing Countries*, Urban Development Technical Paper no. 5, World Bank, Washington DC.

28. Flintoff, F (1976) *Management of Solid Wastes in Developing Countries*, WHO (SEARO), New Delhi.
29. This paragraph draws from Furedy 1990, see note 20.
30. Furedy 1990, see note 20.
31. Cointreau 1982, see note 27.
32. Furedy 1992, see note 21.
33. Furedy 1990, see note 20.
34. Puerbo, Hasan (1991) 'Urban solid waste management in Bandung: towards an integrated resource recovery system' *Environment and Urbanization* vol. 3, no. 1, pp. 60–69.
35. Rabinovitch, Jonas (1992) 'Curitiba: towards sustainable urban development' *Environment and Urbanization* vol. 4, no. 2.
36. Smit and Nasr 1992, see note 25.
37. Smit and Nasr 1992, see note 25.
38. Douglas, Ian (1983) *The Urban Environment*, Edward Arnold, London.
39. Honghai, Deng (1992) 'Urban agriculture as urban food supply and environmental protection subsystems in China' Paper presented to the international workshop on 'Planning for Sustainable Urban Development', University of Wales, 1992.
40. For more details, see Hawkins, JN (1982) 'Shanghai: an exploratory report on food for a city' *GeoJournal* Supplementary issue, pp. 83–98 and Zhongmin, Yan (1988) 'Shanghai: the growth and shifting emphasis of China's largest city' in Victor FS Sit (ed), *Chinese Cities: the Growth of the Metropolis since 1949*, Oxford University Press, Hong Kong, pp. 94–127.
41. To give one example, the reports about the scale and nature of agricultural production in Shanghai is within the Shanghai City Region which had some 12.8 million inhabitants in 1990 within an area of 6340.5 square kilometres. This area included 12 districts and nine rural counties. The central city area of Shanghai only covers a small proportion of the area within the city region boundaries. Around five million inhabitants live in suburbs or rural areas. See Zipei, Zhao (1992) 'Air quality of Shanghai and strategies to control it' Paper presented at an international workshop on 'Planning for Sustainable Urban Development', University of Wales College of Cardiff, 13 pages on the latest population figures. See Zhongmin, Yan (1988) 'Shanghai: the growth and shifting emphasis of China's largest city' in Victor FS Sit (ed), *Chinese Cities: the Growth of the Metropolis since 1949*, Oxford University Press, Hong Kong, pp. 94–127 for a discussion of Shanghai's growth and spatial development.
42. Smit and Nasr 1992, see note 25.
43. Furedy 1990, see note 20.
44. Furedy 1990, see note 20; Smit and Nasr 1992, see note 25.
45. Furedy 1990, see note 22.
46. Smit and Nasr 1992, see note 25.
47. Mara, Duncan and Cairncross, Sandy (1990) *Guidelines for the Safe Use of Wastewater and Excreta in Agriculture and Aquaculture*, World Health Organization, Geneva.
48. Douglas 1983, see note 38; Rabinovitch 1992, see note 35.

49. See vol. 1, no. 2 of *Environment and Urbanization* – special issue on 'Beyond the stereotype of slums – how poor people find accommodation in Third World cities' for more details.
50. For further discussion, see Cairncross, Sandy (1987) 'The private sector and water supply in developing countries: Partnership or profiteering?', *Health, Policy and Planning* vol. 2, no. 2, pp. 180–184.
51. Lee, Kyu Sik (1988) *Infrastructure Investment and Productivity: the case of Nigerian Manufacturing – a framework for policy study*, Discussion paper, Water Supply and Urban Development Division, World Bank, Washington DC.
52. Rabinovitch 1992, see note 35.
53. Cairncross 1990, see note 7.
54. Sinnatamby 1990, see note 5.
55. Furedy 1992, see note 21.
56. Furedy 1992 (see note 21) describes this initiative, which is coordinated by Anselm Rosario of Waste Wise in Bangalore. See also Rosario, A and von der Weid, A (1990) 'Towards socially and environmentally sound solid waste management in Bangalore', *Proceedings of International Workshop on Waste Management and Resource Recovery*, GTZ, Germany.
57. Furedy 1992 (see note 21) describes this project, which Leonarda Comacho initiated. See also Comacho, LN (1991) 'Recycling in Philippines', letter to editor, *Development Forum*, vol. 19, no. 2, March–April.
58. Douglass, Mike (1992) 'The political economy of urban poverty and environmental management in Asia: access, empowerment and community-based alternatives' *Environment and Urbanization* vol. 4, no. 2.
59. Friedmann, John (1990) *Domination and Resistance: the Politics of an Alternative Development*, UCLA/GSUAP, quoted in Douglass 1992, see note 58.
60. Douglass 1992, see note 58.
61. Phantumvanit, Dhira and Sathirathai, Suthawan (1986) 'Promoting clean technologies in developing countries', *Industry and Environment* vol. 9, no. 4, pp. 12–14.
62. Vimal, OP (1983) 'Recycling of organic residues – status and trends in India, *Industry and Environment*, UNEP, Paris, April–June, pp. 7–10.
63. Caballero Almeida, Gilberto (1983) 'Turning sugar into newspapers', *Earthscan Feature*.
64. El Ebiary, MA (1983) 'Disilication of black liquors: a new solution for pollution problems using rice straws', *Industry and Environment*, UNEP–Paris, January–March, pp. 5–9.
65. Halter, Faith (1991) 'Towards more effective environmental regulation in developing countries' in Denizhan Erocal (ed.), *Environmental Management in Developing Countries*, Development Centre, OECD, Paris, pp. 223–254. See also Benavides, Livia, (1992) 'Hazardous waste management for small-scale and cottage industries in developing countries'; paper presented at the International Workshop on Planning for Sustainable Urban Development. Department of City and Regional Planning, University of Wales, Cardiff, for a

discussion of hazardous waste management for small scale industries, including the possibilities presented by collective treatment.

66. Leonard, Jeffrey H. and Morell, David (1981) 'Emergence of environmental concern in developing countries: a political perspective', *Stanford Journal of International Law* vol. 17, issue 2, pp. 281–313.
67. Harris, Nigel (1990) *Environmental Issues in the Cities of the Developing World*, DPU Working Paper no. 20, University College London.
68. Wangwongwatana, Supat (1992) 'Bangkok metropolis and its air pollution problems', Paper presented at the International Workshop on Planning for Sustainable Urban Development, Department of City and Regional Planning, University of Wales, Cardiff.
69. Note should be made that parts of the electronics industry do have special pollution and waste handling problems but these are not on a comparable scale to traditional heavy industry and their resolution is likely to be much cheaper, relative to the value of production. See Chapter 9 of Timberlake, Lloyd (1987) *Only One Earth: Living for the Future*, BBC/Earthscan Publications London, for an interesting case study of the water pollution created by the computer industry, and its health impacts, in California.
70. Calculated from tables in World Bank (1988) *World Development Report 1988*, Oxford University Press, Oxford.
71. Elkington, John and Shopley, Jonathan (1989) *Cleaning Up: US Waste Management Technology and Third World Development*, WRI Papers, World Resources Institute, Washington DC.
72. Elkington and Shopley 1989, see note 71.
73. World Bank (1992) *World Development Report 1992*, Oxford University Press, Oxford.
74. Halter 1991, see note 65.
75. Although it is often assumed that those living in urban centres benefit from 'urban bias' in government expenditures and policies, empirical studies in smaller urban centres have failed to substantiate the fact that their inhabitants benefited from such a bias. Certain major cities have been found to benefit from such a bias but this brought little or no benefit to poorer groups. See Chapters 8 and 9 of Hardoy, Jorge E and Satterthwaite, David (1989) *Squatter Citizen: Life in the Urban Third World*, Earthscan Publications, London.
76. Leonard, Jeffrey, H (1984) *Confronting Industrial Pollution in Rapidly Industrializing Countries – Myths, Pitfalls and Opportunities*, Conservation Foundation.
77. Leonard and Morell 1981, see note 66.
78. Panayotou, Theodore (1991) 'Economic incentives in environmental management and their relevance to developing countries' in Denizhan Erocal (ed.), *Environmental Management in Developing Countries*, Development Centre, OECD, Paris, pp. 83–132.
79. King, Bob (1988) 'Taiwan's industrial pollution bills mount', *Financial Times*, 8 November.
80. Quote drawn from Elkington and Shopley 1989, see note 71.
81. Furedy 90, see note 20

82. Cointreau, Sandra Johnson, Gunnerson, Charles G, Huls, John M and Seldman, Neil N (1984) *Recycling from Municipal Refuse: a State of the Art Review and Annotated Bibliography*, World Bank Technical Paper no. 30, UNDP Project Management Guide no. 1, World Bank, Washington DC.; Elkington and Shopley 1989, see note 71.
83. Rosenberg, Charles E (1962) *The Cholera Years*, University of Chicago Press, Chicago.
84. Wohl, Anthony S (1983) *Endangered Lives: Public Health in Victorian Britain*, Methuen, London.
85. This is based on calculations derived from an aid project database prepared by IIED's Human Settlements Programme. A summary of these figures were printed in UNCHS (Habitat), 'Financial and other assistance provided to and among developing countries on human settlements and on the human settlements activities of the United Nations system', Biennial reports submitted to the Inter-Governmental Commission on Human Settlements in 1987 and 1989, HS/C/9/6 and HS/C/11/6, Nairobi, Kenya.
86. In regard to metros, see Ortuzar, S, (1983) 'Santiago's metro' *Cities* vol. 1, no. 2, pp. 113–116; and World Bank (1988) *World Development Report 1988*, Oxford University Press, Oxford. For examples of water treatment plants, Cohen, Michael A (1987) 'Macroeconomic adjustment and the city' *Cities* vol. 7, no. 1, pp. 49–59. See also Elkington and Shopley 1989 (note 71), Cointreau 1982 (note 27).
87. Drawn from document described in note 85.
88. Guarda, Gian Carlo (1990) 'A new direction in World Bank urban lending in Latin American countries', *Review of Urban and Regional Development Studies* vol. 2, no. 2, pp. 116–124.
89. UNICEF (1988) *Improving Environment for Child Health and Survival*, Urban Examples no. 15, UNICEF, New York.
90. Turner, Bertha (ed.) (1988) *Building Community – A Third World Case Book*, Habitat International Coalition, London.
91. UNICEF 1988, see note 89 and Turner 1988, see note 90.

6 SUSTAINABLE DEVELOPMENT AND CITIES:

1. One notable exception is a collection of papers presented at a colloquium on 'Urbanization and the Environment', University of Toronto, June 1990 and published in Stren, Richard E, White, Rodney and Whitney, Joseph (1992) (eds), *Sustainable Cities: Urbanization and the Environment in International Perspective*, Westview Press, Boulder. A special issue of the journal *Environment and Urbanization* (October 1992) is also devoted to 'Sustainable Cities'.
2. WHO (1992) *Our Planet, Our Health*, Report of the WHO Commission on Health and Environment, World Health Organization, Geneva; Rees, William E (1992) 'Ecological footprints and appropriated carrying capacity' *Environment and Urbanization* vol. 4, no. 2.
3. World Commission on Environment and Development (1987) *Our Common Future*, Oxford University Press, Oxford, p. 8.

4. Rees, William E (1989) 'Defining "sustainable development"', CHS Research Bulletin, University of British Columbia Centre for Human Settlements, Pearce, David, Markandya, Anil and Barbier, Edward B (1989) *Blueprint for a Green Economy*, Earthscan Publications, London; Pezzey, John (1989) *Economic Analysis of Sustainable Growth and Sustainable Development*, Environment Department Working Paper no. 15, World Bank.
5. Meadows, Donella H, Meadows, Dennis L, Randers, Jorgen and Behrens III, William (1974) *The Limits to Growth*, Pan Books Ltd, London.
6. Ward, Barbara and Dubos, Rene (1972) *Only One Earth: Care and Maintenance of a Small Planet*, Penguin, London.
7. See for instance: Mesarovic, Mihajlo and Pestel, Eduard (1974) *Mankind at the Turning Point*, EP Dutton, New York; 'The Cocoyoc Declaration' adopted by the participants of the UNEP/UNCTAD symposium on 'Pattern of Resource-Use, Environment and Development Strategies' in 1974, republished in *World Development* vol. 3, nos. 2 and 3, February–March 1975; Ward, Barbara (1976) *The Home of Man*, Penguin Books; *Catastrophe or New Society* (1976) the Bariloche World Model – International Development Research Centre, Ottawa; Council on Environmental Quality and the Department of State (1979) *The Global 2000 Report to the President: Entering the Twenty-First Century*, vol. 1, Washington DC; Brandt Commission Report (1980) *North–South: a Programme for Survival*, MIT Press, Cambridge, Mass.
8. Centre for Science and Environment (1983) *The State of India's Environment: a Citizen's Report*, New Delhi; Lee-Smith, Diana and Hinchey Trujillo, Catalina (1992) 'The struggle to legitimize subsistence: Women and sustainable development' *Environment and Urbanization* vol. 4, no. 1, pp. 77–88.
9. Centre for Science and Environment (1987) *The Fight for Survival*, New Delhi.
10. Leach, Melissa and Mearns, Robin (1991) *Poverty and Environment in Developing Countries: An Overview Study*, Institute for Development Studies, University of Sussex.
11. Swiss Directorate for Development Cooperation and Humanitarian Aid (1991) *Sustainability of Development Projects: Basic Principles and Application in Practice*, Berne.
12. International Union for Conservation of Nature and Natural Resources (1980) *World Conservation Strategy*, Gland.
13. Pearce, Markandya and Barbier 1989, see note 4.
14. See Ciriacy-Wantrup, S V (1983) *Resource Conservation: Economics and Policies*, University of California; and Bishop, RC (1982) 'Endangered species and uncertainty: the economics of safe minimum standards' *American Journal of Agricultural Economics* vol. 60, pp. 10–18.
15. Svedin, Uno (1988) 'The Concept of Sustainability' in *Perspectives of Sustainable Development – Some Critical Issues Related to the Brundtland Report*, Stockholm Studies in Natural Resource Management no. 1, Stockholm Group for Studies on Natural Resources Management.

16. Conway, Gordon R (1987) 'The Properties of Agrosystems', *Agricultural Systems* vol. 24, no. 2, pp. 95–117.
17. Conway, Gordon R and Barbier, Edward B (1990) *After the Green Revolution: Sustainable Agriculture for Development*, Earthscan Publications, London.
18. Redclift, Michael (1987) *Sustainable Development: Exploring the Contradictions*, Routledge, London and New York.
19. Gore, Charles (1991) *Transport and Sustainable Development*, (mimeo), and (1991) *Policies and Mechanisms for Sustainable Development: the Transport Sector*, (mimeo).
20. WHO 1992, see note 2.
21. Of course in some regions or districts, wastes produced by rural based agricultural production, mining or industries may be much greater than local urban-generated wastes.
22. Chapter 9 of Hardoy, Jorge E and Satterthwaite, David (1989) *Squatter Citizen: Life in the Urban Third World*, Earthscan Publications, London.
23. For a case study of this, see Manzanal, Mabel and Vapnarsky, Cesar (1986) 'The Comahue Region, Argentina' in Jorge E, Hardoy and David Satterthwaite (eds), *Small and Intermediate Urban Centres; Their Role in National and Regional Development in the Third World*, Hodder and Stoughton, UK and Westview USA.
24. Note that in most nations, this conflict can be minimized and urban built-up centres do not encroach on more than 1 or 2 per cent of the total area of national territory.
25. di Pace, Maria, Federovisky, Sergio, Hardoy, Jorge E, Morello, Jorge H and Stein, Alfredo 'Latin America' Chapter 8 in Richard Stren, Rodney White and Joseph Whitney (eds) (1992) *Sustainable Cities: Urbanization and the Environment in International Perspective*, Westview Press, Boulder, pp. 205–227.
26. For an example of this, see Saint, William S and Goldsmith, William D (1980) 'Cropping systems, structural change and rural-urban migration in Brazil', in *World Development* vol. 8, pp. 259–272.
27. Toulmin, Camilla (1990) 'Drylands and Human Settlements', Internal paper, IIED.
28. Poore, Duncan (1989) *No Timber without Trees*, Earthscan Publications, London.
29. Leach, Gerald and Mearns, Robin (1989) *Beyond the Woodfuel Crisis – People, Land and Trees in Africa*, Earthscan Publications, London.
30. Rietbergen, Simon, 'Africa', in Duncan, Poore (1989) *No Timber without Trees*, Earthscan Publications, London.
31. Bhatt, Chandi Prasad (1990) 'The Chipko Andolan: forest conservation based on people's power' *Environment and Urbanization* vol. 2, no. 1, pp. 7–18.
32. Rees, William E (1992) 'Ecological footprints and appropriated carrying capacity: what urban economics leaves out', *Environment and Urbanization* vol. 4, no. 2, October 1992. See also White, Rodney and Whitney, Joe (1992) 'Human settlements and sustainable development: an overview' in Richard

Stren, Rodney White and Joseph Whitney (eds), *Sustainable Cities Urbanization and the Environment in International Perspective*, Westview Press, Boulder, pp. 8–52.

33. The World Bank (1990) *World Development Report* Oxford University Press, Oxford.
34. OECD (1991) *The State of the Environment*, Organization for Economic Cooperation and Development, Paris.
35. Newman, Peter WG and Kenworthy, Jeffrey R (1989) *Cities and Automobile Dependence: an International Sourcebook*, Gower Technical, Aldershot. See Table 3.1, p. 36.
36. OECD (1991), see note 34; Cointreau, Sandra (1982) *Environmental Management of Urban Solid Waste in Developing Countries*, Urban Development Technical Paper no. 5, World Bank, Washington DC.
37. Newman and Kenworthy 1989, see note 35.
38. Newman and Kenworthy 1989, see note 35.
39. Gilbert, Richard (1990) 'Cities and global warming' in James McCulloch (ed.), *Cities and Global Climate Change*, Climate Institute, Washington DC, pp. 182–190.
40. This section draws heavily on a briefing document prepared on this subject by Gerald Leach of the Stockholm Environment Institute.
41. Nishioka, Shuzo, Noriguchi, Yuichi and Yamamura, Sombo (1990) 'Megalopolis and climate change: the case of Tokyo' in James McCulloch (ed.), *Cities and Global Climate Change*, Climate Institute, Washington DC, pp. 108–133.
42. UNEP (1991) *Environmental Data Report, 1991–2*, GEMS Monitoring and Assessment Research Centre, Blackwell, Oxford and Massachusetts.
43. Leach, Gerald *et al* (1979) *A Low Energy Strategy for the United Kingdom*, Science Reviews Ltd, London, for details of how increasing prosperity need not imply increased fossil fuel use.
44. Furedy, Christine (1990) 'Social aspects of solid waste recovery in Asian cities' *Environmental Sanitation Reviews* no. 30, ENSIC, Asian Institute of Technology, Bangkok, pp. 2–52.
45. Gore 1991, see note 19. See also Lowe, Marcia D (1991) *Shaping Cities: the Environmental and Human Dimensions*, Worldwatch Paper 105, Washington DC.
46. Rabinovitch, Jonas (1992) 'Curitiba: towards sustainable urban development' *Environment and Urbanization* vol. 4, no. 2.
47. OECD (1989) *Economic Instruments for Environmental Protection*, OECD, Paris.
48. Leonard, Jeffrey H and Morell, David (1981) 'Emergence of environmental concern in development countries: a political perspective', *Stanford Journal of International Law*, vol. 17, Issue 2, pp. 281–313; and Panayotou, Theodore (1991) 'Economic incentives in environmental management and their relevance to developing countries' in Denizhan Erocal (ed.), *Environmental Management in Developing Countries*, Development Centre, OECD, Paris, pp. 83–132.
49. Leach and Mearns 1989, see note 29.

50. Winpenny, JT (1991) *Values for the Environment: A Guide to Economic Appraisal*, HMSO, London.
51. Pezzey 1989, see note 4.
52. Pezzey 1989, see note 4.
53. Hardoy, Jorge E and Satterthwaite, David (1989) *Squatter Citizen: Life in the Urban Third World*, Earthscan Publications, London; UNCHS (Habitat), (1987) *Global Report on Human Settlements 1986*, Oxford University Press, Oxford; and UNCHS (Habitat) (1990) *The Global Strategy for Shelter to the Year 2000*, United Nations Centre for Human Settlements (Habitat), Nairobi.
54. See for instance Cairncross, Sandy (1990) 'Water supply and the urban poor', Cuentro, Stenio de Coura and Gadji, Dji Malla (1990) 'The collection and management of household garbage'; Goldstein, Greg (1990) 'Access to life saving services in urban areas'; Schofield, CJ, Briceno-Leon, R, Kolstrup, N, Webb, DJT and White, GB (1990) 'The role of house design in limiting vector-borne disease'; and Sinnatamby, Gehan (1990) 'Low cost sanitation' in Jorge E Hardoy *et al* (eds) *The Poor Die Young: Housing and Health in Third World Cities*, Earthscan Publications, London.
55. Gore 1991, see note 19.
56. Stren, Richard E (1989) 'Administration of urban services' in Richard E Stren and Rodney R White (eds), *African Cities in Crisis*, Westview, Boulder.
57. See special issues on the Earth Summit of two journals: *Down to Earth* (published by the Society for Environmental Communications in Delhi) 31 May 1992 and 15 July 1992 and *Third World Resurgence* (published by the Third World Network in Malaysia) no. 24/25; details of both journals are given in the section on 'Further Reading'.

7 CONCLUSIONS

1. McAuslan, Patrick (1984) *Urban Land and Shelter for the Poor*, Earthscan Publications, London; van der Linden, Jan (1982) 'Squatting by organized invasion – a new reply to a failing housing policy?', *Third World Planning Review* vol. 4, no. 4, pp. 400–412; and Sarin, Mahdu (1983) 'The Rich, the Poor and the Land Question' in Angel, Shlomo, Raymon W Archer, Sidhijai Tanphiphat and Emiel A Wegelin (eds) *Land for Housing the Poor*, Select Books, Singapore, pp. 237–253.
2. Douglass, Mike (1992) 'The political economy of urban poverty and environmental management in Asia: access, empowerment and community-based alternatives' *Environment and Urbanization*, vol. 4, no. 2.
3. See Chapter 1, section on 'mega-cities' and Table 1.2 for more details
4. Douglass 1992, see note 2.
5. Arrossi, Silvina, Bombarolo, Felix, Hardoy, Jorge E, Mitlin, Diana and Satterthwaite, David (forthcoming) *Funding Community Level Initiatives*, IIED–América Latina and IIED, sponsored by the UNDP–World Bank–UNCHS Urban Management Programme.

6. Wohl, Anthony S (1983) *Endangered Lives: Public Health in Victorian Britain*, Methuen, London. See also Jones, Kathleen (1991) *The Making of Social Policy in Britain, 1830–1990*, Athlone Press, London and New Jersey.
7. McGranahan, Gordon, (1991) *Environmental Problems and the Urban Household in Third World Countries*, The Stockholm Environment Institute, Stockholm.
8. Cairncross, Sandy, Hardoy, Jorge E and Satterthwaite, David (1990) 'New partnerships for healthy cities' in Jorge E Hardoy *et al* (eds) *The Poor Die Young: Housing and Health in Third World Cities*, Earthscan Publications, London, pp. 245–268. See also two case studies of community development which suggest more participatory, 'process oriented' approaches: Stephens, Carolyn (1991) 'Back to basics: a community based environmental health project in West Point, Monrovia, Liberia' *Environment and Urbanization* vol. 3, no. 1, pp. 140–146; and Hardoy, Ana, Hardoy, Jorge E and Schusterman, Ricardo (1991) 'Building community organization: the history of a squatter settlement and its own organizations in Buenos Aires' *Environment and Urbanization* vol. 3, no. 2, pp. 104–120.
9. Agarwal, Anil and Narain, Sunita (1992) 'Towards green villages; a strategy for environmentally sound and participatory rural development in India' and Lee-Smith, Diana and Hinchey Trujillo, Catalina (1992) 'The struggle to legitimize subsistence: Women and sustainable development', *Environment and Urbanization* vol. 4, no. 1.
10. Gadgil, Madhav and Guha, Ramachandra (1992) 'Interpreting Indian environmentalism', paper presented at the UNRISD Conference on the Social Dimensions of Environment and Sustainable Development, Valletta, Malta, April – to be published in a book *Ecology and Equity; India's Green Alternative*.
11. Kolsky, Peter J (1992) 'Water, health and cities: concepts and examples' Paper presented at the international workshop on Planning for Sustainable Urban Development, University of Wales, July.
12. WHO (1990) *Environmental Health in Urban Development*, Report of a WHO Expert Committee, World Health Organization, Geneva.
13. Pretty, Jules N and Guijt, Irene (1992) 'Primary environmental care: an alternative paradigm for development assistance' *Environment and Urbanization* vol. 4, no. 1.
14. Cairncross *et al* 1990, see note 8.
15. Kalbermatten, John M, DeAnne, Julius S and Gunnerson, Charles C *Appropriate Technology for Water Supply and Sanitation: Technical and Economic Options*, World Bank, Washington DC; Sinnatamby, Gehan, 'Low cost sanitation', Cairncross, Sandy, 'Water supply and the urban poor' and Cuentro, Stenio de Coura and Gadji, Dji Malla, 'The collection and management of household garbage' in Jorge E Hardoy *et al* (eds) (1990) *The Poor Die Young: Housing and Health in Third World Cities*, Earthscan, London.
16. Cairncross, Sandy (1990) 'Water supply and the urban poor' in Jorge E Hardoy *et al* (eds), *The Poor Die Young: Housing and Health in Third World Cities*, Earthscan Publications, London.

17. United States Environmental Protection Agency (1987) *Regulatory Impact Analysis: Protection of Stratospheric Ozone*, Washington DC.
18. Wohl 1983, see note 6.
19. See statistics in the FAO (Food and Agriculture Organization) statistical yearbooks on land use – or drawn from their computerized information service – which has total area, land area, arable land area and land under permanent crops (among other land uses) for each nation.
20. For one example of the amount of high quality agricultural land which is unutilized or underused within a region long known for its rural poverty, see Kutcher, Gary P and Scandizzo, Pasquale L (1981) *The Agricultural Economy of Northeast Brazil*, Johns Hopkins University Press, Baltimore.

21-22. WHO (1992) *Our Planet, Our Health*, Report of the WHO Commission on Health and Environment, Geneva.

Bibliography

Achayo Were, P T (1983) "The development of road transport in Africa and its effect on land use and environment", *Industry and Environment*, UNEP-Paris, April–June, pp. 25–26.

Aga Khan University students 1986 (unpublished) quoted in Harpham, Trudy, Lusty, Tim, and Vaughan, Patrick (eds), (1988) *In the Shadow of the City: Community Health and the Urban Poor*, Oxford University Press, Oxford.

Agarwal, Anil (1983) "The poverty of nature: environment, development, science and technology", *IDRC Report No. 12*, no. 3, Ottawa, Canada, pp. 4–6.

Agarwal, Anil and Narain, Sunita, (1991) *Global Warming in an Unequal World – a Case of Environmental Colonialism*, Centre for Science and Environment, Delhi.

Agarwal, Anil and Narain, Sunita (1992) "Towards green villages; a strategy for environmentally sound and participatory rural development in India" *Environment and Urbanization* vol. 4, no. 1.

Ahmad, Yusuf J (1986) "Saving the Pearl", *The Siren* no. 32, pp. 11–14.

Aina, Tade Akin (1989) *Health, Habitat and Underdevelopment – with Special Reference to a Low-Income Settlement in Metropolitan Lagos*, IIED Technical Report, London.

Aina, Tade Akin (1992) "The environmental problems of Metropolitan Lagos", Paper presented at the International Workshop on "Planning for Sustainable Urban Development", University of Wales College of Cardiff, Department of City and Regional Planning, July.

Amis, Philip (1992) *Urban Management in Uganda: Survival Under Stress*, The Institutional Framework of Urban Government: Case Study no. 5, Development Administration Group, INLOGOV, University of Birmingham, Birmingham, April.

Anandalingam, G and Westfall, Mark (1987) "Hazardous waste generation and disposal: Options for developing countries", *Natural Resources* vol. 11, no. 1, pp. 37–47.

ANAWIM, published by the Share and Care Apostolate for Poor Settlers vol. IV, no. 4, 1990.

Anderson, Ian (1987) "Isotopes from machine imperil Brazilians", *New Scientist* 15 October.

Anderson, Ian (1992) "Dangerous technology dumped on Third World", report of a paper by Nabiel Makarim presented at a conference in Melbourne,

Australia on the trade in hazardous machinery or technologies, *New Scientist*, 7 March.

Apacible, MS and Yaxley, M (1979) "Manila through the eyes of the Malinenos and the Consultant" PTRC Summer Annual Meeting, 1979.

Ard-Am, Orathai (1991) "City background paper: Bangkok" Paper presented at the workshop on "Urban Community-based Environmental Management in Asia", Bangkok, Thailand.

Arrossi, Silvina, Bombarolo, Felix, Hardoy, Jorge E, Mitlin, Diana and Satterthwaite, David *Funding Community Level Initiatives*, IIED-América Latina and IIED, sponsored by the UNDP-World Bank-UNCHS Urban Management Programme, forthcoming.

Asian Coalition for Housing Rights (1989) "Evictions in Seoul, South Korea" *Environment and Urbanization* vol. 1, no. 1, pp. 89–94.

Askoy, M (1976) *et al* "Types of leukaemia in a chronic benzene poisoning", *Acta haematologica* vol. 55, pp. 67–72.

Atkinson, Adrian (1992) "The urban bioregion as a sustainable development paradigm" Paper presented at the International Workshop on Planning for Sustainable Urban Development, Department of City and Regional Planning, University of Wales, Cardiff, July.

Auer, C (1989) *Health Problems (especially intestinal parasitoses) of Children Living in Smokey Mountain, a Squatter Area of Manila, Philippines*, Msc. Thesis, Swiss Tropical Institute, Department of Public Health and Epidemiology, Basel.

Bachmann, Gunter and Hammerer, Max (1984) "80 per cent of losses come from 20 per cent of leaks", *World Water*, October, pp. 48–50.

Barraza, Ernesto (1987) *"Effectos del terremoto en la infraestructura de vivienda"* in *"El terremoto del 10 de octubre de 1986"*, a special issue of *La Universidad*, Nino CXII no. 5, San Salvador.

Bartone, Carl (1990) *Sustainable Responses to Growing Urban Environmental Crises*, Urban Development Division, (mimeo), World Bank, Washington DC.

Bartone, Carl (1991) "Environmental challenge in Third World cities", *Journal of the American Planning Association* vol. 57, no. 4, pp. 411–415.

Baskar, Paul J (1992) "Devastation by leather tanneries in Tamil Nadu" *Development in Practice* vol. 2, no. 2, pp. 127–129.

Basta, Samir S (1977) "Nutrition and Health in low income urban areas of the Third World" *Ecology of Food and Nutrition* vol. 6, pp 113–124.

Beg, M, Arshad, Ali, Mahmood, S Naeem and Sitwat, Naeem (1985) "Environmental problems of Pakistan: Part 1, composition of solid wastes of Karachi", *Pakistan Journal of Science, Industry and Resources* vol. 28, no. 3, pp. 157–162.

Beg, M, Arshad, Ali, Mahmood, S Naeem, Sitwat, Naeem and Yousufzai, AHK (1984) "Land based pollution and the marine environment of the Karachi coast" *Pakistan Journal of Science, Industry and Resources* vol. 27, no. 4, pp. 199–205.

Benavides, Livia (1992) "Hazardous waste management for small-scale and cottage industries in developing countries", Paper presented at the International Workshop on Planning for Sustainable Urban Development, University of Wales College of Cardiff, Department of City and Regional Planning, July.

Bernstein, Janis B (1991), *Alternative Approaches to Pollution Control and Waste Management: Regulatory and Economic Instruments*, Urban Management Programme Discussion Paper no. 3, Urban Management Programme, World Bank, Washington DC.

Bertaud, Alain and Young, M (1990) "Geographical pattern of environmental health in Tianjin, China" Research/Sector Paper, ASTIN, World Bank, Washington DC.

Bhatt, Chandi Prasad (1990) "The Chipko Andolan: forest conservation based on people's power" *Environment and Urbanization* vol. 2, no. 1, pp. 7–18.

Bishop, RC (1982) "Endangered species and uncertainty: the economics of safe minimum standards" *American Journal of Agricultural Economics* vol. 60, pp. 10–18.

Blitzer, Silvia *et al* (1981) "Shelter: People's Needs and Government Response", *Ekistics* no. 286, pp. 4–13.

Bopda, A (1983) "Industrie, urbanisation et pollution", Paper presented at Seminaire National sur la Gestion de l'Environnement, Cameroun.

Bradley, David, Stephens, Carolyn, Cairncross, Sandy and Harpham, Trudy (1991) *A Review of Environmental Health Impacts in Developing Country Cities*, Urban Management Program Discussion Paper no. 6, World Bank, UNDP and UNCHS (Habitat), Washington DC.

Brandt Commission Report (1980) *North–South: a Programme for Survival*, MIT Press, Cambridge, Mass.

Briceno-Leon, Roberto (1990) *La Casa Enferma: Sociologia de la Enfermedad de Chagas*, Consorcio de Ediciones, Capriles CA, Caracas.

Briscoe, John (1986) "Selected primary health care revisited", in Joseph S Tulchin (ed.), *Health, Habitat and Development*, Lynne Reinner, Boulder.

Bubba, Ndinda and Lamba, Davinda (1991) "Local government in Kenya" *Environment and Urbanization* vol. 3, no. 1, pp. 37–59.

Bundey, DAP, Kan, SOP and Rose, R (1988) "Age related prevalence, intensity and frequency distribution of gastrointestinal helminth infection in urban slum children from Kuala Lumpur, Malaysia" *Transactions of the Royal Society of Tropical Medicine and Hygiene* vol. 82, pp. 289–294.

Caballero Almeida, Gilberto (1983) "Turning sugar into newspapers", *Earthscan Feature*.

Cairncross, Sandy (1987) "The private sector and water supply in developing countries: Partnership or profiteering?", *Health, Policy and Planning* vol. 2, no. 2, pp. 180–184.

Cairncross, Sandy (1990) "Water supply and the urban poor" in Jorge E Hardoy *et al* (eds), *The Poor Die Young: Housing and Health in Third World Cities*, Earthscan Publications, London.

Cairncross, Sandy and Feachem, Richard G (1983) *Environmental Health Engineering in the Tropics – An Introductory Text*, John Wiley and Sons, Chichester.

Cairncross, Sandy, Hardoy, Jorge E and Satterthwaite, David (1990) "New partnerships for healthy cities" in Jorge E Hardoy *et al* (eds), *The Poor Die Young: Housing and Health in Third World Cities*, Earthscan Publications, London, pp. 245–268.

Cairncross, Sandy, Hardoy, Jorge E and Satterthwaite, David (1990) "The urban context" in Jorge E Hardoy *et al* (eds), *The Poor Die Young: Housing and Health in Third World Cities*, Earthscan Publications, London.

Cairncross, Sandy and Ouano, EAR (1990) *Surface Water Drainage in Low-income Communities*, WHO, Geneva.

Caputo, Maria G, Hardoy, Jorge E and Herzer, Hilda (compilors) (1985) *Desastres Naturales y Sociedad en America Latina*, CLACSO, Buenos Aires.

Castaneda, Fernando Casas (1989) "The risks of environmental degradation in Bogota, Colombia", *Environment and Urbanization* vol. 1, no. 1, IIED-London, pp. 16–21.

Castleman, BI (1979) "The export of hazardous factories to developing countries", *International Journal of Health Sciences* vol. 9, no. 4, pp. 569–597.

Castleman, Barry I (1987) "Workplace health standards and multinational corporations in developing countries" in Charles S Pearson (ed.), *Multinational Corporation, the Environment and the Third World*, Duke University Press, Durham, USA, pp. 149–172.

Castonguay, Gilles (1992) "Steeling themselves with knowledge" report on the work of Cristina Laurell, *IDRC Reports* vol. 20, no. 1, pp. 10–12.

Catastrophe or New Society, the Bariloche World Model – International Development Research Centre, Ottawa, 1976.

Cauthen, GM, Pio, A and ten Dam, HG (1988) *Annual Risk of Tuberculosis Infection*, World Health Organization, Geneva.

Centre for Science and Environment (1983) *The State of India's Environment – a Citizen's Report*, Delhi, India.

Centre for Science and Environment (1985) *The State of India's Environment: a Second Citizens' Report*, Delhi, India.

Centre for Science and Environment (1987) *The Fight for Survival*, Delhi.

Centre for Science and Environment (1989) "The environmental problems associated with India's major cities" *Environment and Urbanization* vol. 1, no. 1, pp. 7–15.

Chandler, Tertius and Fox, Gerald (1974) *3000 Years of Urban Growth*, Academic Press, New York and London.

Chaturvedi, A (1983) "Bricks versus Food: Delhi's dilemma", *Earthscan Feature*, London.

Ciriacy-Wantrup, SV (1983) *Resource Conservation: Economics and Policies*, University of California.

Clarke, Giles, Hadiwinoto, Suhadi and Leitmann, Josef (1991) *Environmental Profile of Jakarta*, Urban Management and the Environment: Discussion Paper Series.

Cohen, Michael A (1987) "Macroeconomic adjustment and the city" *Cities* vol. 7, no. 1, pp. 49–59.

Cointreau, Sandra (1982) *Environmental Management of Urban Solid Waste in Developing Countries*, Urban Development Technical Paper no. 5, World Bank, Washington DC.

Cointreau, Sandra Johnson, Gunnerson, Charles G, Huls, John M and Seldman, Neil N (1984) *Recycling from Municipal Refuse: a State of the Art Review and Annotated Bibliography*, World Bank Technical Paper no. 30, UNDP Project Management Guide no. 1, World Bank, Washington DC.

Comacho, LN (1991) "Recycling in Philippines", letter to editor, *Development Forum*, vol. 19, no. 2.

Consumer Information and Documentation Centre (1988) *Consumer Currents*, Mar-Apr, International Organization of Consumers Unions, pp. 5–6.

Consumers Association of Penang (1982) *Development and the Environment Crisis – A Malaysian Case*.

Conway, Gordon R (1987) "The Properties of Agrosystems", *Agricultural Systems* vol. 24, no. 2, pp. 95–117.

Conway, Gordon R and Pretty, Jules N (1991) *Unwelcome Harvest*, Earthscan Publications, London.

Conway, Gordon R and Barbier, Edward B (1990) *After the Green Revolution: Sustainable Agriculture for Development*, Earthscan Publications, London.

Costa Leite, L (1988) "Urban disasters in the Third World: The poor first in line", *UN Development Forum*, vol. XVI, no.3.

Council on Environmental Quality and the Department of State (1979) *The Global 2000 Report to the President: Entering the Twenty-First Century*, vol. 1, Washington DC.

Cuny, Frederick C (1987) "Sheltering the urban poor: lessons and strategies of the Mexico City and San Salvador earthquakes" *Open House International* vol. 12, no. 3, pp. 16–20

Das, Ananda Mohan, Bangali, A Mannan, Shabbir, Ahmed and Shahidullah, MD (1990) *An Overview of Health Scenario in Slums and Hazaribag area of Dhaka*, Directorate General of Health Services, Government of Bangladesh, Dhaka.

Davila, Julio D (1987) *Shelter, Poverty and African Revolutionary Socialism: Human Settlements in Guinea Bissau*, IIED, London.

Davis, Ian (1987) "Safe shelter within unsafe cities: disaster vulnerability and raid urbanization" *Open House International* vol. 12, no. 3, pp. 5–15.

de Coura Cuentro, Stenio and Gadji, Dji Malla (1990) "The collection and management of household garbage" in Jorge E Hardoy *et al* (eds), *The Poor Die Young: Housing and Health in Third World Cities*, Earthscan Publications, London, pp. 169–188.

Degg, Martin R (1989) "Earthquake hazard assessment after Mexico" *Disasters* vol. 13, no. 3, pp. 237–246.

di Pace, Maria J, Federovisky, Sergio, Hardoy, Jorge H and Mazzucchelli, Sergio A (1992) *Medio Ambiente Urbano en la Argentina*, CEAL, Buenos Aires.

di Pace, Maria, Federovisky, Sergio, Hardoy, Jorge E, Morello, Jorge E and Stein Alfredo (1992) "Latin America" chapter 8 in Richard Stren, Rodney White and Joseph Whitney (eds), *Sustainable Cities: Urbanization and the Environment in International Perspective*, Westview Press, Boulder, pp. 205–227.

Douglas, Ian (1983) *The Urban Environment*, Edward Arnold, London.

Douglas, Ian (1986) "Urban Geomorphology" in PG Fookes and PR Vaughan (eds), *A Handbook of Engineering Geomorphology*, Surrey University Press (Blackie and Son) Glasgow, pp. 270–283.

Douglas, Ian (1989) "The rain on the roof: a geography of the urban environment" in Dick Gregory and Rex Walford (eds), *Horizons in Human Geography*, Barnes and Noble, New Jersey, pp. 217–238.

Douglass, Mike (1987) "The future of cities on the Pacific Rim", *Discussion Paper no. 3*, Department of Urban and Regional Planning, University of Hawaii.

Douglass, Mike (1989) "The environmental sustainability of development – coordination, incentives and political will in land-use planning for the Jakarta metropolis" *Third World Planning Review* vol. 11, no. 2, pp. 211–238.

Douglass, Mike (1992) "The political economy of urban poverty and environmental management in Asia: access, empowerment and community-based alternatives" *Environment and Urbanization* vol. 4, no. 2.

Down to Earth vol. 1, no. 7, 31 August 1992.

Duerksen, Christopher and Leonard, Jeffrey (1980) "Environmental regulations and the location of industries: an international perspective" *Columbia Journal of World Business*, Summer, pp. 52–58.

Duhl, Leonard J (1990) *The Social Entrepreneurship of Change*, Pace University Press, New York.

Earthscan (1980) *The Gulf: Pollution and Development*, Press Briefing Document, London.

Ebwele, P (1983) "Urbanisation et environnement", Paper presented at Seminaire National sur la Gestion de l'Environnement, Cameroun.

Edgerton, Lynne (1990) "Warmer temperatures, unhealthier air and sicker children", in James McCulloch (ed.), *Cities and Global Climate Change*, Climate Institute, Washington DC, pp. 145–148.

Ekblad, Solvig *et al* (1991) *Stressors, Chinese City Dwellings and Quality of Life*, D12, Swedish Council for Building Research, Stockholm.

El Clarin, "Emergencia ambiental en Mexico por el alto indice de contaminacion", 24 March 1992 Buenos Aires.

El-Hinnawi, Essam (1981) "Three environmental issues", *Mazingira* vol. 5, no 4, pp. 26–35.

El Sayed, MK (1989) "Implications of relative sea level rise on Alexandria" in R Frassetto (ed.), *Cities on Water: Proceedings of the First International Meeting of Sea level Rise on Cities and Regions*, Venice, Italy.

El Ebiary, MA (1983) "Disilication of black liquors: a new solution for pollution problems using rice straws", *Industry and Environment*, UNEP-Paris, January–March, pp. 5–9.

El Raey, M, Nasr, S and Frihy, O (1990) "National assessment of the impact of greenhouse induced sea-level rises on the northern coastal regions of Egypt" in SP Leatherman (ed.), *National Assessments of Sea-level Rise Vulnerability*, Centre for Global Change, University of Maryland.

El Sammani, Mohamed O, El Hadi Abu Sin, Mohamed, Talha, M, El Hassan, BM and Haywood, Ian (1989) "Management problems of Greater Khartoum", in

Richard E Stren,and Rodney R White (eds), *African Cities in Crisis*, Westview Press, USA, pp. 246–275.

Elkington, John and Shopley, Jonathan (1989) *Cleaning Up: US Waste Management Technology and Third World Development*, WRI Papers, World Resources Institute, Washington DC.

Environmental Protection Council (1988) *Ghana Environmental Action Plan* vol. 1, Accra.

ESCAP (1986) *Study and Review of the Human Settlements Situation in Asia and the Pacific*, vol. II; Country Monographs, United Nations, Bangkok.

Escobar, Jairo (1988) "The south-east Pacific", *The Siren* no. 36, pp. 28–29.

Espinoza, Vicente (1988) *Para una Historia de los Pobres de la Ciudad*, Ediciones SUR, Santiago.

Esrey, SA and Feachem, RG (1989) "Interventions for the Control of Diarrhoeal Disease: Promotion of Food Hygiene", WHO/CDD/89.30, World Health Organization, Geneva, quoted in WHO 1992, see note 3.

Faria, Vilmar Evangelista (1988) chapter on São Paulo in Mattei Dogon and John D Casada (eds), *The Metropolis Era vol. 1*, Sage Publications, Beverley Hills and London, pp. 294–309.

Flintoff, F (1976) *Management of Solid Wastes in Developing Countries*, WHO (SEARO), New Delhi.

Friedmann, John (1990) *Domination and Resistance: the Politics of an Alternative Development*, UCLA/GSUAP, manuscript, quoted in Douglass 1992, see note 58.

Fundacao SEADE 1990, quoted in Leitmann, Josef (1991) "Environmental profile of São Paulo" Urban Management and the Environment: Discussion Paper Series, UNDP/World Bank/UNCHS.

Furedy, Christine (1990) "Social aspects of solid waste recovery in Asian cities" *Environmental Sanitation Reviews* no. 30, ENSIC, Asian Institute of Technology Bangkok, pp. 2–52.

Furedy, Christine (1990) "Urban wastes and sustainable development: a comment on the Brundtland Report" in Nicolas Polunin and John H Burnett (eds), *Maintenance of the Biosphere*, Proceedings of the 3rd International Conference on Environmental Future, Edinburgh University Press, Edinburgh, pp. 213–218

Furedy, Christine (1992) "Garbage: exploring non-conventional options in Asian cities" *Environment and Urbanization* vol. 4, no. 2.

Furedy, Christine and Alamgir, Mohammed (1992) "Street pickers in Calcutta slums", *Environment and Urbanization*, vol. 4, no. 2.

Gadgil, Madhav and Guha, Ramachandra (1992) "Interpreting Indian environmentalism", paper presented at the UNRISD Conference on the Social Dimensions of Environment and Sustainable Development, Valletta, Malta, April – to be published in a book *Ecology and Equity; India's Green Alternative*.

Gakenheimer, Ralph and Brando, CHJ (1987) "Infrastructure Standards", in Lloyd Rodwin (ed.), *Shelter, Settlement and Development*, Allen and Unwin, Boston and London, pp. 133–150.

Garza, Gustavo (1991) "The metropolitan character of urbanization in Mexico, 1900–1988", (mimeo).

Gennino, Angela and Shorrock, Tim (1982) "South Korea: paying a high price for an 'economic miracle'", *Not Man Apart*, July, pp. 10–11.

Gilbert, Richard (1990) "Cities and global warming" in James McCulloch (ed.), *Cities and Global Climate Change*, Climate Institute, Washington DC, pp. 182–190.

Goldstein, Greg (1990) "Access to life saving services in urban areas" in Jorge E Hardoy, *et al* (ed) *The Poor Die Young: Housing and Health in Third World Cities*, Earthscan Publications, London.

Gomes Pereira, M (1989) "Characteristics of urban mortality from Chagas' disease in Brazil's Federal District" *Bulletin of the Pan American Health Organization* vol. 18, no. 1.

Gore, Charles (1991) *Transport and Sustainable Development*, (mimeo).

Gore, Charles (1991) *Policies and Mechanisms for Sustainable Development: the Transport Sector*, (mimeo).

Greenway, DR (1987) "Vegetation and slope instability" in ME Anderson and KS Richards (eds), *Slope Stability*, John Wiley and Sons, Chichester.

Guarda, Gian Carlo (1990) "A new direction in World Bank urban lending in Latin American countries", *Review of Urban and Regional Development Studies* vol. 2, no. 2, pp. 116–124.

Guimaraes, JJ and Fischmann, A (1985) "Inequalities in 1980 infant mortality among shantytown residents and non-shanty town residents in the municipality of Porto Alegre, Rio Grande do Sul, Brazil", *Bulletin of the Pan American Health Organization* no. 19, pp. 235–251.

Gunnerson, CG (1987) *Resource Recovery and Utilization in Shanghai*, UNDP/World Bank Global Programme of Resource Recovery.

Gupta, Joyeeta (1990) "A partnership between countries and cities on the issue of climate change – with special reference to the Netherlands" in James McCulloch (ed), *Cities and Global Climate Change*, Climate Institute, Washington DC, pp. 66–89.

Haigh, Nigel (1984) *EEC Environmental Policy and Britain – an Essay and a Handbook*, ENDS, London.

Halter, Faith (1991) "Towards more effective environmental regulation in developing countries" in Denizhan Erocal (ed.), *Environmental Management in Developing Countries*, Development Centre, OECD, Paris, pp. 223–254.

Hamer, Andrew M (1984) *Decentralized Urban Development and Industrial Location Behaviour in São Paulo, Brazil: A Synthesis of Research Issues and Conclusions*, Discussion Paper, Water Supply and Urban Development Department, World Bank, Washington DC.

Hamza, Ahmed (1983) "Management of industrial hazardous wastes in Egypt", *Industry and Environment* Special Issue on Industrial Hazardous Waste Management no. 4, UNEP-Paris Office, pp. 28–32.

Hamza, Ahmed (1989) "An appraisal of environmental consequences of urban development in Alexandria, Egypt", *Environment and Urbanization* vol. 1, no. 1, pp. 22–30.

Hardoy, Ana, Hardoy, Jorge E and Schusterman, Ricardo (1991) "Building community organization: the history of a squatter settlement and its own organizations in Buenos Aires" *Environment and Urbanization* vol. 3, no. 2, pp. 104–120.

Hardoy, Jorge E (1975) "Two thousand years of Latin American urbanization" in JE Hardoy (ed.), *Urbanization in Latin America: Approaches and Issues*, Anchor Books, New York.

Hardoy, Jorge E. and Satterthwaite, David (1981) *Shelter: Need and Response; Housing, Land and Settlement Policies in Seventeen Third World Nations*, John Wiley and Sons, Chichester.

Hardoy, Jorge E. and Satterthwaite, David (1989) *Squatter Citizen: Life in the Urban Third World*, Earthscan Publications, London.

Harpham, Trudy, Garner, Paul and Surjadi, Charles (1990) "Planning for child health in a poor urban environment: the case of Jakarta, Indonesia" *Environment and Urbanization* vol. 2, no. 2, pp. 77–82.

Harpham, Trudy, Vaughan, Patrick and Lusty, Tim (eds) (1988) *In the Shadow of the City: Community Health and the Urban Poor*, Oxford University Press, Oxford.

Harris, Nigel (1990) *Environmental Issues in the Cities of the Developing World*, DPU Working Paper, no. 20, University College, London.

Hasan, Arif (1989) "A low cost sewer system by low-income Pakistanis" in Bertha Turner (ed.), *Building Community: a Third World Case Book*, Habitat International Coalition, London.

Hasan, Arif (1990) "Community organizations and non-government organizations in the urban field in Pakistan" *Environment and Urbanization* vol. 2, no. 1, pp. 74–86.

Hawkins, JN (1982) "Shanghai: an exploratory report on food for a city" *GeoJournal* Supplementary issue, pp. 83–98.

Hofmaier, VA (1991) *Efeitos de poluicao do ar sobre a funcao pulmonar: un estudo de cohorte em criancas de Cubatao*, Doctoral thesis, São Paulo School of Public Health.

Hogan, Daniel Joseph (1992) "Migration dynamics, environmental degradation and health in São Paulo" Proceedings of the Congress on *El Poblamiento de las Americas* vol. II, International Union for the Scientific Study of Population, Veracruz, pp. 279–299.

Honghai, Deng (1992) "Urban agriculture as urban food supply and environmental protection subsystems in China" Paper presented to the international workshop on Planning for Sustainable Urban Development, University of Wales.

Hughes, Bob (1990) "Children's play – a forgotten right" *Environment and Urbanization* vol. 2, no. 2, pp. 58–64.

IIED (1992) "Environmental synopsis of Ghana" prepared for ODA, London.

IIED-América Latina, *Problemas Ambientales en Ciudades Argentinas*, Medio Ambiente y Urbanizacion special issue, no. 37.

IIED-América Latina with CEA and GASE (1992) "Sustainable development in Argentina" *Environment and Urbanization* vol. 4, no. 1.

International Union for Conservation of Nature and Natural Resources (1980) *World Conservation Strategy*, Gland.

IPCC (1990) *Potential Impacts of Climate Change: Report to IPCC from Working Group II*, World Meteorological Organization and the United Nations Environment Programme.

IRENA (1982) *Taller International de Salvamento y Aprovechamiento Integral del Lago de Managua*, vol. 2, no. 2.

Izeogu, CZ (1989) "Urban development and the environment in Port Harcourt", *Environment and Urbanization* vol. 1, no. 1, pp. 59–68.

Jacobi, Pedro (1990) "Habitat and health in the municipality of São Paulo" *Environment and Urbanization* vol. 2, no. 2, pp. 33–45.

Jacobs, Jane (1965) *The Death and Life of Great American Cities*, Pelican, London.

Jarzebski, LS, (1991) "Case Study of the Environmental Impact of the Non-Ferrous Metals Industry in the Upper Silesian Area", Paper prepared for the WHO Commission on Health and the Environment.

Jeune Afrique (1979) *Republique Unie de Cameroun*, les Atlas Afrique, Editions j.a., Paris.

Jimenez, Rosario D and Velasquez, Sister Aida (1989) "Metropolitan Manila: a framework for its sustained development", *Environment and Urbanization* vol. 1, no. 1, pp. 51–58.

Jimenez Diaz, Virginia (1992) "Landslides in the squatter settlements of Caracas; towards a better understanding of causative factors" *Environment and Urbanization* vol. 4, no. 2.

Jones, Kathleen (1991) *The Making of Social Policy in Britain, 1830–1990*, Athlone Press, London and New Jersey.

Jones, Gavin W (1983) "Structural change and prospects for urbanization in Asian countries", Papers of the East-West Population Institute no. 88, East-West Centre, Honolulu.

Kagan, AR and Levi, L (1975) "Health and environment: psycho-social stimuli – a review", in L Levi (ed.), *Society, Stress and Disease – Childhood and Adolescence*, Oxford University Press, Oxford.

Kalbermatten, John M, DeAnne, Julius S and Gunnerson, Charles C (1980) *Appropriate Technology for Water Supply and Sanitation: Technical and Economic Options*, World Bank, Washington DC.

Kebe, Moctar (1988) "The West and Central African Action Plan", Interview in *The Siren* no. 37, pp. 31–34.

Khan, Akhter Hameed (1991) *Orangi Pilot Project Programmes*, Orangi Pilot Project, Karachi.

Kim, Ik Ki (1991) "The environmental problems of poor communities in Seoul", Paper presented at the workshop on "Urban Community-based Environmental Management in Asia", Bangkok, Thailand.

King, Bob, (1988) "Taiwan's industrial pollution bills mount", *Financial Times*, 8 November.

Kishk, MA (1986) "Land degradation in the Nile Valley", *Ambio* vol. XV, no 4, pp. 226–230.

Kolsky, Peter J (1992) "Water, health and cities: concepts and examples" Paper presented at the international workshop on Planning for Sustainable Urban Development, University of Wales, July.

Kone, Sidiki (1988) "Stop Africa from becoming the dumping ground of the world", *The Siren* no. 37, pp. 2–3.

Krupa, SV and Manning, WJ (1988) "Atmospheric ozone: formation and effects on vegetation" *Environmental Pollution* vol. 50, pp. 101–137.

Kulaba, Saitiel (1989) "Local government and the management of urban services in Tanzania", in Richard E Stren and Rodney R White (eds), *African Cities in Crisis*, Westview Press, USA, pp. 203–245.

Kutcher, Gary P and Scandizzo, Pasquale L (1981) *The Agricultural Economy of Northeast Brazil*, Johns Hopkins University Press, Baltimore.

Lagos Group for the Study of Human Settlements, *The Environmental Problems of Metropolitan Lagos*, draft (to be published in 1993).

Lamba, Davinder *et al* (1992) *Environmental Problems of Nairobi*, (draft report), Mazingira Institute, Nairobi.

Leach, Gerald *et al* (1979) *A Low Energy Strategy for the United Kingdom*, Science Reviews Ltd, London.

Leach, Gerald and Mearns, Robin (1989) *Beyond the Woodfuel Crisis – People, Land and Trees in Africa*, Earthscan Publications, London.

Leach, Melissa and Mearns, Robin (1991) *Poverty and Environment in Developing Countries: An Overview Study*, Institute for Development Studies, University of Sussex.

Lee, James A (1985) *The Environment, Public Health and Human Ecology*, World Bank, Johns Hopkins University Press, Baltimore and London.

Lee, Kyu Sik (1988) *Infrastructure Investment and Productivity: the case of Nigerian Manufacturing – a framework for policy study*, Discussion paper, Water Supply and Urban Development Division, World Bank, Wasington DC.

Lee-Smith, Diana, Manundu, Mutsembi, Lamba, Davinder and Gathuru, P Kuria (1987) *Urban Food Production and the Cooking Fuel Situation in Urban Kenya* Mazingira Institute, Nairobi.

Lee-Smith, Diana and Schlyter, Ann (eds) (1991) *Environment and Urbanization* special issue on "Women in Environment and Urbanization", vol. 3, no. 2.

Lee-Smith, Diana and Trujillo, Catalina Hinchey (1992) "The struggle to legitimize subsistence: Women and sustainable development" *Environment and Urbanization* vol. 4, no. 1.

Lee-Wright, Peter (1990) *Child Slaves*, Earthscan Publications, London.

Leitmann, Josef (1991) "Environmental profile of São Paulo" Urban Management and the Environment: Discussion Paper Series, UNDP/World Bank/UNCHS.

Leitmann, Josef (1991) *Tianjin Urban Environmental Profile*, Urban Management and the Environment: Discussion Paper Series, UNDP/World Bank/UNCHS.

Leitmann, Josef, Bartone, Carl and Bernstein, Janis (1992) "Environmental management and urban development: issues and options for Third World cities" *Environment and Urbanization* vol. 4, no 2.

Leonard, Jeffrey H (1984) *Confronting Industrial Pollution in Rapidly Industrializing Countries – Myths, Pitfalls and Opportunities*, Conservation Foundation, Washington DC.

Leonard, Jeffrey H and Morell, David (1981) "Emergence of environmental concern in Developing countries: a political perspective", *Stanford Journal of International Law* vol. 17, issue 2, pp. 281–313.

Linn, Johannes F (1982) "The costs of urbanization in developing countries" *Economic Development and Cultural Change* vol. 30, no. 3.

Listorti, James A (1990) *Environmental Health Components for Water Supply, Sanitation and Urban Projects*, World Bank Technical Paper no. 121, Washington DC.

Lopez, Jose Manuel (1988) "The Caribbean and Gulf of Mexico", *The Siren* no 36, pp. 30–31.

Lowe, Marcia D (1991) *Shaping Cities: the Environmental and Human Dimensions*, Worldwatch Paper 105, Washington DC.

Lungo Ucles, Mario (1987) "*El terremoto de octubre de 1986 y la situacion habitacional de los sectores populares*" in "*El terremoto del 10 de octubre de 1986*", a special issue of *La Universidad*, Nino CXII no 5, San Salvador, January–March.

Lungo Ucles, Mario (1988) "San Salvador: el habitat despues del terremoto", *Medio Ambiente y Urbanizacion* no. 24, September 1988, pp. 46–52.

MacKenzie, Deborah and Mpinga, James (1988) "Africa wages war on dumpers of poisonous waste", *New Scientist*, 23 June 1988, pp. 30–31.

Macklin, Debbie *South Magazine*, March.

Maheswaran, A (1982) "Water pollution in Malaysia; problems, perspectives and control", *Development and the Environment Crisis – A Malaysian Case*, Consumers Association of Penang.

Makil, Perla Q (1982) "Slums and squatter settlements in the Philippines" Concerned Citizens of the Urban Poor Series no. 3, Manila.

Manciaux, M and Romer, CJ (1986) "Accidents in children, adolescents and young adults: a major public health problem" *World Health Statistical Quarterly* vol. 39, no. 3, pp. 227–231.

Manzanal, Mabel and Vapnarsky, Cesar (1986) "The Comahue Region, Argentina" in Jorge E Hardoy and David Satterthwaite (eds), *Small and Intermediate Urban Centres; Their Role in National and Regional Development in the Third World*, Hodder and Stoughton (UK), and Westview (USA).

Mara, Duncan and Cairncross, Sandy (1990) *Guidelines for the Safe Use of Wastewater and Excreta in Agriculture and Aquaculture*, World Health Organization, Geneva.

Marco del Ponte, Louis (1984) "El crimen de la contaminacion", Universidad Autonoma Metropolitana-Atzcapotzaldo, Mexico.

Maskrey, Andrew (1989) *Disaster Mitigation: A Community Based Approach*, Oxfam Development Guidelines no. 3, Oxford.

Matte, TD, Figueroa, JP, Ostrowski, S, Burr, G *et al* (1989) "Lead poisoning among household members exposed to lead-acid battery repair shops in Kingston, Jamaica (West Indies)" *International Journal of Epidemiology* vol. 18, pp. 874–881.

Mazzucchelli, Sergio A (1991) "San Carlos de Bariloche: La problematica ambiental urbana" *Medio Ambiente y Urbanizacion* no. 37, pp. 75–92.

Mbuyi, Kankonde (1989) "Kinshasa: problems of land management, infrastructure and food supply", in Richard E Stren and Rodney R White (eds), *African Cities in Crisis*, Westview Press, USA, pp. 148–175.

McAuslan, Patrick (1984) *Urban Land and Shelter for the Poor*, Earthscan Publications, London.

McGee, TG (1987) "Urbanization or Kotadesasi – the emergence of new regions of economic interaction in Asia", Working paper, East-West Center, Honolulu.

McGranahan, Gordon (1991) *Environmental Problems and the Urban Household in Third World Countries*, The Stockholm Environment Institute, Stockholm.

McGranahan, Gordon (1992) "Household environmental problems" Paper presented at the International Workshop on Planning for Sustainable Urban Development, University of Wales College of Cardiff, July 1992.

Meadows, Donella H, Meadows, Dennis L, Randers, Jorgen and Behrens III, William (1974) *The Limits to Growth*, Pan Books Ltd, London.

Meekyaa, Ude James and Rakodi, Carole (1990) "The neglected small towns of Nigeria", *Third World Planning Review* vol. 12, no. 1, February, pp. 21–40.

Meith, N (1989) *High and Dry: Mediterranean Climate in the 21st Century*, United Nations Environment Program Athens.

Mekvichai, Banasopit, (1992) "The Bangkok Metropolitan Region: sustainable development or resource management?" Paper presented at the International Workshop on Planning for Sustainable Urban Development. University of Wales, Cardiff, July.

Mesarovic, Mihajlo and Pestel, Eduard (1976) *Mankind at the Turning Point*, EP Dutton, New York.

Michaels, David, Barrera, Clara and Gacharna, Manuel (1985) "Economic development and occupational health in Latin America: new directions for public health in less developed countries" *American Journal of Public Health* vol. 85, no. 5, pp. 536–542.

Misra, Harikesh (1990) "Housing and health problems in three squatter settlements in Allahabad, India" in Jorge E Hardoy *et al* (eds), *The Poor Die Young: Housing and Health in Third World Cities*, Earthscan Publications, London.

Misra, HN (1986) "Rae Bareli, Sultanpur and Pratapgarh Districts, Uttar Pradesh, North India" in Jorge E Hardoy and David Satterthwaite (eds), *Small and Intermediate Urban Centres; their role in Regional and National Development in the Third World*, Hodder and Stoughton (UK) and Westview (USA).

Mitlin, Diana (1992) "Sustainable development: a guide to the literature" *Environment and Urbanization* vol. 4, no. 1.

Moreno, Gloria (1980) "Drinking Water: black with foam on top", *Earthscan Feature*, London.

Moser, Caroline ON and Peake, Linda (eds), (1987) *Women, Human Settlements and Housing*, Tavistock Publications, New York and London.

Muhtab, FU (1989) *Effect of Climate Change and Sea level Rise on Bangladesh*, Report prepared for the Commonwealth Expert Group on Climate Change and Sea Level Rise, Commonwealth Secretariat, London.

Murphy, Denis (1990) "Community organizations in Asia" *Environment and Urbanization* vol. 2, no. 1, pp. 51–60.

Murphy, Denis (1990) *A Decent Place to Live – Urban Poor in Asia*, Asian Coalition for Housing Rights, Bangkok, 130 pages.

Murthy, BS (1979) "India: environmental aspects of motor vehicles", *Industry and Environment*, UNEP-Paris, April–June, pp. 6–7.

Myers, Robert (1991) *The Twelve Who Survive: Strengthening Programmes of Early Child Development in the Third World*, Routledge, London and New York.

Needleman, Herbert L, Schell, Alan, Bellinger, David, Leviton, Alan and Allred, Elizabeth N (1991) "The long-term effects of exposure to low doses of lead in childhood: an eleven year follow up report" *The New England Journal of Medicine* vol. 322, no. 2, pp. 83–88.

Newman, Peter WG and Kenworthy, Jeffrey R (1989) *Cities and Automobile Dependence: an International Sourcebook*, Gower Technical, Aldershot.

Newman, Oscar (1972) *Defensible Space: Crime Prevention through Urban Design*, MacMillan, New York.

Ngom, Thiecouta (1989) "Appropriate standards for infrastructure in Dakar" in Richard E Stren and Rodney R White (eds), *African Cities in Crisis*, Westview Press, USA, pp. 176–202.

Nishikawa, Jun (1982) "The strategy of Japanese Multinationals and South-east Asia", *Development and the Environment Crisis – A Malaysian Case*, Consumers Association of Penang.

Nishioka, Shuzo, Noriguchi, Yuichi and Yamamura, Sombo (1990) "Megalopolis and climate change: the case of Tokyo" in James McCulloch (ed.), *Cities and Global Climate Change*, Climate Institute, Washington DC, pp. 108–133.

OECD (1989) *Economic Instruments for Environmental Protection*, OECD, Paris.

OECD (1991) *The State of the Environment*, Organization for Economic Cooperation and Development, Paris.

Office of Technology Assessment *Serious Reduction of Hazardous Waste*, Congress of the United States Summary, quoted in Elkington and Shopley (1989).

Onono, Ondja and Mebenga, A (1983) *"Le probleme de la pollution au Cameroun"*, Paper presented at *Seminaire National sur la Gestion de l'Environnement*, Cameroun.

Ortuzar, S (1983) "Santiago's metro" *Cities* vol. 1, no. 2, pp. 113–116.

Pacheco, Margarita (1992) "Recycling in Bogota; developing a culture for urban sustainability" *Environment and Urbanization* vol. 4, no. 2.

Panayotou, Theodore (1991) "Economic incentives in environmental management and their relevance to developing countries" in Denizhan Erocal (ed.), *Environmental Management in Developing Countries*, Development Centre, OECD, Paris, pp. 83–132.

Parry, Martin (1992) "The urban economy", presentation at *Cities and Climate Change*, conference at the Royal Geographical Society, 31 March.

Patel, Sheela (1990) "Street children, hotels boys and children of pavement dwellers and construction workers in Bombay: how they meet their daily needs", *Environment and Urbanization* vol. 2, no. 2, pp. 9–26.

Pearce, David, Markandya, Anil and Barbier, Edward B (1989) *Blueprint for a Green Economy*, Earthscan Publications, London.

Pearson, Charles S (1987) "Environmental standards, industrial relocation and pollution havens" in Charles S Pearson (ed.), *Multinational Corporation, the Environment and the Third World*, Duke University Press, Durham, USA.

Pepall, Jennifer (1992) "Occupational poisoning" reporting on the work of Mohamad M Amr in *IDRC Reports* vol. 20, no. 1, Ottawa, 15.

Pezzey, John (1989) *Economic Analysis of Sustainable Growth and Sustainable Development*, Environment Department Working Paper, no. 15, World Bank, Washington DC.

Phantumvanit, Dhira and Sathirathai, Suthawan (1986) "Promoting clean technologies in developing countries", *Industry and Environment* vol. 9, no. 4, pp. 12–14.

Phantumvanit, Dhira and Liengcharernsit, Wanai (1989) "Coming to terms with Bangkok's environmental problems", *Environment and Urbanization* vol. 1, no. 1, pp. 31–39.

Pimenta, JCP (1987) "Multinational corporations and industrial pollution control in São Paulo, Brazil" in Charles S Pearson (ed.), *Multinational Corporations, Environment and the Third World: Business Matters*, Duke University Press, Durham.

Ping, Li (1991) "Eco-farming on Huaibei Plain, *Beijing Review* vol. 34, no. 28, pp. 8–16.

Pio, A (1986) "Acute respiratory infections in children in developing countries: an international point of view", *Pediatric Infectious Disease Journal* vol. 5, no. 2, pp. 179–183.

Poore, Duncan (1989) *No Timber without Trees*, Earthscan Publications, London.

Prasad, Raj Mangal and Furedy, Christine (1992) "Small businesses from urban wastes: shoe renovation in Delhi" *Environment and Urbanization* vol. 4, no. 2.

Pretty, Jules N. and Guijt, Irene (1992) "Primary environmental care: an alternative paradigm for development assistance" *Environment and Urbanization* vol. 4, no. 1.

Puerbo, Hasan (1991) "Urban solid waste management in Bandung: towards an integrated resource recovery system" *Environment and Urbanization* vol. 3, no. 1, pp. 60–69.

Rabinovitch, Jonas (1992) "Curitiba: towards sustainable urban development" *Environment and Urbanization* vol. 4, no. 2.

Redclift, Michael (1987) *Sustainable Development: Exploring the Contradictions*, Routledge, London and New York.

Rees, William E (1991) (1989) "Defining 'sustainable development'", CHS Research Bulletin, University of British Columbia Centre for Human Settlements.

Rees, William E "Conserving natural capital: the key to sustainable landscapes" *International Journal of Canadian Studies* Fall 1991, vol. 4, pp. 7–27.

Rees, William E (1992) "Ecological footprints and appropriated carrying capacity: what urban economics leaves out", *Environment and Urbanization* vol. 4, no. 2.

Reichenheim, M and Harpham, T (1989) "Child accidents and associated risk factors in a Brazilian squatter settlement" *Health Policy and Planning* vol. 4, no. 2, pp. 162–167.

Republic of the Philippines, City of Manila Health Department Statistics Division of Preventable Diseases, Manila, 1973; Food and Nutrition Research Center Survey for four regions and Greater Manila, 1973; and unpublished survey of 6000 households by the Nutrition Foundation of the Philippines and Tondo Foreshore Development Authority, May 1975. All three sources quoted in Basta 1977.

Richardson, Harry W (1984) "Planning Strategies and policies for Metropolitan Lima" in *Third World Planning Review* vol. 6, no. 2.

Rietbergen, Simon (1989) 'Africa', in Duncan, Poore *No Timber without Trees*, Earthscan Publications, London.

Rocky Mountain Institute (1991) *Water Efficiency: A Resource for Utility Managers, Community Planners and other Decision Makers*, Water Program, Snowmass.

Rohde, JE (1983) "Why the other half dies: the science and politics of child mortality in the Third World", *Assignment Children* vol. 61/62.

Romieu, Isabelle *et al* (1990) "Urban air pollution in Latin America and the Caribbean: Health perspectives", *World Health Statistics Quarterly* vol. 23, no. 2, pp. 153–167.

Rosario, A and von der Weid, A (1990)"Towards socially and environmentally sound solid waste management in Bangalore", *Proceedings of International Workshop on Waste Management and Resource Recovery*, GTZ, Germany.

Rosenberg, Charles E (1962) *The Cholera Years*, University of Chicago Press, Chicago.

Rothenburg, Stephen J, Schnaas-Arrieta, Lourdes, Perez-Guerrero, Irving A *et al* (1989) *"Evaluacion del riesgo potencial de la exposition perinatal al plombo en el Valle de Mexico" Perinatologia y Reproduccion Humana* vol. 3, no. 1, pp. 49–56.

Ruddle, Kenneth (1983) "Inshore marine pollution in Southeast Asia", *Mazingira* vol. 7, no. 2, pp. 32–44.

Sahabat Alam (1983) *The State of Malaysian Environment 1983–4* – Towards Greater Environmental Awareness, Malaysia.

Sahabat Alam (1986) *Environmental News Digest* no. 4.

Sahil (1988) "Marine pollution and the Indus Delta", vol. 1 House journal of National Institute of Oceanography, Karachi, Pakistan, pp. 57–61.

Saint, William S and Goldsmith, William D (1980) "Cropping systems, structural change and rural-urban migration in Brazil", in *World Development* vol. 8, pp. 259–272.

Sani, S (1987) "Urbanization and the atmospheric environment in Southeast Asia", in *Environment, Development, Natural Resource Crisis in Asia and the Pacific*, Sahabat Alam Malaysia.

Sapir, D (1990) *Infectious Disease Epidemics and Urbanization: a Critical Review of the Issues*, Paper prepared for the WHO Commission on Health and Environment, Division of Environmental Health, WHO, Geneva.

Sarin, Mahdu (1983) "The rich, the poor and the land question" in Shlomo Angel, Raymon W Archer, Sidhijai Tanphiphat and Emiel A Wegelin (eds) *Land for Housing the Poor*, Select Books, Singapore, pp. 237–253.

Schaeffer, B (1990) "Home and health – on solid foundations?", *World Health Forum* vol. 11, pp. 38–45.

Schofield, CJ, Briceno-Leon, R, Kolstrup, N, Webb, DJT and White, GB (1990) "The role of house design in limiting vector-borne disease" in Jorge E. Hardoy *et al* (eds) *The Poor Die Young: Housing and Health in Third World Cities*, Earthscan Publications, London.

Schteingart, Martha, chapter on Mexico City in Mattei Dogon and John D Casada (eds) (1988) *The Metropolis Era Volume 2*, Sage Publications, Beverly Hills, London and New Delhi.

Schteingart, Martha (1989) "The environmental problems associated with urban development in Mexico City", *Environment and Urbanization* vol. 1, no. 1, pp. 40–49.

Secrett, Charles (1988) "Deadly offer poor countries find hard to refuse", *The Guardian*, July, p 11.

Sestini, G., Jeftic, L and Milliman, JD (1990) *Implications of Expected Climatic Changes in the Mediterranean Region: an Overview*, UNEP Regional Seas Reports and Studies no. 103, UNEP, Nairobi.

Showers, Victor (1979) *World Facts and Figures*, John Wiley and Sons, Chichester.

Shrivastav, PP (1982) "City for the citizen or citizen for the city: the search for an appropriate strategy for slums and housing the urban poor in developing countries – the case of Delhi" *Habitat International* vol. 6, no. 1/2, pp. 197–207.

Singh, Abha Lakshmi (1992) "Land degradation around Aligarh" Paper presented at the International Workshop on Planning for Sustainable Urban Development, Department of City and Regional Planning, University of Wales, Cardiff, July.

Sinnatamby, Gehan (1990) "Low cost sanitation" in Jorge E Hardoy *et al* (eds) *The Poor Die Young: Housing and Health in Third World Cities*, Earthscan Publications, London.

Sivaramakrishnan, KC and Green, Leslie (1992) *Metropolitan Management – The Asian Experience*, Oxford University Press (for the World Bank).

Smil, Vaclav (1984) *The Bad Earth: Environmental Degradation in China*, ME Sharpe, New York and Zed Press, London.

Smit, Barrie (1990) "Planning in a climate of uncertainty" in James McCulloch (ed.), *Cities and Global Climate Change*, Climate Institute, Washington DC, pp. 3–19.

Smit, Jac and Nasr, Joe (1992) "Urban agriculture for sustainable cities: using wastes and idle land and water bodies as resources" *Environment and Urbanization* vol. 4, no. 2.

Songsore, Jacob (1992) *Review of Household Environmental Problems in the Accra Metropolitan Area, Ghana*, Stockholm Environment Institute, Stockholm.

Soto Sierra, Javier, Pedro (1977) "Transformacionen el sector urbano", VI Congreso Interamericano de Vivienda, Interhabitat 77.

SPP (1984) *Programa de Desarrollo de la ZMCM y de la Region Centrale*, Mexico, quoted in Harris 1990.

Stephens, Carolyn (1991) "Back to basics: a community based environmental health project in West Point, Monrovia, Liberia" *Environment and Urbanization* vol. 3, no. 1, pp. 140–146.

Street, Annie (1981) "Nicaraguans cite Pennwalt, US company has poisoned its workers and Lake Managua", *Multinational Monitor* vol. 2, no.5, pp. 25–26.

Stren, Richard E (1986) *The Ruralization of African Cities: Learning to Live with Poverty*, Project Ecoville working paper no. 34, University of Toronto.

Stren, Richard E (1989) "Administration of urban services" in Richard E Stren and Rodney R White (eds), *African Cities in Crisis*, Westview.

Stren, Richard E, White, Rodney and Whitney, Joseph (eds) (1992) *Sustainable Cities: Urbanization and the Environment in International Perspective*, Westview Press, Boulder.

Svedin, Uno (1988) "The Concept of Sustainability" in Stockholm Studies in Natural Resource Management no. 1, *Perspectives of Sustainable Development – Some Critical Issues Related to the Brundtland Report*, Stockholm Group for Studies on Natural Resources Management.

Swiss Directorate for Development Cooperation and Humanitarian Aid (1991) *Sustainability of Development Projects: Basic Principles and Application in Practice*, Berne.

Tahal (1981) *Accra-Tema Water Supply and Sewage Project Review of Master Plan*, Final Report vol. 2, Report prepared for the Ghana Water and Sewage Corporation (Accra), quoted in Songsore (1992).

The Cocoyoc Declaration adopted by the participants of the UNEP/UNCTAD symposium on "Pattern of Resource Use, Environment and Development Strategies" in 1974, republished in (1975) *World Development* vol. 3, nos. 2 and 3.

The Economist, 18–24 February 1989.

The Siren no. 38, October 1988, UNEP, Nairobi.

Timberlake, Lloyd (1987) *Only One Earth: Living for the Future*, BBC/Earthscan Publications, London.

Timberlake, Lloyd and Thomas, Laura (1990) *When the Bough Breaks...: Our Children, Our Environment*, Earthscan Publications, London.

Toksoz, Sadik (1983) "Impacts of the growth of Mexico City through water supply and waste disposal", UNCHS (Habitat), Nairobi, Kenya, reported in *Habitat News* vol. 5.

Toulmin, Camilla (1990) "Drylands and Human Settlements", Internal paper, IIED.

Turner, Bertha (ed.) (1988) *Building Community – A Third World Case Book*, Habitat International Coalition, London.

Turner, John FC (1976) *Housing By People – Towards Autonomy in Building Environments*, Ideas in Progress, Marion Boyars, London.

Turner, John FC and Fichter, Robert (eds) (1971) *Freedom to Build*, Macmillan, New York and London.

Turner, RK, Kelly, PM and Kay, RC (1990) *Cities at Risk*, BNA International, London.

UNCHS (Habitat) (1986) "Low cost sanitation project in Bihar, India" *Project monograph*, UNCHS (Habitat), Nairobi.

UNCHS (Habitat) (1987) *Global Report on Human Settlements 1986*, Oxford University Press, Oxford.

UNCHS (Habitat) (1988) "Seismic risk mitigation in the planning of the historic centre of Mexico City" *Project Monograph*, UNCHS (Habitat), Nairobi.

UNCHS (Habitat) (1988) *Refuse Collection Vehicles for Developing Countries*, UNCHS (Habitat), Nairobi, Kenya.

UNCHS (Habitat) (1990) *The Global Strategy for Shelter to the Year 2000*, United Nations Centre for Human Settlements (Habitat), Nairobi.

UNCHS (Habitat), "Financial and other assistance provided to and among developing countries on human settlements and on the human settlements activities of the United Nations system", Biennial reports submitted to the Inter-Governmental Commission on Human Settlements in 1987 and 1989, HS/C/9/6 and HS/C/11/6, Nairobi, Kenya.

UNEP and WHO (1988) *Assessment of Urban Air Quality*, Global Environment Monitoring Service, United Nations Environment Programme and World Health Organization, MARC, London.

UNEP/WHO (1987) *Global Pollution and Health* – results of health-related environmental monitoring, Global Environment Monitoring System.

UNEP (1988) *Strategic Resources Planning in Uganda*, vols. II to X.

UNEP (1991) *Environmental Data Report, 1991–2*, GEMS Monitoring and Assessment Research Centre, Blackwell, Oxford and Massachusetts.

UNFPA (1980) Presentation at the Conference on Population and the Urban Future, Rome.

UNICEF (1988) *Improving Environment for Child Health and Survival*, Urban Examples no. 15, UNICEF New York.

UNICEF (1992) *Environment, Development and the Child*, Environment Section, Programme Division, UNICEF, New York.

UNIDO, *A Statistical Review of the World Industrial Situation in 1980*, February 1981.

United Nations (1980) *Urban, Rural and City Populations 1950–2000, as assessed in 1978*, Population Division, Department of Economic and Social Affairs, ESA/P/WP.66, New York.

United Nations (1987) *Population Growth and Policies in Mega-Cities: Bangkok*, Population Policy Paper no. 10, Department of International Economic and Social Affairs, ST/ESA/SER.R/72, New York.

United Nations (1988) *Population Growth and Policies in Mega-Cities: Karachi*, Population Policy Paper no. 13 Department of International Economic and Social Affairs, ST/ESA/SER.R/77, New York.

United Nations (1991) *World Urbanization Prospects 1990; Estimates and Projections of Urban and Rural Populations and of Urban Agglomerations*, United Nations, ST/ESA/SER.A/121, New York.

United States Environmental Protection Agency (1987) *Regulatory Impact Analysis: Protection of Stratospheric Ozone*, Washington DC.

US AID (1990) *Haiti Shelter Sector Assessment*, Office of Housing and Urban Development.

US AID (1980) *Ranking Environmental Health Risks in Bangkok*, Office of Housing and Urban Programs, Washington DC.

van der Linden, Jan (1982) "Squatting by organized invasion – a new reply to a failing housing policy?", *Third World Planning Review* vol. 4, no. 4, pp. 400–412.

Vimal, OP (1982) "Recycling of organic residues – status and trends in India, *Industry and Environment*, UNEP Europe, Paris, April–June, pp. 7–10.

Waller, Robert E (1991) "Field investigations of air" in WW Holland, R Detels and G Knox (eds), *Oxford Textbook of Public Health* vol. 2 (2nd edn), Oxford University Press, Oxford, New York, pp. 435–450.

Wang, Jia-Xi and Bien, Yong-Mei (1985) "Fluoride effects on the mulberry-silkworm system" *Environmental Pollution* vol. 52, pp. 11–18.

Wangwongwatana, Supat (1992) "Bangkok metropolis and its air pollution problems", Paper presented at the International Workshop on Planning for Sustainable Urban Development, Department of City and Regional Planning, University of Wales, Cardiff, July.

Ward, Barbara and Dubos, Rene (1972) *Only One Earth: Care and Maintenance of a Small Planet*, Penguin, London.

Ward, Barbara (1976) *The Home of Man*, Penguin Books.

Warner, DB and Laugeri, L (1991) "Health for all: the legacy of the water decade" *Water International* vol. 16, pp. 135–141.

White, Rodney R (1992) "The international transfer of urban technology: does the North have anything to offer for the global environmental crisis?" *Environment and Urbanization* vol. 4, no. 2.

White, Rodney and Whitney, Joseph (1992) "Cities and the environment: an overview" in Richard Stren, Rodney White and Joseph Whitney (eds), *Sustainable Cities Urbanization and the Environment in International Perspective*, Westview Press, Bouldner, pp. 8–52.

WHO (1989) *Urbanization and its Implications for Child Health: Potential for Action*, World Health Organization, Geneva.

WHO (1990) *Environmental Health in Urban Development*, Report of a WHO Expert Committee, World Health Organization, Geneva.

WHO (1990) *Global Estimates for Health Situation Assessments and Projections 1990*, Division of Epidemiological Surveillance and Health Situation and Trend Analysis, World Health Organization, WHO/HST/90.2, Geneva.

WHO (1992) *Report of the Panel on Energy*, WHO Commission on Health and Environment, WHO/EHE/92.3, Geneva.

WHO (1992) *Report of the Panel on Industry*, WHO Commission on Health and Environment, WHO/EHE/92.4 WHO Geneva.

WHO (1992) *Our Planet, Our Health*, Report of the Commission on Health and Environment, Geneva.

Winpenny, JT (1991) *Values for the Environment: A Guide to Economic Appraisal*, HMSO, London.

Wohl, Anthony S (1983) *Endangered Lives: Public Health in Victorian Britain*, Methuen, London.

World Bank (1984) *Staff Appraisal Report: Brazil Second Health Project*, São Paulo basic health care and national health policy studies, Population, Health and Nutrition Department, Washington DC.

World Bank (1988) *World Development Report 1988*, Oxford University Press, Oxford.

World Bank (1989) "Adult health in Brazil: adjusting to new challenges", Report No 7808-BR, Brazil Department, Washington DC.

World Bank (1990) *World Development Report 1990*, Oxford University Press, Oxford.

World Bank (1991) *World Development Report 1991*, Oxford University Press, Oxford.

World Bank (1991) *Urban Policy and Economic Development: An Agenda for the 1990s*, Washington DC.

World Bank (1992) *World Development Report 1992*, Oxford University Press, Oxford.

World Commission on Environment and Development (1987) *Our Common Future*, Oxford University Press, Oxford.

World Resources Institute (1992) *World Resources 1991–92: a Guide to the Global Environment: Toward Sustainable Development*, Oxford University Press, Oxford.

Yhdego, Michael (1991) "Urban environmental degradation in Tanzania" *Environment and Urbanization* vol. 3, no. 1, pp. 147–152.

Zhao, D and Xiong, J (1988) "Acidification in southwestern China" in H Rohde and R Herrera (eds), *Acidification in Tropical Countries*, SCOPE Report no 36, John Wiley and Sons, Chichester.

Zhao, D and Sun, B (1988) "Atmospheric pollution from coal combustion in China" quoted in UNEP and WHO 1988.

Zhongmin, Yan (1988) "Shanghai: the growth and shifting emphasis of China's largest city" in Victor FS Sit (ed.), *Chinese Cities: the Growth of the Metropolis since 1949*, Oxford University Press, Hong Kong, pp. 94–127.

Zipei, Zhao (1992) "Air quality of Shanghai and strategies to control it" Paper presented at an international workshop on "Planning for Sustainable Urban Development", University of Wales College of Cardiff, July.

Zorrilla, Silvia and Guaresti, Maria Elena (1986) *Sector Agua Potables y Saneamiento: Lineamientos para una Estrategia Nacional*, PNUD (UN Development Programme), Buenos Aires.

Further Reading

Below are suggestions for further reading for those who want to follow up the points raised in this book. These are organized under the following headings:

1. General works
2. Journals and newsletters
3. City case studies
4. Health and the urban environment
5. Groups at risk
6. Water, sanitation and drainage
7. Air pollution
8. Garbage/solid waste management
9. Water pollution
10. Food in the city
11. Regional impact of cities
12. Sustainable development and cities

1. General works

Stren, RE, White, R and Whitney J (eds) (1992), *Sustainable Cities: Urbanization and the Environment in International Perspective*, Westview, 5500 Central Avenue, Boulder, Colorado 80301-2847, USA; includes chapters on urban environmental problems in each of the world's regions.

Douglass, Mike (1992), "The political economy of urban poverty and environmental management in Asia: access, empowerment and community-based alternatives" and other papers in the special issue of *Environment and Urbanization* vol. 4, no. 2 on "Sustainable cities: meeting needs, reducing resource use and recycling, re-use and reclamation" available from IIED, 3 Endsleigh Street, London WC1H ODD, UK, £9.00 (Third World orders £5).

Douglas, Ian (1983), *The Urban Environment*, Edward Arnold, London; includes chapters explaining how cities function within the physical, chemical and biological characteristics of their site and region.

WHO (1992), *Our Planet, Our Health*, Report of the Commission on Health and Environment, Geneva (especially informative on the links between environment and health); order from the Publications Office, WHO, 1211 Geneva 27, Switzerland.

Papers from an international workshop on "Planning for Sustainable Urban Development; Cities and Natural Resource Systems in Developing Countries" in July 1992. Over 30 papers were presented on different aspects of urban environmental problems. The complete set is £40 although individual papers can be ordered at a cost of between £1 and £2, depending on length; for a list of the papers or for ordering the complete set, write to Dr. Carole Rakodi, Department of City and Regional Planning, University of Wales College of Cardiff, PO Box 906, Cardiff CF1 3YN, UK.

McGranahan, Gordon (1991), *Environmental Problems and the Urban Household in Third World Countries*, The Stockholm Environment Institute, Stockholm. For this and details of other SEI publications on the urban environment, write to SEI, Box 2142, S-103 14 Stockholm, Sweden.

India: The two citizen reports on *The State of India's Environment* produced by CSE in Delhi have detailed coverage of both rural and urban environmental problems, integrated within a concern for development. To order, write to CSE, F-6 Kailash Colony, New Delhi 110048, India; international money order or bankers draft US$21 for either of the Reports ($25 if you want it sent airmail).

China: Although there are many works on environmental issues in China, Smil, V (1984), *The Bad Earth: Environmental Degradation in China*, ME Sharpe, New York and Zed Press, London covers both rural and urban environmental problems and includes within it considerable detail on environmental problems in China's largest cities.

Malaysia: Two NGOs publish a range of literature on environmental problems, including urban environmental problems: for details, write to the Consumers Association of Penang, 87 Jalan Cantonment, Pulau Penang 10250, Malaysia; and Sahabat Alam Malaysia, 43 Salween Road, 10050 Pulau Pinang, Malaysia.

2. Journals and newsletters

Environment and Urbanization – a twice yearly journal available from IIED, 3 Endsleigh Street, London WC1H ODD, UK, £17 for annual subscription (£8 for Third World subscribers; some free subscriptions available for Third World NGOs and teaching/training colleges). Each issue is on a special theme and recent themes include:

- Environmental problems in Third World cities (October 1989)
- Community based organizations (April 1990)
- Children and the environment (October 1990)
- Women in environment and urbanization (October 1991)
- Sustainable development and the global commons (April 1992)
- Sustainable cities (October 1992)

Medio Ambiente y Urbanizacion – a quarterly journal in Spanish published by IIED–America Latina in Buenos Aires and available from IIED, 3 Endsleigh Street, London WC1H ODD, UK, £25 for annual subscription. Recent issues include:

- Health and Habitat (September 1991)
- Environmental Problems in Argentine Cities (December 1991)
- Sustainable Development: Reality or Utopia (June 1992)
- A Retrospective on the Earth Summit (September 1992)

Down To Earth – Science and Environment fortnightly. This new journal concentrates on environment and development issues in the Third World with a combination of detailed descriptions of environmental and developmental problems, news, analyses, interviews and reviews of new books and films. Individual subscriptions $65 (cheaper rates available for those in Southeast Asia) write to *Down to Earth*, F-6 Kailash Colony, New Delhi, 110048, India.

Environmental News Digest – draws together extracts from very wide range of publications reporting on environmental issues; published four times a year by Sahabat Alam Malaysia, 43 Salween Road, 10050 Pulau Pinang, Malaysia.

Industry and Environment produced by the Paris office of the United Nations Environment Program is a useful source of information, especially about industrial pollution and about techniques and processes for reducing pollution. Most articles can be understood by a general reader – although it is aimed principally at a specialist audience. Published four times a year, it is available from the Industry and Environment Office, UNEP, Tour Mirabeau, 39-43 quai Andre-Citroen, 75739 Paris Cedex 15, France.

3. City case studies

Stren, RE and White RR (eds) (1989), *African Cities in Crisis*, Westview, 5500 Central Avenue, Boulder, Colorado 80301-2847, USA. Includes overview chapters and chapters which focus on particular cities which have a lot of information on deficiencies on water supply, sanitation and solid waste disposal and on the inadequacies of local government.

Sivaramakrishnan, KC and Green, L (1986), *Metropolitan Management – The Asian Experience*, Oxford University Press has separate chapters on various major Asian cities; some include detailed information about environmental problems and problems with water supply, sanitation and garbage disposal.

The Urban Management Programme, World Bank-UNDP-UNCHS (Habitat) have produced a series of environmental profiles of cities – for details write to Josef Leitmann, Urban Management Programme, World Bank, 1818 H Street NW, Washington DC 20433, USA.

By mid or late 1993, a series of detailed case studies of different Third World cities based on research currently underway will be available: Nairobi (Mazingira Institute, PO Box 14550, Nairobi, Kenya); Lagos (Lagos Group for the Study of Human Settlements, c/o AAA Consult, Belgravia House – Second floor, 1A Birrel Avenue, Yaba, Lagos, Nigeria); and Accra, Jakarta and Sao Paulo (SEI, Box 2142, S-103 14 Stockholm, Sweden).

4. Health and the urban environment

Bradley, D et al (1991), *A Review of Environmental Health Impacts in*

Developing Country Cities, Urban Management Program Discussion Paper No 6, World Bank-UNDP-UNCHS (Habitat); available from Urban Management Programme, World Bank, 1818 H Street NW, Washington DC 20433, USA.

Harpham, T, Vaughan P and Lusty T (eds) (1988), *In the Shadow of the City: Community Health and the Urban Poor*, Oxford University Press, Oxford.

Jacobi, P (1990), "Habitat and health in the municipality of Sao Paulo" *Environment and Urbanization* vol. 2, no. 2, October, pp. 33-45.

Cauthen, GM, Pio A and ten Dam HG (1988), *Annual Risk of Tuberculosis Infection*, World Health Organization, Geneva. Write to Publications, WHO, 1211 Geneva 27, Switzerland.

Listorti, JA (1990), *Environmental Health Components for Water Supply, Sanitation and Urban Projects*, World Bank Technical Paper Number 121; write to Publications, World Bank, 1818 H Street NW, Washington DC 20433, USA.

WHO (1992), *Our Planet, Our Health* (see under general works).

Schofield, CJ et al (1990) "The role of house design in limiting vector-borne disease" in Hardoy JE et al (eds) *The Poor Die Young: Housing and Health in Third World Cities*, Earthscan Publications; available from IIED, 3 Endsleigh Street, London WC1H ODD, UK.

5. Groups at risk

Lee-Smith, D and Schlyter A (eds) (1991), special issue of *Environment and Urbanization* on "Women in Environment and Urbanization", vol. 3, no 2; available from IIED, 3 Endsleigh Street, London WC1H ODD, UK.

Lee-Wright, P (1990), *Child Slaves*, Earthscan Publications, London.

Manciaux, M and Romer CJ (1986), "Accidents in children, adolescents and young adults: a major public health problem" *World Health Statistical Quarterly* vol. 39, no. 3, pp. 227-231.

Moser, CON and Peake L (eds) (1987), *Women, Human Settlements and Housing*, Tavistock Publications, New York and London; available from International Thompson Publishing Services, North Way, Andover, Hants SP10 5BE, UK.

Myers, R (1991), *The Twelve Who Survive: Strengthening Programmes of Early Child Development in the Third World*, Routledge, London and New York, 468 pages.

Patel, S (1990), "Street children, hotels boys and children of pavement dwellers and construction workers in Bombay: how they meet their daily needs", and Omer, MIA (1990), "Child health in the spontaneous settlements around Khartoum", *Environment and Urbanization* vol. 2, no. 2.

Pio, A (1986), "Acute respiratory infections in children in developing countries: an international point of view", *Pediatric Infectious Disease Journal* vol. 5, no. 2, pp. 179-183.

UNICEF (1992), *Environment, Development and the Child*. Write to Environment Section, Programme Division, UNICEF, 3 UN Plaza, New York, NY 10017, USA.

6. Water, sanitation and drainage

Cairncross, S (1990), "Water supply and the urban poor" and Sinnatamby, G (1990), "Low cost sanitation" in Hardoy JE et al (eds), *The Poor Die Young: Housing and Health in Third World Cities*, Earthscan, London; write to IIED, 3 Endsleigh Street, London WC1H ODD, UK.

Kalbermatten, JM, Julius DS and Gunnerson C (1981), *Appropriate Technology for Water Supply and Sanitation: a Summary of Technical and Economic Options*, World Bank – available from Publications Division, the World Bank, 1818 H Street NW, Washington DC, 20433, USA or regional offices of the World Bank. One of many publications from a UNDP-World Bank-WHO Programme on water supply, sanitation and garbage disposal; ask for a complete publication list from this same address.

UNCHS (1986), *The Design of Shallow Sewer Systems*, Nairobi; write to Publications, UNCHS (Habitat), PO Box 30030, Nairobi, Kenya for this and for details of other relevant publications.

Cairncross, S and Ouano EAR (1990), *Surface Water Drainage in Low-income Communities*, WHO, Geneva; write to Publications, WHO, 1211 Geneva 27, Switzerland.

Hasan, A (1988), 'Orangi Pilot Project: a Low Cost Sewer System by Low Income Pakistanis', in Turner B (Ed), *Building Community: A Third World Case Book*, Habitat International Coalition, £12.50 available from Building Communities Books, 5 Dryden Street, London WC2E 9NW, UK.

7. Air pollution

Romieu, I et al (1990), "Urban air pollution in Latin America and the Caribbean: Health perspectives", *World Health Statistics Quarterly* vol. 23, no 2, pp. 153-167.

UNEP and WHO (1988), *Assessment of Urban Air Quality*, Global Environment Monitoring Service, United Nations Environment Programme and World Health Organization, 100 pages, Nairobi.

Waller, RE (1991), "Field investigations of air" in Holland WW, Detels R and Knox G (eds), *Oxford Textbook of Public Health* Volume 2 (second edition), Oxford University Press, Oxford and New York, pp. 435-450.

WHO (1992), *Our Planet, Our Health* (see under general works) and WHO (1992), *Report of the Panel on Energy*, WHO Commission on Health and Environment, WHO/EHE/92.3, Geneva; write to Publications Office, WHO, 1211 Geneva 27, Switzerland.

8. Garbage/solid waste management

Furedy, C (1992), "Garbage: exploring non-conventional options in Asian cities" and Pacheco, M (1992) "Recycling in Bogota; developing a culture for urban sustainability" *Environment and Urbanization* vol. 4, no 2; available from IIED, 3 Endsleigh Street, London WC1H ODD, UK.

Furedy, C (1990), "Social aspects of solid waste recovery in Asian cities" *Environmental Sanitation Reviews* No. 30, ENSIC, Asian Institute of Technology Bangkok, December 1990, pp. 2-52. Available from ENSIC, Asian Institute of Technology, PO Box 2754, Bangkok 10501, Thailand.

Elkington, J and Shopley J, *Cleaning Up: US Waste Management Technology and Third World Development*, WRI Papers; available from World Resources Institute, 1709 New York Avenue NW, Washington DC 20006, USA.

Cointreau, S (1982), *Environmental Management of Urban Solid Waste in Developing Countries*, Urban Development Technical Paper No 5, The World Bank; for this and other publications on solid waste management, write to World Bank Publications, 1818 H Street NW, Washington DC 20433, USA.

9. Water pollution

UNEP (1992), *Chemical Pollution: a Global Overview*, Earthwatch; write to UNEP, PO Box 30552, Nairobi, Kenya.

Lee, JA (1985), *The Environment, Public Health and Human Ecology*, The World Bank, Johns Hopkins University Press, Baltimore and London.

See also WHO 1992 and general works on India and China listed in section 1.

10. Food in the city

Smit, J and Nasr J (1992), "Urban agriculture for sustainable cities: using wastes and idle land and water bodies as resources" *Environment and Urbanization* vol. 4, no 2. These authors also have a more detailed report being published soon; write RCD Consultants, 1711 Lamont Street NW, Washington DC 20010, USA.

Several case studies have been published by the *Food–Energy Nexus* programme of the UN University. Write to UNU/FEN, Bureau 311, Maison des Sciences de l'Homme, 54, Boulevard Raspail, 75270 Paris Cedex 06, France.

Lee-Smith, D et al (1987), *Urban Food and Fuel Study*, Mazingira Institute, covering Nairobi and other urban centres in Kenya, available from Mazingira Institute, PO Box 14550, Nairobi, Kenya.

11. Regional impact of cities

Douglass, M, "The environmental sustainability of development – coordination, incentives and political will in land use planning for the Jakarta metropolis" *Third World Planning Review* vol. 11, no. 2, pp. 211-238.

Rees, WE (1992), "Ecological footprints and appropriated carrying capacity: what urban economics leaves out", *Environment and Urbanization* vol. 4, no 2, October.

Conway, GR and Pretty JN (1991), *Unwelcome Harvest*, Earthscan Publications, London, 1991, 645 pages (especially for impact on agriculture of urban air and water pollution); write to IIED, 3 Endsleigh Street, London WC1H ODD, UK, £15.

See also general works on India listed in section 1.

12. Sustainable development and cities

Redclift, M (1987), *Sustainable Development: Exploring the Contradictions*, Routledge, London and New York.

WHO (1992), *Our Planet, Our Health* (see section on general works).

Newman, PWG and Kenworthy JR (1989), *Cities and Automobile Dependence: an International Sourcebook*, Gower Technical, Aldershot.

Lowe, MD (1991), *Shaping Cities: the Environmental and Human Dimensions*, Worldwatch Paper 105; order from Worldwatch Institute, 1776 Massachusetts Avenue NW, Washington DC 20036, USA, $5.

UNCHS (1990), *Human Settlements and Sustainable Development*, HS/214/90E, Nairobi; order from UNCHS Publications Office, PO Box 30030, Nairobi, Kenya, 1990.

Turner, RK, Kelly, PM and Kay, RC (1990) *Cities at Risk*, BNA International, London, 108 pages.

Index